Anonymous

Jubilee Volume: The Archdiocese Of Toronto, 1842-1892, And Archbishop Walsh

Anonymous

Jubilee Volume: The Archdiocese Of Toronto, 1842-1892, And Archbishop Walsh

ISBN/EAN: 9783744653374

Printed in Europe, USA, Canada, Australia, Japan

Cover: Foto ©ninafisch / pixelio.de

More available books at **www.hansebooks.com**

1842.   *Jubilee Volume.*   1892.

THE
ARCHDIOCESE OF TORONTO

AND

Archbishop Walsh.

WITH

An Introduction by His Grace the Archbishop.

ILLUSTRATED.

TORONTO:
GEO. T. DIXON, PUBLISHER.
1892.

To

THE MOST ILLUSTRIOUS AND MOST REVEREND

John Walsh, D.D.,

ARCHBISHOP OF TORONTO,

THIS VOLUME

IS RESPECTFULLY DEDICATED AS A

MEMORIAL OF HIS MANY YEARS OF DISTINGUISHED SERVICE IN THE CHURCH,

AND AS A TRIBUTE OF AFFECTION

UPON THE

SILVER JUBILEE

OF HIS

EPISCOPAL CONSECRATION.

"And thou shalt sanctify the fiftieth year, and shalt proclaim remission to all the inhabitants of the land: for it is the year of jubilee."

LEVITICUS, XXVI., 10.

The Editor's Notice.

While we leave the introduction of our work to abler hands, we feel that a word from the Committee to whom the preparation of this volume was entrusted is not out of place; the more so, as the Archbishop, in his remarks, has omitted to touch upon one of the notable events which this book is intended to commemorate, viz: the Silver Jubilee of his own consecration as Bishop. Dr. Walsh, who was elevated to the episcopal rank on the 10th of November, 1867, has, by his labors extending over quarter of a century, well entitled himself to a lasting regard in the memory of his people. And no more favorable opportunity could be presented of reviewing a life replete with honor for its subject and good for those amongst whom it has been cast, than the auspicious occasion when we also glance back upon the first golden tide of our family history as children of this Metropolitan See. This also must be considered: that twenty-two years of his Grace's distinguished career have been passed away from Toronto. His life, therefore, occupies a special place in this volume: it is not so much history of the archdiocese, as a biographical sketch, and rightly serves to divide, according to our title page, our volume into two parts, the first of which is more directly intended as a lasting tribute to our venerable Father in Christ.

The other aims, scope and purposes of the work, the mode of preparation, as well as the moral lessons to be derived from its perusal, are clearly set forth by his Grace in the Introduction: to which we shall add a brief note concerning the Editor's more direct task of preparing the notices of the parishes. These are founded upon sketches which were supplied by the incumbents of last year (1891). Some of the notes were meagre on account of the pastors not being acquainted with the early history of the diocese;

and also because of the very simplicity of those times. Visiting families who were scattered through the depths of a Canadian forest, superintending the erection of a log chapel, instructing once or twice a year a settlement of pious people, are deeds apostolic in their character and most important in their results; but they afford little variety for the historian and call forth little enthusiasm in a materialistic age. As far as possible we have carefully compared and re-written these reports in order to avoid discrepancies and repetitions.

We return our thanks to his Grace the Archbishop, who has been our support throughout, and to the generous priests of the archdiocese whose co-operation has enabled us to place the book before the public. We are also grateful to our many friends who have otherwise aided us with material for the more complete success of the work in hand. With this parting word we commend ourselves and our labors to the consideration of our readers, in the hope that they will not be entirely dissatisfied with the Jubilee Volume.

J. R. TEEFY,
Editor.

St. Michael's College, Toronto,
Feast of St. Michael, September 29, 1892.

THE CLERGY
OF
THE ARCHDIOCESE OF TORONTO.
1892.

THE MOST REV. ARCHBISHOP WALSH.

Monsignore F. P. Rooney, V. G.	St. Mary's, Toronto.
Very Rev. J. J. McCann, V. G.	St. Michael's Cathedral, Toronto.
Rev. Allain, L. A. H.	St. Catharines.
Very Rev. Bergin, W., Dean	Barrie.
Rev. Beaudoin, F. J.	Lafontaine.
" Best, D. F., O. C. C.	Niagara Falls.
" Best, P. A., O. C. C.	Niagara Falls.
" Brennan, L., C. S. B.	St. Basil's, Toronto.
" Brogan, S., C. SS. R.	St. Patrick's, Toronto.
Very Rev. Campbell, K. A., Archdeacon	Orillia.
Rev. Cantillon, C.	Apto.
Very Rev. Cassidy, E., Dean	St. Helen's, Toronto.
Rev. Cherrier, L. E., C. S. B.	St. Basil's, Toronto.
" Christian, M., C. S. B.	Toronto.
" Colin, J.	Midland.
" Collins, J., C. S. B.	Toronto.
" Coyle, P.	St. Mary's, Toronto.
" Crespin, J.	St. Basil's, Toronto.
" Cruise, J. M.	St. Mary's, Toronto.
" Duffy, F. W.	Orillia.
" Egan, J. J.	Thornhill.
" Finan, A. P.	House of Providence, Toronto.
" Frachon, F. R., C. S. B.	St. Basil's, Toronto.
" Gallagher, E. F.	Schomberg.
" Gearin, M. T.	Apto.
" Gibbons, J.	Penetanguishene.
" Gibney, H. J.	Alliston.
" Gibra, L.	Barrie.
" Guinane, J. J., C. S. B.	St. Basil's, Toronto.
" Hand, J. L.	Oshawa.
" Harold, P. J.	Niagara.
Very Rev. Harris, W. R., Dean	St. Catharines.
Rev. Jeffcott, M. J.	Pickering.
" Keane, P. J.	Uxbridge.

Rev. Kelly, J. J. .... Toronto.
  "   Kiernan, E. J. .... Collingwood.
  "   Kiernan, P. .... Vroomanton.
  "   Kilcullen, J. .... Colgan.
Very Rev. Kreidt, A. J., O.C.C., Superior...... Niagara Falls.
Rev. Krein, S., C.SS.R. .... St. Patrick's, Toronto.
  "   Laboureau, T. F. .... Penetanguishene.
  "   Lafontaine, A. .... Toronto.
  "   Lamarche, P. .... Sacred Heart, Toronto.
  "   Lawler, E. B. .... Toronto.
  "   Lynch, J. J. .... St. Paul's, Toronto.
  "   Lynett, J. F. .... Merritton.
  "   McBrady, R., C.S.B. .... St. Basil's, Toronto.
  "   McBride, J. F. .... St. Helen's, Toronto.
  "   McCall, P. J. .... Fort Erie.
  "   McCarthy, J., C.SS.R .... St. Patrick's, Toronto.
  "   McEntee, J. J. .... Port Colborne.
Very Rev. McInerney, A. J., C.SS.R., Superior.. St. Patrick's, Toronto.
Rev. McMahon, P. .... Brechin.
  "   McPhillips, H. J .... Orangeville.
  "   McRae, K. .... Smithville.
  "   McSpiritt, F. .... Wildfield.
Very Rev. Marijon, V., C.S.B., Provincial....... St. Basil's, Toronto.
Rev. Minehan, L. .... St. Paul's, Toronto.
  "   Morris, D. .... Newmarket.
  "   Moyna, M. .... Stayner.
  "   Murray, E., C.S.B. .... St. Basil's, Toronto.
  "   O'Malley, D. T., O.C.C. .... Niagara Falls.
  "   O'Reilly, M. Mc. .... St. Joseph's, Toronto.
  "   Redden, J. .... St. Paul's, Toronto.
  "   Rohleder, F. F. .... St. Michael's Cathedral, Toronto.
  "   Ryan, F. .... St. Michael's Cathedral, Toronto.
  "   Smyth, F. .... St. Catharines.
  "   Sullivan, T. .... Thorold.
  "   Teefy, J. R., C.S.B. .... St. Basil's, Toronto.
  "   Trayling, J. .... Dixie.
  "   Voissard, J. A. .... Fort Erie.
  "   Walsh, F., C.S.B. .... St. Basil's, Toronto.
  "   Walsh, J .... Our Lady of Lourdes, Toronto.
  "   Whitney, P. .... Caldwell.

TABLE OF CONTENTS.

INTRODUCTION.. (11)

PART I.

The Life of the Most Reverend John Walsh, D. D., Archbishop of Toronto............ i

PART II.

CHAPTER I.

The Indian Missions in Western Canada.. 1

    The Indian—The Missionary—The Recollets or Franciscans—The Jesuits—Brebeuf and Lalemant—The Sulpitians.

CHAPTER II.

Early History of the Church in Upper Canada.. 37

    The Old Province of Quebec—Early Missions and Pioneer Priests—Early Catholic Settlements—Statistics—Missionary Work—The Church and State—The Clergy Reserves—Bishop Plessis—Division of the Diocese of Quebec.

CHAPTER III.

The Life and Times of Bishop Macdonell.. 67

    The Diocese of Kingston—Bishop Macdonell—The Early Clergy—Cardinal Weld—Visitation of the Diocese—The Parishes—Bishop Gaulin—The Troubles at York—New Missions—An Interesting Event—1835 to 1838—Statistics—Bishop Macdonell's Death and Burial.

CHAPTER IV.

The Life and Times of Bishop Power.. 107

    Bishop Gaulin—Diocese of Kingston divided—Diocese of Toronto—Bishop Power—The First Diocesan Synod—The Clergy—The Coming of the Jesuits—Notable Events—St. Michael's Cathedral—Pastorals—Death of Gregory XVI., and Accession of Pius IX.—The Bishop visits Europe—The Typhus—Death of Bishop Power.

Table of Contents.

CHAPTER V.

The Life and Times of Bishop De Charbonnel 141

Family—Ordination and Entry to St. Sulpice—Coming to America—Services among the Fever Patients—Bishop of Toronto—Separate Schools—Return to France—Propagation of the Faith—Archbishop of Sozopolis.

CHAPTER VI.

The Life and Times of Archbishop Lynch 169

Birth and Education—Missionary Career—College of the Holy Angels—Bishop of Toronto—Archbishop—Silver Jubilee—Death.

CHAPTER VII.

The Religious Communities and their Work 197

The Basilians—Father Soulerin—Father Vincent—The Christian Brothers—The Sisters of Loretto—The Sisters of St. Joseph—The House of Providence—The Nuns of the Precious Blood—The Sisters of the Good Shepherd—The Sisters of the Holy Cross—The St. Vincent de Paul Society—The Lady Visitors to the Hospital.

CHAPTER VIII.

Separate Schools 249

Early Legislation—Acts of 1851, 1853, 1855, 1863—Separate School Law of Ontario under British North America Act—Recent Legislation—Separate Schools of the Archdiocese.

CHAPTER IX.

The Parishes of the Deanery of Toronto 275

Introduction—St. Michael's Cathedral—St. Paul's—St. Mary's—St. Basil's—St. Patrick's—St. Helen's—St. Joseph's—Sacred Heart—Adjala—Brock—Caledon—Dixie—Newmarket—Orangeville—Oshawa—Pickering—Schomberg—Thornhill—Uxbridge—Toronto Gore.

CHAPTER X.

The Parishes of the Deanery of St. Catharines 323

St. Catharines—Merritton—Niagara-on-the-Lake—Niagara Falls—Port Colborne—Smithville—Thorold.

CHAPTER XI.

The Parishes of the Deanery of Barrie 341

Barrie—Alliston—Brentwood—Brechin—Collingwood—Flos—Mara—Midland—Orillia—Penetanguishene—Stayner—Ste. Croix.

LIST OF ILLUSTRATIONS.

Archbishop Walsh.................... Frontispiece.

	PAGE
St. Peter's Cathedral	xx
John De Brebeuf	2
The Portage	19
Bishop Plessis	38
Map of Quebec under Act of 1774	40
St. Joseph's Church, Kingston, 1808	44
Bishop Macdonell	68
Guelph, 1827	80
Niagara Church, 1836	84
Bishop Power	108
Bishop De Charbonnel	142
Archbishop Lynch	170
Very Reverend Father Vincent, V. G.	198
St. Michael's College	202
Loretto Abbey	212
St. Joseph's Convent	224
House of Providence	231
Chevalier Macdonell	246
Brother Tobias	250
Very Reverend Dean Cassidy	276
St. Michael's Cathedral	280
Very Reverend Father McCann	282
St. Paul's Church	284
Bishop O'Mahony	286
St. Mary's Church and School	288
Monsignore Rooney	292
Sanctuary of St. Helen's	301
Our Lady of Lourdes	304
Adjala and Penetanguishene	311
Very Reverend Dean Harris	324
St. Catharines' Church and School	326
Thorold and Port Colborne	338
Very Reverend Dean Bergin	342
Bishop O'Connor	344
Barrie	346
Orillia	356

INTRODUCTION.

When it was proposed to us to take some recognition of the fiftieth anniversary of the establishment of the diocese of Toronto, which occurs in the year of grace 1892, we suggested as one means of commemorating this epoch a volume which would record the history, as far as ascertainable, of the foundation, growth and progress of the Catholic Church in Ontario, and more particularly in that portion comprised within the present limits of the archdiocese of Toronto. A number of gentlemen kindly acted upon the suggestion, and contributed, each the chapter or chapters to which his name is attached. This Committee consisted of: The Very Rev. W. R. Harris, B. D., Dean of St. Catharines; the Rev. J. R. Teefy, B. A., C. S. B., Superior of St. Michael's College, Toronto; D. A. O'Sullivan, Esq., M. A., LL. D.; the Hon. T. W. Anglin, ex-Speaker of the House of Commons of Canada; H. F. McIntosh, Esq.; and J. F. White, Esq., Inspector of Separate Schools. The Reverend Father Teefy was appointed Editor.

The purpose of the volume is to record and preserve the trials, sacrifices and labors of the bishops, priests and people who have gone before us, and who planted the mustard seed of our holy faith in this province, who watered it with tears until it has grown up into a great tree overshadowing the whole land. It is not pretended that this is a complete history of the subject. It is rather an earnest attempt to gather up fragments of traditions and family history which every year were becoming more scattered, but which must have an abiding interest for the younger generation. It is the erection of a memorial tablet over the first fifty years of our existence as a diocese. We cannot claim the veneration due to antiquity, or proudly point to a long line of saintly prelates, and institutions dating to the dawn of civilization; for we are of yesterday compared with many of the dioceses of the Church. Armagh celebrated its thousandth anniversary about the time that Columbus discovered America; Cologne is older still, and

Marseilles completed its Golden Jubilee before the christian dispensation had closed its first century. But there are in our midst treasures of faithful memories, revered names, and well established homes of charity and halls of learning worthy of a place in the imperishable annals of history. The heroic footsteps of the missionaries who first trod this country are retraced in simple narrative; and their tragic sufferings are told as a reminder that our soil is watered with the blood of martyrs. A second chapter upon the early English occupation of the country forms a link between the Huron missions and the episcopate of Bishop Macdonell, the latter part of whose career is within the memory of living men. These two chapters may be regarded as pre-historic; for, strictly speaking, the scope of the work lies within the fifty years which closed last May. What was the state of this country in those times? People found themselves in the face of savage nature, and had to engage in a deadly struggle to compel it to yield even a bare subsistence. These poor settlers, habitually deprived of the consolations of religion, of its holy word and holier bread of life, its saving truths, its sanctifying prayer and heavenly sacrifice, gradually grew careless; and it is not surprising that on reviewing the past we have reason to mourn the loss of many a family whose fathers came to this country rich in faith and the love of their ancestral Church.

The Scotch Catholics in Glengarry and the French in Essex were more fortunate in this respect than their Irish co-religionists in the other parts of Upper Canada. They always had the happiness of having their religious guides in their midst. Glengarry was a centre whence a considerable number of good, intelligent and devoted Catholics spread throughout the province, and formed rallying points around which Catholic immigrants gathered and grew into congregations. The French in Essex, being cut off by language from the other inhabitants and clinging tenaciously to their homes, had little share in the spread of the faith elsewhere.

But while the Irish had many difficulties which people of other nationalities had not, and while amongst them there were many losses to deplore, still it will ever be our pride in the new world, as in the old, that they have as a people remained faithful. Whether deep in Canadian woods, or in the wind-swept prairies of the west, or in the crowded cities of the United States, the sons and daughters of Erin have been, in the face of all their hardships, true to the cause of their religion, generous in its support and loyal to its teaching. The men who hewed our forests and dug our canals are they who built our churches and established our institutions—and as long as these monuments of faith survive, so long shall be published to the world the undying attachment to the Church of the apostolic Irish who came to these shores poor in this world's goods but rich in the treasures which religion alone can bestow.

Fifty years ago, when Toronto was created an Episcopal See, the Catholic Church in this section was in its infancy—no religious institutions, no Catholic schools, and many of our immigrants poor and unfriended. Our readers will follow through these pages its advancement from such small beginnings until, at our Golden Jubilee, we see two new dioceses sprung from Toronto; about two hundred priests; one hundred and eighty-five thousand faithful; a sufficient number of churches, many of them beautiful structures; colleges and academies for the purposes of higher education, Catholic schools, orphanages, hospitals for the suffering, and homes for the infirm and poor. The labors, struggles and sacrifices which have led up to this prosperous and gratifying condition of affairs are recorded in the following pages.

These pages will be found absorbing in interest, instruction and edification; and we commend the work to the patronage and favour of the public in general, and of our Catholic people in particular. If encouraged and patronized, as it deserves, this volume will doubtless be the precursor of others descriptive of the work of the Church in other dioceses of Ontario; and thus material will be supplied for a full and complete history of the Catholic Church in this premier province of the Dominion of Canada.

We cannot close these introductory remarks without putting on record our heartfelt thanks to the gentlemen who have so generously and disinterestedly given their time and talents to the laborious research and patient study requisite for the composition of their various chapters. They deserve well of the Church and of the country. May their names be written in the book of life!

† John Walsh,
Archbishop of Toronto.

THE LIFE

OF

THE MOST REV. JOHN WALSH, D.D.,

SECOND ARCHBISHOP OF TORONTO

BY

REV. JOHN R. TEEFY, B.A., C.S.B.,

SUPERIOR OF ST. MICHAEL'S COLLEGE, TORONTO.

THE LIFE OF THE MOST REV. JOHN WALSH, D.D.

> "I saw another Ruler rise;
> His words were noble, good and wise;
> With the calm sceptre of his pen
> He ruled the minds and thoughts of men."
> —ADELAIDE PROCTER.

TO write the history of a generation still alive is a delicate and difficult task. Public acts develop their consequences slowly. Witnesses remain with their own impressions and recollections of the various scenes, even after the actors have passed off the stage. But the biographical sketch of one who has still before him many years of usefulness and honor is necessarily unfinished. The interest claimed by the past is more or less absorbed by the unwritten future. True as this may be, our readers will feel that the career of the Most Rev. Dr. Walsh, the present Archbishop of Toronto, affords abundant material for the historian and special interest for this volume. Like a land sloping upwards from the sea, and ever presenting, as it rises, wider plains of fruitful soil, so, from boyhood to early manhood and on to riper age, the life of this venerable prelate is one continued advance in dignity and extending sphere. Besides, his Grace is no stranger to us. Coming to the diocese a young man, its Vicar-General for several years, Bishop in the ecclesiastical province, and returning to Toronto as its Archbishop, he has been closely connected with forty out of the fifty years which this work is intended to commemorate.

John Walsh was the son of James Walsh and Ellen Macdonald, and was born in the parish of Mooncoin in the County of Kilkenny, Ireland, May 23rd, 1830. This parish is adjacent to the "gentle" Suir,

> "That making way
> By sweet Clonmel adorns rich Waterford,"

and is situated in one of the most charming sections of Leinster's charming Province.

The Walsh family (written also Wallis) is a very old and honored one. The first members in Ireland were two Barons of Cornwall, David and

Philip, who accompanied Earl Strongbow in 1171. The former was created Baron of Carrickmaine by Henry II.; the latter, who had settled in Kilkenny, Baron of Pildon. Here in the course of time they acquired large possessions, which to the present day bear the name of the "Walsh Mountains." This property was afterwards confiscated during the different persecutions. Nor was property the only sacrifice they were called upon to make; the family could pride themselves in having distinguished martyrs amongst their number: one, William Walsh, Bishop of Meath, suffering under Elizabeth; another, who was Archbishop of Cashel, suffering under Cromwell. During the time of the Commonwealth and in the reign of William III., the elder branch engaged in the military service of France and Austria. In the former country the title of Count Servant was conferred upon the representative of the family. The branch which remained at home, and to which the subject of our sketch belongs, lived for generations in a condition of comfort and independence which the better class of farmers enjoy. Such homes in Ireland have been shrines of simplicity, parental authority and filial affection. Their greatest wealth has lain in their energy; their coronet is their faith; their crest their patriotism. From them have gone forth to all quarters of the globe earnest, devoted priests, who might have won distinction at home had they not chosen devotion in exile.

John Walsh is an excellent example. Evincing at an early age a desire to study for the priesthood, he was sent in due time to St. John's College, Waterford, where he made his preparatory studies with great success, standing first in his class of philosophy. He remained at St. John's to make one year of theology, when he decided that his vocation lay in the vast field of foreign missions. Accordingly, breaking all the endearing ties of home, friends and native land, he left for Canada in April, 1852. The following autumn, when studies began, the young Mr. Walsh entered the Grand Seminary of Montreal as a student of the diocese of Toronto. His industry and talent, his exemplary conduct, his strict observance of rule won the approbation of his superiors, and justified hopes concerning his future which have since been realized. He received tonsure from Bishop La Rocque at Trinity, 1853, and minor orders from Bishop Bourget, December 17th, the same year. At the close of the Seminary the following summer, when on his way from Montreal, Mr. Walsh nearly died from a severe attack of the cholera which was raging in Canada during that season. After his recovery he visited Toronto for the first time. On October 22nd, 1854, Bishop de Charbonnel ordained him sub-deacon in the Bishop's private chapel, and deacon on October 29th. On November 1st following, the Feast of All Saints, the same prelate raised him to the holy priesthood in St. Michael's Cathedral. After ordination, Father Walsh was attached to no particular curacy; his duty consisted in attending every place that happened to be vacant—in those days only too numerous. To these scattered districts he went, catechising the young, preparing children for first communion, bearing spiritual consolation to the dying, sowing the seeds of eternal life in the hearts of all. The following year (1855) he was appointed to the Brock mission, bordering on Lake Simcoe, of which parish he was the first resident pastor. It was a trial for a young priest fresh from college to be so situated—far removed from any clerical society, in the midst of a rural population whose time and energy were taken up with the gigantic task of clearing the farms, with no railroad accommodation and with worse than indifferent roads. But it was a good school for one upon whom God had such high designs. It drove the young priest to the choicest companions he could have—his books. For the two years that Father Walsh was in this mission, he cultivated his mind with constant study. It was easy for him to do so. He was a student by nature. Endowed with a clear judgment, possessing an extraordinary memory and a rich imagination, he has all the qualifications which form an earnest, successful student. It was therefore a pleasure, as well as an obligation imposed by his surroundings, for him to have time which he might employ to such advantage for himself and his future.* But not even to the present day has Archbishop Walsh ceased studying. Whenever the duties of his sacred calling leave him any spare moments, or even when enjoying a brief season of well earned relaxation, his books are never laid aside or neglected. Nor does he take to books because he is a recluse. On the contrary, he is most congenial and delights in the society of priests. None can come within the magnetic influence of his company without being attracted by his urbanity and amiability. His fund of stories, his powers of conversation seem exhaustless; while his various travels and extensive reading, his shrewd observance of men and things, his keen sense of humor,

* His Grace, when asked a short time ago by a distinguished scholar where he had made his studies, replied that he had made some of his most useful studies by the light of the tallow candle and of the log fire in the shanties of "the settlers" of the backwoods.

have enriched him with treasures which a marvellous memory preserves only too well.

In April, 1857, Father Walsh was removed from Brock and placed in charge of the more important parish of St. Mary's in Toronto. A priest's life in the city is a very busy one. The religious community which calls for constant attention, the young people more exposed to danger, the poor more numerous and more afflicted, the pious penitent and the stubborn wanderer, all make heavy demands upon a pastor's zeal and time, while the schools require as much care as the church does administration. Full of the spirit of his holy vocation, Father Walsh applied himself to all his manifold duties with energy and constancy. Loretto Convent found in him a devoted chaplain, the schools a self-sacrificing champion, and the parish a father and friend. But amidst all he still found time to give himself to study and the careful preparation of sermons, which soon earned for him a well deserved reputation as a pulpit orator. Advancing time and more exalted state, as well as his own continued industry as a student, have increased this reputation. Archbishop Walsh's dignified appearance, rendered more dignified by the insignia of his office, his rich voice, rendered richer with a sweet, native brogue still clinging to it, his deep, earnest manner, rendered more earnest by the subjects which he treats, serve to give weight to his well balanced sentences and finely rounded periods. In style ornate, in treatment practical, in thought logical, rich in imagery and choice in language, Dr. Walsh, as a speaker, is never commonplace, always impressive, and in many passages brilliantly eloquent. The following eulogy on the Catholic priesthood is taken from his sermon on the occasion of the late venerable Father Dowd's golden jubilee, which was celebrated in St. Patrick's Church, Montreal, May 26th, 1887 :

" There is no body of men," said Bishop Walsh, " known to history that have rendered mankind such great and inappreciable services as the Catholic priesthood. They redeemed the world from barbarism and conferred upon it the blessings of christian civilization. They freed the slave and opened the doors of the dungeon to persons unjustly detained. They redeemed millions of captives from Mahometan prisons. In every centre of population they erected and supported hospitals for the sick and suffering, and houses for the poor and helpless. They invented a language for deaf mutes, and thus opened up God's glorious creation, with all its beauties, wonders and meanings, and all the fountains of knowledge and the saving truths of religion to minds hitherto imprisoned behind the adamantine walls of unbroken silence and deafness, and shrouded in more than Egyptian darkness. The great universities of the world that flamed out like beacons on a dark and stormy sea, they founded and endowed. Parish schools for children were established by them. To the working classes they taught trades, as well as agriculture. They taught the rich the duty of helping the poor, and they defended and upheld human rights and liberties against the tyrant and oppressor. The arts and sciences were brought to perfection by them. Printing, sculpture, music, architecture, eloquence and poetry were by them christianized, perfected and immortalized. They have been the greatest benefactors of mankind, the most virtuous, the most enlightened, the most disinterested, the most useful body of men that ever lived. To say that some of them fell from their high estate and lofty ideals, and were stained with sin and vice, is to admit that they were human, and liable to the influence of human passions and the seductions of the flesh; but the fallen were the few; and the great body, having on the panoply of God, led lives of purity, justice and holiness, and by their great learning and splendid virtues have made a track of light across the waste of centuries."

Very soon after the consecration of Dr. Lynch in 1859, Father Walsh was appointed rector of St. Michael's Cathedral. It was the following September, when the Prince of Wales visited Canada, that the new rector of the Cathedral came forth more publicly, and displayed some of that force of character which has ever since made him a leader amongst men. He was chief organizer of a mass meeting of Catholics called to "take into consideration most important matters connected with the visit of the Prince of Wales." A large and influential meeting was held, over which Father Walsh presided, and which he addressed at some length. He said: "They had assembled to deliberate on the part the Catholics of Toronto should take in the reception of the Prince of Wales in this city. The peculiar circumstances in which they were placed by the action of a portion of their fellow citizens, who were intending to make this reception the occasion of insulting the feelings of Catholics, compelled them to adopt this procedure, in order to give expression to their feelings and to concert together as to the line of action they ought to pursue. Fain would they wish to be permitted to join in the intended demonstration in honor of the Prince of Wales with all their fellow citizens, without distinction of sect or country. Fain would they wish to be permitted to join the mighty throng that would assemble on that occasion to greet their royal visitor, and like the waters of the St. Lawrence, which gathered strength and body from the tributaries that flowed into it, until they poured, a mighty flood, into the ocean, so would they wish to pour their feelings of attachment and loyalty to the Queen, through her son, in the same broad stream with those of all their fellow citizens. Catholics were loyal by principle, and not by caprice; they were loyal because their Church taught loyalty to lawfully constituted authorities. They were no believers in the divine right of kings, as the doctrine was understood nowadays; nor were they believers in the creed of the revolutionists, but they were loyal by principle, loyal according to the dictates of their Church, which taught them to be subject to the powers that be. To the taunts of disloyalty flung against them from time to time, it would be beneath them to reply. The soil of their native country had been repeatedly reddened by the blood of their martyred fathers in the struggle with traitors who had imbrued their hands in the blood of their lawful king.

"To those taunts of disloyalty their Catholic fellow countrymen of Lower Canada had given a good answer by their brilliant illuminations, by the roar of their artillery, and by their loud shouts of applause and welcome which greeted the royal visitor to our shores. Fain would they wish to take up those shouts and cheers of welcome, and cause them to echo along the borders of our blue Ontario, but they must be permitted to do so without having their feelings insulted and their self-respect trampled on, and without forfeiting those rights which they hold dearer than life. Catholics stood on a platform of equality with other denominations in this country, and should they now abate their rights in order to pander to the feelings and malicious designs of a particular class? They were aware that he alluded to the fact that the Orangemen of this country had expressed their determination to walk in full regalia on the occasion referred to; and that not content with this, not content with carrying their offensive party emblems and playing their offensive party tunes, they were now actually employed in the erection of an Orange arch, to be decorated by their Orange flags and insulting insignia, and intended that the Catholics of this city should walk beneath their yoke, in token of their bondage and slavery. Every citizen possessed of good sense would admit that this was not an occasion to be seized upon to insult the feelings of any portion of the community. Why should the Orangemen take this opportunity of raking up from the tomb of the past the ashes of our fathers, defeated by overwhelming numbers and foreign mercenaries, and flinging those ashes in our face? Orangeism, which was born in the defeat of our fathers, which, springing into existence in order to commemorate that defeat, and which raised its throne on the wreck of our common liberties, that institution should not be planted on our virgin soil to perpetuate the hatred and discord that cursed our native land. It had been planted here by one whom they all knew to be of a very reputable character, and he must say the offspring was worthy of its immaculate sire. He was proud to inform the meeting that the most influential citizens of Toronto, men not professing the same creed as themselves, had set their face against this proposition of the Orangemen, and had denounced it in no measured terms. He believed the vast majority of the impartial Protestants of Toronto denounced the proceedings as an insult to themselves as well as to Catholics, because they considered this was an occasion on which all citizens ought to act together. It would be proposed that this meeting should memorialize the Duke of Newcastle, the Prince's adviser, telling him how they would feel if any formal recognition of the Orange body was given by the Prince or his advisers."

Father Walsh concluded by urging upon his hearers quiet and peaceable behavior whatever might be the issue of their remonstrance, so that they might not place themselves on the same low level with those who flaunted their yellow colors in the face of the midday sun.

A deputation, consisting of Captain Elmsley, Colonel Baldwin and J. G. Moylan, Esq., was appointed to present to the Duke of Newcastle a memorial protesting against the erection of such an arch, and that it would be "the means of preventing your memorialists from participating in the welcome of His Royal Highness to this part of Canada." It went on to say:

"That on an occasion like the present your memorialists most anxiously desire to participate in the joyful pleasure of tendering a hearty welcome to the heir apparent of the British Crown to this prosperous and noble dependency of the Empire, but in view of the contemplated action of the Orange association, a feeling of self-respect must preclude your memorialists from joining in the demonstration to His Royal Highness, as under no circumstances can they submit to the degradation of passing under an arch displaying offensive emblems, calculated to provoke a breach of the peace.

"That your memorialists, having appealed to the local authorities in vain, and endeavored by every means in their power to avert this offensive display, now as a last resource appeal to your Grace to aid them in discountenancing this insulting demonstration of party spirit on the part of a sworn secret society, with whose history your Grace is doubtless familiar, whose acts have very often led to sanguinary conflicts, and at the present time have called for the action of the Imperial Parliament.

"Wherefore, your memorialists humbly pray that your Grace, so long distinguished in the councils of your country for liberal and just views of policy, may be pleased to represent to His Royal Highness the nature of the wanton insult about to be offered to a large class of Her Majesty's loyal subjects, the danger to be apprehended to the peace of the city if it be allowed to pass unmarked by his disapprobation, an insult which would not be permitted to take place in England or Ireland without summary punishment.

"And your petitioners, as in duty bound, will ever pray," &c.

As a result of this meeting and memorial the Prince of Wales refused to recognise the existence of the arch in question, and Orangeism received a blow from which it did not rally for years.

On Easter Sunday, April 20th, 1862, Father Walsh was made Vicar-General of the diocese. In September of the same year, resigning his rectorship of the Cathedral, he returned as pastor to St. Mary's Church. In May, 1863, he attended the third Provincial Council of Quebec as theologian to the Bishop of Toronto. The following spring Vicar-General Walsh, after having been twelve years away, determined on visiting Ireland. His friends availed themselves of the opportunity to testify their regard by presenting him with a gold watch bearing the inscription: "A token of affectionate esteem to the Very Rev. J. Walsh, V. G., from his friends in St. Michael's parish, Toronto." They also, with great delicacy and thoughtfulness, sent to Father Walsh's mother a present of a gold cross, very massive and beautifully wrought with wreaths of shamrocks, bearing on the reverse side the following engraving: "A souvenir sent from Toronto, C. W., to the mother of the Very Rev. J. Walsh, V. G., from his admiring friends." We quote one paragraph from the address which accompanied these offerings, as showing the pleasing relations which the subject of our sketch retained with all the Catholic citizens of Toronto:

"In the great and holy works of the sacred ministry you have labored with earnest zeal and patient ability. While bearing the heat and burthen of the day, you have given evidence of an industry whose main inspiration is God's honor and the people's good. By the simple combination of the rare qualities united in the good priest and citizen, you have gained the good will and commanded the respect of every one who is capable of appreciating the merits of one who wears to this day 'the white flower of a stainless life.'"

Father Walsh replied: "Your good nature attributes to me qualities which even my self-love cannot convince me that I possess. The picture which you draw of what I am, and of what I have done in the holy ministry, is truly beautiful—it is the most flattering photograph I have yet seen; but, unfortunately, it is not mine—it is but the ideal of what I ought to be, and of what I, indeed, would wish to be. The image which I am accustomed to see on the mirror of my conscience is not quite so pleasing, though it is a faithful reflex of the original. But those who look through the prism of friendship will see the most beautiful and the most varied lights of virtue shining on the path of one who, after all, plods the weary journey of life under no brighter sky than do the most ordinary mortals."

Nor was he forgotten by his people of St. Mary's, who presented him with a purse and an address expressive of the deep affection in which he was held by his flock.

Upon this occasion the Vicar-General paid his first visit to the Eternal City. He was received most graciously by the Venerable Pius IX., who manifested the deepest interest in the Canadian Church. After travelling some time in Europe, Father Walsh spent a few months in Ireland, visiting again the home of his childhood. Sorrow had thrown its shadow over the hearthstone by removing his father, who had died the year previously. But he had the joy of offering up beneath the parental roof the holy sacrifice for those from whom he had been so long separated, but with whom he was ever closely united in ties of affection and bonds of faith.

During all this time Father Walsh was a busy writer and speaker. Amidst his many parochial duties he still found time to be a constant contributor to the press and to deliver sermons innumerable. We read of him preaching at the Mass for Cardinal Wiseman in 1865, at the blessing of St. Michael's Cathedral bell in 1866, at the laying of the corner stone of Guelph Church; while the demands for him on anniversaries of different kinds were too many for him to fulfil.

The health of Dr. Pinsonneault, Bishop of Sandwich, becoming impaired it was necessary to select a successor. Accordingly the hierarchy of the ecclesiastical province of Quebec unanimously nominated Vicar-General Walsh as future bishop. The choice was in due time ratified by bulls from the Holy See.

The consecration took place in St. Michael's Cathedral, Toronto, November 10th, 1867. The following Bishops were present: Rt. Rev. E. Langevin of Rimouski, L. Lafleche of Three Rivers, J. J. Conroy of Albany, N. Y., E. Horan of Kingston, J. Farrell of Hamilton, and J. E. B. Guigues of Ottawa. The consecrating Bishop was Mgr. Baillargeon, then Archbishop of Quebec; the assistant Bishops were the Rt. Rev. J. Bourget, Bishop of Montreal, and Rt. Rev. J. J. Lynch, Bishop of Toronto. Rev. J. M. Bruyere, Vicar-General of Sandwich, acted as assistant priest to the bishop elect, and the Very Rev. Father Rice, C. M., of the College of Our Lady of Angels, Suspension Bridge, and the Rev. H. Moreau of Montreal, performed the same function towards the assistant consecrating bishops. The Very Rev. J. F. Jamot, V. G., was archpriest. The deacons of honor near the archiepiscopal throne were the Very Rev. Dean Crinnon of Stratford, and Very Rev. F. P. Rooney, Toronto; while the deacon and sub-deacon of the Mass were Very Rev. C. Vincent, President of St. Michael's College, and Rev. M. Gagnon of Quebec. The Very Rev. G. Northgraves of Barrie acted as notary to the Archbishop. The master of ceremonies upon the occasion was the Rev. T. Morris. Besides those mentioned there were fifty-two other priests present. The sermon of the day was preached by the Very Rev. Father Dowd of Montreal, "upon the substance of the great act which these ceremonies so expressively accompany." "The consecration of a new bishop in the Catholic Church," continued the preacher, announcing his divisions, " is the perpetuating of that lawful succession of pastors in the apostolic line through which, by the ordinance of God, true doctrine is preserved and taught to all nations to the end of time. The new bishop is a new heir of the apostles, inheriting from them, and in the same plenitude, the divine commission of Jesus Christ: 'Go teach all nations.'"

The clergy of Toronto presented his Lordship with a mitre, crozier, pectoral cross and ring on the eve of his consecration. The address accompanying the present, while it congratulated him upon his elevation to the purple, expressed very deep regret at parting with a dearly beloved brother. After referring to the many acts of kindness and friendship which they, the priests of Toronto, had experienced at the hands of Bishop Walsh, the address expressed the most ardent wishes and fervent prayers for God's choicest blessings upon his episcopacy. His Lordship replied in most touching terms, dwelling upon the consolation afforded a priest by his confreres in the ministry, "who are animated by the spirit of their holy state, whose lives are in beautiful accord with the requirements of their holy calling. . . . . It is hard to part with priests—the companions of happy years—who have endeared themselves to me by their many kindnesses—their never wavering confidence and steady friendships—hard to be withdrawn from the care of a holy bishop, who was to me at once a father and friend, as well as a bright example of the virtues which I should practise; but the voice of God calls, and I must obey. But, go where I will, rest assured, that the bishop and priests of the diocese of Toronto shall ever occupy a large place in my heart and in my memory. Adieu, friends, for ever dear, and be sure that I will not fail to remember you there where remembrance is indeed precious—at the holy altar."

Besides this address many others were presented. The institutions of the city, the personal friends of his Lordship, his old parish of St. Mary's, all vied with one another in doing honor to the memorable occasion, and sent him forth loaded with the prayers and blessings of faithful souls and the handsome presents of generous hearts.

The newly consecrated bishop, accompanied by the Bishops of Kingston and Hamilton and a large number of clerical friends, reached London, en route for Sandwich,* on the 13th of November. After the formal reception

---

* Bishop Pinsonneault, who had been consecrated Bishop of London, transferred the See to Sandwich in 1859.

of his Lordship had taken place at St. Peter's Cathedral, Dean Crinnon read the following address of welcome:

"MY LORD: The priests of the diocese here assembled respectfully approach your Lordship with feelings of joy, to offer you our sincere and hearty welcome to the diocese. We know that in taking charge of this diocese you have made many sacrifices. In your former position as pastor of St. Mary's and Vicar-General of the diocese of Toronto, you had no extraordinary fatigue to endure or difficulties to overcome, and enjoyed the love and esteem of all. You have, my Lord, in obedience to the voice of the Holy Father, made this noble and generous sacrifice to enter a diocese in which there are many wants and pressing difficulties; but the cross has no terror for a true disciple of his Heavenly Master. He who called you to this responsible office will supply the necessary grace to enable you to discharge it. We know how much the welfare of a diocese depends on its bishop; we were, therefore, filled with joy when we heard of your appointment to the See of Sandwich; for your Lordship's known ability, zeal and prudence are sure guarantees for the future welfare of this new diocese. We are truly thankful to God for giving us a bishop so endowed with talent and virtue; and to you, my Lords, we are grateful for selecting one so capable of advancing the interests of our holy religion, which is so dear to us all. In conclusion, my Lord, we beg to assure you that we will cheerfully co-operate with you in all you undertake for the glory of God and the salvation of souls."

This was the key-note of the success of Bishop Walsh's administration. The confidence pledged on that occasion between the priests and their bishop was kept faithfully on both sides. Twenty years and three went by with all the changes which such a length of time is sure to bring before the relations then established were broken; and all that time the mutual confidence developed, veneration for the episcopal dignity gave way to warm affection for him who bore it, and casual acquaintance developed into life-long friendship.

The following day, November 14th, his Lordship was duly installed in the Cathedral of Sandwich.

In January, 1868, Bishop Walsh removed the episcopal residence from Sandwich to London, to which city the See was again transferred by a decree from the Propaganda dated November 15th, 1869.

In this large field of Christ's vineyard his Lordship immediately applied himself with extraordinary resolution and ability to the important duties of his exalted office. Beginning by a thorough examination into the affairs of the diocese, he found the outlook very unpromising, and requiring all his courage and spirit of sacrifice. A large and pressing debt of about $35,000 had to be liquidated; the reorganization of the clergy and missions was urgent; a number of priests had to be provided; in many parishes churches and presbyteries had to be built, or restored and enlarged; the interests of education demanded earnest, immediate attention; asylums for the orphan and the infirm had to be established.

All this, if any good was to be done, required arduous and constant labor, and Bishop Walsh was equal to the occasion. Nothing daunted by the difficulties which surrounded him, he set himself with earnestness about putting his house in order. He visited every mission in his diocese; and everywhere he administered confirmation, delivered eloquent exhortations, founded churches and schools where required, catechised the young, encouraged the old, and appealed to all to help in removing obligations which were preventing him from doing the good he contemplated. Nobly seconded by a faithful clergy and a generous laity, he succeeded within three years in paying off the heavy debt which had at first confronted him. His success, however, was achieved at the risk of his life. The physical and mental strain so long endured, undermined his Lordship's health to such a degree, that his medical adviser insisted upon a long period of rest and a change of scene. The bishop accordingly visited Ireland for the second time in 1870. He was thus prevented from attending the Vatican Council which had begun its sittings towards the end of the year previous. His Lordship's interests in this great assembly were no less keen. In May, 1869, he issued an erudite pastoral "upon the magisterial authority of the Church in matters of faith," "as also upon the nature of General Councils and their great importance and bearing in Catholic theology on articles of faith." In 1875, when the Hon. W. E. Gladstone, in a celebrated pamphlet, attacked the decree of Papal Infallibility, Bishop Walsh contributed a lengthy and very learned essay upon the subject. But controversial writing makes heavy reading. The precious stones of historical evidence and logical proof which the controversialist draws from the deep mines of tradition need the jeweller's setting before they adorn the writer or please the reader. Bishop Walsh has afforded this setting in the numerous pastorals which he has issued in the course of his long episcopate. As compositions these pastorals bear in form the impress of a polished writer; and in matter the riches of a well stored mind. Replete with Sacred Scripture, the holy fathers, the history and practice of the Church, they are pregnant with instruction upon the various subjects treated. Practical in their bearing, a spirit of earnest piety, so natural to their author, breathes from every page; and their language is that of a kind father teaching his children the most important lessons of life, and bidding them love God, the Sacred Heart, the Blessed Mother, the Church, the dead. His Lordship has also published a very touching little work upon the Sacred Heart. We regret that we cannot dwell any longer upon writings which, by their number and quality, well deserve more careful notice. We hope that those who come after us will collect in fitting manner the pastorals and other works of the subject of our sketch, and so prevent them being consigned to the dust of shelves or the grave of oblivion.

In 1876 he paid his official visit as Bishop to Rome. Upon his return he gave an interesting abstract of the report made to the Holy See of the religious growth during the decade then completed. After speaking about the payment of the diocesan debt, his Lordship proceeded: "Twenty-eight new churches have been raised to the glory of God, and for the purposes of religion. All these edifices, with few exceptions, are of brick and stone, and many of them are splendid and costly structures. Besides, five churches have been greatly enlarged and improved. Seventeen commodious presbyteries have been built for the accommodation of the parochial clergy. An episcopal residence, second to none in the Province, has been constructed, and not a cent of debt has been left upon it. Three convents have been built. Mount Hope has been purchased and paid for, and a splendid new orphanage has been erected on it; and besides, a handsome new college in Sandwich has been built by the self-sacrificing zeal of the Basilian Fathers. In fine, more than a quarter of a million dollars has been actually expended in church improvement within the last nine years. These facts are extremely creditable to the public spirit of the laity of the diocese, as well as to the zeal and self-sacrifice of the priests. If they had not husbanded their resources instead of expending them on their families, and had not put them apart for the service of God's Church, these splendid results had never been achieved. We know, dearly beloved brethren, that a good and efficient priesthood are, in a certain sense, the life and soul of the church. They are the representatives of God, the ambassadors of Jesus Christ, the dispensers of the sacred treasures of His sufferings and death. Without them, religion languishes and immortal souls are starved for want of the bread of life. Twenty-three pious and efficient priests have been ordained during the last nine years ; five have been regularly affiliated to the diocese, and nine Basilian Fathers have come to take charge of two parishes, and to conduct the College of Sandwich. About ten thousand children have received the sacrament of Confirmation, and most of them have been pledged to abstain from the use of intoxicating drinks until they shall have attained their majority. This is a summary of the work done in the last nine years."

"The Holy Father," continued the Bishop, "bestowed upon me many favors, for which I hope to be forever thankful, and some of which I trust the diocese will hold in grateful recollection. One of these was that, at my request, he bestowed upon our Vicar-General, the Very Rev. J. M. Bruyere, the dignity of a Roman prelate, in consideration of his virtues and talents, and the eminent services he has rendered the church in Canada during the last twenty-five years. You, who know the Vicar-General well, will agree with me in saying that the dignity of the Roman purple was in this case well deserved and very fittingly bestowed. His Holiness also gave me free places for two ecclesiastical students in the College of the Propaganda, the alma mater of some of the most distinguished men that ever shed a lustre on the church by their genius and their virtues."

On November 28th, 1877, the clergy of the diocese assembled in London to tender their congratulations upon the tenth anniversary of Bishop Walsh's elevation to the episcopate. They presented a very complimentary address, which they accompanied with a generous gift of $3,000, in testimony of their affectionate esteem and their appreciation of his sterling qualities of heart and mind. The priests whom the bishop had ordained since his arrival in the diocese also presented him with an address and a very valuable ostensorium. The former address, after mentioning the various works which had been accomplished since Bishop Walsh's consecration, amongst others, "the creation and establishment, on a permanent basis, of St. John's Society, which provided for the decent support of the infirm and aged priests of the diocese," spoke of his Lordship personally: "While thus adverting to your ability in administration, we must not omit to mention that whereas energy and zeal are often accompanied by harshness, your Lordship has been able to reconcile the successful administration of an important charge with a suavity of manner which has endeared you to all, so that you are regarded by all as a kind father; and it is this quality, more especially, which has secured to you the filial affection of both clergy and laity in the diocese, and the respect and admiration of all with whom you have intercourse. Permit us, then, on behalf of the laity as well as for ourselves, to tender to you our congratulations on the prosperity of the diocese, which, after the providence of God, is due chiefly to your Lordship."

But not only was Bishop Walsh honored by his subjects; he received at the time a signal mark of the confidence reposed in him by his superiors in Rome. The late Dr. Lynch, Archbishop of Toronto, either signified to the Propaganda his wish to resign, or had actually sent in his resignation. What circumstances led up to this important step, and what others checked the successful issue of the proposed arrangement, are irrelevant to this biographical sketch. Suffice it to say that Dr. Conroy, delegate of the Holy See, wrote Bishop Walsh from Montreal, 16th September, 1877, as follows: " You will probably have already received Cardinal Franchi's letter announcing that the Sacred Congregation of the Propaganda, with the approval of his Holiness, has designated you as Coadjutor for Toronto." Again he writes to Bishop Walsh in December of the same year: " I congratulate you on the interesting meeting* of the other day, in which your Clergy paid you so splendid and so well merited a compliment. I do not wonder that you shrink from exchanging the diocese which, through you, has been blessed with such men, for the difficult honor of being Coadjutor to an Archbishop."

It is also a matter of history that Toronto was not the only archdiocese which Rome urged upon Bishop Walsh to accept.

On November the 16th, 1879, Bishop Walsh celebrated the silver jubilee of his sacerdotal ordination. The clergy of the diocese read him an address " expressing their heartfelt wishes for his welfare and paying due

* His Lordship refers to the meeting in London of the clergy related above.

homage to his virtues and talents," accompanying it with the presentation of a complete set of the Greek and Latin Fathers. In returning thanks his Lordship thus reviewed the past :

" You congratulate me on the twenty-fifth anniversary of my ordination to the holy priesthood. Would that these precious years had been more profitably spent! Twenty-five years are but a speck of time in the life of the immortal Church, but they are a great deal in the life of an individual, spanning, as they do, the golden vale of his existence. In looking back through these vanished years, whilst there are many things in the retrospect to trouble the individual conscience for duties omitted or imperfectly performed, yet there are many things also calculated to comfort and encourage. Within that period, short as it is, the progress of the church in Ontario has been very great indeed. There are nearly as many priests in one diocese now, as there were twenty-five years ago in the four dioceses and the vicariate apostolic that constituted the ecclesiastical province of Ontario. There were vast districts then without priest or church. Children grew up without religious instruction, and many of them were in consequence lost to the faith. The little ones of Christ were famishing for the bread of life, and there was no consecrated hand to break it unto them. The holy sacrifice of the Mass, the great central act of christian worship, for which the most glorious structure that ever was designed by human genius and raised by human hands is too unworthy, was offered up at distant intervals in the smoky cabin or the humble log chapel. Now this sad state of things has utterly disappeared; and instead, we behold the Church and her institutions in a hopeful and flourishing condition. The Separate School system, greatly amended, is being worked with efficiency and with beneficial results ; there is a sufficient number of colleges and conventual academies for higher education, whilst the orphans and the aged poor are provided for in institutions established for the purpose.

" To the holy bishops and zealous priests, some of whom have passed to their reward, and others of whom still remain to edify us by their example, this happy state of things is, under God, mainly due. They bore the burthen of the day and the heats; they sowed in tears that we might reap in joy ; 'sowing they went and wept, casting their seeds; but we, coming with joyfulness, carry the sheaves.' (Ps. cxxv., 6.) It is for us to take up the great work they began, and as far as in us lies to carry it to a successful issue. Canada is a free and happy country. No penal law has ever soiled the virgin page of its statute book ; no state trammels hamper the action and clog the activity of the Church. Here the bride of Christ may walk forth in all her majesty and loveliness, like unto the spouse of the canticles coming up from the desert, like the morning rising, and fragrant with perfumes of sweetest odor. Here there is open to the divine energies and zeal of the Church a field of labor as fair and free as that on which the eyes of the patriarch rested when about to separate from Lot. Great, then, are our opportunities, and great also our responsibilities ; may we not be wanting to them. Such are thoughts that are uppermost in my mind to-day, and to which I have thus ventured to give expression. I thank you once again for your extreme kindness, and I humbly pray that the blessing of our heavenly Father may descend upon you and abide with you always."

The diocese was by this time placed upon a solid basis : religion had its shrines and priests ; learning, its college, its academies and its schools ; charity, its houses for the infirm and the poor. One thing the diocese did not possess : a cathedral worthy of the name. Accordingly Bishop Walsh, who had long set his heart upon it, now devoted his energies to the building of a stately temple, which, to quote his own words, " would be the enduring monument of the faith and hope and charity of the apostolic people who planted the mustard seed of the Catholic faith in this country." The time was now ripe for carrying out the cherished design. On the 22nd of May, 1881, the corner stone was laid, bearing upon its eastern face the following inscription :

<pre>
         Hunc lapidem angularem
             Benedixit ac posuit
         Revmus Joannes Walsh,
            Episcopus Londinensis,
          XXII Maii Anno Domini
                MDCCCLXXXI.
</pre>

The sermons were preached by Archbishop Lynch of Toronto in the morning, and Bishop Cleary of Kingston in the evening.

The Cathedral consists of nave and chancel with transepts, chapels, baptistery, and towers, sacristy, morning chapel and chapter-house. The last two, as well as the spires which are intended to surmount the towers, are not yet completed. A cloister will connect the adjacent episcopal residence with the chapter-house and the cathedral. The total length of

St Peter's Cathedral, London

the cathedral proper is over two hundred feet, and total breadth about one hundred and fifteen feet. From the ground to the ridge of the main roof is about ninety feet, while each tower with its cross and vane will rise to the height of two hundred and twenty feet. The walls are composed of fine brown-red stone laid in blue Ohio sandstone and Queenston limestone for the finer and bolder dressings respectively, and Scotch granite for the shafts of the pillars. The style of architecture is of the early French period. Three magnificent doorways give entrance to the body of the church, while two others give access to the transepts. The great rose window in the front gable over the main door, and the minor wheel window in each transept, give a charm to the principal façade. Entering by the front vestibule the view of the majestic nave, with its lofty clere-story and loftier groined roof, ending in the distant octagonal apse, gorgeously lighted with its splendid coronal of stained glass windows, is most striking. The main altar, of very chaste design, is of beautiful white marble, with other species for pillars supporting the tabernacle; and when the reredos proposed is in its place, it will greatly enhance the beauty of a beautiful church. We do not compare it with any of the English cathedrals; for it is as yet incomplete. Like many of them it stands forth on an extensive green sward and shows to greatest advantage. But Canadian cathedrals must differ from those old minsters and shrines. The shadows cast by the gray towers of the one are the shadows of morning twilight, with future glory rising over them; while the shadows of the others are those of night, whose sun has long gone down, and whose morrow seems very distant. But in point of architecture St. Peter's Cathedral will rank with many of them, and is a credit to the architect, Mr. Joseph Connolly, as it is a glory to Bishop Walsh, his devoted priests, and his generous people of London diocese.

It reached its present state in 1885, and was ready to be opened. On April 19th of that year, when, for the last time, religious services were held in old St. Peter's, his Lordship alluded most touchingly to the memories of the venerated edifice which they were about to vacate for the new and stately cathedral which, when dedicated, would also bear the cherished title of their old and beloved church. Within a short time the cathedral was ready for divine worship, it being dedicated with becoming pomp on June 28th by Bishop Walsh. Besides his Lordship, seven other prelates and a large number of clergy, both from the diocese and elsewhere, were present upon the occasion. The Rt. Rev. Dr. McQuaid, Bishop of Rochester, preached in the morning, pontifical high Mass being sung by Bishop Jamot of Peterborough, with the Very Rev. M. J. Walsh, V. G., of Philadelphia, as assistant priest; the Very Rev. E. L. Heenan, V. G., of Hamilton, as deacon; the Rev. Jas. Lonergan of Montreal, as subdeacon. In the evening, Bishop Walsh sang Vespers, assisted by the Very Revs. O'Connor of Sandwich and Delavigne of Montreal. The Rt. Rev. Dr. O'Farrell, Bishop of Trenton, N. J., preached.

At a banquet given at Mount Hope Orphanage in the afternoon, Bishop Walsh, returning thanks to the visiting prelates and priests, spoke thus of the work which had received the crown of religious blessing and dedication: "I care not what the worldly-wise may now or hereafter say about the wisdom or folly of that undertaking which we have this day brought to a partial completion, but I am satisfied that christian men will admit that in a material age, when great and colossal structures are raised for the purposes of commerce and the worship of mammon, the clergy and laity of this diocese have deserved well of religion, and have done a noble christian work by building this beautiful and stately temple for the glory of God and of His Christ, the honor of Holy Church, and the sanctification of immortal souls. I cannot close without paying the tribute of my thanks and praise to the accomplished christian architect, Mr. Joseph Connolly, under whose creative genius the unconscious stones of our Cathedral have grown into shape and beauty, and the symmetry and perfection of life. Thanks are also due to the clerk of works, Mr. John Wright, and to all; for all," concluded his Lordship, "have faithfully done their duty and justly deserved gratitude and commendation."*

---

*The following is a letter of congratulation from Bishop de Charbonnel to Mgr. Bruyere:

LYONS, July 23rd, 1885.

RT. REV. AND DEAR FRIEND,—I have just finished reading the five long pages in the *Catholic Record*, containing a description of the dedication of your splendid Cathedral. I send you my hearty congratulations on this magnificent result. It is his Lordship Bishop Walsh who should be specially happy on this occasion. His undertaking must have appeared rash to some; I myself would never have dreamt of even thinking of such a tacky, and behold an immense success obtained! It is to my mind an additional proof that an Irish priest who is zealous and exemplary can do any amount of good with his compatriots, with his faith and so great a heart. Please, tell his Lordship how largely I share in his joy, in his triumph, and, above all, in all the good that is safe to flow from this *chef d'oeuvre* of zeal, prudence, patience, business tact, and refined taste. The description given of the church in the "Record," as well as of all the circumstances of the solemnity, has struck me with admiration, and I wish you to convey to the editor my sincere compliments therefor.

The present letter being written solely to express my delight, I will conclude by embracing with you, his Lordship the Bishop, and you also, my dear friend of other days in Toronto. I had nearly forgotten the magnificent collection taken up on the occasion of the dedication. I never heard or knew of the like before.

Yours devotedly in Christ,

† ARMAND F. M. de CHARBONNEL.

Another church, St. Joseph's of Chatham, requires a brief mention in this chapter, as due to the fostering zeal of Bishop Walsh. It was dedicated by his Lordship October 23rd, 1887; upon which occasion he preached one of his most eloquent sermons upon the Catholic Church as "the house of God and the gate of heaven." This Church, erected by the Franciscan Fathers who have charge of Chatham, is pure Roman in architecture, with a fine clere-story. Two towers rising to the height of 175 feet give the front a very striking appearance. In the interior, eleven stone columns on each side, adorned with Corinthian capitals, separate the central nave from the two aisles, and two more beautifully decorated columns separate it from the sanctuary. It is 74 feet wide by 190 feet long with a transept of 110 feet in width. When completed, it will cost $100,000.

Resuming the biography which the above descriptions interrupted, we find Bishop Walsh again crossing the ocean on a visit to Ireland in July, 1882. In 1864 he had assisted at the laying of the corner stone of the O'Connell monument in Dublin, and, by a happy coincidence of events, he took part, on the 15th of August, 1882, in the ceremony of the unveiling. Upon his return to Canada, his Lordship was presented with a very complimentary address by the citizens of London and the substantial gift of $1,000, "as a voluntary testimony of esteem." A few days after, he was entertained at a public dinner in the London Club by a number of influential citizens.

In the fall of 1884, Bishop Walsh, by special invitation, assisted at the third Plenary Council of Baltimore.

At the close of the twentieth year of his episcopate, November, 1887, his Lordship again repaired to Rome to make the official returns of his diocese. Before his departure the clergy made him a personal present of over one thousand dollars, besides sending $5,200 as an offering to the Holy Father. The Bishop assisted at the Pope's Jubilee, which was celebrated in St. Peter's on December 31st, 1887. Upon arriving home his Lordship issued a pastoral giving an interesting account of the memorable event and the lessons which it contained.

While Bishop Walsh was on his way back to this country, Archbishop Lynch of Toronto laid down in death the crozier which for twenty-eight years he had carried with so much zeal, having appointed in his illness the Very

Rev. Fathers Rooney and Laurent Administrators. The former, who had the actual management of affairs, conducted the diocese with a prudence and firmness which had always characterized the different periods when he had been in charge. Administrators are not expected to make history. Their success lies in them not doing so. Father Rooney succeeded admirably; for while he earnestly maintained the activity of religion, no event occurred special enough to be recorded. In the mean time all eyes were turned towards London; Rome spoke; Bishop Walsh gave his placet; and from one end of the country to the other all acknowledged the wisdom of the Holy Father's selection. Thus by a brief from Rome, dated August 27th, 1889, was closed his Lordship's brilliant and successful career as Bishop of London. What were the good Bishop's feelings in parting may be best described by quotations from his farewell pastoral of November 1st, 1889:

"For twenty-two years we have labored together—bishop, priests and people—in our respective spheres for the glory of God and the progress of our holy religion. We have worked together in mutual confidence, in unity of purpose, and with disinterested and magnanimous co-operation; and God has blessed and fructified, as with the dews of heaven, our united labors, our arduous undertakings for the honor and weal of the Church within the diocese, and the spiritual welfare of its people.

"The ties that bind us to the diocese of London are the closest and most intimate. We have spent the best part of our sacerdotal life amongst you. Twenty-two years form a great part of a man's life. We have ordained the great majority of the priests of the diocese, and raised them to a participation in the eternal priesthood of Christ. This is a unique and sacred relationship between priests and their bishop, that can never be broken. We have given the sacrament of confirmation to many generations of our young people, thereby strengthening them in the profession of the faith, and marking them with an ineffaceable character as soldiers of Jesus Christ. We have dedicated your churches and institutions to the glory of God, and for the purposes of religion. In a word, we have lived and planned and toiled with you for twenty-two years in the Lord's vineyard, sharing with you the burthen of the day and the heats, until our heart's affections have grown and gathered around you as a diocese, even as ivy grows and clings to the walls of some holy building. In parting with you, therefore, we are wrenching our heart-strings from persons and institutions

to which they would fain cling to the end. God knows that we had no
other ambition or desire in this matter than to be allowed to end our days
amongst you, and in death to occupy a crypt in our beautiful cathedral,
where we had hoped to be remembered by our spiritual children, and to
have a share in their prayers and suffrages, and in the expiatory merits of
the holy sacrifice daily offered on its altars. But God has willed otherwise,
and it is our duty to obey His call. But though the ties that bound us be
severed, and though separated by distance from each other, we trust that
we shall ever remain united in loving memory and in the sweet inter-
communion of holy prayer.

"We can never forget you; we are deeply grateful for all your kindness;
we love you all in the Sacred Heart of Jesus. We leave you with heart-felt
regrets, for you are in our hearts, to die together and to live together.
(II. Cor., vii., 3.) We recommend ourselves most earnestly to your prayers,
and we shall not fail, in turn, to ask that the grace of our Lord Jesus Christ
and the charity of God and the communication of the Holy Ghost may be
with you all." (II. Cor., xiii.)

On November 27th, 1889, Archbishop Walsh preached his last official
sermon in London Cathedral, and took farewell of his priests and the
congregation. The clergy presented him with an address congratulating
him upon his exaltation, calling to mind all that had been accomplished
during his administration in the diocese, "which never could be obliterated
from the grateful, affectionate and, on that day, alas! stricken hearts of the
priests." The laity also presented an address; and, joining with the
clergy, made his Grace a gift of $2,000 for the purchase of an archiepiscopal
outfit.

Accompanied by Archbishop Cleary of Kingston, Bishop Dowling of
Hamilton, a large number of the London priests, and several laymen, his
Grace left his home of many happy years for that of his earlier manhood.
And that evening in St. Michael's Cathedral, many who had witnessed his
consecration, and had received his first episcopal benediction, now knelt to
receive his blessing as Archbishop of Toronto. The hand which gave it
still wore its strength and vigor of old. Time had dealt gently with Dr.
Walsh. The form was erect; the voice full and rich as erst it rang through
those vaulted walls. The silver hair showing beneath the mitre alone told
the story that years had passed and age was coming on. But we are

anticipating. His Grace was met at Hamilton by a large deputation of the clergy and laity from Toronto. Immediately upon their arrival at the last named city, a procession was formed, and upon reaching the Cathedral, the Archbishop was received by the Administrators of the Archdiocese according to the ceremonial. The only thing which had marred the proceedings was the spirit shown while the distinguished company were advancing from the station to the Church. Insulting songs were yelled and missiles hurled at the principal carriages, one stone striking his Grace a severe blow on the arm. At the conclusion of the religious ceremony in the Cathedral, Father McCann read the following address to his Grace :

"MOST REV. FATHER— We, the priests of the Archdiocese of Toronto, hail with gladness your advent to this archiepiscopal city. Joy fills our hearts because once more we have a father to love, a spiritual chief to guide, and authority divine in its origin to sustain and direct us.

"The sorrow-stricken Church of Toronto, which has bitterly deplored the loss of the good and illustrious Archbishop Lynch, at last lays aside the garb of mourning and puts on the robes of gladness. A new era has dawned upon her. New life and energy are about to be infused into the religious work of the archdiocese. Its progress will be made commensurate with the material advancement of this great city. Your presence will weld more closely the priests, religious communities and faithful into one united and harmonious body.

"Years ago your distinguished career in the priesthood of Toronto created bright anticipations of a glorious future in the Church of God. These anticipations have been abundantly realized. Your fellow priests and devoted people in this diocese hailed with unfeigned joy your elevation to the episcopate. Your successful labors and illustrious regime in the diocese of London have been at once our distinction and our pride.

"It is not necessary to recall all the good that your administration has effected: the majestic cathedral you have reared, the many charitable, educational and religious institutions your activity and zeal have originated and fostered for the glory of God, the sanctification of souls, the advancement of learning, and the solace of human suffering. With a learned and zealous priesthood, a faithful and pious people, you have built up in sublime proportions the mystical body of Christ.

"Great indeed is the sacrifice you have been called upon to make. When, in the natural course of events, you should be expected to rest from labor and enjoy the well earned fruits of your long and energetic career as Bishop of London, the voice of Christ's Vicar calls you to a more extended field of action and puts on your already tired shoulders the heavier burden of the archiepiscopate in the great metropolis of Ontario. You have magnanimously responded to that voice. You were the first of the priests of Toronto honored with a mitre. You are again to bear upon your hallowed shoulders the pallium of metropolitan jurisdiction. The brilliancy and lustre that distinguished your rule in London will be excelled in the important charge of governing the Archdiocese of Toronto. We assure your Grace, as far as in us lies, the burden will be made light by the devotedness, love and obedience of the clergy, whose chief you have now become.

"May your sojourn in our midst be a long and prosperous one. That heaven may crown your labors with its choicest blessings, is now, and ever will be the prayer of your obedient, devoted children, the priests secular and regular of the Archdiocese of Toronto, who humbly ask your paternal benediction."

Archbishop Walsh, replying, thanked them for the kind things they had said of him, and continued : " I come to do my utmost in co-operating with you for the glory of God and for the salvation of souls. I count largely, reverend Fathers, upon your help and co-operation, for as a general can do nothing without his soldiers, so a bishop can do nothing without his priests. You are necessary to me as I am necessary to you. You are nothing without the authority of the bishop, and the bishop is useless in the diocese without the help of his priests. We are surrounded in this free and noble country by a loyal and devoted laity, and it is for us to work for them and to expend ourselves for their salvation and sanctification, and for the spiritual welfare and progress of the Church of God in this country. The holy Catholic Church was the first religion in this country, except paganism, which deserves not that holy name. The Catholic Church, in the blood of her priests, consecrated the country to God ; and, please God, we shall hold it and work in this country, no matter what opposition we may meet with ; and we shall, with the grace of God and the blessing of our Divine Saviour, work together in unity and harmony with priestly zeal, for the honor and glory of God and the triumph of our holy religion. I thank you, my reverend and dear Fathers, for your words of promise, which bring great consolation to me; and I shall bear them in mind, and I know that you will at all times loyally and faithfully co-operate with your Archbishop. For my part, it will be my pleasure to become amongst you as I was with the clergy in the diocese of London, rather a father than bishop; to enter into relations of friendship with you, as Christ said to His diciples; *non dicam vos servos sed amicos.*"

An address of welcome from the laity was also presented. After replying to it his Grace ascended the pulpit, and having thanked the people for this reception, spoke at some length upon the office of bishop, and more particularly upon the great examples he had before him in the venerable prelates who had preceded him in his See of Toronto, and with whose memories that Cathedral was filled. "You are no strangers to me," concluded his Grace, "for I spent thirteen years of my priesthood amongst you. During that time I learned to respect, esteem and love the Catholics of Toronto, and acquaintances were then made and friendships formed that have never since been forgotten. I left you in the summer of my life; I return in its advanced autumn. I come back to you, changed in appearance, it is true, for time and labors and cares have left their marks upon me; but unchanged, I am sure, in my heart's best wishes for you. I trust, therefore, that we shall labor together in harmony, good will and zeal for the furtherance of the great interests of our holy religion."

After the ceremonies of the installation had taken place, the priests of the archdiocese of Toronto entertained the visiting prelates and clergy at a banquet. Thus joyously closed the day of Archbishop Walsh's return to Toronto.

A round of visits to the various institutions followed; each had its special word of welcome; and each received a special word of thanks and fatherly encouragement best suited to its own circumstances.

Then upon an appointed evening, December 4th, 1889, came the Societies with blaze of banner and blare of music, testifying their loyalty and respect. His Grace, having received their many addresses, spoke to them upon the interest he had ever taken in Catholic Societies, upon the dignity of labor and the Catholic Church as guardian of the working man, and as the one society to which we all owed religion and obedience.

The influence and character of Archbishop Walsh were very soon felt, combining as he does to a wonderful degree, suavity of manner and firmness of purpose. Respect for authority was shown with a cordiality which proved that authority had won confidence and love whilst firmly requiring obedience. Friction ceased in matters which for a long time had caused irritation. The erection of Sunnyside Chapel, the renovation of St. Michael's Cathedral, the visitation of the archdiocese, the encouragement of students for the priesthood, are some of the marks of progress made by religion since his Grace's arrival. These are of such late date that we either record them in the history of the institution or parish to which they belong, or leave them with their undeveloped consequences to the memory of our readers.

At London on October 18th, 1890, Archbishop Walsh, assisted by Bishops Foley, of Detroit, and Dowling of Hamilton, consecrated the Rt. Rev. Denis O'Connor, D. D., C. S. B., his successor to the See of London. Dr. O'Connor, who had been Superior of Assumption College, Sandwich, since its start, and to whose energy it owed its state of efficiency, had been appointed administrator of London diocese when his Grace left for Toronto. The choice was therefore not unexpected; while the new Bishop's deserved reputation gives every confidence that his Grace has entrusted his London crozier into most worthy hands.

On September the 18th of this year his Grace administered confirmation in St. Mary's Church, Toronto, and informed the congregation present that he had a most pleasing duty to fulfil, namely, that of investing his old friend, their beloved pastor, with the robes of a Roman prelate, and conferring the honor of a domestic prelate of the Holy Roman Church upon Monsignore Rooney. The following is a translation of the bulls containing the appointment:

"*To our well beloved son, Francis Patrick Rooney, Vicar-General of the Diocese of Toronto, health and apostolic benediction :*

"It is always pleasing to us to give special marks of our apostolic favor to those ecclesiastics who have distinguished themselves by virtue, learning and zeal. Now, since we have the most weighty testimony of his Grace the Archbishop of Toronto regarding the remarkable success with which you have discharged the office of vicar-general, and the wisdom and energy that have characterized your administration, it is our pleasure to confer upon you an exalted ecclesiastical dignity as a reward of your eminent services and as an evidence of our good will towards you.

"Wherefore by these presents we create and appoint you a Roman prelate of the Papal household.

"Moreover, we grant you the privilege of wearing the purple of a Roman prelate, and also the rochet, worn in the Roman Curia, together with all the other privileges, rights and marks of dignity which others bearing this distinguished rank by right or custom enjoy.

"Given at Rome, under the Ring of the Fisherman, this 29th day of July, 1892, the 15th year of our Pontificate.

S. CARDINAL VANNUTELLI."

With this gracious act towards a most venerable and most faithful faithful Vicar-General we close our imperfect sketch. Our task, which to us has been a labor of love, is now finished. And we offer it as a homage of esteem to our revered Archbishop, in admiration of his career and character, in gratitude for the sacred unction of the priesthood which he poured out upon us as upon one "out of due season."

"What is writ is writ,
Would it were worthier."

NOTE.—Our thanks are due the publishers of the "Catholic Record" of London for reports of sermons, &c., by the Archbishop.

THE INDIAN MISSIONS IN WESTERN CANADA.

BY THE

VERY REVEREND W. R. HARRIS,

DEAN OF ST. CATHARINES.

JOHN DE BRÉBEUF, JESUIT MISSIONARY.
BORN 25th MARCH, 1593.
MARTYRED 16th MARCH, 1649.

Jubilee Volume.
of the
Archdiocese of Toronto.

CHAPTER I.
1615-1760.

SKETCH OF THE EARLY MISSIONS IN WESTERN CANADA.

The Indian—The Missionary—The Recollets or Franciscans—The Jesuits—Brebeuf and Lalemant—The Sulpicians.

THE INDIAN.

> "Ye say their cone-like cabins,
> That clustered o'er the vale,
> Have fled away like withered leaves
> Before the autumn gale;
> But their memory liveth on your hills,
> Their baptism on your shore;
> Your everlasting rivers speak
> Their dialect of yore."
> — MRS. SIGOURNEY.

BEFORE entering upon a history of the heroism and self-denial of the Priests of the Catholic Church who attempted the reclamation and conversion of the nomadic tribes of North America, let us rapidly survey the divisions, subdivisions and general moral condition of the fierce and crafty race of men who roamed the forests of Canada along the banks of the St. Lawrence and on the margins of the great lakes.

Of the eight great families of savages, divided into four hundred and sixty-five tribes, who occupied the vast prairies and desolation of wilderness lying between the Esquimaux country of Labrador, the Mississippi and

Atlantic, three only claimed the exclusive privilege of calling the waters and hunting-grounds of this great Dominion their own. These were the Algonquins, the Huron-Iroquois and the Sioux or Dacotah. These nations, having each a generic language, were divided into tribes, which were again subdivided into clans or families.

The Huron-Iroquois nation was composed of eleven or twelve separate tribes speaking a common language, but differing in patois or dialect. The Attiwendarons of the Niagara Peninsula, the Tinnontates or Tobacco Nation of the Blue Ridge, the Erie or Cat Nation, and several other tribes occupying lands stretching from Lake Huron to Lake Erie and along the Niagara River, were members of the Huron Nation that, in the fifteenth century, broke apart from the Iroquois and formed a separate and distinct confederacy.

The nations, tribes and families were recognized and distinguished by symbolic signs or emblems called totems. There was the national totem, akin to the English lion; then the tribal totem, similar to the heraldic emblem of a Scotch clan; and the family totem, like unto the House of York or the English Howards. The wolf, bear, beaver, deer, snipe, heron, hawk, turtle or snake painted on the doors of their wigwams indicated the family of the occupants. It is worthy of note that the Wild Oats of Lake Michigan had for their tribal totem an eagle perched on a cross. A remarkable fact, which goes far to prove that the American savage was familiar with the disastrous effects of intermarriage with blood relations, was that no warrior ever took a wife from a family that bore the same totem as his own.

The moral debasement of the tribes was something appalling. A frightful heirloom of entailed and indefeasible accursedness in association with senseless ignorance and brutal customs was the only inheritance to which they could look forward. All their lives the victims of unrestrained and brutal passions that opened wide the door to every species of hard-heartedness and every degree of cruelty, their regeneration would never have come from themselves, and could only be accomplished by men dowered with tireless patience and God-like attributes. The insatiable and loathsome cruelty that overshadowed the land and its people was calculated to awe the stoutest heart that dared to redeem them.

If now, when we move amid the green mounds that mark their graves, or with curious eye inspect their rude trinkets and only treasures—the clay pipe, the arrow-head and the wampum—the soft sadness of pity steals over us, we must not forget that their inhuman hard-heartedness was unparalleled in the history of our fallen humanity. "They are not men," moaned an unfortunate woman whose child the Iroquois had torn from her breast, boiled and devoured in her presence, "they are wolves."

It is difficult to conceive a more atrocious refinement of cruelty than that of exposing a living naked body in a broiling sun on the margin of some marsh where the victim perished from famine or an accumulation of torture induced by reptiles and mosquitoes. Yet this was not an uncommon method of punishing their enemies.

There is a subtle connection between cruelty and lust which no metaphysical enquiry has yet satisfactorily explained; and hence we are not surprised to read that they had no conception of morality, even in the abstract. In truth, until the coming among them of the Priests of the Catholic Church they had no word to give expression to the idea of virtue, morals, religion, faith and the like. The Jesuit, Father Le Moyne, than whom no man was better qualified to know, wrote to his Superior in France that "Morality was unknown among the tribes, and a shocking license of unrestrained intercourse everywhere obtained among them."

Among a people who had no regard for chastity it was not to be expected that any respect would be had for the sanctity of a woman's nature. Hence, among them woman was treated with a callous disregard for the weakness of her sex, the memory of which sends a blush to the cheek of our manhood. Affrighted man recoils with horror from the perusal of woman's degradation as penned by the eloquent Le Jeune. The honor and heart of man can never be impeached with meaner or fouler crimes than are there recorded. All the menial offices of the camp, the heavy burdens of the chase, the labors of the corn-field, in a word, all that implied hard work was her allotted portion. Her infirmities excited no commiseration; and, with the crippled, maimed and the weak, she was more often a victim of contempt than an object of pity. Is it any wonder then that woman became so utterly shameless, hard-hearted and cruel—that, in vindictiveness and fierceness, she surpassed, as Chaumonot tells us, the brutality of man?

The crowning infamy of all the inhuman abominations of the American Indian was his utter contempt and disregard for human life. Savage as he was by inheritance and brutal as his passions had made him, it was yet to be hoped that the instinct which moves one animal to spare another of its own species would have lingered amid the wreck and ruin of his fallen nature. Such, however, was not the case. The most trivial accident or a thirst for blood at times led to a war which often ended in the dispersion or annihilation of a tribe. Frequently, and for no end than acquiring renown or scalps, the Indian warrior gathered his braves around him and, after haranguing them on the bloody deeds of their ancestors and their own past and prospective exploits, raised the familiar war-whoop and moved out to a mission of bloodshed and pillage. With the cunning of the fox and the ferocity of the tiger they fell upon their prey in the darkness of night or in the dawning morning and indiscriminately slaughtered men, women and children. "They approached like foxes," writes one of the Missionaries, "attacked like lions and disappeared like birds." Their prisoners were treated with unparalleled brutality. Some were mutilated inch by inch until they expired from extremity of suffering; others were reserved to be tortured by fire, and, by a refinement of cruelty surpassing belief, their agonies were prolonged from day to day. There was a tradition among the Mohawks that the night after a great battle between the Iroquois and the Eries the forest was lighted by a thousand fires, at each of which an Erie was roasting alive. Others of their captives they cut to pieces, boiled and devoured with unspeakable relish. "I saw the Iroquois," writes Father Bressani, "tear out the heart from a Huron captive, whom they had killed, and in the presence of the other prisoners roast and devour it." "In a word," says the heroic Lalement, "they eat human flesh with as much appetite and more relish than hunters eat the meat of the deer."

It would appear that they set no value on the attributes of nature which made them superior to the animals around them. Ferocity, strength, activity and endurance alone excited their admiration; and, as a result, they approached as near as it was possible for human beings to the condition of the wild beasts in which these qualities predominate. To make a hero of the American Indian, as is often done by writers of fiction, is to raise a monument to cruelty on a pedestal of lust.

Their religious conceptions were no higher than their moral actions. They believed all things to be animated with good or bad spirits; and, when on the war trail, they not unfrequently sacrificed human beings to propitiate the Okis or Manitous that influenced the future of the tribes. "On the third day after my arrival among the Iroquois," writes Father Jogues, "they sacrificed an Algonquin woman in honor of Ageskone, their war-god, inviting the grim demon, as if he were present, to come and feast with them on the murdered woman's flesh." They had no idea of God, as we understand the word. The sighing of the winds, the melancholy moan of the midnight forest, the crash of thunder or the gleam of lightning were the voices of the shadow-phantoms that hovered in the air around them. Every animal was animated with a spirit; and diseases, plagues and pestilence were the awful effects of the anger of some spirit.

In the vile abominations of their lives there were, however, some redeeming features. They were true to each other in their friendships, held eloquence in high repute, were remarkably hospitable, and, in times of famine, divided with each other the morsel that chance or the fortune of the hunt cast in their way. They were a courageous people, but their valor was disgraced by its brutality; and no form of vice, however loathsome, or cruelty to an enemy, however fiendish, met with condemnation, or, indeed, attracted attention.

Such, briefly, were the prevailing traits in the character and life of the American savage. Day after day for many a dreary age the sun looked down upon their enormous wickedness till, wasted with desolation, they faded from off the face of the earth, supplying by their ruin additional strength to the prophecy of Isaiah, that "The people who will not serve God shall perish."

If the enemies of Christianity seek for evidence of the grandeur of man when emancipated from the thraldom of religion, priest and altar, it will do them no harm to read carefully the history of the American Indian, to whom the boundless liberty of free thought and free speech gave the untrammelled freedom of an essentially independent man.

The Missionaries—The Recollet.

To fight the battles of the Cross, Christ's chosen ones are sent—
Good soldiers, and great victors—a noble armament.
They use no earthly weapon, they know not spear or sword,
Yet right and true and valiant is the army of the Lord.
              ADELAIDE PROCTOR.

We have now to ask ourselves, what manner of men were they who conceived, and, under accumulated hardships, in a measure bore into effect the magnificent resolve of Christianizing these half humanized hordes. The men who were selected by the Church from her missionary and teaching orders were, many of them, members of noble and honorable families. They had graduated in the best schools of Europe, and some of them—like Galinée, the Sulpician—had a European reputation for scholarship; others had cultivated a literary taste so remarkable for its chasteness and purity as to merit the praises of the ablest scholars and historians of America. They were cultured and refined, animated with an ardent zeal for the salvation of souls, and a courage so heroic as to elicit the admiration of savage warriors, who were themselves the embodiment of courage and endurance.

When Champlain disembarked at Stadacona—now Quebec City—on the 3rd day of July, 1607, he was told by an Algonquin Chief that, from that cliff to the great Lake of the Hurons and beyond, there roamed a numerous people broken up into tribes and families that lived by fishing and hunting.

Eight years later, at the request of Champlain, then Governor of Canada, and with the authority of the Pope, four members of the Franciscan Order—Joseph Le Caron, Denis Jamay, John Dolbeau and Pacifique Duplessis—arrived at Quebec. On the 1st of July, 1615, in company with a band of Hurons and Algonquins of the Ottawa, Father Joseph LeCaron started on his wondrous journey of nine hundred miles to the shores of the great Lake of the Hurons. Sailing up the St. Lawrence amid a silence broken only by the splash of the paddle they entered the Ottawa, passed the two lakes of Alumet and, at length, reached the tributary water of the

Mattawan. For forty miles or more they continued their journey. Bearing the canoes on their shoulders they crossed a portage and, through an opening in the forest, LeCaron—the first of white men—looked out upon the placid waters of Lake Nipissing. Skirting along its picturesque shores they entered French River, whose pleasant current bore them to the great Lake of the Hurons—precisely one month before Champlain's canoes shot into its waters. For more than a hundred miles they sailed through the tortuous channels of the Georgian Bay. The great Manitoulin lay directly in their front; they hugged the eastern shore, sailed by Byng Inlet, Parry Sound, and beached their canoes at the entrance to the Bay of Matchedash to the west of the harbor of Penetanguishene. Following, through woods and thickets, an Indian trail, they passed broad meadows, fields of maize, beds of vegetables, and entered the palisaded Huron town of Otoucha. Here, in what is now the northern and western portion of Simcoe County, embracing the peninsula formed by the Nottawasaga and Matchedash Bays, the River Severn and Lake Simcoe, were the fishing and hunting grounds of the great nation of the Wyandot or Hurons, comprising a population of twenty or thirty thousand souls,* a confederacy of four distinct tribes, afterwards increased to five by the addition of the Tionnontates.

Perhaps of all the races of red men the Hurons were the least liable to be attracted or to become attached to the practices of a Christian life. They were given over completely to sensuality, feasting and pleasure. "Their every inclination," writes the good missionary, "was brutal. They are naturally gluttonous, having their farewell feasts, their complimentary feasts, war, peace, death, health and marriage feasts."

Father LeCaron was, however, received hospitably by them. A wigwam was built for his convenience in the town of Caragouha, near Nottawasaga Bay, where he offered his first Mass. He was joined one month afterwards by Champlain. Mass was again chanted, a Te Deum sung and the Cross, the emblem of man's salvation, planted on the shores of Lake Huron. Thus, two hundred and seventy-seven years ago, with solemn Mass, with holy blessing and the Te Deum, the standard of the Cross was elevated, the law of the Gospel proclaimed, and the work of Christianizing the Canadian

---

* Very careful statistics made since the time of Champlain go to show that his figures are exaggerated. The inference of the census commissioners would lead one to suppose that ten or twelve thousand would be a fair estimate. See Census of Canada, 1871, Vol. iv., page 52, for details.

tribes begun. For six months this great Franciscan missionary, amid the hardships and perils of his solitary life, continued to study the language of the tribe, and, with a patience and zeal truly heroic, endeavored to make known to them the great saving truths of Christianity.

On February 1st, 1616, he visited the Tionnontates, or Tobacco Nation, who occupied lands in what are included now within the limits of Collingwood, Nottawasaga and Sunnidale Townships; but, being received with fear and suspicion, he was cruelly treated and compelled to return to Caragouha, where he spent the winter instructing the Wyandot tribes and preparing the first dictionary of the Huron language. On the 20th of May, 1616, in company with a band of Hurons who were going down to Three Rivers to exchange their furs and peltries, he left for Montreal; and, in the spring of 1623, accompanied by Father Nicholas Viel and Brother Gabriel Sagard (afterwards the historian of the Huron Missions), he returned to the tribes, who received him with open arms, built him a chapel at Ossosanee, where he said Mass every day and gave instructions in the Faith. This chapel he dedicated to St. Joseph, whom he chose as Patron of the country.

The mission now took a definite character, and the labors of the Fathers began in earnest. "It would be difficult to tell you," writes Father Le Caron, " the fatigue I suffer, being obliged to have my paddle in hand all day long, and run with all my strength with the Indians. I have more than a hundred times walked in the rivers over the sharp rocks, which cut my feet, in the mud, in the woods, where I carried the canoe and my little baggage, in order to avoid the rapids and frightful waterfalls. I say nothing of the painful fast which beset us, having only a little sagamity, which is a kind of pulmentum composed of water and the meal of Indian corn, a small quantity of which is dealt out to us morning and evening. Yet I must avow that amid my pains I felt much consolation. For alas! when we see such a great number of infidels, and nothing but a drop of water is needed to make them children of God, one feels an ardor, which I cannot express, to labor for their conversion and to sacrifice for it one's repose and life." " Meat was so rare with us," adds Sagard, " that we often passed six weeks or two whole months without tasting a bit, unless a small piece of dog, bear or fowl given to us at banquets." Father Viel, having by heroic patience and perseverance acquired a fair knowledge of the language, began giving the Indians instructions and teaching them the "Our Father," the "Hail

Mary," and the "Creed." His success, however, was not encouraging. He sent a letter to Father Le Caron, who had gone to Quebec on business of the Mission, that more help was wanted. Le Caron, with characteristic disinterestedness, wrote to France, inviting the Jesuit Fathers to come to their assistance. Here, virtually, end the labors of the Recollect or Franciscan Fathers in northern Canada.

In spite of the zeal and self-sacrifice of these heroic and generous men, circumstances did not permit of their mission assuming a permanent form. Father Le Caron never again visited the Hurons. He returned to France, where, in 1632, worn out with labors, he died in the odor of sanctity. Father Nicholas Viel, if not a martyr, had a martyr's will. He was on his way to Quebec to procure some necessary articles for the mission of St. Joseph, when, according to the historian Le Clercq, he was hurled by his Indian companion into the last rapid of the Riviere Des Prairies, known to this day as the "Sault au Recollect." Father Viel had already completed Le Caron's dictionary of the Huron language, and left at the Mission interesting and valuable notes of his labors.

Sagard, who returned to France, also wrote a dictionary of the Huron language, and a series of narratives that to this day furnish a source of ethnological, geographic and historic data for all writers on early Canadian history.

The Recollects or Franciscans established missions at Tadousac and Gaspe for the Montagnais Indians, at Miscou for the Micmacs, at Three Rivers and on the Georgian Bay for the Hurons. The missions of New Brunswick, Nova Scotia and Gaspé were under the care of Father John Dolbeau, with three assistants, one of whom, Father Sebastian, perished of starvation on his way to a mission on the St. John River. The others, despairing of softening the hardened hearts of the Micmacs and Montagnais, returned to Quebec. One of them, Father William Poullain, was afterwards captured by the Iroquois, who stripped him for the torture, when he was providentially preserved from the horrors of mutilation by the arrival of a messenger from the French with an offer of exchange.

"The country," writes the historian Kingsford, "owes the Order (the Franciscans) a debt of gratitude which history has only imperfectly paid; any mention of their name has been merely perfunctory, without acknowledgment or sympathy."

THE JESUIT.

But wondrous is the love of God! who sends His shining host
From age to age, from race to race, from utmost coast to coast;
And wondrous 'twas in our own land—e'en on the spot we tread
Ere yet the forest monarchs to the axe had bow'd the head,
That in our very hour of dawn a light for us was set,
High on the royal mountain side whose lustre guides us yet.
                                        THOMAS D'ARCY MCGEE.

What manner of men were they who succeeded them? It is no compliment to the honesty and intelligence of our age that even now, with the imperishable parchment of their heroic deeds unrolled before us, there are to be found those whose partiality is so pronounced that they cannot think of the Jesuits without associating with them blood, poison and daggers. The repeated and time-worn calumnies of secrecy, unscrupulous agents, conspiracies and the like, make up the religious and literary rubbish that too often passes for delectable reading at many a rural fireside. The conventional Jesuit is a familiar figure and a terrible one. He is as grotesque as he is unreliable and intangible. But we of the household of their faith have known the Jesuits and their works from the day that Ignatius Loyola, in the grotto of Manreza, threw himself heart and soul into the militia of Jesus Christ. We have studied their lives from the hour that Francis Xavier asked himself the portentous question—"What will it profit a man to gain the whole world if he lose his soul?" down to the present day, and our hearts go out in love and reverence towards them. From the halls of their Institutes come men whose names are beads of gold, worthy to be filed on the Rosary of Fame; men of saintly lives and of a transcendent greatness that raises them high above the level of even good men, and whose sacrifices for Christ and humanity challenge the admiration of the brave, and stagger faith itself. Of these were the men who, breaking with the fondest ties, forsaking the teeming fields and pleasant vineyards of sunny France, faced the storms of northern climates and buried themselves in the revolting companionship of fierce and inhospitable hordes.

"Away from the amenities of life," writes Bancroft, "away from the temptations of vain glory, they became dead to the world and possessed their souls in unalterable peace. The few who lived to grow old, though by the toils of a long mission, still kindled with the fervor of apostolic zeal.

The history of their labors is connected with the origin of every celebrated town in the annals of French America. Not a cape was turned, nor a river entered, but a Jesuit led the way."

"Maligners may taunt the Jesuits if they will," says the industrious and learned Parkman, "with credulity, superstition and blind enthusiasm, but slander itself cannot accuse them of hypocrisy or ambition." Among those who came to Canada in the sixteenth century were many who were influenced by motives of avarice and ambition. Among them was the high-spirited cavalier, bound on romantic enterprise; the fearless sea rover in quest of new laurels in unsailed seas; the restless adventurer wooing the charm of novelty in unexplored lands, and the disgraced courtier resolved by reckless daring to wipe out the memory of his humiliation. With them sailed the dark-robed Soldiers of the Catholic Church, brave as the bravest among them, fearless and undaunted in the shadow of the land but yesterday pressed by the boot of civilization.

To-day, dispassionately and calmly examining the historical and documentary evidence of the zeal, courage and piety of the great missionary orders, it is difficult to know to which of the three orders, the Franciscans, the Sulpicians or the Jesuits, belongs the palm of excellence. The great Jesuit Order, as Lord Macaulay called the Society, bathed the country with the blood of its members; but the indomitable courage and self-denial of the Franciscans and the Christian willingness with which the Sulpicians fearlessly entered upon the most dangerous missions assigned them, are conclusive evidence that, if circumstances demanded it, they also were prepared to furnish for the faith and the salvation of souls a bead-roll of martyrs.

Towards the end of May, 1625, Fathers Charles Lalemant, Enemond Masse and Jean de Brebeuf, in answer to the invitation of the Franciscans, arrived at Quebec. Their first act on reaching shore was to kneel down and kiss the earth, the scene of their future labors; then they thanked the Holy Trinity for having chosen them for the work of the mission, saluted the guardian angels of the land, and rose to their feet, prepared to spend or be spent in the service of their Master. Father Masse had already passed some time with the Micmacs of Nova Scotia, and was, in a measure, inured to the hardships of Indian life. Father Charles Lalemant remained at Quebec, and in the following year wrote the first letter of the now famous "Relations of the Jesuits."

Jean de Brebeuf, the descendant of a noble family, was selected for the Huron Mission. He passed the autumn and winter with a roving band of Montagnais Indians, endured for five months the hardships of their wandering life, and all the penalties of filth, vermin and smoke—the inevitable abominations of a savage camp. During these months he acquired a fair knowledge of their language; and when spring opened it found him prepared to start, in company with Father Joseph de la Roche Daillon, a Recollect of a noble French family, for the shores of the great lake of the Hurons.

In company with a band of Indians, who had come down from the Georgian Bay to the French settlements, and were now returning, after bartering to advantage their furs and peltries, the two Priests bade good-bye to their friends and embarked with their swarthy companions, whose canoes were headed for the Huron hunting-grounds in northern forests. Brebeuf was a man of broad frame and commanding mien, endowed with a giant strength and tireless endurance. His stay among the Montagnais taught him that physical superiority invited the respect of the savage when Christian virtues often provoked his ridicule. Stroke for stroke with the strongest of the Hurons he dipped his paddle from morning till night, and, to the amazement of his savage companions, showed no sign of fatigue. Thirty-five times in that weary journey of nine hundred miles Brebeuf and his associate bore their share of the heavy burdens across the portages. Through pestilent swamp and stagnant pool they waded, across the stony beds of shallow streams, over fallen trees and prostrate trunks, they made their devious way; descending, climbing, clambering over sharp and jagged rocks, till their clothes hung around them in shreds, these soldiers of the Cross kept pace with the stubborn march of their leggined and moccasined companions. Now and then the comparatively feeble Daillon, worn with the hardships of the journey, weakened under his load. In spite of his indomitable will his strength would fail him, and his manly but feeble attempts to hold the pace of his red companions—whose every fibre and muscle were hardened by years of hunting and canoeing—but provoked their laughter and ridicule. The heroic Brebeuf, flying to his assistance, would then relieve him of his burden, and, to the astonishment of the band, continue for hours bearing his double load. The Hurons themselves were often spent with fatigue, and marveled at an endurance that distance could not tire nor fatigue conquer.

When they arrived at the Mission of St. Joseph they found Father Viel's bark chapel still standing. Here they remained for three years, devoting themselves to their labors with the patience of saints and the heroism of martyrs. In the meantime Father Daillon visited the Neutral Nation, or Attiwindarons, a fierce and exceedingly superstitious people, on whose hardened hearts he could make no impression. Their hunting-grounds stretched from the Niagara river up to Detroit. Unfortunately Father Daillon left no record of his journey or stay among them. If he saw the Falls he would have been the first white man that ever gazed upon the great cataract. He returned the same year to his Huron Mission, where, with Father Brebeuf, he remained until 1629, when Quebec was taken by the English fleet, commanded by Admiral Kertk, a French Huguenot, the two Priests were summoned to return, and the Huron Mission was abandoned until 1632, when, by the treaty of St. Germain-en-laye, Canada was restored to France.*

Owing to the opposition of the Algonquins of the Ottawa river, who refused passage through their country to the French, the Fathers who had returned to Quebec in 1633 were unable to go to their northern missions. At length all obstacles having been overcome, Fathers Daniel, Davost and Brebeuf embarked with a party of Hurons, and after four weeks of incredible hardship finally reached the Huron country at Ihonatiria. Father Brebeuf was received with rapturous welcome. "Echon is come again," the children cried; "Echon is come again." "Echon" was the Indian name given to Father Brebeuf when he dwelt among them six years before. The Fathers, scarcely giving themselves time to recover from the fatigue of their long and trying journey, began at once the erection of a log building, which served them for house and chapel. Day after day, in the frosts of winter and the burning heat of summer, these men of God went from village to village, from hut to hut, censuring vice, correcting abuses, and patiently taming, by the influence of their teaching and example, the savage natures around them. At every opportunity they gathered the children together, and, clothed in surplice and baretta, for greater solemnity, taught them the "Our Father," the children repeating it after them. In language suited to their understanding, Brebeuf instructed them in the Commandments, and

---

* The Missionaries were made prisoners by order of Admiral Kertk, who allowed the Recollect Fathers to return to France; but entertaining an implacable enemity to the Jesuits, he brought Brebeuf a prisoner to England, where he remained for some time, but was finally permitted to leave for France.

with words of encouragement, accompanied with some trifling presents, dismissed them for the time. Later on he might be seen encircled by a curious crowd of warriors, sagamores and squaws, explaining the mysteries of religion, describing Heaven and Hell, and picturing with all the strength of his vigorous eloquence the horrors of eternal fire and the tortures of the damned, till their hardened hearts quailed in the presence of the verbal picture of their approaching doom.

The success which attended the preaching of Brebeuf alarmed the Medicine Men, or "Sorcerers," of the tribe, and they publicly charged the Fathers with conspiracy to destroy their crops by suspending for weeks the rain in the Heavens. They said the Cross, which was planted before the residence of the Fathers, was a fetich, or instrument of witchcraft, and threatened to destroy it. Brebeuf, after petitioning St. Joseph, and asking the prayers of his two companions, met the Medicine Men in a council of the Sachems, and succeeded in convincing the chiefs that neither the Fathers nor the Cross were responsible for the drought.

The Fathers arrived in the Huron country in 1634, and in the following year Fathers Pierre Pigàrd and Francis Le Mercier came, and with this addition to his numbers Father Brebeuf was now able to extend his field of labors. Nothing was more apostolic than the life which they led. "All their moments," writes Charlevoix, "were marked by some heroic action, by conversions or by sufferings, which they considered as a real indemnity when their labors had not produced all the fruit which they had hoped for. From the hour of four in the morning, when they rose, till eight they generally kept within; this was the time for prayer, and the only part of the day which they had for their private exercises of devotion. At eight each went whithersoever his duty called him; some visited the sick, others walked into the fields to see those who were engaged in cultivating the earth, others repaired to the neighboring villages which were destitute of pastors. These excursions answered many good purposes, for in the first place no children, or at least very few, died without Baptism; even adults, who had refused to receive instruction while in health, applied for it when they were sick. They were not proof against the ingenious and indefatigable charity of their physicians." The missionaries lived with their spiritual children, adopted their mode of life, in so far as it was possible, shared their privations, accompanied them in their fishing and hunting expeditions, and became all to all that they might gain their souls for Christ. The constancy and courage of the human heart were perhaps never put to a severer trial than that which they experienced when the smallpox broke out among the tribes. The filthy habits of the Indians, the offal and garbage of the camp that lay reeking around every wigwam invited disease, and, as a result, their bodies offered a rich pasturage for the epidemics that periodically fed upon them. Whole villages, while the plague lasted, were more like charnel-houses than homes of living men; and day after day, for many a dreary month, men, women and children, from whose bones the flesh had rotted, sank under the accumulation of their sufferings.

The heroism of the Fathers in these trying ordeals provoked the astonishment of the Hurons, whose stubborn natures yielded but to miracles of self-denial and contempt of danger. With all the patience and tenderness of Sisters of Charity, they went from wigwam to wigwam, instructing some, consoling others, baptising those who would receive the sacrament, and to all bringing consolation and relief. The suffering they endured and the hardships they encountered may be learned from the letters filed among the archives of their Order. Even the indomitable Brebeuf, whose chivalric nature rose superior to complaint, wrote to his Superior in France: "Let those who come here, come well provided with patience and charity, for they will become rich in troubles; but where will the labouring ox go when he does not draw the plough; and if he does not draw the plough how can there be a harvest." The Sorcerers of the tribe, or Medicine Men, charged the Fathers with being the cause of all their affliction. The chanting of their sacred litanies and the ceremonies of the Mass were incantations casting a malign spell upon the crops and people, paralyzing the arm of the brave in war, and destroying the swiftness of the hunter in the chase. The dangers of infection from the plague were trivial compared to the peril of the tomahawk. Brebeuf and his companions, in solemn council of the Sachems, were doomed to death, and were only saved, as they piously believed, through the intercession of the Blessed Virgin and St. Joseph. Amid all the discomforts and privations of savage life the Fathers were sustained by a holy enthusiasm that conquered all natural fears. When Brebeuf heard that the sentence of death was passed upon them, he strode fearlessly into the council-house, and, to the amazement of the chiefs, demanded to be heard. He was master of their language; and, being naturally eloquent, harangued the assembly in words so forcible and persuasive as to obtain a reversal of the sentence passed upon the Fathers. The plague spent itself in a short time, and with it died out the bitterness against the missionaries.

Towards the end of the year Fathers Daniel and Davost returned to Quebec, bringing with them three boys whom they proposed to place in a Huron school which they intended to found, that some of the Huron boys might be trained up in religion and in the arts of life. On the Ottawa River they met Fathers Garnier and Chatelain, who had left Quebec a few days before in company with Amons, a chief of the Hurons, and embarked for the Northern Missions. When the Fathers reached Three Rivers, Father Jogues, who had shortly before arrived from France, was there to receive them. He was amazed at the poverty and outward wretchedness of the Missionaries. "They were," said he, in a letter to his mother, "barefoot and exhausted, their underclothes worn out and their cassocks hanging in rags on their emaciated bodies; yet their faces were expressive of content and satisfaction with the life which they led, and excited in me, both by their looks and conversation, a desire to go and share with them the crosses to which the Lord attached such unction."

The desire of the illustrious priest, the future martyr of the Mohawks, was soon to be gratified. A party of Huron braves, on their departure from Quebec for their forest homes, asked Jogues to accompany them; and, having received the permission of Father Le Jeune, Superior of the Missions of Canada, he got ready for the voyage. It was not without a certain feeling of emotion that, bare-footed, he took his place in the birch canoe, and with his swarthy companions began the ascent of the great river. Father Jogues was in a measure familiar with the difficulties of his perilous voyage from the instructions and wise counsel addressed by Brebeuf to the Fathers stationed at Quebec. "Easy as the journey may appear," writes this model of missionaries, "it will, however, present difficulties of a formidable nature to the heart that is not strengthened by self-denial and mortification. The activity of his Indian companions will neither shorten the portages, make smooth the rocks, nor banish danger. The voyage will take at least three or four weeks with companions whom he perhaps never before met : he will be confined within the narrow limits of a bark canoe, and in a position so painful and inconvenient that he will not be free to change it without exposing the canoe to the danger of being capsized or injured on the rocks. During the day the sun will scorch him, and at night the mosquitoes will allow him no repose. After ascending six or seven rapids his only meal will be of Indian corn steeped in water, his bed will be the earth, or a jagged and uneven rock. At times the stars will be his blanket, and around him, night and day, perpetual silence."

On the 11th of September, 1636, Father Jogues arrived at the village of Ihonatiria, where were the mission of St. Joseph and the residence of the Fathers. Needless to say he was received with open arms. It was at first

THE PORTAGE.
(From an old engraving.)

the intention of the missionaries to establish permanent missions in the principal Huron towns; but when the smallpox decimated the village of Ihonatiria, and compelled its inhabitants to seek another and healthier locality, the Fathers divided themselves between the town of Ossossane, which they called "Conception," and that of Teanaustayae, to which they gave the name of St. Joseph, in memory of their first mission at Ihonatiria. The establishment of these two missions, however, did not equal their expectations, nor were they sufficient for the wants of the country. They became satisfied that a permanent and central residence which would serve as their headquarters for Northern Canada was a necessity. They chose a solitary piece of ground north-east of the Huron peninsula on the banks of what is now known as the river Wye. A chain of buildings, including a large chapel, an extensive residence, and a hospital built on solid stone foundations rose, in the midst of the country of the Attaronchronons, who beheld with astonishment and delight the growth of those wondrous buildings that, they thought, would never stop till they pierced the clouds. When the series of buildings was completed, they dedicated them to the Blessed Virgin under the title of "Residence Sainte Marie."

The Fathers, who were now eight in number, had already visited every Huron town, and were in most of them hospitably received and invited to return. It cannot be said that their success was commensurate with their hopes; but with a sublime confidence in God, and a constancy as heroic as it was admirable, they continued their missionary labours. The wisdom of their action in establishing this Residence now became apparent. New missions were opened, converts began to increase, and hope dawned anew for these devoted men. Among the mountains at the head of Nottawasaga Bay, forty-eight hours journey from the Huron towns, dwelt the Tionnantates, known to the French as the Petuns or Tobacco Nation, from the large quantities of tobacco raised by them for purposes of trade with neighboring tribes.

In the month of December, 1639, Fathers Jogues and Garnier, unable to obtain a guide among the Hurons, fearlessly plunged into the forest, and after three days and nights of incredible hardships entered at eight o'clock in the evening the first Tobacco town. The Indians of this tribe were told that the pest which had annihilated the town of Ihonatiria was brought about by the prayers and invocations of the "Black Sorcerers," as the Jesuits were known to them. When the two Priests stood at the margin of their village, boldly outlined against the northern sky, terror took possession of them all: they fled to their cabins screaming that the demons of Famine and Pest were here to blight them. The door of every wigwam was closed against the Priests, and nothing but the feeling of fear and awe which they excited saved them from the deadly blow of the tomahawk. From town to town they travelled, loaded with curses and maledictions, unable to obtain a hearing, and on every side meeting with scowling brows and murderously furtive looks. The children, as they passed, cried with fear, and from out the cabins came the pleadings of the squaws, appealing to the young braves to lay open their heads. The Priests bore a charmed life; but finding that the time had not yet come to establish a permanent mission among the Petuns, they returned to Sainte Marie. "Nowhere," adds Parkman, "is the power of courage, faith and unflinching purpose more strikingly displayed than in the mission of these two Priests." Their visit, however, was not barren of results; they became familiar with the journey, learned something of the habits of the people, and prepared the way for Father Charles Garnier, who, the following year, took up his abode with the tribe, and established in their midst the Mission of the Apostles.

In 1641 a deputation of Ottawas, representing the great Algonquin Nation, came down from the shores of Lake Superior to visit some of their Algonquin countrymen, and to be present at their great Feast of the Dead. This particular Algonquin tribe, now visited by the Ottawas, dwelt for some time on the northern margin of the Huron country, with whose people they were on terms of familiarity. Father Charles Raymbault, who spoke their language fluently, visited them from time to time, and had already made many converts among them. On the 17th September, 1641, accompanied by Father Jogues, he returned with the Ottawa flotilla and spent some weeks with the tribe, whose villages were planted at Sault Sainte Marie and in its neighborhood. The two Priests were the first Europeans that ever passed through the Sault and stood on the shore of the great Northern Lake.*
"Thus did the religious zeal of the French," writes Bancroft, commenting on the faith and daring of the Priests, "bear the cross to the banks of the St. Mary and the confines of Lake Superior, and look wistfully towards the homes of the Sioux, in the valley of the Mississippi, five years before the New England Eliot had addressed the tribe of Indians that dwelt within six miles of Boston harbor."

The Sachems of the Ottawas invited the Jesuits to dwell among them; but the time was not yet ripe for the establishment of a fixed mission, and the Fathers returned to St. Mary's, on the Wye.

On the north shore of Lake Erie, stretching along both banks of the Niagara River, and embracing the fertile lands of the Niagara peninsula, lived the Nation of Attiwandarons, or as they were known to the French, Neutrals. Physically they were, perhaps, the finest specimen of the then existing American Indian. The Recollect, Father Daillon, who

---

* The Franciscan historian Sagard, who wrote in 1632, says that: "Etienne Brule, the companion of Champlain, left that explorer at Toanche and started with an associate named Grenolle on a voyage to the Upper Lakes. On his return to Quebec, bringing with him a large ingot of copper, he claimed to have visited the Sault, and gave an elaborate description of Lake Superior; but all this information he could have obtained from the Wild Oats of Lake Michigan, who traded with the Algonquins of the North."

visited them in 1626, did not see a single deformed person among all the members of this Nation. They numbered about twelve thousand souls; their climate was mild the winter comparatively short, snow falling scarcely more than three or four inches in depth. The country was filled with game, the beaver, moose, wildcat, wolf, buffalo, wild goose, turkey, crane and squirrel existing in abundance. The people were steeped in a licentiousness so shameless and revolting as to excite the surprise of their Huron and Iroquois neighbors. They burned female prisoners, a practice unknown to the Northern tribes. In summer the men had no other clothing than a tatooing of powdered charcoal. They kept their dead in their wigwams until putrefaction was very far advanced, when they scraped the decaying flesh from off the bones, which they carefully preserved for years until the communal burial of the Feast of the Dead.

On the second of November, 1640, Fathers John Brebeuf and Joseph Chaumont set out for the Neutral Country, and after nine days' journey reached its first town. Terrible reports of their awful power for evil preceded them. They were represented as sorcerers whose very presence produced a withering blight on all things. Their beads, crucifixes, crosses and breviaries were held in awe and looked upon as instruments of necromancy calculated to bring on plagues and diseases that would eventually destroy the people. The Fathers visited eighteen towns, but were everywhere received, as were Jogues and Garnier among the Petuns, with a storm of execrations and maledictions. Every door was closed against them under the impression that if they were once admitted a curse would fall upon the cabin. For months they went from town to town suffering from cold and hunger, and were only saved from death by repeated miracles. Their mission was barren of any other results than the self-denial and mortifications which assured them a harvest of eternal glory. In despair of accomplishing the object of their mission the Fathers prepared to leave the country. On the night of their departure, while Brebeuf was communing with God in prayer, he beheld in a cloudless sky the ominous vision of a blood-red cross moving towards him from the land of the Iroquois. He spoke of the apparition to his brother Priests on his return. "Was it large?" they asked him. "Large enough," answered Brebeuf, "to crucify us all." I wonder if the indomitable spirit of this heroic Priest quailed in the presence of this portentous and prophetic sign, or did he welcome the apparition as foretelling the near approach of his hopes and prayers for the martyr's crown.

In the year 1648, the Jesuit Fathers beheld, with increasing hope, the approaching realization of their great labors. Flourishing missions were established and churches built in what are now the townships of Sunnidale, Tiny, Medonte, Tay, Matchedash and North Orillia. Scattered through these townships were the missions of the Conception—St. Michael, St. Joseph, St. Ignatius, Mary Magdelane, and the mission of Holy Mary. Among the Algonquins of Lake Nipissing and those that dwelt on the northern coast of Lake Huron were erected the missions of the Holy Ghost and of St. Peter. Even among the Tobacco Nation, where, a few years before, Fathers Jogues and Garnier were so roughly treated, two missions were permanently established. The missions were attended by eighteen Fathers, who, looking forward to the arrival of others from France and Quebec, began now to cast wistful eyes towards the Dacotahs of the Mississippi, the Sioux of the plains, and Algonquins of the north. The Puants and the Nation of Fire dwelling along the shores of Lake Michigan asked to have missionaries sent among them. In one year were baptized eighteen hundred persons; and though the Fathers attending outlying stations were subject to frightful hardships, they were consoled in their sufferings with the prospect of ultimate success. Every day added to the number of their converts; and if it were not for the events we are about to relate, the whole Huron Nation would in a few years have been enrolled under the banner of the Cross.

For a long time a deadly feud existed between the Iroquois and the Hurons, and had, at the period at which we write, reached the proportions of a war of extermination. In 1647, the terrible Iroquois, who dwelt in Central New York, south of Lake Ontario, and for a considerable distance along the north and south shore of the St. Lawrence, had almost annihilated the Neutrals. They were the most warlike and ruthless among the American Indians. The word Iroquois was a generic term for a confederacy of five tribes composed of the Senecas, Mohawks, Oneidas, Onondagas and Cayugas, afterwards joined by the Tuscaroras, thus forming the familiar confederacy of the Six Nations. In the Spring of 1648, emboldened by repeated successes, a large war-party crossed the St. Lawrence, and urged by an implacable hate of their hereditary foes, the Hurons, burst upon the frontier village of St. Joseph, near what is now the prosperous town of Barrie, and indiscriminately slaughtered men, women and children. For weeks before the massacre they infested the forest, lying in ambush here and there till a favorable opportunity presented itself, when they sprang like a tiger on his prey, rending the forest with demoniac yells of triumph and victory.

Father Daniel was in charge of this mission, and when the Iroquois stormed the town he had just finished Mass. The mission chapel was crowded, and as the dread war-whoop broke upon the doomed people they became paralyzed with fear and terror. Two days before the attack the fighting men had gone on a hunting expedition, and only old men, woman and children were there to meet the enemy. Father Daniel tried to rally them to the defence, but his efforts were vain. He then called to them to fly for their lives, while he himself would remain to face the enemy. He returned to the chapel, followed by a crowd of women and children. Turning again to them he exclaimed : " My children, fly and retain your faith until death." Among them was a large number the Father was instructing for Baptism. Dipping his handkerchief in water he baptised them by aspersion collectively, and to those who had already received the sacrament he gave a general absolution.

The village is now burning; the Iroquois approach the chapel; the Priest turns to the people saying : " We will die here and shall meet again in Heaven ;" and then, striding to the door, he serenely confronts the enemy. The Mohawks are struck with astonishment, and for a moment remain rooted with surprise that one should alone have the hardihood to meet them. At length they discharge at him a sheaf of arrows ; but, though pierced and rent with wounds, he continued to exhort his catechumens till death in mercy ended his sufferings. " He died murmuring the name of Jesus, surrendering his soul to God like the Good Shepherd who gives his life for his flock."* Chapel, Priest, and congregation were consumed together. The wilderness is their grave ; their ashes, floating upon the air, drop sanctified fertility on the land ; and while no man knows their resting-place, their monument is so large that though its foundations are on the earth its apex touches the great white Throne of the Eternal.

So died the first martyr of the Huron mission in the forty-eighth year of his age, after spending eighteen years on the Northern missions. Twice after his death he appeared to the Fathers assembled in council, radiant in

---

* Letter of F. Ragueneau, 1648.

the sweetest form of celestial glory. The mission of St. Joseph became a charred ruin; seven hundred of its inhabitants perished by fire, torture or the tomahawk. The warning ought to have been sufficient for the other Huron towns to prepare for the impending conflict. The winter passed away without further disturbance, and the Fathers continued to hope that all danger was at an end.

Martyrdom of Brébeuf and Lalemant.

On the morning of the 17th of March, 1649, Father Ragueneau, who had charge of the mission of St. Mary's, was on his knees before the Blessed Sacrament, after having offered up the Holy Sacrifice of the Mass, when a Huron runner, breathless and bleeding from a bullet wound, entered the village and announced to the terrified people that the Iroquois had captured the fortified town of St. Louis, slaughtered the men, women and children, and might at any hour attack St. Mary's. "Where are Fathers Lalemant and Brebeuf?" asked the Priest, who, hearing the commotion, left the chapel and strode into the crowd of bewildered Hurons. "They are dead," spoke back the runner. "Dead!" Father Ragueneau fell back aghast with horror and returned to the altar of the Blessed Sacrament. The courier was mistaken; the two Priests were not dead, but their end was not far off.

One thousand Iroquois, chiefly Senecas and Mohawks—the tigers of the forest and the boldest and fiercest warriors of North America—had, late in the autumn, taken the war-path, wintered amid the forests of Nipissing, and early in March captured the Huron town of St. Ignatius, tomahawked, scalped and butchered its inhabitants. Then, smearing their faces with the blood of their victims, to give additional horror to their savage appearance, they moved out on the run for the neighboring village of St. Louis through a forest whose silence was at intervals broken by the echoes of their pitiless war-whoops. Despite the desperate valor of the Hurons, who fought like demons, the Iroquois carried the fort, set fire to the town, and flung in among the burning cabins the women and children, whose shrieks of agony rose above the whoops and yells of their conquering foe.

The Iroquois retraced their path to St. Ignatius, dragging with them a number of prisoners, among them the lion-hearted Brebeuf and his delicate and gentle companion, Lalemant. Three times, while the enemy were storming St. Louis, the Huron warriors urged the Priests to fly, as the road was still open to St. Mary's. "We cannot," answered the stalwart Brebeuf. "Where should the Priest be found but with his people?" Amid a pelting rain of bullets and arrows they continued giving absolution and baptism to souls that were fast leaving bodies, mutilated and torn by the deadly missiles of the Senecas. When the Iroquois entered the town Brebeuf rose from the side of a wounded brave and confronted them with a face whose calmness was in strange contrast to his stormy surroundings. Lalemant, frail of constitution and delicate from childhood, was unequal to similar display of fortitude; his slender body trembled in the presence of the tomahawk raised to brain him; his weakness was but for a moment, when, summoning his faith to his assistance, he looked his enemy in the face and bowed his head for the blow. He was reserved for a more cruel and horrible fate.

Four hours after the capture of St. Louis, while the ashes from its ruins were still floating over the virgin forests, John de Brebeuf was stripped of his clothes, led to a stake, to which he was bound, and his torture began. The courage of Brebeuf was of that indomitable character that rises superior to fear. He foresaw the appalling sufferings that awaited him, but when the Iroquois closed in on him they looked in vain for any sign of cowardice or symptom of weakness. They tore the flesh in strips from his body and devoured it in his presence, plucked out his finger-nails, and scorched him with burning brands. "You do not scream, Echon,"[*] they said to him. "Why do you not moan? We will make you." Heating red hot a collar of hatchets they flung it over his head till the flesh on his broad shoulders shrivelled up to the consistency of burned leather. The odor of burning flesh made them demons. They glared upon him like tigers; and when the unconquerable Priest raised his voice in withering denunciation of their wickedness, they tore away his lips and cut out his tongue. Still they wrung from him no cry of pain. With torn lips and mutilated tongue he endeavored to warn them of God's awful punishments. They replied with shouts of derision, obscenity and filthy songs, cut off his fingers, joint by joint, and scorched him with brands from head to foot; but the iron frame and unconquerably

---

[*] Father Brebeuf's Indian name. After Brebeuf's death Father Chaumonot fell heir to his title: Father Le Moyne, who discovered the salt springs at Onondaga, was known among the Iroquois by the title of Ondersouk.

resolute nature of the indomitable Priest did not quail, and even they, stolid and brutal as they were, marveled at a courage that gave no sign of weakness. They poured boiling water on his head, and in mockery of the sacrament of Baptism cried out: "We baptise you, Echon, that you may be happy in Heaven—for you black gowns tell us that no one can be saved without baptism." Despairing of overcoming his wondrous fortitude they tore the scalp from his head, laid open his side, and scooping up his blood in their hands, drank it with the hope that they might partake of some portion of his marvelous courage. A chief then advanced, and burying his hunting-knife in the Priest's breast, tore out the palpitating heart, and holding it aloft that all might see it, began to devour it with unspeakable relish.

The lustre of the eye is dimmed, the power of utterance is gone forever, his countenance is marred and pitiable to look upon, and like his Divine Master when the horrors of His crucifixion swept over Him, "There is no beauty in his face nor comeliness." Thus died John de Brebeuf, Priest of the Catholic Church, and one of the grandest men that ever trod the American Continent. From that memorable day when, kneeling on the rock at Stadacona, he dedicated his life to the conversion of the tribes, he never wavered in his high resolve. For twenty-four years of laborious and unceasing sacrifice, amid perils as fearful as ever tried the heart of man, he walked the furrow to the martyr's stake, nor cast one halting, lingering look behind. His zeal, his courage, his fidelity to duty in the presence of the greatest dangers, his fortitude under hunger, weariness and excessive fatigue, his angelic piety and his prodigious heroism under the excruciating ordeal of Indian torture preach an eloquent sermon, and its burden is: "All ye that seek the kingdom of God behold the paths that lead ye to it."

Brebeuf's companion, Father Lalemant, was tortured with atrocious cruelty. His body was swathed in birch bark smeared with pitch and the torch put to it. In this state he was led out while they were rending the body of Brebeuf; and when he beheld the unutterable condition of the heroic Priest, whom he loved with the love of a brother, his agitation overcame him, and throwing himself at the feet of the dying martyr he exclaimed: "My God! we're made a spectacle to the world, to angels and to men." He was then dragged away, and for seventeen hours from sunset to sunrise was tortured with a refinement of cruelty that fills us with affright and bewilderment. By a slow process he was literally roasted alive; from head to foot there was no part of his body that was not burned, even to his eyes, in the sockets of which were placed live coals.

The Tobacco Nation shared the fate of the Hurons. With them perished Father Garnier; he was shot down in the act of giving absolution to a dying Indian, and, while still breathing, his head was laid open with the blow of a tomahawk. Father Chabanel, his companion, was killed on his way from the mission of St. Matthias by a Huron renegade, who, after murdering him, threw his body into the river. He evidently had a presentiment of his fate, for, before leaving St. Mary's on the Wye, he wrote to his brother that he anticipated death, and probably by fire, at the hands of the Iroquois.

The charred remains of the martyred Priests, Brebeuf and Lalemant, were gathered together, their bones brought to Quebec, and there sacredly guarded till they were removed to France.* The bodies of the other three Priests were given a grave in the wilderness, and the Huron Nation became their mourners. No monument of granite or marble is there to challenge the attention of passing man, and tell him that here lie the ashes of heroes and of saints. Around them rise in stately grandeur the swaying pines whose youth the martyrs saw; the waters of the broad Huron still lave the fertile shores, the scene of their mighty deeds; and the same sun that, three hundred years ago, shone upon their heroism to-day warms the green turf that shrouds their sanctified remains. They and their tawny converts are gone forever; but on the altar of a neighboring church is still celebrated the same unchangeable sacrifice that the martyred Priests offered to the Adorable God centuries ago. A broad-shouldered, fair complexioned people now listen to the same immortal truths that Brebeuf and his companions preached to the dark-haired Hurons in the forests of Ihonatiria; and while these unalterable truths are wedded to the soul of man, the memory of the dead Priests will live in the hearts of the brave and the true.†

The Hurons, despairing of ever recovering from the disastrous effects of the sudden onslaught made upon them, and unable to cope with the terrible

---

* The skull of Father Brebeuf is preserved in a silver reliquary in the Hotel Dieu at Quebec, and may be seen by anyone desirous of venerating the sacred relic.

† Mr. Douglas Brymner, the Canadian Archivist, in his report for 1884 inserts an orginal account of the martyrdom of the two Jesuit Fathers. It was written by Christopher Regnaut, a lay brother attached to the mission of St. Mary's on the Wye, and gives a graphic description of the horrible tortures of the martyrs. To Mr. Byrmner belongs the credit of discovering and giving this document to the public.

Iroquois, resolved to abandon their country. All was over with them; and having determined upon flight, they at once carried the resolution into effect. Inside of twelve days scarcely a Huron was left in the country; they put the torch to fifteen of their towns, fearing that the Iroquois would take shelter in them. They disappeared in bands of twenty and thirty families. Some sought refuge with the Neutrals; others again found an asylum among the Algonquins on the northern shore of Lake Huron; while others were given a temporary home with the Tobacco Nation. One large party, under the leadership of Father Ragueneau took up their quarters on Charity Island, called by them the Island of St. Joseph. Even here they were not free from the attacks of the Iroquois, who were continually prowling in the woods or lying in ambush for days awaiting a favorable opportunity for a shot. The winter was a terrible one for them; famine added to the horrors of their position; disease lingered continually with the tribe.

At length, broken-hearted and discouraged, they left the Island early in the spring, accompanied by their Priests, and began their perilous journey to Quebec. On their way to French River they skirted along the coast of their own familiar country, now a land of horror and of desolation. Lake Nipissing, on whose shores there dwelt a few years before a once numerous and powerful tribe, was stillness itself. From the fringe of the Georgian Bay to the mouth of the Ottawa the land was a vast grave-yard, over which there brooded the silence of death. On their way down the Ottawa they met Father Bressani returning with a party of French and Hurons with supplies for the mission of St. Joseph. On learning that the Island was a desert and no living soul left upon it, Father Bressani retraced his route, and in a few weeks the whole company reached Quebec. They settled in a place some thirteen miles from the city, now called Lorette, where still dwell all that remains of that mighty race of hunters and fighters once known as the Huron Nation. "It may be asked," writes Bancroft, "if these massacres quenched enthusiasm. I answer that the Jesuits never receded one foot; but as in a brave army new troops press forward to fill the places of the fallen, they were never wanting in heroism and enterprise on behalf of the cross."*

The scattered bands of Hurons were accompanied by their Priests. Father Grelon, whose soutane hung in rags around him, clothed himself in

---

* Bancroft, iii. vol. pg. 141; ed. 1846.

the skins of animals, and northward by the shores of Lake Huron, amid the islets and rocks of its desolate coast, searched for the remnants of his scattered flock. Another plunged into the forest with a company of famishing proselytes; and, amid their miserable rovings through thicket and mountain, endured for months the horrors of cold and hunger. Father Simon Lemoyne, years afterwards, visits the Onondagas, and is the first white man to ascend the St. Lawrence River.* Pere Chaumonot and Claude Dablon follow him a year after; and to the fierce Iroquois who, a few years before, had perpetrated such atrocious cruelties on the Hurons, preached the saving truths of Christianity. René Menard, in 1656, takes up a permanent abode with the Cayugas; and Chaumonot, the following year, fearlessly enters the dens of the lions—the villages of the Senecas. In 1656 Fathers Gabriel Druillettes and Leonard Garreau—the one having already carried the cross through the forests of Maine, and the other, eighteen years before, a missionary with the Tobacco Nation, are captured by the Mohawks after having started to visit the great Sioux Nation.† Thus before the expiration of the year 1656 the Jesuit Priests, taking their lives in their hands, began the conversion of those war-hawks of the wilderness—the five nations of the Iroquois.

In 1660 the aged Menard, after weeks of great hardship and suffering, visited the southern shore of Lake Superior; and having begun a mission among the scattered Hurons found in this region, plunged into the forest to visit an inland tribe, and is never again heard of. The lion-hearted Claude Allouez steps into the breach made by his death, and for thirty years this Confessor of the Faith becomes the companion of roving Algonquins. He gave the name Ste. Marie to the waters dividing Lakes Superior and Huron, where he established the first permanent mission on the spot consecrated twenty-five years before by the visit of the martyr Jogues and the saintly Raymbault. This extraordinary Priest established missions during his long sojourn in the upper country among more then twenty different nations, including Miamis, Saulteurs, Menomonies, Illinois, Chippewas,

---

* Father Lemoyne discovered the salt mines at Salina on August 16, 1654, two weeks after his ascent of the great river. Father Joseph Poncet, in 1653, made the first descent of this river from Ogdensburg to Montreal.

† Father Garreau, when on his way in 1656 to open a mission among the Ottawas of the Lake Superior region, was killed by the Iroquois. He arrived in Canada in 1643, and in the following year was a missionary among the Hurons. He was distingnished for great piety and child-like obedience to his Superiors.

Sacs, Winnibagoes, Foxes, Potawatomies of Lake Michigan, Kickapoos, and among the scattered Hurons and Ottawas.

In 1668 Fathers Dablon, Nicolas and Marquette, soon to enter upon the exploration of the Mississippi, are with the tribes that occupy the vast regions extending from Green Bay to the head of Lake Superior, " mingling happiness with suffering and winning enduring glory by their fearless perseverance."

Truly there were giants in those days; and it is impossible not to admire the sublime influence of the Catholic Church on the hearts of men—an influence which then, as now, inspired Priests to turn aside from the allurements of civilized society, and, untrammeled with wives or families, devote themselves unreservedly to the elevation of the savage races that were buried in the darkness of the Valley of Death.

FLIGHT OF THE TIONNONTATES.

South of the Nottawasaga Bay, and about two days journey west of the Huron towns, were situated nine or ten villages of the Tionnontates or Tobacco Nation, known to the French as Petuns. They numbered between fifteen and twenty thousand souls when they joined the Huron Confederacy in 1630.* They shared to a large extent in the ruin and dispersion of that unhappy people. Among them the martyred Priests Garnier and Chabanel had charge of the mission of St. John, while Fathers Garreau and Grelon looked after the mission of St. Matthias. Their piety, zeal and self-denial were softening the flinty hearts of the Petuns; and when the Iroquois began their war of extermination the light of conversion was already breaking above the horizon. When driven from their country the remnant of this great clan held together and retained its tribal organization. There is not in modern history, and taking no account of numbers, perhaps none in all history, an event less generally known or more striking to the imagination than the flight of this tribe across the boundless plains and through the forests of North America. In the intense sufferings of the men, women and children there is much that appeals to the sympathy and pity of humanity. The gloomy vengeance of the ruthless enemy that hung upon the rear of the

---

* Mr. David Boyle, the **Canadian Archæologist**, in an interesting paper on this tribe published 1889, would lead us to infer, from **the remains of their** villages and burial-mounds, that they were not only a numerous people, but, in **point of intelligence, superior to the other tribes of North America.**

fugitive band was like the solitary Miltonic hand pursuing through desert spaces a rebellious host and overtaking those who believed themselves already within the security of darkness. The reverses sustained by the tribe, the untravelled forests through which it opened a path, the foe ever doggedly hanging to its skirts, and the hardships that became a part of its very existence invest its exodus with melancholy interest. The anabasis of the younger Cyrus, and the subsequent retreat of the ten thousand to the shores of the Black Sea; the Parthian expeditions of the Romans, especially those of Crassus and Julian, and the retreat of the French soldiers from Moscow, whilst more disastrous in the loss of life, were not more pitiful in the sufferings endured.

In 1652 they fled to Michilimackinac, and now the history of their wanderings becomes intensely pathetic. The daring and ferocious Iroquois drove them thence, and with the pertinacity of blood-hounds hung upon their trail, forcing them to seek refuge with the Puants of Green Bay. From here they were driven to the number of five hundred, and continued their wanderings till they reached the country of the Illinois. No hospitable greeting awaited them; and, worn out and discouraged, they addressed a most pathetic appeal to the Andastes, pleading for shelter among them. "We come from the land of souls, where all is sorrow, dismay and desolation. Our fields are covered with blood, our wigwams are filled but with the dead, and we ourselves have only life enough to beg our friends to take pity on a people drawing near their end." Such was the burden of their melancholy appeal; but the Andastes, fearing to provoke the anger of the Iroquois, turned a deaf ear to their petition and the unhappy people began anew their wearisome journey, this time, towards the plains of the Mississippi. The Sioux met them and drove them back. They next faced towards Lake Superior, and after many adventures and reverses found a resting-place at Ashland Bay, Wisconsin, where Father Allouez met them in 1665. Their stay here was but temporary, when, under the care of Father Marquette, after twenty years of wandering on the plains and in the forests, they returned to the Mackinac Country. After remaining here for some years they removed to Detroit and Sandusky; and, engaging in the wars of Pontiac, eventually as a tribe disappeared from off the face of the earth.

During the long and weary years of the rovings of the Wyandots the Fathers of the Society of Jesus had, when possible, faithfully attended to their spiritual wants. Fathers Dablon, Marquette, Pierson, Marest, Nouvel, Enjalran, De Carheil, and many others, were with them from time to time and kept alive the Faith in their midst. So exemplary were the lives of these Priests, and such their devotion to their Indian flocks, impelling them to follow the tribes in their wanderings, that Sir William Johnson, writing to the Lords of Trade, complained that Protestant missionaries were failures, and might never look for success in converting the Indians till they could practise sufficient self-denial to do as the Priests were doing.[*]

In 1748 Father J. B. Salleneuve built the first church at Sandwich, Ont., where for some years he ministered to a small remnant of the Tobacco Nation. He was succeeded by Father J. B. Marchand, a Sulpician Priest from Montreal, who remained in charge from 1796 to 1825.

THE BAY OF QUINTE MISSION.

The Jesuit Fathers, as already stated, secured a permanent foothold among the five nations. "In the spring of 1668," Father Francis Mercier says in his Relation, "a large detachment of the Cayugas left western New York and settled on the northern shores of Lake Ontario." Early in the autumn this tribe sent a deputation to Montreal, asking that Priests be sent among them, as the Jesuit Fathers with the Iroquois were too few in numbers to attend to their spiritual wants. Bishop Laval invited the Sulpician Fathers of Montreal to take charge of the work; and, in obedience to his wish, Fathers Fenelon and Trouve left La Chine for the Bay of Quinte, arriving there 28th of October, having been twenty-six days making the voyage. They were received with a hospitable welcome, began their labors without delay, and were filled with hopes of encouragement for the future. That a spirit of affectionate cordiality between the Jesuits and Sulpicians existed, even at this early day, is evident from what appears in the Jesuit Relations of this year. "Two fervent missionaries of the Seminary of St. Sulpice, Fathers Fenelon and Trouve, were despatched this year to the family of the Iroquois called Oiogouens, who for some time had been camping on the northern shore of Lake Ontario. These people require pastors to confirm in them the spirit of Faith which for two years we fanned and kept alive." The Priests met with comparatively little success

---

[*] Note Col. History, Vol. vii., p. 580.

in the conversion of the adult population. They were consoled, however, in being permitted to baptise the daughter of the chief, the children, and many of the grown people on their death beds. The Cayugas at this period occupied four villages. Keint-he and Canagora were situated thirty miles north of Lake Ontario, some distance north of the Bay of Quinte.* The villages of Tiot-hatton and Canohenda were five miles southward of these, necessitating the Priests to be continually moving amid incredible hardships and fatigues.

In 1669 Father Fenelon, worn out with labor, but still full of zeal, went to Quebec, making his first call upon Bishop Laval, that he might pay the tribute of respect and reverence due to the great prelate and his exalted office; after a most affectionate and fraternal greeting his lordship questioned him concerning his apostolic labors, intimating that he wished to preserve the details of his work among the Episcopal archives. "My Lord," replied the saintly Priest, "the greatest kindness you can show us is to say nothing at all about our work." He was accompanied on his return to the Bay of Quinte by Father Lascaris d'Urse, who, in preparation for the life of a missionary, wished to learn the Iroquois language and become familiar with the habits and methods of life necessary for one who was to devote himself to the Christianising of the savages. As soon as Father Fenelon arrived at Quinte a deputation of the Cayugas, representing the Indians of Gandaseteiadon, waited upon him, asking that he would open a mission at their town. Leaving Fathers d'Urse and Trouve at Quinte, he accompanied the deputation and passed the winter ministering to the spiritual wants of the people of Gandaseteiadon. In the winter of 1668 Fathers Dollier de Casson and Barthelmy joined the Fathers already at Quinte. De Casson, after a short stay, left for Lake Nipissing and passed the winter with a roving band of Ottawas, who had come together after their dispersion by the Iroquois and settled for a time on the shores of the Lake. During his stay among these people he obtained information of innumerable tribes that dwelt along the banks of the Mississippi; and burning with zeal for the conversion of souls, he returned to Montreal, where, joining to himself Father Galinee, a distinguished mathematician and Priest of his own Order, he started with La Salle, the explorer, and on the 30th September, 1669,

---

* Mr. Kingsford, the historian, is of the opinion that the missions of Quinte were situated somewhere in the Townships of Frederickburgh and Marysburgh; but Wentworth Greenhalgh says, in his Report, that in 1677 he visited all the Cayuga villages on the north shore of Lake Frontenac (Ontario). He places the first two thirty miles north of the Lake, and the others five miles southward of these.

reached the Grand River. Here La Salle's health gave out, and he was compelled with his party to return to Lake Ontario. The Priests continued their journey and made the first recorded ascent of the Detroit River to Lake Huron, and on the 25th of May arrived at the Sault Ste. Marie, where they were met by Fathers Dablon and Marquette, who extended to them a hospitable welcome. Failing in their attempts to obtain a guide and interpreter to accompany them on their journey to the Mississippi, they returned home, visiting on their homeward journey the Straits of Mackinaw, and reached Montreal on the 18th of June, 1670.

The Sulpician Fathers who had charge of the Quinte Missions continued to labor with apostolic zeal. After years of incredible labor and fatigue they constructed central mission buildings, similar to those built by the Jesuits years before at St. Mary's on the Wye. The difficulties that confronted them were, however, of a nature that paralyzed their sublimest efforts for the conversion of the Cayugas. The restless nature of the tribes was continually impelling them to change their quarters. It was impossible to follow them in their rovings, and the Fathers abandoned the missions, satisfied that their attempts for their reclamation, no matter how long continued, would inevitably end in disappointment. A combination of fatuous circumstances beyond the control of the Fathers brought about their departure. Their courage and zeal were undaunted; but their expectations realized but comparative disappointment.

The Recollect Fathers, under the impression that the hardships of missionary life were too much for the zeal of the Sulpicians, then entered the abandoned field. Fathers Louis Hennepin, Luke Buisset and Francis Wasson labored for years with the heroism of martyrs, but reaped no harvest of success, and in utter despair of accomplishing much good they left the country forever, and in 1687 all traces of the missionaries, and, it may be said, of the Indians of the Quinte district, disappear from the pages of history.

NOTE.—We append for the instruction of our younger readers a list of the discoveries of the early Missionaries: Fathers Joseph Le Caron, in 1615, discovered Lake Nipissing, and was the first European that stood on the shores of Lake Huron. In 1641 Fathers Jogues and Rayambault discovered Lake Superior. In 1646 Father DuQuen discovered Lake St. John, and passed two months on its north-western shore preaching to a Montagnais band known as the "Tribe of the Porcupine." On August 16th, 1654, Father Le Moyne discovered the salt mines at Salina. In 1616 Father John D'Albeau left with a roving band of Montagnais and met the Esquimaux. In 1660 the Jesuits traced on a map the highway of waters from Lake Erie to Lake Superior, showing Lake Michigan. In 1669 Fathers Galinee and De Casson made the first recorded ascent of the Detroit River. In this year Father Galinee drew the first map of the country from Montreal to Detroit, including Lake Ontario and the south shore of Lake Erie. Father Le Moyne, in 1649, discovered the salt wells at Onondaga. In 1653 Father Poncet was the first white man that ever sailed down the St. Lawrence River. Father Le Moyne, in 1654, was the first European that ever ascended the same river. Father Charles Albanel was the first man that ever made the overland journey to Hudson Bay. He left Quebec on 6th of August, 1671, reached Lake St. John in September, and wintered there. On June the 25th he discovered Lake Nemiskau, and on July the 5th from the mouth of the Rupert River looked out upon the waters of Hudson Bay. In 1661 Father Dablon penetrated ninety miles north of Lake St. John, preceding Chouart and Pierre D'Esprit eighteen years. In 1671 the Jesuits drew the first map of the Upper Lakes, and gave to the world the first authentic information of the Wisconsin and Minnesota regions. In 1665 Father Allouez confirmed the report of the existence of copper on the islands of Lake Superior. Father Joseph Lafitau, in 1716, discovered the plant jen-sing. The first church in Canada was built at Tadousac by Father Le Caron in 1616. Father Louis Hennepin was the first European that saw the Niagara Falls. In the same year, 1678, he discovered the Falls of St. Anthony. On June 17th, 1673, Father Marquette, in company with Louis Joliet, discovered the Mississippi.

EARLY HISTORY OF THE CHURCH IN UPPER CANADA.

BY

D. A. O'SULLIVAN, M.A., LL.D.,

ONE OF HER MAJESTY'S COUNSEL.

THE RIGHT REVEREND JOSEPH OCTAVE PLESSIS,
ELEVENTH BISHOP OF QUEBEC.
BORN AT MONTREAL 3rd MARCH, 1763.
DIED AT QUEBEC 4th DECEMBER, 1825.

CHAPTER II.

1760 to 1826.

EARLY HISTORY OF THE CHURCH IN UPPER CANADA.

The Old Province of Quebec—Early Missions and Pioneer Priests—Early Catholic Settlements—Statistics—Missionary Work—The Church and State—The Clergy Reserves—Bishop Plessis—Division of the Diocese of Quebec.

"The life of a Missionary Priest is never written, nor can it be. He has no Boswell. His biographer may record the Priest's public and official acts. He may recount the churches he erected, the schools he founded, the works of religion and charity he inaugurated and fostered, the sermons he preached, the children he catechized, the converts he received into the fold; and this is already a great deal. But it only touches upon the surface of that devoted life. There is no memoir of his private daily life of usefulness and of his sacred and confidential relations with his flock. All this is hidden with Christ in God, and is registered only by His recording angel."—CARDINAL GIBBONS.

THE fate of the Huron Missions at Penetanguishene, as recorded in the preceding chapter, forms a remarkable episode in our missionary annals. In the varied experience of the Catholic Church she has seen her priests massacred and her churches laid in ruins; but these, from her exhaustless resources, she replaces with others, and continues on in her work. But when, in the middle of the seventeenth century, the churches around Georgian Bay had been destroyed and the Jesuit Fathers martyred, there was no need of replacing them. The Hurons were annihilated and the missions and their history brought to an abrupt conclusion.

We have therefore no thread of narrative to take up from the foregoing pages; and for the next one hundred years and over, Western Canada has really no history of any sort. Lying between Quebec on the east and the Hudson Bay Territory on the northwest, it was beyond the reach of civilization; and, with the exception of a few forts or trading posts, was totally uninhabited. When the Seven Years' War was terminated by the Treaty of Paris in 1763 Canada by the fortunes of war fell to the share of the English, and it was not till about twenty years later that Western Canada began to be settled. By the Quebec Act of 1774 the original province of Quebec was extended westward to include not only what is now

40   *Early History of the Church in Western Canada.*

Upper Canada, but also five or six states of the present American Union. The American Revolution reduced the area of that immense Province, but Western Canada along the Lakes remained part of the province of Quebec until the year 1791. In that year Upper Canada was carved out of the province of Quebec, and corresponded substantially in geographical limits to the present province of Ontario. Within a dozen years after the time that England became possessed of Canada she lost her American colonies; and it so happened that many of her old subjects preferred to live under the British, rather than the American flag. These settled in Western or Upper Canada. They are known in our history as United Empire Loyalists, and they form a very important feature of the early portions of it. These came in the years 1783-84, and the very great majority of them were Protestants; but they were not the first settlers. As in the ancient days of this country so it was in those of this Province--the pioneer settlement in Western Canada was Catholic and the first missionary a Priest.

QUEBEC UNDER THE ACT OF 1774.

In these early days and down in fact to the year 1820 the religious care of the Canadian and the immigrant was in charge of the Bishop of Quebec. That ancient See not only embraced what is now the Dominion of Canada, but extended to the south along the Mississippi as far as the Gulf of Mexico.

Within its vast limits there was no settlement nor trading post nor fort without a priest in charge; though it was no longer the Jesuit or Franciscan that ministered to its wants, but the secular Priest of the Diocese of Quebec. It was no longer also the untutored savages that formed his little congregations or their surroundings, but the Scotch or Irish immigrants and the descendants of the ancient French settler. We accordingly have to begin anew in our narrative and deal with other people and under very altered conditions.

> Still stands the forest primeval; but under the shade of its branches
> Dwells another race with other customs and language.

Whatever difficulties there may have been, and they were not a few, that confronted the earlier missionary around the camp fires, they were all one class of dangers and came from one direction; but the difficulty of establishing or maintaining the Catholic religion in any part of the British Empire one hundred years ago was something not to be readily imagined by us to-day. That religion was barely tolerated and its adherents regarded with suspicion and distrust. All the terrors of penal legislation were evoked for its destruction. Nevertheless Catholic immigrants found their way to this country; the charges of disloyalty were proved to be groundless; the legal difficulties were dissipated; and the Church soon asserted its rights and was secured and maintained in them.* It is to the events of this pioneer period that attention is directed in this chapter.

EARLY MISSIONS AND PIONEER PRIESTS.

Such information respecting the early settlement of Western Canada as comes within reach of the general reader does not contain much that is interesting or useful from a religious or ecclesiastical point of view. So long as Canada remained French the missions in these western wilds flourished; after the cession to England they languished, and some of them died out altogether. Their struggles are untold and unknown; their chronicles come to an end.

---

* The freedom of the Church was guaranteed by the Treaty of Paris and the Quebec Act, though it was not fully recognized till after the war of 1812. The reader will note the importance of the Quebec Act, when the territory embraced in it is seen by the map on the preceding page to include all the present Province of Ontario. In marked contrast to the freedom allowed in Canada was the rabid intolerance manifested by the American colonies—Maryland perhaps the sole exception. See Essays on the Church in Canada in the American Catholic Quarterly Review, 1885, by the writer of this chapter.

"The cession of Canada to the British by the French," says Dr. Canniff, "had been followed by a withdrawal of troops from many of the forts, around which had clustered a few hamlets, specks of civilization in a vast wilderness, and in most places things had lapsed into their primal state. And when rebellion broke out in the colonies of Britain there were but a few posts whereat were stationed any soldiers or where clustered the white settlers. There were a few French living at Detroit and at Michilmacinac, and to the north-east of Lake Huron."*

In the North-West, in what is now Canada, and the Illinois country, there were only four priests, of whom Father Bocquet was at Detroit and Father La France at Mackinac. The Sandwich mission, dating from 1748, had Father Potier at the time of the cession. Niagara was deserted, and the Penetanguishene country still tenantless.

After the Revolution or rebellion of the American Colonies immigrants from the British Islands came to Canada. Many of them came not only to make a living, but to be allowed as Catholics to exist, to escape the persecution they endured elsewhere on account of their religion. The first of these, Abbe Ferland tells us, were Highlanders who followed an Irish Priest named Father McKenna. At that time M. Mongolfier, Superior of the Sulpicians, had charge of Montreal and the Western Country, and in 1776, the Abbe says,† he spoke of Father McKenna in these terms: "That Missionary has been charged with accompanying a new colony of Highlanders, about 300 in number, who, they say, are going to settle in Upper Canada, where they hope to enjoy the Catholic religion without molestation. They have already arrived at Orange, and intend to fix altogether in the same place with their missionary, who alone understands their language. I have given him the ordinary powers for ministering to his ambulating parish." Many years after, according to the Abbe, "Mr. Alexander MacDonell joined to his first troop a part of the Highlanders who had been licensed; the whole formed the settlement of Glengarry."

The troop of Highlanders here referred to did not reach Upper Canada until the lapse of nearly thirty years; but it is likely that this was not only

---

* Canniff's Settlement of Upper Canada, page 192. The north-east of Lake Huron did not seem to have any missionary at this period.

† Abbe Ferland's Life of Bishop Plessis, page 32. See also Le Foyer Canadien.

the first settlement of Catholics, but the pioneer settlement in Western Canada.* They came out to the Mohawk valley, in the Province of New York, under the auspices of Sir William Johnson, in 1773, but were driven therefrom by reason of the bigotry of the Dutch.

Not much is known of Father John McKenna, except that he was educated at Louvain, and was the first resident Priest among the settlers in New York since the Jesuit Fathers in Governor Dongan's time, nearly a century before. He took up his abode in Montreal with the Jesuit Father Flocquet; and when the Hessians arrived in Canada, finding that many of them were Catholics, he went from company to company preaching and confessing in German, a language which he spoke fluently.†

Regarding Father McKenna's successor, Chevalier Macdonell, who cites this reference in his Reminiscences of the late Bishop Macdonell, adds : " The next Priest in that section seems to have been the Rev. Alexander Macdonell, ordained in 1768, misssionary at New Johnson, Upper Canada, in 1796, died at Montreal, 9th July, 1803, aged 61 years."‡ In the census of Canada, to be referred to presently, this clergyman was stationed at Oswegatchie in the year 1783, and the Rev. Roderick Macdonell was near at hand in charge of the noted mission of St. Regis. Twenty years later, when a second Father Alexander McDonell came with other Highlanders from Scotland they joined the old settlement then in existence, and it has never died out, and is to-day the See of a Bishop.

It is said that the Highlanders who settled in the neighborhood of St. Andrew's, in the Township of Cornwall, put up a chapel soon after their arrival. It was a humble structure, in fact, a log house, but in it the services of the church were conducted until the first stone church was built. This was commenced about 1788, but was not completed for some time. It was continued in use till 1864, when the new church was consecrated. For many years after the first settlement was formed there was no resident Priest; the Rev. Roderick McDonell, who was then stationed at St. Regis, came occasionally to St. Andrew's to conduct the services.‖

---

* The U. E. Loyalists did not come to Canada till after the Treaty of 1783, when England recognized the American Union.

† His name does not appear in Abbe Tanguay's list. This is on the authority of Dr. Shea in his history of the Church in the United States, Vol. ii., page 142.

‡ Abbe Tanguay's Repertoire General du Clerge Canadien, page 124.

‖ Cornwall Freeholder, July, 1864, cited by Judge Pringle in his history of Lunenburg ,or the old Eastern district. See Mr. John McLennan's paper on " Glengarry," which was read before the Celtic Society of Montreal, referring to this matter.

The first regular parish priest of St. Andrew's was the Rev. Mr. Fitzsimmons, who was appointed in 1805. About the same time the Rev. Alex. McDonald took charge of Glengarry, on the decease of the Rev. Mr. Macdonell (Scotus). Mr. Fitzsimmons returned to Ireland in 1807, and for thirteen years thereafter the late Venerable Bishop McDonell ministered to the people both of Stormont and Glengarry, assisted by the then pastor of St. Raphael's. Father Gaulin, afterwards Bishop of Kingston, was here for four years, from 1811 to 1815. The Rev. Mr. O'Meara took charge of St. Andrew's in 1821, and was there until 1827.*

Kingston, formerly Cataraqui, was a seigniory of La Salle's in 1675, and subsisted as Fort Frontenac rather than as a trading post down into

ST. JOSEPH'S CHURCH, KINGSTON, BUILT 1808.†

British rule. A large number of Iroquois savages having declared their willingness to embrace Christianity, it had been proposed to establish a

---

* See Judge Pringle's reference to Cornwall, in History of the Eastern district, pages 234-5; also pages 192-196 as to the U. E. Loyalists.

† Since the erection of St. Mary's Cathedral, about half a century ago, that little church has been used for a school, under care of the Sisters of the Congregation de Notre Dame, and was divided into several compartments for the purpose of classification of pupils. It was at all times unsuited for school

mission in the vicinity of Fort Frontenac. Abbe Piquet, a zealous missionary in whom the natives evinced much confidence, was especially fitted for the task. The missionary station and fort were however not established at Frontenac, but further down the River St. Lawrence on the southern shore, at what is now the city of Ogdensburg. Father Piquet arrived here in 1749, at the River then called Presentation, and laid the foundation of a church, the corner-stone of which is yet preserved in the City of Ogdensburg. As early as 1751 the Abbe, accompanied by an escort, sailed around Lake Ontario, calling at Fort Niagara, and receiving a grand reception at Kingston on his return. Some years later, when Canada was lost to his countrymen, he traversed these places again, and he returned to France by way of Louisiana. He died in 1781; he is known as the Apostle of the Iroquois.* In 1783 about 700 of the U. E. Loyalists, some of whom were Catholics, arrived at Kingston. It was visited in 1801 by Bishop Denaut on his way to Detroit; and in Smith's Upper Canada we find it stated that there was a Roman Catholic Chapel in Kingston in 1812. The old French church in Kingston was built in 1808, the Rev. Angus McDonell, V.G., being in charge. Father Perinault and Father James McDonald were stationed there three years later, and Father Salmon in 1817. He was followed by Father Fraser, bringing us down to about the time of the establishment of that place as the Episcopal See of Upper Canada. Bishop Plessis included Kingston in his itinerary of Upper Canada in 1816, and the Catholic population was then said to number 75 families, of which more than two-thirds were French Canadians. No doubt the archives of this city, so important in our ecclesiastical history, have many interesting particulars, but their details are beyond the limits assigned to this chapter.

Niagara, at the other end of the lake, was a fort early in the 18th century, about the year 1720. There was then a chapel and a Recollect Father in charge. Father Crespel was here in 1730, but for no considerable time; and we find that Father Legrand, a missionary at Vincennes, died in

---

purposes and Inspectors made frequent complaint of it. Recently the structure had become weakened in various parts and the walls bulged out. This gave occasion to more urgent complaints on the part of the Inspectors, and last year they officially condemned it as unfit and dangerous, and threatened to withdraw the annual grant. Early this year the Kingston City Commissioner likewise condemned it as a peril to the lives of the citizens. Hence it became necessary to take it down and build a new school in its place. The new edifice is already nigh to completion.

I am indebted to Mr. Flanagan, City Clerk of Kingston, for a photograph (Henderson & Co.) from which the accompanying cut was taken. The engraver erased the supports which were on the side and front of the church.

* Documentary History of New York.

1742, on his way between these two places. The services were continued after Father Piquet's first visit; but in 1760 they ceased, and the Niagara records are lost. It is supposed that they were carried away by Sir William Johnson. A report on the Church of England states there was no clergyman at this point during the war of 1776, but this may have reference to clergymen of that church. The earliest name I find, in connection with British Niagara, is that of Vicar General Burke, who was stationed there in 1796 to 1798. He apparently did duty then at York, and seems to have been on intimate terms with the members of the Provincial Government.*
He and Father McKenna are the pioneer Irish priests in this Province. It may be that Father Roderick McDonnell was an Irishman, but some written testimony and fair inferences from it point the other way.

In 1785 an Irish Bishop, in acceding to the desires of the Halifax Catholics, offered some Irish priests for the assistance of the Diocese of Quebec; and on the faith of this Mgr. D'Esglis, then Bishop, wrote to the Abbe Hussey at London, and begged of him to obtain from the British ministry permission for Irish or English priests to come to Canada. These were intended as teachers in the seminaries, and also for missionary work among the Indians. It was probably a consequence of this recommendation that M. Hussey sent Father Roderick McDonell and Father Burke to this country. The former, for nearly five years, had charge of the Iroquois mission at St. Regis with great success and edification.† Father Burke was one of the directors of the Quebec Seminary in 1786, where he taught philosophy and mathematics, and did missionary work, as we have seen, in Niagara and also labored in Cornwall. Vicar General Burke was consecrated Vicar Apostolic for Nova Scotia in 1817, and made titular Bishop of that Province in the following year. The name of the priest that preceded Father Burke is not given; but there were services in 1792 at Niagara, because Navy Hall, the governor's residence, was alternately used for members of the Church of England and the Church of Rome.‡ Father Des Jardins was there in 1802. The importance of Niagara declined when the seat of government was transferred to York, and there is little further

---
* There is in the Toronto Public Library, MSS, A 11, an original letter written by him to Hon. Mr. Smith, Surveyor-General. See an extended sketch and portrait in Dr. Shea's History of the Church in America, Vol. II., page 571.

† Mandements, etc., of the Bishops of Quebec, Vol. ii., page 428. Dr. Shea regards Father McDonnell as a Scotchman.

‡ Rochefoucault Liancourt Travels in 1795 in Upper Canada.

information in the first quarter of this century. It was not until May, 1832, that Bishop Macdonell secured four acres of land in Niagara, whereon Father Edward Gordon built a church.

Sandwich, or the old Assumption Parish, is the oldest mission in western Canada. It dates back to 1744, and the Huron church was built there in 1748. Father Potier, the last of the Jesuits of the west, was here nearly 40 years, and died in 1781. For upwards of one hundred and fifty years this ancient mission has, under French and English masters, continued to exist, and is now the centre of many flourishing parishes.

There is abundant information to be had in reference to the early missions in this western peninsula of Ontario, but it could not be condensed satisfactorily within the limits of this chapter; only a few dates and facts are given.

The Detroit mission is closely connected with the early settlements at Sandwich and Malden, and is in a sense the parent mission of these in the western peninsula of Upper Canada. It began in the first years of the 18th century, and in point of antiquity reaches further back than Niagara. Like Niagara it had the honor of including in its missionaries a Vicar General, who was afterwards a bishop in the church.

The mission was founded, some say, in 1700, others in 1702, but in the third year of the century Father De Lhalle was in charge, though for no considerable time; he was put to death by the Ottawas in 1706. Abbe Tanguay has collected from the registers of Detroit that a Father Bonaventure, Recollect Missionary, was then in charge of that post. Then we find in the same painstaking writer that Father Du Jaunay was there in 1724. It is probable that the wars of 1759 and 1776 created some confusion in this mission, but there is no evidence that it was at any time abandoned. In the census of 1783 we find two priests, Father F. X. Dufaux and Father Frechette. Father Dufaux is buried at Sandwich. He was Vicar General and missionary at Detroit up to his death in 1796. In that year Detroit and the Illinois country became part of the United States.

M. Hubert, afterwards Bishop of Quebec, solicited as a favor and procured permission to go as a missionary of the Hurons at Assumption, Detroit. This was in 1781, and he remained at that mission until 1784, when he was named coadjutor to Mgr. D'Esglis.* He afterwards, in 1789, sent a pastoral letter to these Hurons, in which he counselled them to be true to their religion, and to the King—George III.† In 1790 the Catholics of Detroit numbered 2,330. After Father Dufaux came Father Francis Ciquard, and at the same time we find Father Marchand for Sandwich. At this point the mission of Detroit belongs to another country, and henceforth we are concerned only with the Canadian Mission.‡ Nevertheless in 1801 Father Felix Gatien, in charge of Detroit, is included as one of the priests of the Quebec diocese. Father Marchand was in charge of Sandwich from 1796 to 1825, with some assistance from Father Crevier, who succeeded him for a short time. Father Crevier was missionary at Malden and on the Thames, and was transferred to Penetanguishene, but subsequently retired to Lower Canada. In 1817 there was one church with two priests at Sandwich, and one priest with one church at Malden. The population of Malden was given at 675.∥ At this time there does not seem to be any other priest or church west of Niagara. In 1816 Sandwich had a population of 1,500 souls. "The old parish of St. Peter on the Thames (Riviere de la Tranche)," adds Chevalier Macdonell in his Reminiscences of Bishop Macdonell, "of which the wooden church still stands in the midst of St. Clair flats, contained with the settlement at Malden about 450 souls. These two establishments were on the confines of civilization; beyond them commenced the great solitudes of the west, known as the "Upper Country," or "North West," where many Canadians were employed in the service of the Hudson Bay and other fur trading companies."

•When the seat of Government of Upper Canada was transferred in 1797 from Niagara to York (Toronto), it is probable that some priest visited this place shortly thereafter. In 1805 Father Macdonell (afterwards Bishop) came to Toronto, as we find in that year, December 11, that he secured for the Church the block of land on Dundas street, and in the following year, the property on the corner of George and Duke streets in this city. This property was conveyed to the Hon. J. Baby, Reverend A.

---

* Mandements, etc., of the Bishops of Quebec, Vol. ii., page 341.
† See the original of this letter, vol. ii. of the Mandements, page 384.
‡ See Dr. Shea as to the Detroit mission and the boundaries of the Quebec and Baltimore dioceses, vol. ii., page 465, et passim.
∥ Gourlay's Canada.

Macdonell, and John Small, Esquire, in trust for the Roman Catholic Church, for the purpose of erecting a chapel thereon. Subsequently these trustees represented to the Parliament of Upper Canada that this lot of land was insufficient and inconvenient; and accordingly power to sell was granted in 1821. The Act also authorized the trustees to purchase other land for the use of the Roman Catholic congregation of York and its vicinity. In pursuance of this the present site of St. Paul's on Power street was purchased.*

The late Mr. C. P. Mulvaney, in his "Toronto Past and Present," says, that the "Church of Rome began her ministrations in York about the year 1801. The first services were conducted by missionary priests on their way to visit the French settlements, which ever since the Conquest lingered around Detroit and the River St. Clair. At first these services were held at the private residences of those Catholics who were prominent citizens or members of the government; at length, in 1826, St. Paul's Church was built, and is described by travellers of that time as the handsomest edifice in Little York." Mr. Talbot, who was here in 1824, is one of the travellers referred to, and he described the village or town as containing 1,336 inhabitants, occupying about 250 houses. "The public buildings are, a Protestant Episcopal Church, a Roman Catholic Chapel, a Presbyterian and Methodist meeting house, the Hospital, the Parliament House, and the residence of the Lieutenant-Governor. The Episcopal Church is a plain timber building of tolerable size, with a small steeple of the same material. The Roman Catholic Chapel, which is not yet completed, is a brick edifice, and intended to be very magnificent." Dr. Scadding in several places gives an account of old St. Paul's. "The material of the north and south walls was worked into a kind of tesselated pattern, which was considered something very extraordinary. The spire was originally surmounted by a large and spirited effigy of the bird that admonished St. Peter, and not by a Cross. It was not a flat movable weathercock, but a fixed solid figure covered with tin."†

The ground for St. Paul's was purchased in 1821, but the date at which building operations began is not known definitely. As we have seen

---

* II Geo IV., cap. xxix. This was the first Act passed by our Canadian Legislature in reference to the Catholic Church. The school property on Jarvis and Lombard streets was secured by an order in Council passed in 1817. See preamble to Act of Ontario Legislature, exchanging this for the property on Duke street; Acts of 1884, page 383, drafted by the writer of this chapter.

† Toronto of Old, page 203.

in Talbot's account, it was in course of erection in 1824. On the 1st of March, 1829, a collection was taken up in aid of the fund to liquidate the debt, and £55 8s. 6d. was realized, the Attorney-General giving £5, and many other Protestants contributing generously. The Solicitor-General, Hon. W. W. Baldwin, M.P., Simon Washburn and James Fitzgibbon, Esquires, were the collectors.*

Regarding other missions in Upper Canada a paragraph must suffice at this place.

In 1812, it is said, there was a church at Cornwall, and three years later Father Perinault was doing missionary work at Perth. After him we have Father De La Mothe, who was succeeded by Father Sweeny, or Swiney as the Quebec Almanac for 1820 gives it. Mention is made of Father Angus McDonell at Rideau, and a Father Morin at Raleigh. Father Haran, set down in the Quebec Almanacs for Richmond, 1824-6, was the first missionary at Bytown (Ottawa), 1827. The returns published in 1825 add two parishes, St. Andrew's and Cornwall, in charge of Father O'Meara, and York, in charge of Father Crowley. The following is the list for 1826:

MGR. ALEX. MCDONELL, Bishop.
MR. CROWLEY, York.   MR. HARAN, Richmond.
MR. WM. FRASER, Kingston.   MR. O'MEARA, St. Andrew's.
MR. JEAN MACDONELL, Perth.   MR. ANGUS MCDONELL, St. Raphael's.
MR. CREVIER, Sandwich and Malden.
MR. FLUET, Vicaire.†

EARLY CATHOLIC SETTLEMENTS.

When Canada passed over to the English in 1763 the total population was put down at 70,000, of whom 350 or 400 were Protestants and all the others Catholics. A few thousands would represent all west of Montreal. After the lapse of a dozen years we have an estimate by Mr. Bouchette that

---

* See Memorial Volume of Toronto, 1884, for list and further particulars. Father O'Grady, was then in charge of Toronto.

† Of these pioneers and others already mentioned, we may say that Father Perinault died in Montreal, 1821. Father De La Mothe left Perth in that year and was in Kingston for the following year; he then went to Lower Canada, and died in 1847. Father Marchand was at Sandwich for nearly 30 years, and died there in 1825. Father Crevier was about 10 years at the same place, and then went to Penetanguishene, and finally to Lower Canada. Father Sweeney, after two years in Perth, left that place in 1821 for the United States. Father Des Jardins left Niagara in 1802 and returned to France, where he died in 1833. Two Fathers Alex McDonnells died in 1803; the others will be mentioned in the next chapters. See infra, page 54, as to Father Ahearn of Peterborough.

the population had then reached 80,000. We come to definite figures in 1783, when, at the request of the Governor, the Bishop of Quebec directed a census to be taken of the Canadian Catholics. The number reached 113,008, with 135 Priests and 234 Nuns. Four of the Priests were stationed in Western Canada—two in Glengarry and two at Detroit, as already mentioned. There is no possibility of estimating exactly the Catholic population at these places, but it was probably between three and four thousand. It is material to make some calculation, as in this year (1784) the settlement of Western Canada began.

When the War of Independence in the United States was ended by the Peace of Versailles in 1783, there was a number of the old colonists there who did not favor this disruption of the Empire. Several regiments of British soldiers were disbanded in 1783, and not caring; or not being allowed to remain in the Union, they determined to come to Canada. These were the United Empire Loyalists, and it is uncertain how many came to this Province. A pretty common estimate is that in 1784 ten thousand of these Loyalists settled along the shores of the St. Lawrence. They received liberal grants from the Government, and in fact they had the choice of the best land in this Province. In early times they came in for a large share of abuse, not only from the Americans, but also from the English.* In Western Canada they were supreme—they were the owners of the soil—the nation-builders. In later days they have taken up the cudgels in their own defence, and there is a large and increasing literature now written by their descendants. Many of them, Dr. Canniff says, were Roman Catholics; and Mr. J. A. Macdonell of Greenfield in his sketch of the life of Bishop Macdonell gives a number of particulars in regard to them which are well worth perusal.

In the space of one short year, Western Canada received such an accession to its population as ordinarily would not come in a quarter of a century. In 1790 the population of Canada had increased to 161,311, of whom 134,374 were Catholics, and settled chiefly in the eastern part of the Province. These were attended to by 142 priests in active service. The

---

* Dr. Howison, in his Sketches of Upper Canada, says: "They are still the untutored, incorrigible beings that they probably were when, the ruffian remnant of a disbanded regiment, or the outlawed refuse of some European nation, they sought refuge in the wilds of Upper Canada, aware that they would neither find means of subsistence, nor be countenanced in any civilized country. Their original depravity has been confirmed and increased by the circumstances in which they are now placed." Dr. Canniff replies in strong language, to this " stupid Englishman."

British Government, finding itself possessed of a colony composed of two races and two religions, determined to divide the old Province of Quebec, and this was effected in the following year by the Canada Bill. The division took effect in 1792. From that date we have to deal with Upper Canada, or Canada West, as it was subsequently called. Though Upper Canada was mainly Protestant we find only Mr. Stuart of Kingston, Mr. Bryan of Cornwall, and a missionary named Langhorn doing duty for the Church of England; while Mr. Bethune, a Presbyterian clergyman, was the only other representative of the Protestant Church. Things were in a bad state, according to a report on the State of Religion, 1790. Amongst other things the report says: " The neglect of church duty appears, from repeated accounts sent to the Bishop of London, and the society, to be most shameful. There is not a single Protestant Church in the whole Province. The French Minister at Quebec, a reformed Jesuit, cannot preach in English, and is very negligent in his duty. The minister of Trois Rivieres is a most dissolute character," * * * * and more of this sort. At that time there were settlements on the Bay of Quinte, at Johnstown on the Grand River, 40 miles above Niagara. The report also adds that there was not a resident clergyman at Niagara during the whole war.*

In 1794 the State of the Diocese of Quebec was reported by the Bishop to the Propaganda at Rome; and there were then 160 priests, of whom four were in Upper Canada. One of these was a grand vicar. " This small number of priests," the report goes on to state, " suffices there for the present; but as this new country is being opened up and rapidly peopled, it will require a large number of priests to attend to it."†

As regards the drifting of the Catholic emigrants, when they reached Upper Canada, there is not much direct information before 1842. In that year a census by Religions was given, and the Catholics then were about one in eight of the population. The largest number was in the Eastern district, then the Home district—that is, the counties around Toronto—and next to that the Western district—the counties in the southwestern part of the Province. These, with the Midland and Dalhousie districts, made up more than one-half the entire Catholic population. In the census of 1852 the Catholics had generally increased in the preceding

---

* Archives of Canada, 1889, page 48.
† Mandements, Vol. ii., p. 474. In 1790 in the United States there were but 1 Bishop, 5 Churches, and 24 priests. Rev. Dr. Middleton, O.S.A., Records Am. Cath. Hist. Society, vol. i., page 47.

decade; and out of a total population of 952,000, over 167,000 were Catholics. Glengarry takes the lead; and Carleton, Essex, Toronto, Hastings come in that order with over 7,000 in each. The best test is the comparative proportion, and we find that Bytown (Ottawa) is the most thickly settled with Catholics, and that they were a majority of the whole population; that Prescott comes next; then Glengarry; and no other county, except Essex, approaches to a majority. There were, however, large settlements in Simcoe, Wellington, Wentworth, Northumberland and Peterborough. In Toronto, Kingston, Bytown, Hamilton and London, the aggregate Catholics formed about one-eighth of the entire Catholic population.

Whatever index these figures may be of the previous settlements, it is likely that the Catholics in Canada in early times, kept within reach of a town, if possible, in order that they might be within the call of a priest. It is characteristic of the whole settlement of America. The Irish immigrants especially have been often censured for it. The censure has been passed by those who did not, perhaps, take all the circumstances of the situation into account. Where there is no injunction to go to church on Sunday, and no penalty in not complying with the rules of one's church—if there be rules at all—it is easy enough for settlers to go where they please in a new country; but it is otherwise with Catholics who profess to live up to the requirements of their church. To be enabled to go to Mass on Sunday, or once a month, or even at rarer intervals, has often determined the choice of our immigrants, and invited them to accept what onlookers would regard as undesirable locations in the country, and inferior positions in the cities. The past is not now easily judged in this matter.

We have seen that the first Catholic immigrants in Western Canada were Highlanders, who settled in Glengarry and adjoining counties as early as 1776. The next perceptible increase was the addition of whatever Catholics there were with the U. E. Loyalists in 1784. There was no further increase, except by the immigration of the times, until Father Alexander Macdonell (afterwards Bishop) came out here in 1803 with the Glengarry Fencibles, a Scotch regiment of which he was Chaplain. They settled in Glengarry and were very numerous. The first number of Irish Catholic immigrants arrived at Perth, and these were falsely reported as riotous and mutinous, and an application made to the Home Government to have them put down. Bishop Macdonell said he was willing to pledge his life for their good conduct if they got fair play.* This was about the year 1823, and the Government had no reason to regret accepting the assurance of the Bishop. It was probably the disturbance created at this time that drove Father Sweeney out of Perth. The Perth mission continued to exist and Irish immigrants increased there and elsewhere.

In May, 1825, four hundred and fifteen families, numbering 2,024 souls, sailed from Cork, and, arriving in Upper Canada, settled chiefly in the present county of Peterborough, north of Rice Lake. These were popularly known as Robinson's emigrants, having come out under the patronage of the Hon. Peter Robinson. One hundred acres of land were granted to each family of five persons, and grown up sons were entitled to the same. The settlers petitioned the Governor General, setting out that they were in need of clergymen and school teachers. Some of these settlers and their descendants took up land around Lindsay and were the beginning of the flourishing mission established there.† In 1826 Father Ahearn was in Peterborough, and after an interval we find Father Crowley in charge of that place.

There was another settlement in 1831; 150 persons were sent out to Canada by the Marquis of Bath, and 100 commuted prisoners and their families, with 1,700 emigrants who came at their own expense. These were located in the Township of Dummer, Peterborough County, under the direction of Sir John Colborne.‡ As in the case of the Irish Catholics at Perth, a cry of disloyalty was raised against these settlers. But that question has been authoritatively settled by no less a personage than Sir Francis Bond Head. Writing to Sir R. W. Horton, May 31st, 1838, he says: "On receiving intelligence that Toronto had been attacked by a band of rebels, the settlers to whom you have alluded were amongst those who at once marched from the Newcastle district, in the depth of winter, nearly 100 miles, to support the Government."‖

---

* See Bishop Macdonell's letter cited by Chevalier Macdonell, Reminiscences, page 52.
† See Maguire's Irish in America, 103. History of the County Peterborough, published by Hunter, Rose & Co. (No author given).
‡ Mr. Rubidge's evidence before the Emigration Committee cited in Horton's Ireland and Canada, vol. x., page 59; Canada Miscellaneous Tracts, Parliamentary Library, Ottawa.
‖ Ibid, page 78. See letter to Rev. Father Crowley, Douro, 1826, from Hon. Thomas A. Stewart, as to the conduct of these settlers, given in Poole's Peterborough, page 10.

And so, while the Scotch held their own and became a power in the land, the Irish soon appeared, and were to be found everywhere throughout the Province. Their missions, once established, became permanent and advanced with the growth of the country.*

With the ancient Indian missions it was sadly otherwise. The Quinte mission languished and died out altogether. Father Fenelon returned to France, and Father Trouve was taken prisoner, but released, and subsequently served for many years in Nova Scotia. The Lake Erie mission of Dollier and Galinier was gone without a vestige, and Penetanguishene laid waste. In the report already mentioned as sent to Rome in 1794 on the state of the church in Canada, we are told that the Indian missions were reduced to eight or ten, all attended by Secular Priests in place of the ancient Jesuits. The most numerous of these missions did not exceed 500 souls. They were reduced to one-tenth of what they were on the discovery of Canada.†

MISSIONARY WORK.

The Catholic Priest begins to care for man at the cradle, follows him with his ministry through all the phases and vicissitudes of life, and does not abandon him even when the last sod is put on his grave. He follows him into the eternal world by his blessed ministrations, praying and offering sacrifice for his departed soul. Like his Divine Master, he goes about doing good, reclaiming the sinner, reconciling neighbours, bringing peace into families torn by dissensions, instructing the ignorant, visiting the sick, comforting the afflicted, helping the poor, protecting the widow and the orphan; in a word, giving glory to God in the highest and bringing peace and happiness to men of good will.—ARCHBISHOP WALSH.

The organized missionary work in Upper Canada began with this century. In the summer of 1801 Bishop Denaut journeyed as far west as Kingston and Detroit; and in the following February, on his return, visited

---

* There was a projected French settlement in the County of York about 1779, which is deserving of some mention. Dr. Scadding, in his Toronto of Old, has made short references to it; but since he wrote in 1873, much further information has come to hand. On account of the disturbed state of France after the Revolution, a number of French refugees who were in England wished to settle in Canada. Some correspondence was held in 1798 between the Duke of Portland and Peter Russell, who was then President of the Council or Government here in York (Toronto), as to regulations, grants of land, &c., for these Loyalists. The Loyalists were represented by Count De Puisage, a Lieutenant General, and there were many others of rank in France among their numbers. It was intended to settle them in the northern part of the County of York and form them into a military corps. The authorities at York did not want them at all, and Osgoode, the Chief Justice, raised objections to the land grants, though finally they were located adjoining the Oak Ridges and north of the present townships of Markham and Whitchurch. Some few settled in Niagara. After suffering great hardships the little colony was broken up, and the survivors went away greatly dissatisfied with the treatment they had received. The land on which they were located was of the poorest description, and the settlers were purposely kept as far as possible from the other French speaking inhabitants of Canada. See Canadian Archives, 1888, for lists and correspondence, &c.

† See report from the Diocese of Quebec to the Propaganda, vol. ii. of the Mandements, &c., page 480. This report was written by Father Plessis (afterwards Bishop Plessis), and contains a great deal of information respecting the Indians.

St. Andrew's and St. Raphael's, and confirmed 2,000 persons at these latter places.*

In the same year (1802) the Bishop issued his first pastoral letter to the "Inhabitants of Upper Canada." It was written in French; but being intended for the parishes of Glengarry, was directed to be translated into Gaelic. One copy was sent to Mr. Alex. Macdonell, and the other to Mr. Roderick McDonnell, and the letter itself was dated from Longueuil, 25th April, 1802. There are eight regulations in it—the 1st and 2nd constituting the County of Glengarry and other places served by Father McDonnell into a parish under the invocation of the Archangel Raphael. The third referred to payment of tithes, as in the other parts of the Diocese; 4th, the appointment of three churchwardens and their duties, &c.; 5th, a parish registry and what it should contain; 6th, a baptismal registry and regulations respecting it; 7th, regulations as to ornaments, &c., of the church—the whole containing a great number of details.†

The future Bishop subsequently wrote as to the task before him: "Upon entering upon my pastoral duties I had the whole of the Province in charge, and without any assistance for the space of ten years. During that period I had to travel over the country from Lake Superior to the Province line of Lower Canada, carrying the sacred vestments, sometimes on my back, and sometimes in Indian birch canoes, living with savages without any other shelter or comfort but what their fires and their fares and the branches of the trees afforded: crossing the great lakes and rivers and even descending the rapids of the St. Lawrence in their dangerous and wretched craft. Nor were the hardships and privations which I endured among the new settlers and emigrants less than those I had to encounter among the savages themselves, in their miserable shanties exposed on all sides to the weather and destitute of every comfort."‡

A few years later Father McDonell was made Grand Vicar of Upper Canada. "I am busy now," wrote Bishop Plessis in 1807, "with a difficult task, that is, to get the Government to agree to the establishment of a

---

* Mandements, &c., of the Bishops of Quebec, vol. ii., page 505. Bishop Pontbriand had visited Detroit and Ogdensburg half a century before this—in 1755.

† Mandements, vol. ii., page 523. The original is too long for transcription. It can be seen in the Toronto Public Library.

‡ Bishop Macdonell in 1836. See extracts from Canniff's Settlement of Upper Canada, page 305.

Catholic Bishop in Upper Canada. If the thing turns out well I shall have the honor of recommending to the Holy See the subject who seems to be best calculated for that place, and whom I have already placed among the number of my Grand Vicars." The war of 1812 prevented this recommendation from being made, and other difficulties delayed the matter for upwards of ten years. The question was first broached in 1789 under Bishop Denaut, and subsequently his successor called attention " to the impossibility of a single bishop extending his solicitude with any success from Lake Superior to the Gulf of St. Lawrence. That space contains more than 200,000 Catholics, and yet there are only 180 priests to supply all their wants. Add to that the numerous difficulties from their entanglement with a Protestant population, and the constant vigilance necessary to avoid being compromised with a Government which views things only through the medium of its own principles, and is constantly making some new effort to establish the supremacy of the King."*

This was in 1806, and the total Catholic population of Upper Canada at that time was a few thousand out of the 70,718 inhabitants. Bishop Denaut died in this year and was succeeded by his Coadjutor, Bishop Plessis, whose career will call for some extended remarks. When Bishop D'Esglis was consecrated in 1784 he called, as we have seen, Father Hubert from Detroit as his successor. The Bishop died four years afterwards, and Bishop Hubert, his coadjutor, governed the diocese for nine years. In 1789 the Diocese of Baltimore was detached from the Diocese of Quebec and seven years later took with it the Illinois country, cut off by Jay's Treaty of 1795.† The Bishop at this time proposed a separation of Western Canada, but Cardinal Antonelli was opposed to it. Unfortunately Bishop Hubert had difficulties with Governor Prescott respecting the creation of new parishes, and these difficulties were greatly increased by the action of his successor, Bishop Denaut, until the liberties of the Church were greatly imperilled. Were it not for the bold stand taken by Bishop Plessis there might have been in Canada a repetition of the scenes under the so-called Gallican Church of France. It may not be out of place here to advert briefly to the relations

---

* Bishop Plessis' Letters.

† The reader of American history will remember that the Declaration of Independence, 1776, and the Treaty of 1783, affected only the old 13 colonies along the Atlantic seaboard. The Illinois country was claimed as British territory till Jay's Treaty was signed in 1795. As we have seen, Detroit was a Canadian parish in that year. See map ante page 40.

then existing between the Church and State in Canada, rendered more antagonistic by the Act which brought Upper Canada into existence in 1791.

THE CHURCH AND STATE IN CANADA.

When it is said that a Catholic colony in the middle of the last century fell under the control of a government so Protestant as England then was, the reader will appreciate at once the position of the Canadian Catholics in 1763 and thereafter. When the Treaty of Paris of that year was signed there was no sort of recognition or toleration for a Catholic in the British Islands. The British law did not recognize any such person. The penal laws were in force against him. But these laws, with one notable exception, did not, however, extend to the colonies. The exception was a statute passed in the first year of Queen Elizabeth, and it was in effect to abolish the supremacy of the Pope in the British possessions, at home and abroad. It was passed in the year 1558 when Canada belonged to the French. In 1763, when Canada was handed over to the English, the fourth section of the Treaty of Paris provided that the new Roman Catholic subjects of His Majesty George III. should have freedom of religion, so far as the laws of Great Britain would permit. A learned but not very sensible Attorney General of Canada, named Mazeres, unearthed this old statute of Elizabeth; and though, if the terms of the Treaty were to be regarded at all, common sense would have indicated that this obsolete statute could not apply in Canada, learned opinions were given to the effect that Catholics were indeed to enjoy their religion, but that the King of England and not the Pope of Rome was the head of it. British statesmen, who were not concerned with running counter to the Elizabethan statute—who saw at once the absurdity of it—removed this difficulty in passing the famous Quebec Act of 1774, by which, practically, an oath of allegiance was substituted for the "supremacy" inconsistency. After that Catholics were allowed to breathe; but it was the one aim of the Canadian Governors to bring the Catholic Church under the civil law, as an Establishment. This was so notoriously the issue in the time of Bishop Plessis that the whole question was fought out then and decided. The struggle terminated in favor of the Church; but long before the result was reached the Church of England had secured the Clergy Reserves as a material foothold for itself, and then the

Church of Scotland also secured its share, and secured also its recognition as a church.

Such, briefly, was the position the Catholic Church held before the law when and after Upper Canada came to be settled. The Church of England and the Church of Scotland were the only other religious bodies then known to the law. The Catholics in Western Canada were no more than tolerated, but in the East there was not much change from early times. They were too numerous and too necessary to be persecuted on the score of religion; and in the face of governors, under-secretaries and English Churchmen, the British Government kept the terms of the Treaty of Paris in view, and, all things considered, dealt fairly with the Canadian Catholics.*

The Clergy Reserves.

When the British Parliament, in 1774, passed the Quebec Act, it was intended to be a measure of relief for the French Canadian and the Catholic Church. In 1791 the same Parliament passed the Canada Bill, as it is called, for the relief of the English settlers and the Church of England. This relief was more substantial for the English Church and people than the earlier measure had been for the Canadian and his Church. It provided that one-seventh of all the public lands granted were to be reserved for the support and maintenance of a Protestant clergy. This reservation did not constitute an act of appropriation; but it put by part of the public domain for an object specified and incapable of being otherwise applied—unless, of course, at the will of the Home Government. The reserved lands in Upper Canada amounted to about two millions of acres. This Church endowment was intended to be the basis of Church rectories; in 1819 the Home Government instructed the Colonial authorities to erect a Church of England rectory in every township. This instruction was unheeded; and seven years later another instruction, much to the same effect, came, and it also was disregarded. Then came an agitation against these Reserves, and in a very short time the Church of Scotland proved to the English law-officers of the Crown that it was as good a church as the Church of England ever

---

* After 1775 the Bishop of Quebec received £250 per annum from the Government, and in 1813 this was increased to £1,000. This latter sum was regularly paid to Mgr. Plessis, Mgr Panet, and Mgr., Signay. On the death of Mgr. Signay the payment ceased. The Protestant Bishop, Dr. Mountain, was paid £3,000 per annum. The Catholic Church received 400 acres of the Clergy Reserve between 1789 and 1833, the Church of Scotland 1,160 acres, and the Church of England 22,345 acres.

was. The legal opinion went to this limit, but held that all other denominations were excluded. The other denominations, accordingly, arrayed themselves against these two claimants; and before five years had elapsed the Imperial Government declared that it abandoned the Reserves, and desired that they should fall back into the general public lands of the Crown. The popular feeling in Canada was against the reservation, but the Church of England had strong friends in England and in this country. The elective branch of the old U. C. Legislature declared on sixteen different occasions for devoting these lands to general public purposes, but the other branch of the Legislature effectually blocked that disposition of them. Then they engendered McKenzie's Rebellion; and after it was suppressed, Lord Sydenham, the Governor in Canada, procured a local bill dividing the lands among a few favored denominations. The Church of England got the lion's share, but that was not enough for the Archbishop of Canterbury; he prevailed on Lord John Russell to alter the bill. The alteration scarcely suited the Archbishop, and displeased the Canadians, and nothing came of it. Many years after Upper and Lower Canada were united,* a bill was passed by which the proceeds of the sales of these lands were handed over to the different municipalities in the Province; thus putting an end to this unfortunate enactment, which, for upwards of sixty years, disturbed this country. In 1857 Dr. Ryerson, the Chief Superintendent of Education in Upper Canada, wished these moneys to be spent on educational improvement—on furnishing schools with maps, globes, &c., and especially with libraries. He wanted the public to believe that the moneys ought to go in that direction. By this means he filled each school section with books to his own liking, and was taken to task for it by Father Bruyere, and vanquished in a controversy published in the old Toronto Leader.

These two matters of the status of the Church and the Clergy Reserves are important enough for the digressions, and we will now resume the missionary work of Upper Canada in 1806, and recur to the bishop then in charge.

Bishop Plessis.

The Right Reverend Joseph Octave Plessis was born in Montreal in 1763, and was ordained priest in 1786. He was for a time professor in St. Raphael's College, and was subsequently Secretary of the Bishop of Quebec.

---

* In 1854.

In 1797 he was named Coadjutor to Bishop Denaut, and obtained the Royal acceptance through General Prescott. By reason of the captivity of Pius VI. the bulls for his appointment were delayed for some time; but in April, 1800, the new Pontiff, Pius VII., appointed him Bishop of Canathe, with the right of succession to the see of Quebec. He was consecrated Bishop of Quebec in January, 1801.* Bishop Denaut died in 1806, and on the 27th of January of the same year Mgr. Plessis took possession of the See. The new Bishop appointed Abbe Panet as his Coadjutor, and took the oath of fidelity to the King in presence of the members of the Legislative Council.† The Government of the time disputed his right to be called Bishop of Quebec; and for the first ten years of his episcopate there was a contest, as to his status before the law, between him and Governors Craig and Prevost, largely at the instigation of the new Anglican Bishop, Dr. Mountain. In 1811 Bishop Plessis prepared an elaborate memorial on the position of the Church since the cession, and the reader is referred to Abbe Ferland's memoir for particulars of it.

In that important document‡ the Bishop set out the position of the Church, both before and after the cession of Canada to England in 1763, and the position he contended it must occupy in the future. Ryland, the Governor's Secretary, went to England to consult the Colonial Secretary, but effected nothing. The Bishop subsequently went to Europe and travelled to Rome, interviewing the French King on his return. The war of 1812 put a new face on the question;§ the conduct of the Bishop in en-

---

* See life of Mgr. Plessis by Abbe Ferland; Morgan's Celebrated Canadians; also l'Abbe Gosselin's History of the Church of Canada. In each of these, different dates are given for the early events in the life of the Bishop.

† The officious Ryland, the Governor's Secretary, endeavored to get the Bishop to take the oath under the Elizabethan and other statutes, but the Bishop indignantly refused. The Governor sent Ryland the following day to apologize to the Bishop.

‡ See also Christie's Canada, Appendix for valuable documents.

§ The aid given by the Catholic Church to the authorities in Canada has on more than one occasion preserved this colony to the British Crown. In 1775, in 1812, and in 1837, its influence was in this country, as it has been in every country and at all times, on the side of legitimate authority. In 1775 the Bishop issued a pastoral letter exhorting the faithful to be true to British allegiance and repel the American invaders. This was the time that Franklin, Chase, and Father Carroll, came to Montreal to influence the Canadians and endeavour to get them to join in the American revolution. They were coldly received, and their mission proved a failure. No wonder Governor Carleton declared publicly in that year that if the Province of Quebec had been preserved to Great Britain, it was owing to the Catholic Clergy.

"Warriors," said Bishop Plessis, addressing the Militia in 1812, "to you belongs the task of opposing yourself as a wall to the approach of the enemy and to disconcert their measures." And the Government gracefully acknowledged his assistance. So did the Prince Consort for the services of Bishop Macdonell in 1837.

couraging and supporting the militia drew on him the friendly regard of the Home and Colonial Secretary ; and the result was that the Home Secretary recognized the Bishop as Bishop of Quebec, settled a pension on him for life, and declined to decide adversely the various points raised against the position of the Church. Subsequently, by a circular letter of Lord John Russell, the title of Lord was added to the name of the Catholic Bishop.* In 1817 the Bishop was called as a member of the Legislative Council of Quebec, and remained as such till his death in 1825. In 1818 he was named Archbishop of Quebec, but deemed it prudent not to assume the title, which lay dormant till 1844."†

In 1816 Bishop Plessis visited Upper Canada, giving confirmation at St. Raphael's, at Kingston, and at Sandwich, and westward to the confines of civilization. He visited Malden and the Thames Settlement. (See Itinerary for 1816.) In trying to carry out the plan of Cardinal Gerdil in 1796, he aimed to have three Coadjutors—one for Montreal, the second for Upper Canada, and the third for the Gulf Provinces. In 1806 he wrote: " My first attempt will be for Upper Canada."‡

Division of the Diocese of Quebec.

In time the Bishop took into consideration the division of his vast Diocese. He formed a permanent mission in the North-West, which became an accomplished fact in 1819; in July, 1817, Nova Scotia was detached, and erected into a Vicariate Apostolic ; and Upper Canada, with New Brunswick and Prince Edward Island, were detached from Quebec and erected into Provinces in 1819. In 1820 Bishop Plessis visited Upper Canada, and went also to the North-West and Red River. At this time he desired to divide up Quebec into five Dioceses: Gaspe, Quebec and Three Rivers; the Gulf Country; Montreal; Upper Canada; and the Hudson Bay Country. This was not acceptable at London, but finally four were agreed on. The North-West was substituted for the Hudson Bay Country, and there was only one Bishop along the Atlantic Coast.‖ The Bishop set out for Europe in this year to lay his plans before the Courts of Rome and St. James. The only condition imposed by the English Court was that the

---

* See Essays on the Church in Canada, by the present writer, Chap. VII., for this whole question.
† In 1820 when Mgr. Plessis was in Rome the Pope was satisfied with the prudence of this step.
‡ Mandements, &c., Bishops of Quebec, vol. iii., page 19.
‖ Vol. iii., page 170, of the Mandements.

new titularies were to depend completely on the Bishop of Quebec.* The Court of Rome, in 1820, approved of the project, giving an Administrator for the District of Montreal, and a Vicar Apostolic for the North-West. In 1820, therefore, we find Upper Canada with an Auxiliary Bishop; and it continued in this state for the following six years, till the Diocese of Kingston was erected.

Father Macdonell was nominated Bishop of Resina—in partibus infidelium—and Vicar Apostolic of Upper Canada on the 12th of January, 1819. He was consecrated on the 31st December, 1820, in the Church of the Ursuline Convent, Quebec.† Upper Canada was erected into a Bishopric on the 14th of February, 1826, and Bishop Macdonell appointed first Bishop under the title of Regiopolis, or Kingston. It is said to be the first Diocese erected in a British colony since the so-called Reformation in England. The particulars of the life of this illustrious man, and of his labors in Upper Canada, will be the subject of the next chapter.

This bird's-eye view of the Church in Western Canada down to 1826 is necessarily imperfect; but it contains some of the elements, and shows some of the characteristics of Church history. To the French Missionaries in Canada must be accorded the first place. They colonized this country and planted the Cross on its citadels and settlements. They mastered the dialects of the savages, and taught them to pray in their own tongue. They began and continued the evangelization of the native Indian. When the British immigrant came, they took up the work of the mission on his behalf, and obtained missionaries suitable for him, addressed him in his own tongue, and continued their assistance till the immigrants could look after themselves.

Of these the Scotch are entitled to the premier rank. In Glengarry and in Kingston, and along the St. Lawrence, Scotch settlements were established and Scotch Priests were to be found. The first Bishop was a Scotchman. When Lord Sidmouth, in 1802, raised objections to the Highlanders coming to Upper Canada, from his apprehension that the hold the parent State had

---

* Abbé Gosselin, Histoire de l'Eglise du Canada, page 125.
† In 1823 a circular letter in English was addressed by Bishop Plessis to the Clergy of Upper Canada. Bishop McDonell was in Europe at the time, and the Rev. Anthony Manseau was appointed to superintend the missions. Mandements, vol. iii., page 180. Father Manseau was never stationed in Upper Canada. He was at Soulanges 1817 to 1827, and died in 1866. He is named a Vicar General. See Tanguay, page 162.

of the Canadas was too slender to be permanent, Father McDonnell assured him " that the most effectual way to render that hold strong and permanent was to encourage and facilitate the emigration of Scotch Highlanders and Irish Catholics into these colonies."

The Irish Catholics, now so important in the Church in Western Canada, come indeed next in importance, but they came in such numbers as soon to constitute the bone and sinew of the Church in this country. The pioneer Priest, even amongst the early Highlanders, that came before Father McDonnell reached America was Father McKenna, an Irishman; and it may be that Father Roderick McDonnell, who labored at St. Regis for twenty years before the Glengarry Fencibles crossed the Atlantic, was of the same nationality. The first Bishop of this Diocese was an Irishman.*

When the prejudice against the Irish immigrant died out or was stifled large numbers of Irish came to Upper Canada, and the succeeding chapters of this volume will be occupied chiefly in showing what they have done here. The Catholic Church puts no one nationality before another—it recognizes all nations and embraces all within her capacious bosom. While the three we have referred to are prominent in our history there are yet substantial services to be recorded from her children in England—a country to which the church in all America is greatly indebted. Pausing at this point, not 70 years ago, we find in this Province one bishop with eight priests—3 Scotch, 3 Irish and 2 French—and with parishioners scattered over the whole Province, and numbering perhaps less than ten thousand souls. For 200 years prior to 1826 French Canada was indeed known and inhabited; but Western Canada, until 1784, was a desolation. Then all at once an English-speaking and intensely Protestant band of immigrants landed in this country in great numbers and the colony, Minerva-like, sprang at once into existence. The Catholic Church that was here in the beginning of our civilization, and had ministered all along to her own children and to the native Indians, suddenly found herself as an alien in her own territory. The loyalty of the Catholics was suspected and the position of their spiritual advisers questioned. Favors were heaped on what was the State Church in England, and obstacles put in the way of the Catholic Church and her

---

* But the Irish Priest, as a rule, went to the sea coast, as we have seen that Vicar General Burke did in 1798. In Abbe Tanguay's volume we find dozens of Irish Priests going to Newfoundland and what are now the Maritime Provinces, while only three or four remained in this country.

adherents. At first she was menaced with the statute of Elizabeth, depriving her of all recognition; and secondly she was offered the more deadly alternative of falling into the embrace of the State and becoming a mere establishment by law. But amid all these and other difficulties the Church maintained her own course and preserved her own position. British connection depended continuously on her aid, which was cheerfully given, and the State learned that the Catholics are loyal to every legitimate form of government. Then prejudice slowly disappeared; and though the Emancipation Act was delayed for Ireland, Catholics in Canada, in the midst of a Protestant population, enjoyed freedom of religion. And so the Church pursued her steady course through all the varying fortunes of this country. "One great fact," says Parkman, "stands out conspicuously in Canadian History—the Church of Rome. More even than the royal power she shaped the character and destinies of the colony. She was its nurse and almost its mother; and wayward and headstrong as it was it never broke the ties of faith that held it to her. These ties formed under the old regime the only vital coherence in the population. The Royal Government was transient. The English conquest, shattered the whole apparatus of civil administration at a blow, but it left her untouched. Confusion, if not anarchy, would have followed but for the parish priests, who, in a character of double paternity, half spiritual and half temporal, became more than ever the guardians of order throughout Canada."

Notwithstanding this continuity of the Church and this customary devotion of her priesthood, common facts on the surface of history, there yet remained difficulties for the British immigrants and the French Canadians that were sufficient to depress, if not to dishearten them. They were scattered over an area of territory immense and inaccessible; they were discovered and ministered to under circumstances of unusual hardships; and when the country became less thinly inhabited they found themselves wedged in amongst the adherents of a hostile faith. The Church could no longer count on the support of the great French Catholic nation, and English-speaking missionaries were needed and not readily obtained. In the face of all these and other obstacles, there have been great strides made in the Catholic Church in this western country during the last century and a half. Even in the 50 years reviewed in this chapter, from Father McKenna's time in 1776 to the establishment of the Diocese of Kingston, the Church acquired a solid footing in Canada and her children shared creditably in its vicissitudes and prosperity. "We can look history in the face," says Thomas D'Arcy McGee, "and putting our hands on any part of the fabric of the State, we can say as a people, THIS was partly our work."

CRITICAL NOTE.—It would be difficult to indicate the sources from which the reader might get additional information from the foregoing other than the Ecclesiastical Archives at Rome, Quebec, and Kingston. The mandements of the Bishops of Quebec, published recently in three volumes, are important and will repay looking into. They give the Bishops' letters, and some reports, public documents, &c. Next in point of information come the archives of Canada, issued by D. Brymner, at Ottawa. These are indispensable, and frequent use has been made of them in the foregoing. After these, for personal information as to priests, Abbe Tanguay's Repertoire General du Clerge Canadien is very interesting, but very brief. For public documents the last volume of Christie's Canada is of great value, and could not be overlooked. Garneau's Canada has an immense amount of information; but in dealing with the Church the author has laid himself open to criticism, and has received it in several quarters. Abbe Ferland's Life of Bishop Plessis is interesting; many facts are given in brief in Abbe Faillon of Canadian History; Gosselin's little catechism of Church history has facts and dates, but is too short; Chevalier Macdonell's Reminiscences of Bishop Macdonell, and Mr. J. A. Macdonell's sketch of the same person, are both entertaining little brochures, while a number of other writers contribute here and there facts respecting this period. The U. E. Loyalists have a number of historians and apologists, the writings of whom are to be found in most public libraries. The Clergy Reserves question has been discussed in a number of books and by a number of writers. The legal aspect of the period has been written in French by Mr. Pagnuelo of Montreal and in English in Essays by the present writer. There are some local histories worth looking into, Judge Pringle's Eastern District, Leavitt's Leeds and Grenville, Scadding's Toronto of Old, and others.

*LIFE AND TIMES OF THE HONORABLE AND RIGHT REVEREND
ALEXANDER MACDONELL.*

BY

H. F. McINTOSH, Esq.,

CORRESPONDING MEMBER OF THE AMERICAN CATHOLIC HISTORICAL SOCIETY
OF PHILADELPHIA.

The Honorable and Right Reverend Alexander Macdonell.
Born at Glen Urquhart, Scotland, July 17th, 1762.
Died at Dumfries, Scotland, January 14th, 1840.

CHAPTER III.

1819-1840.

THE LIFE AND TIMES OF BISHOP MACDONELL.

The Diocese of Kingston—Bishop Macdonell—The Early Clergy—Cardinal Weld—Visitation of the Diocese—The Parishes—Bishop Gaulin—The Troubles at York—New Missions—An Interesting Event—1835 to 1838—Statistics—Bishop Macdonell's Death and Burial.

THE DIOCESE OF KINGSTON.

> "Endeared to all by the simplicity of his manner, by the benevolence of his disposition, and by the affectionate warmth of his heart, his death was deplored by those who knew him, almost as a domestic calamity; his loss was regarded as one whose place could never be supplied. With his neighbors of every creed and of every shade of opinion, he lived in habits of familiar and unreserved intercourse. Ardently attached to his religion himself, imbued with a deep sense of the sanctity of its precepts, and the divine authority of its doctrines, he sought to extend its influence among others, not by the jarring elements of disputatious criticism, not by wounding the prejudices, or challenging the hostility of his Protestant brethren, but by the innocence of his life, by the modesty of his demeanour, and by the exercise of all the calm, quiet, unobtrusive virtues, which adorn the character of the Christian."
>
> REV. M. A. TIERNEY'S, "Memoir of Dr. Lingard."

THE time had now come when the Church in Upper Canada was to enter upon a new epoch in her history. Hitherto she had formed but a part of the vast Diocese of Quebec; but now she was to enter upon a corporate existence of her own and take her place in that world-wide circle of episcopal sees which cluster round and draw their refulgence from the See of Peter, the mother and mistress of churches. The division of the Diocese of Quebec was a project which had occupied the thoughts of Bishop Plessis from the very beginning of his episcopate, and had formed the subject of frequent addresses to the Propaganda; but a multitude of untoward circumstances which shall presently be summarized, had delayed its realization. When he paid his first episcopal visit to the Province in 1816 and saw with his own eyes the promising state of the missions at St. Raphael, Kingston and Sandwich, he was more than ever convinced of the necessity of placing them directly under the care of a resident bishop. But such was the position of the Church at that time that he felt the necessity of first coming to a satisfactory understanding with the British Government as to his own title ere he broached the subject of new bishoprics. Surprising as it may now seem, objections had been taken to his use of the title, Bishop of Quebec, although it had been borne by his predecessors for more than a century. The ruling power made strenuous efforts to enforce the Royal Supremacy, and, by claiming the right to nominate the parish priests, sought to make the Church the creature and slave of the State. But this question has already been gone into at some length, and it is enough now to say that Bishop Plessis, who was not a man to be easily daunted, steadfastly contended for the freedom and dignity of his office ; and, as not infrequently is the case, patience and courage gained the day. His title being at length conceded to him, he lost no time in taking up again the project of the division of his Diocese. At his instance Father Alexander Macdonell, who was known to have great influence with the Court of St. James, proceeded to England in 1816 to lay before the Ministers of the Crown the project which Bishop Plessis had already brought to the notice of the Holy See. On arriving in England Father Macdonell waited upon Viscount Sidmouth, who introduced him to the Colonial Secretary, Earl Bathurst. Thanks to the influence which the Vicar General had with these Ministers, born of his services to the Crown at an earlier period, he, to a certain extent, succeeded in his mission.* Strange as it may appear, the Home Government, though not too kindly inclined towards its own Catholic subjects, was disposed to take a more liberal view of colonial affairs. Profiting by the lesson of the revolt of the Thirteen Colonies, they were anxious to conciliate the Canadas, and accordingly put no obstacle in the way, but rather favored the erection of new bishoprics, as proposed to them by Father Macdonell. Accordingly, as a first step in this direction, in July, 1817, with the consent of the British Government, the Holy Father separated Nova Scotia from the Diocese of Quebec and erected it into a Vicariate Apostolic. About the same time an agreement was arrived at between the Courts of Rome and London to erect two other Vicariates, one in Upper Canada and the other to comprise New Brunswick, Prince Edward's Island and the Magdalen Islands. This was but a portion of the ecclesiastical divisions considered necessary by Bishop Plessis : he desired to place a bishop in the district of Montreal and another in the North-west Territory, but this general division of his diocese he hoped

---

* For a more extended account of his negotiations see Mgr. Tetu's "Les Eveques de Quebec:" Quebec, 1889.

to obtain only after protracted negotiations at London and at Rome. Father Macdonell had, in the meantime, returned to Canada.

Not having been apprised of the understanding which had been arrived at between the Holy See and the British Government, Bishop Plessis himself was urged by the most influential members of the Canadian clergy to proceed to England. Sir John Sherbrooke before quitting Quebec in August, 1818, had strongly advised the Bishop to make this voyage, which he foresaw would be of great advantage to Canada and to the Church. So many solicitations, joined to the powerful motives suggested by the interests of religion, decided Mgr. Plessis to cross the ocean to draw down more efficaciously on the Church the benediction of the Pope and the favor of the Sovereign. He accordingly sailed from Quebec on July 3rd, 1819. Shortly after his arrival in London he was surprised to learn by letter from Canada that within a few hours of his departure Bulls had been received from the Holy See appointing him Archbishop of Quebec, and giving him as suffragans two bishops, one in charge of Upper Canada, the other of New Brunswick and Prince Edward's Island. This was more than he contemplated; for, as the British Government had not been apprised of the matter, there was reason to fear that objections might be raised to the erection of Quebec into a Metropolitan See. He therefore hastened to wait upon Lord Bathurst, and frankly explained the state of affairs. As he anticipated, the news was not well received, and Lord Bathurst informed him that he had better allow the title to remain in abeyance until some more convenient time. At the same time he was assured that no objection would be taken to the appointment of the new bishops, provided they did not assume the titles of their respective Sees, but remained for the present Vicars Apostolic and Coadjutors to the Bishop of Quebec. Thereupon Mgr. Plessis proceeded to Rome and sought an audience with the Holy Father. Kneeling at the feet of the Father of Christendom, he begged permission to lay aside the title of Metropolitan until such time as the British Government should cease to be opposed to it. The well-known merit of Mgr. Plessis and his influence at the Court of St. James induced Pius VII. to approve the measure, and to grant the Bishop the privilege of deciding the time when prudence would permit him to assume publicly the title of Archbishop of Quebec; it accordingly remained in abeyance until 1844, when it was revived by Mgr. Signay, and has been borne by the subsequent occupants of the See.

The Bulls appointing Father Macdonell Bishop of Resina and Vicar Apostolic of Upper Canada were issued by Pope Pius VII. on January 12th, 1819. His consecration did not, however, take place until two years later, the ceremony being performed by Bishop Plessis in the Church of the Ursuline Convent, Quebec, on December 31st, 1820. The new Bishop at once returned to Upper Canada and entered upon the duties of his high office with that zeal and determination characteristic of the man. Notwithstanding he was close upon his sixtieth year, he became more than ever the apostolic missionary, traversing the country in every direction and laying broad and deep the foundations of the now flourishing Church of Ontario.

Although Upper Canada was now under the care of a Vicar Apostolic the full desire of Bishops Plessis and Macdonell was yet to be realized. Under the freedom and independence which the Church of to-day enjoys in this thriving Province, it is difficult to realize the obstacles by which she was hampered in the discharge of her Divine mission three quarters of a century ago. It is an unpleasant fact to recall that she should have been dictated to by the civil government in things solely of the spiritual order. Yet so it was; and if, after lengthy negotiations, she was permitted to send a Bishop into the new Province to administer her affairs, that Bishop was not allowed to take the title of his See or to exercise fully his prerogatives. But Bishops Plessis and Macdonell, who had fought so valiantly for the rights of the Church, did not now relax in vigilance or determination. They continued negotiations with the Ministers in London to induce them to withdraw opposition to the appointment of titular bishops in Canada, and the better to further this end Bishop Macdonell visited England in 1825.* There he found, to his relief and delight, that the Ministers of the Crown were disposed to take a more reasonable view of things, and were now willing to accede to the desires of the Canadian prelates. Bishop Macdonell accordingly proceeded to Rome; and having there reported to the Holy Father and to the Propaganda the altered state of affairs, he returned to Canada in January of the following year.† During his absence Bishop Plessis, worn

---

* The Bishop had been in England also in 1823.

† While in England in 1823 Bishop Macdonell had called upon Mr. John Galt, the well-known Scottish novelist, who was agent in England for those of the principal inhabitants of Upper Canada who had claims against the Government for losses incurred during the invasion of the Province by the armies of the United States in 1812-15. The information given to Mr. Galt by the Bishop at this time resulted shortly afterwards in the formation of the Canada Company. See Mr. Galt's "Autobiography."

out by the cares and fatigues of the episcopate, had died and been succeeded at Quebec by Mgr. Panet.

On February 14th, 1826, Leo XII. erected Upper Canada into a diocese and appointed Bishop Macdonell its first Bishop under the title of Regiopolis or Kingston, Kingston being chosen as the episcopal city. The diocese comprised the whole of the present Province of Ontario, which has since been subdivided into the eight dioceses of Kingston, Toronto, Ottawa, Hamilton, London, Peterborough, Pontiac (Pembroke) and Alexandria.

Bishop Macdonell.

Bishop Macdonell was born in Glen Urquhart, on the borders of Loch Ness, Inverness-shire, Scotland, on July 17th, 1762,[*] and being from his infancy destined for the Church, was, at an early age, sent to Douay, then to the Scottish College at Paris, and subsequently to the Scottish College at Valladolid in Spain, where he was ordained priest on February 16th, 1787. On leaving Valladolid he returned to Scotland and served for four or five years as a missionary priest at Badenoch and the Braes of Lochaber, so celebrated in the old Jacobite song, "Lochaber no more."

Towards the end of the last century a large proportion of the smaller tenants in the Highlands of Scotland were reduced to the greatest distress by reason of ejectments from their holdings, which the proprietors had determined to convert into sheep-walks. At the same time the restrictions of the emigration acts prevented them from emigrating to the colonies.[†] In this dilemma, Father Macdonell, who labored amongst the poor people and was a daily witness to their sufferings, sought and obtained employment in the manufactories of Glasgow for seven or eight hundred of the dispossessed Highlanders, the greater part of whom were Catholics. This was in 1792. Here they remained until 1794, giving full satisfaction to their employers and, notwithstanding the bitter hostility against Catholics characteristic of the time,[‡] earning the

---

[*] "Reminiscences of Bishop Macdonell," by Chevalier Macdonell, K.H.S.; Toronto, 1888. Another account states that he was born in Inchlaggan in Glengarry in 1760, but the weight of testimony is in favour of the former. See also Tanguay's: "Repertoire General du Clerge Canadien," Quebec, 1868. For information relating to the Bishop's career in Scotland I am mainly indebted to the interesting "Reminiscences" above quoted.

[†] See Lord Selkirk's "Present State of the Highlands of Scotland."

[‡] Only a few years before (1780) a riotous mob led by Lord George Gordon had burned and sacked the Catholic Chapel and priest's house in Glasgow.

friendship and good-will of their Protestant fellow-workmen. In the latter year, owing to the troubles on the continent and the consequent stagnation of the British export trade, there ensued a general failure among the cotton manufacturers of Glasgow. The result was that the greater part of the operatives, Catholics as well as others, were thrown out of employment, and were obliged by necessity to enlist in the numerous military organizations then being formed for the defence of the country. Finding that the Catholics under his charge were obliged to enlist in these bodies, and compelled, according to the then universal practice, to declare themselves Protestants, Father Macdonell conceived the idea of embodying them into one corps as a Catholic regiment. With this view a meeting of Catholics was held at Fort Augustus in 1794, and a loyal address to the King drawn up, offering to raise a Catholic corps under command of young Macdonell of Glengarry ; a deputation was sent to London, and the address was most graciously received by the King, a letter of service being issued to raise the first Glengarry Fencible Regiment as a Catholic corps, the first raised as such since the so-called Reformation. Father Macdonell, though contrary to the then existing law, was gazetted chaplain.* In the summer of 1795 the regiment was ordered to the Isle of Guernsey, and in 1798 was transferred to Ireland on the breaking out of the troubles in that country.

During the peace of 1802 the Glengarry regiment was disbanded and its members again reduced to great straits, the Scottish manufacturing trade having been so circumscribed by the late sanguinary war that the Highlanders could not find an asylum or employment in their own country. Father Macdonell then began to entertain the hope of establishing a claim upon the Government, so far at least as to obtain for them grants of land in Upper Canada, where many of their race were already settled on lands obtained as rewards for services rendered during the American Revolutionary War. Father Macdonell lost no time in putting his scheme into execution. He proceeded to London about the year 1802 to lay before the Premier, Right Hon. Henry Addington (afterwards Lord Sidmouth), the claims of the disbanded Highlanders. After protracted negotiations success at length crowned his efforts, and in 1803 he obtained the Sign Manual for a grant of land for every officer and soldier of the Glengarry Regiment whom he should introduce into Upper Canada. Despite the opposition of the Highland

* Chevalier Macdonell's "Reminiscences."

proprietors, who were loath to see their people emigrate, and in consequence threw every obstacle in their power in the chaplain's way, the first batch of his Highlanders left Scotland and landed in Quebec in 1803, where Father Macdonell soon joined them; others followed at intervals during that and the following year and proceeded to Upper Canada, where, in what is now the County of Glengarry, their indomitable leader had, on the presentation of his credentials to the then Lieutenant-Governor, Lieutenant-General Hunter, obtained the land stipulated for his followers according to the order of the Sign Manual.

This was the third considerable settlement of Catholics in Upper Canada, and if the circumstances which led up to it have been dwelt upon at some length, it is because of the importance of their bearing upon the future of the Church in this Province.

Father Macdonell, as already related, had, immediately on his arrival in Canada, been appointed to the mission of St. Raphael in Upper Canada, and in 1807 he became Vicar-General. Here he devoted himself in earnest to the duties of his sacred calling. "For more than thirty years," says his biographer, "his life was devoted to the missions of Upper Canada. He travelled from the province line at Coteau du Lac to Lake Superior, through a country without roads or bridges, often carrying his vestments on his back, sometimes on horseback, sometimes on foot, or in the rough waggons then used, and sometimes in Indian bark canoes; traversing the great inland lakes and navigating the rivers Ottawa and St. Lawrence, to preach the Word of God and administer the rites of the Church to the widely scattered Catholics, many of whom were Irish immigrants who had braved the difficulties of settling in our Canadian woods and swamps. By his zeal, his prudence, his perseverance and good sense, these settlers, as they multiplied around him, were placed in that sphere and social position to which they were justly entitled."*

The Early Clergy.

On the erection of Upper Canada into a diocese in 1826 there were but seven priests in the entire Province, viz.: Father William Fraser at Kingston, Father Angus Macdonell at St. Raphael, Father John Macdonald at Perth, Father James Crowley at York, Father Patrick Harm at

---

* Chevalier Macdonell's "Reminiscences."

Richmond on the Ottawa, and Fathers Joseph Crevier and Louis Joseph Fluet in charge of the missions at Sandwich and Malden.* Churches and schools were few in number, and the Catholic settlers, scattered here and there through the Province,† were forced to depend upon the occasional visit of a priest for instruction and the consolations of religion.

Father Fraser, or "Priest" Fraser as he was more familiarly called, was a native of Inverness, Scotland, and was born in 1788. He was ordained priest at Quebec in 1819, and was at St. Raphael to welcome Bishop Macdonell after his consecration in 1820. He was removed to Kingston in 1822, where he built a fine stone presbytery, afterwards occupied by Bishop Macdonell during his residence in Kingston, and subsequently used as an academy by the Nuns of the Congregation. He died at Kingston in 1836 after a life of exceptionally fruitful labor.

Father Angus Macdonell was born in Glengarry in 1791, and ordained priest in 1822. He subsequently became Vicar General, and was in his day one of the most influential and best known of the Upper Canadian clergy.

The priest at that time in charge of the Perth mission deserves more than a passing notice. Father John Macdonald was one of the most noteworthy characters in the Province, and no history of the Church in Ontario could make any pretence to completeness which failed to make mention of him. He had been ordained at Quebec in 1814, coming to Upper Canada in the following year, and settling at Kingston, where he remained until he was appointed to Perth in 1822. He lived to a great age, dying only a few years ago. Here is a pen-picture of him by a writer who visited him not long before his death: "The great object of interest, love and pride of all classes throughout the country was 'The Vicar,' old Father John Macdonald, who had held their spiritual rule for over half a century, and who was still living, hale and hearty, in a pleasant cottage in Glengarry. * * * This fine old priest was, without exception, the most venerable and patriarchal figure the writer ever looked upon. He was nearing his hundredth year of age. His massive head and trunk were unbent by years, and sound in every function. Only the limbs that had travelled so many a weary mile, in days when the whole country was but an

---

* Quebec Almanac, 1826.
† We have no means of estimating the number of Catholics in the Province at this time. The total population was 166,379.

untracked wilderness, had yielded to time and fatigue and could no longer bear up the colossal frame. Wallace himself had not passed through more bold adventures than this old Highland chief. * * * The reverence and love that centred in him in his old age gave proof of his benign and salutary use of his mighty sway."* "Father John" is the subject of many interesting and amusing anecdotes, which, however, would be out of place here.

Of Father Crowley, the pastor of St. Paul's, York, until 1829, very little is known. On leaving York he went to Peterborough, remaining there until 1835, when his name disappears from the published lists of the Upper Canadian clergy. What became of him is not known.

Father Patrick Haran† was pastor of Richmond from 1826 until 1830, when the parish was amalgamated with that of Bytown. Whether Father Haran died about that time or left the Province has not been ascertained. At any rate he is not mentioned in the clergy-lists after that year.

Father Crevier, who succeeded Father Marchand in charge of the Sandwich mission, was born in 1786, ordained priest in 1816, and in the same year became Father Marchand's vicar. On the latter's death in 1825 he succeeded him and remained in charge until 1831.‡ During his incumbency a community of Nuns were induced to come to Sandwich to take charge of the Girls' school; but a project which had been entertained of building a convent for them having fallen through, the religious soon after left the parish.

This same year was marked by the arrival in the Province of Rev. William Peter Macdonald, afterwards Vicar-General, who took up his residence at St. Raphael with the idea of taking charge of the Bishop's intended seminary for ecclesiastics.§ This well-known ecclesiastic was born in Scotland in 1771, and was educated at Douay and at the Scottish College at Valladolid in Spain, at which latter place he was ordained on Nov. 29th,

---

* "Canadian Sketches" in "Irish Ecclesiastical Record," Nov., 1887.
† There was a Father Ahearn at Peterborough in 1826, but whether he was the same man I have not been able to ascertain. The spelling of priests' names in the almanacs and other publications of the time varies so much that it is sometimes difficult to identify them.
‡ Abbé Tanguay's "Repertoire General."
§ "The seminary," says Chevalier Macdonell, "was a very modest affair; but it had the honor to produce some of the most efficient missionaries of the time, among whom may be mentioned Rev. George Hay of St. Andrew's, Rev. Michael Brennan of Belleville, and Rev. Edward Gordon of Hamilton."—"Reminiscences."

1790. Returning to Scotland he served for twelve years on the missions in different parts of the country. He was subsequently in the service of the British Government in several important capacities, latterly as an attache of the British Embassy in Spain. "He was," says one who knew him well, "a thorough scholar and a polished gentleman. Possessed of a refined poetic taste, he left many pleasing productions of his pious muse, most of which are still in manuscript."* He published a newspaper called "The Catholic" at Kingston in 1830, and afterwards resumed it at Hamilton from 1841 to 1844. He died at St. Michael's Palace, Toronto, on April 2nd (Good Friday), 1847, and his remains are buried in the Cathedral, under the Gospel side of the altar.

CARDINAL WELD.

In the Fall of 1826 occurred another event having an important bearing on the development of the Church in Upper Canada. Advancing age and increasing responsibility had caused Bishop Macdonell, when in Rome in 1825, to ask of the Holy See the appointment of a coadjutor to assist him in the work of his extensive diocese, naming at the same time Rev. Thomas Weld of Lulworth Castle in England. Leo XII. graciously acceded to his request, and on Aug. 6th, 1826, Mgr. Weld received episcopal consecration as Bishop *in partibus* of Amycla. This estimable prelate was a descendant of one of the oldest English Catholic families, whose name is held in benediction by reason of its princely benefactions to the Church. He was born in London on Jan. 22nd, 1773, and was educated entirely at home. He early gave proofs of piety and munificent charity, and on the death of his father he succeeded to the estates of the family at Lulworth in Dorsetshire. In the meantime he had married and been blessed by the birth of a daughter, who subsequently became the wife of Lord Clifford. Mrs. Weld died in 1815, and not long afterwards her husband resigned his estates into the hands of his brother, and retired on a pension to Paris to study for the priesthood. He was ordained in April, 1821, by the Archbishop of that city, and, returning to England, entered on the duties of the priesthood at Chelsea, where he remained until his appointment as coadjutor to Bishop Macdonell. After his consecration he took up his residence at the Benedictine Convent at Hammersmith. Being in poor health he deferred his

---

* Many of Father Macdonald's poems are of exceptional merit, and if collected and published would form a notable addition to our slender stock of Catholic literature in this Province.

departure for Canada and occupied himself with the direction of the Benedictine Community, with whom he resided. His health, however, did not improve, and by the advice of his physicians he continued to reside in England until summoned to Rome by Pope Pius VIII. in 1830. On the 25th of May in that year he was named Cardinal, and in the enjoyment of that august dignity he took up his permanent residence in the Eternal City. He died on April 10th, 1837, and is buried in the Church of St. Marcello, where a handsome monument, from designs by Signor Giorgioli, is erected to his memory. His funeral discourse was preached by Dr. (afterwards Cardinal) Wiseman, Rector of the English College at Rome,* who, in his "Recollections of the Last Four Popes," says of his Eminence : "Seldom has a stranger been more deeply and feelingly regretted by the inhabitants of a city than was this holy man by the poor of Rome." The presbytery and great church of St. Raphael in Glengarry were erected in anticipation of Mgr. Weld coming to Canada. Bishop Macdonell received many favours from Rome through the influence of his former coadjutor, who, while he lived, ever retained a deep interest in the well-being of the Church in Upper Canada. Several generous gifts from him of money, vestments and church plate are recorded in Bishop Macdonell's correspondence.

Visitation of the Diocese.

In 1827 Bishop Macdonell began a visitation of his immense diocese. Under his own immediate supervision there were parishes at Kingston, still presided over by Father Fraser; at Perth, under the charge of Father Macdonald ; at Richmond, of which Father Haran was pastor ; and at St.

---

* The following is that portion of Dr. Wiseman's sermon relating to Canada: "In accepting this office (coadjutor to Bishop Macdonell) there could certainly be no room for ambition. It would lead him into a far country, where for the rest of his days an ocean would roll between him and all that was dear to him on earth. The field of his exertions would have been, in great measure, a district but lately colonized—very unsettled, and unprovided with many of those resources which long custom had rendered almost indispensable for his happiness. In fact, it was at the risk of life that he consented to accept his nomination; for already was his constitution enfeebled, and unequal to the unhealthy climate of so cold a latitude. The remonstrances of his domestic and medical advisers, and the business of his new district to be transacted in London, joined to other causes, detained him three years in England; but though it delayed his departure from time to time, he never abandoned the intention of proceeding to America. In the meantime he was not unemployed. He could no longer discharge the public duties of the ecclesiastical state; but he found means of compensation by assuming a charge which enabled others to fill his place. He retired into the Convent of Hammersmith, and devoted himself to the spiritual direction of edifying the Community. But Providence now designed him for a higher dignity, and a more extensive circle of usefulness. The health of his beloved daughter required the experiment of a milder climate ; and he took the opportunity of accompanying her, to visit, before leaving Europe, the tomb of the Apostles. He had not been long in Rome before he was invested by Pope Pius VIII. with the dignity of Cardinal. His nomination took place on the 15th of March, 1830."

Andrew's, in charge of Father Macdonell. The church at St. Raphael's the Bishop presided over in person. Between Kingston and York there was no resident priest. Arriving in York, the Bishop found the few Catholics then in the place still under the pastoral care of Father Crowley, St. Paul's church being the only Catholic place of worship in the town.

Proceeding on his journey westward, Bishop Macdonell reached Guelph, where he found his old friend, Mr. John Galt, whom he had not seen since his visit to England in 1823. Mr. Galt, who had come to Canada but a few months before as Commissioner of the Canada Company, was the projector and founder of Guelph, the first tree on the site of the town having been felled, with befitting ceremonies, on April 23rd of the same year (1827). The Bishop remained for several days as the guest of the Commissioner, who had already erected a substantial log house on the banks of the river Speed, where he dispensed a generous hospitality.* In recognition of Bishop

GUELPH, 1827.
Showing Macdonell street and the site on which the Church now stands.

Macdonell's services in the formation of the Canada Company, Mr. Galt presented him with a block of land on a commanding site on a hill overlooking the settlement, on which to erect a church.† An incident with

---

* This house, which was the first erected in Guelph, still stands in perfect preservation, and is now used by the C. P. R. as a railway station. It was formerly known as "The Priory."
† Galt's "Autobiography."

reference to this gift is worth recording. As a compliment to the Bishop, Mr. Galt at once set men to work to open an avenue* through the forest, extending from the river's brink to the summit of the hill on which the church of the future was to be built. On the crest of the hill a large elm tree was left standing in the midst of the clearing, "forming," says a chronicler, "a very prominent feature in the landscape which the place then presented." On the exact site of this tree the present magnificent church of the Jesuit Fathers now stands, overlooking the city and surrounding country. It is the first object that strikes the eye of the traveller approaching Guelph from any direction.†

Leaving Guelph, Bishop Macdonell continued his journey westward to the Talbot Settlement, where was a considerable number of Catholics scattered through the townships bordering on Lake Erie. This settlement had been made and was then presided over by the celebrated Colonel Talbot, whom the Bishop had met in York a short time before. Though a member of the Church of England, Col. Talbot was not unkindly disposed towards Catholics, and, on this occasion, extended a warm-hearted hospitality to the Bishop, who remained in that vicinity as his guest for several days.‡ Indeed it was to the urgent representations of Col. Talbot that the visit of Bishop Macdonell was due. As a result of the Bishop's observations, Father Campion, then stationed at Niagara, was directed to visit St. Thomas and London twice a year.

From the Talbot Settlement the Bishop proceeded to the missions along the Detroit River, then in charge of Fathers Crevier and Fluet. Of these the principal, as we have seen, was Sandwich, presided over by Father Crevier in person, while his vicar looked after Malden. Here the

---

* This street still bears the Bishop's name.

† Mr. Galt seems to have been of a prophetic turn of mind. Writing from Guelph to a friend in England he said: "Hitherto we have had no adventure in Guelph, not even one Sabine scene; but an incident in the clearing was magnificent. Desirous of seeing the effect of a rising ground, at the end of a street where a popish church, about twice the size of St. Peter's at Rome, is one day to be built (the site was chosen by the Bishop, and we have some expectation that his coadjutor, Mr. Weld, of Lulworth Castle, is coming here), I collected all the choppers in the settlement to open a vista, and exactly in two hours and ten minutes, 'by Shrewsbury clock,' or my own watch, an avenue was unfolded as large as the Long Walk in Windsor Park, and of trees that, by their stature, reduce to pigmies all the greatest barons of the English groves."—*Fraser's Magazine, 1830*. While the present noble structure is far from being "twice the size of St. Peter's," it may at least be said to be one of the largest and most beautiful in Ontario. Whether it was intended that Mgr. Weld, in the event of his coming to Canada, should take up his residence in Guelph or not, as mentioned above, is not definitely known. Had he done so Guelph might have become permanently an episcopal city. A gift is recorded of £1,000, from Cardinal Weld to Bishop Macdonell towards the erection of a church or college there.

‡ St. Thomas "Journal."

Bishop again met Mr. John Galt, who was also on a tour of the Western Province. Mr. Galt, in his "Autobiography," states that on reaching Detroit he was told that Bishop Macdonell was at the "seminary" on the other side of the river. He probably meant the presbytery, as there was no college erected there until many years after this date. The parish at Sandwich was in a flourishing condition, and possessed a substantial church (the Assumption), erected in 1782, a presbytery and a school. The Catholics were more numerous than in any other district west of Glengarry, and their spiritual wants had been well looked after by a succession of zealous and devoted pastors.

Whether, on this tour, Bishop Macdonell visited the old Indian missions on Manitoulin Island and along the shores of Lake Superior does not appear. But no priest attended there regularly until 1835, when Father Proulx took up his residence at Penetanguishene, and from that out, for many years, devoted himself to the welfare of the Indian.

The result of this protracted visitation of the diocese was a great impetus to religion and the establishment of several new missions. As we have seen, the number of priests in the Province in 1826 was seven; by 1830 they had increased to sixteen, and many new churches were erected or in prospect.

The Parishes.

As already stated, the only church in York at this time was old St. Paul's. Father Crowley continued in charge of the parish until 1828, when he was removed to Peterborough, where, so far as can be ascertained, he was the first resident priest. He was succeeded at York by Father O'Grady, an active man, but, as the sequel proved, greatly lacking in that humility which should ever characterize the true priest. One of Father O'Grady's first acts in York was to raise funds towards liquidating the debt on the church. To this end he called together his parishioners and had a committee appointed to take the matter in hand. As a result of their deliberations a collection was made on Sunday, March 1st, 1829, which amounted, including donations, to £55 8s. 6d. Among those who contributed, as appears from an advertisement in the "Loyalist," of March 14th, were: The Attorney-General, Hon. Thomas Clark, Hon. W. Dickson, Col. W. Chewett, Rev. Dr. Phillips, Dr. Widmer, Dr. Diehl, John S. Baldwin,

Esq., Captain Baldwin, R.N., Robert Baldwin, Esq., Robert Sullivan, Esq., W. R. Prentice, Esq., and Samuel P. Jarvis, Esq. At a subsequent meeting of the committee (March 9th), Lawrence Heyden, Esq., J.P., presiding, the following resolution was adopted: "That we hail the liberality which our Protestant and dissenting brethren manifested on this interesting occasion as a certain prelude to future concord among all classes of the community: That the Solicitor General, W. W. Baldwin, Esq., M.P., Simon Washburn and James Fitzgibbon, Esquires, are justly entitled to our best thanks for having acted as collectors."* An instance of toleration and liberality such as this is recorded with pleasure, as proving conclusively that acts of a less happy nature which have marred the fair fame of Toronto at sundry times, have not emanated from the better class of our Protestant fellow-citizens.

About this time the Bishop took up his residence in York. He had been named a member of the Legislative Council of Upper Canada, and his civil duties as such required his presence in the capital during the Parliamentary sessions. He lived in the house still standing, though somewhat altered, on the south-east corner of Jarvis (then Nelson) and Duchess streets.† Dr. Scadding is the authority for the statement that the Bishop also resided at one time in Russell Abbey, formerly the residence of Hon. Peter Russell, on Princes street.‡ The episcopal private chapel, a large frame building, afterwards known to fame as the "Soup Kitchen," which was nearly opposite the Bishop's residence on Nelson street, was removed only a few years ago.

In 1827 Father James Campion was placed in charge of the mission at Niagara. His parish, however, may be said to have extended from York to the Detroit River, and this immense district he was accustomed to traverse once or twice in the year. He was the first priest to visit Guelph, St. Thomas, London, and other settlements, since Bishop Macdonell's visit in 1827. Father Campion remained in charge of this mission until 1830, when he was removed to Prescott. He was a most devoted missionary, and is said to have been a personal friend of the famous Father De Smet, whose career in the wider field of the "Far West" he emulated in

---

* "Toronto: Past and Present." (Memorial Volume), p. 92.
† "Reminiscences of Bishop Macdonell," p. 26.
‡ "Toronto of Old," p. 54.

the forests and clearings of Upper Canada. He was succeeded by Father John Cullen; and he, in 1833, by Father Bollan (or Polin), who remained until the appointment of Father Edward Gordon in 1835.

In 1832 Bishop Macdonell secured from the Government a grant of four acres of land at Niagara, being part of the military reserve. Here, on the advent of Father Gordon about 1835, a church was built under the title of St. Vincent de Paul, which continues in use to the present day. Father Gordon, who was a convert,* was destined to become one of the best-known and most influential priests in Upper Canada. He continued in charge at Niagara until the division of the Diocese of Kingston in 1842, and for some time afterwards. Subsequently he be-

CHURCH OF ST. VINCENT DE PAUL, NIAGARA.
Erected about 1836.

came Vicar General of the Diocese of Toronto under Bishop de Charbonell, and resided in Hamilton. On the erection of the Diocese of Hamilton in 1857, Bishop Farrell made him his Vicar-General, in the enjoyment of which dignity he continued for the rest of his life.

The years 1828 and 1829 were marked by the rise of parishes in Peterborough, Belleville, Prescott and Bytown (Ottawa). Of Peterborough,

---

* On the occasion of Father Gordon's visit to Great Britain in 1843, he said, in reply to an address from his flock: "The individual who is the cause of my absenting myself for a short time from you is an only brother in the decline of life—a brother to whom I am bound by every endearing tie—one to whom, under Providence, I owe my conversion to the Catholic faith, and who has never ceased to exhort me to the practice and faithful discharge of all my spiritual and temporal duties."—"The Catholic," July 12th, 1843.

Father Crowley, as already stated, was the first pastor, and continued as such until 1835, when he was succeeded by Father John Butler, who, for a long term of years, labored with great success on that mission. On Feb. 18th, 1834, Bishop Macdonell secured a grant of land in Peterborough in trust for the erection of a church, etc. This grant consisted of lots 1 and 2, south of Brock street and west of George street; Nos. 1 and 2, north of Hunter street and west of George street; No. 14, new survey, fronting Hunter street, and park lot 6. On this land Father Butler began the erection of a church, which is the present Cathedral of St. Peter.

The first resident priest at Belleville was Father Michael Brennan, who continued to minister to the Catholics of that mission during the lifetime of Bishop Macdonell, and for many years afterwards.

Father Timothy O'Meara's name first appears as resident pastor of Prescott in 1830. He was probably placed in charge the previous year. He was succeeded by Father James Campion, already referred to, who built the priest's residence and the building known as Grenville College, which was intended to provide the Catholic youth of the time with the means of a higher education. Dr. Thomas Rolph, in his "Canada and the West Indies," published at Dundas in 1836, describes this structure as "a very elegant stone building, 84 feet in length, with two wings, one at either end, 40 feet each in length, extending in a fine garden geometrically arranged, and lying between them and a splendid stone mansion erected for his (Father Campion's) own residence." The zealous priest, however, attempted too much;* the building, though still standing, was never used as a college, but was diverted to other purposes. Father Campion went to the United States in 1838, and some time afterwards died at Lewiston, N. Y. The next priest whose name appears in the clergy lists as in charge of this mission is Father James Clarke,† who rebuilt the front of the church and erected thereon a tablet with an inscription to that effect.

Bytown, then a frontier settlement, but destined, under the name of Ottawa, to become the capital of the Dominion and the seat of an arch-

---

* In connection with this establishment Father Campion intended to have a library for general circulation. This library was to have been bought at the public expense, and the proceeds were to be devoted to the purchase of clothing for poor children, who would receive gratuitous instruction at the college. This benevolent design, like that of the college, seems never to have been realized.

† Chevalier Macdonell states that after Father Campion, and before Father Clarke, Revs. William P. Macdonald (afterwards Vicar General) and Patrick Foley resided at Prescott in the order named.

bishopric, had for its first pastor Father Angus Macdonell, who remained until about 1831 or 1832, when he was succeeded by Father John Cullen, and he, in 1835, by Very Rev. Wm. Peter Macdonald, Vicar General, who had for his curate, or vicar, Father J. F. Cannon. On the removal of the Vicar General to Hamilton in 1838, Father Cannon was installed as pastor, and continued as such for some years. He it was who built the church now known as the Basilica.

As we have already seen, Father Fraser was parish priest at Kingston in 1826, and continued as such until 1828 or 1829, when he gave place to Father W. P. Macdonald, V. G. Father Macdonald had as assistants, first Father Murth Lawlor from 1830 to 1832, and then Father Edward Gordon until 1835. Although Kingston was Bishop Macdonell's titular city, he did not make it his permanent residence for some years after this, and the Vicar General was in consequence first in authority. On the removal of Father Macdonald to Bytown in 1835, his place was taken by Fathers Daniel Downie and J. H. McDonagh. Father Angus Macdonell's name also appears in the published lists as residing at Kingston from 1836 to 1838, although at this time he was cure of Sandwich. He was, however, absent from Sandwich for three years without resigning his office,* and it is likely he spent this period in Kingston, though for what reason does not appear.

Perth was in charge of Father John Macdonald until 1838. Here, in 1834, a grant of land was secured from the Government for a church and burying ground, and shortly afterwards a church was erected thereon.

At St. Andrew's in Glengarry, there resided, during Bishop Macdonell's episcopate, Fathers Angus Macdonell, Fraser, O'Meara and George Hay in the order named. Dr. Thomas Rolph, writing in 1836,† refers to the church at St. Andrew's as "a large building." It could not then have been built but a short time.

Father Angus Macdonell was pastor of St. Raphael until the erection of a parish at Bytown in 1829 when he removed thither. He was succeeded by Father Fraser, and he by Father John Macdonald. Bishop Macdonell resided here for many years and built the great church which, had the

---

* "History of the City and Diocese of London," by Rev. J. F. Coffey, M.A., 1885.
† "Observations on Canada and the West Indies."

Bishop Gaulin.

Since the elevation of Mgr. Weld to the Cardinalate in 1830, and his consequent resignation of the coadjutorship of the Diocese, no successor had been appointed until Mgr. Remigius Gaulin was consecrated Bishop of Tabracca, 20th Oct., 1833, with right of succession to Kingston.* This prelate was a native of Quebec, where he was born on June 30th, 1787. He was ordained priest in 1811, and from that date until his episcopal consecration he zealously discharged the duties of the ministry on various missions throughout Canada. His last station was at Sault au Recollet, near Montreal. After his consecration he, for a time, took charge of the Seminary at St. Raphael, and subsequently removed to Kingston. On the death of Bishop Macdonell in 1840 he, as we shall see, succeeded him as Bishop of Kingston.

The Troubles at York.

We now return to the Church in York, still under the charge of Father O'Grady. The subject is approached with diffidence as the name of this unfortunate priest would be best consigned to oblivion. But, on the other hand, it is well that in the interests of historical truth the true facts should be recorded. Father O'Grady's name first appears in the published clergy lists as parish priest at York in 1829. Where he came from is not now known, but he appears to have been a man of uncommon energy, though not too well grounded in prudence or discretion. From the first he was an

---

* The coadjutorship of Kingston appears to have been offered to but declined by Father John Larkin, a Sulpician Priest of Montreal, at the time of Cardinal Weld's resignation. On the death of Bishop Power in 1847 the same priest, then a Jesuit, was nominated for the Diocese of Toronto, which dignity he likewise declined. On the latter occasion he used these precise words in the presence of several brother priests, one of whom was Father Michael Nash, S.J., of New York, to whom I am indebted for the information: "Do they think," said Father Larkin, "that after having refused the whole of the great diocese of Kingston, I will now accept a portion of it." Father Allen Macdonell, S.J., of Keyser Island, Conn., a grand nephew of Bishop Macdonell, states that it is a continued, unquestioned tradition in the family that Father Larkin refused the nomination to Kingston though urged to accept it by both Cardinal Weld and Bishop Macdonell, and that in anticipation of his acceptance the Cardinal sent to him his crozier and other articles belonging to the office. On Father Larkin's refusal a new list of candidates for the office was sent to the Holy See. Among them were Rev. John Murdoch of Glasgow and Rev. James Gillis of Edinburgh. The choice fell upon the former, and the bull for his appointment was actually drawn up, but, on the strong representations of the Scottish Vicars Apostolic, was cancelled. Father Murdoch was soon after nominated coadjutor of the Western District of Scotland and Father Gillis became Vicar Apostolic of the Eastern District. See Rev. J. F. S. Gordon's "Scotichronicon."

ardent politician, and when his spiritual duties clashed with his political views, the latter got the upper hand. He allied himself to the political party of William Lyon Mackenzie, and that fiery politician did not himself espouse his cause with greater zeal than did the pastor of St. Paul's. Father O'Grady's political creed was, possibly, his own affair, but when, not satisfied with holding certain opinions as an individual, he dragged them into the sanctuary and made the pulpit a political rostrum, the Bishop considered it time to call a halt. With the merit or demerit of the political questions which agitated the public mind in this Province sixty years ago it is not our place here to deal. Feeling certainly ran high and found expression in violent language, later in violent deeds. Catholics were to be found in the ranks of both parties. Bishop Macdonell, who was conspicuous for his attachment to the British Crown and his loyalty to the established authorities, deemed that Catholics as a body had been dealt with in a fair and generous spirit by the Government, which, therefore, did not merit abuse from them. Especially, in face of the troubles that were brewing, did he consider it the duty of a priest to fulfil his mission as peace-maker rather than to spur men on to violence. He accordingly felt constrained to rebuke Father O'Grady for the part he was playing and to insist on discontinuance of it. But he was met with a defiant rejoinder, and the rebellious priest carried his insubordination so far as to leave the Bishop, in vindication of his office and for the best interests of his flock, no other alternative than to resort to extreme measures. Father O'Grady was accordingly silenced. Whatever grounds for sympathy his friends may thus far have imagined themselves to have had, there could be none in the face of the priest's conduct in this crisis. He openly defied the Bishop, and, disregarding all authority, continued to exercise the functions of the priestly office and to exhort the people to side with him. This a few misguided spirits did; but, to the credit of the Catholics of York be it said, the majority were true to the instincts of their faith and upheld the hands of their Bishop in this trying crisis. Bishop Macdonell proceeded to St. Paul's, and, having caused Father O'Grady to be ejected, he installed another in his place. With the subsequent career of the unfortunate priest we are not concerned. He continued his unpriestly conduct, and when summoned before the Committee on Grievances of the House of Assembly to give evidence as to the state of affairs in the Province, made a series of wanton and malicious charges against the Bishop, which, however, were proved to be utterly without foundation. For instance, he charged him with misappropriation to his own private purposes of funds granted by the Government for the support of churches and schools; and whereas the Bishop had discretionary powers to appropriate such portion of the grant to school purposes as he deemed necessary, it was charged that he was bound to devote a fixed portion, but did not. The evidence, as printed in the Seventh Report of the Committee on Grievances, proves the utter groundlessness of O'Grady's charges. The truth is, Bishop Macdonell had impoverished himself in building up the Church in Upper Canada. In a letter to Father O'Grady before any trouble had arisen between them, he says: "If I be called thither (to York) ex-officio, I shall go, but not otherwise. For besides the fatigue of so long a journey, the precarious state of the weather, and want of accommodation in this inclement season of the year, I find my funds so completely drained and myself so much involved by educating, boarding and clothing seven or eight ecclesiastics for so many years at my own expense without the smallest assistance from any other quarter except the few pounds that you have been remitting to the two of them that have been teaching here, that I could hardly command to-day what would defray my travelling expenses to and from York." Again: "Although upwards of five thousand pounds behind-hand between the new church of this parish (St. Raphael) and other churches, with the expenses of supporting my ecclesiastics, and other outlays for religion, I am unwilling to appropriate any of the small property given for the use of the Church as long as I can, in full reliance that His Divine Majesty for whose honor and glory I have involved myself in difficulties, will, in His gracious goodness, extricate me out of them." And, writing to Sir Francis Bond Head, "under circumstances," says Dr. Canniff, "which precluded the possibility of any statement accidentally creeping in which could not be fully substantiated,"* he used these words: "As to the charges brought against myself, I feel very little affected by them, having the consolation to think that fifty years spent in the faithful discharge of my duty to God and to my country, have established my character upon a foundation too solid to be shaken by the malicious calumnies of two notorious slanderers." And continuing, he said: "In this way (travelling the country under great difficulties in discharge of his spiritual duties) I have been spending my time and my

---

* "The Settlement of Upper Canada." Toronto: 1872.

health, year after year, since I have been in Upper Canada, and not clinging to a seat in the Legislative Council and devoting my time to political strife, as my accusers are pleased to assert. The erection of five and thirty churches and chapels, great and small, although many of them are in an unfinished state, built by my exertion; and the zealous services of two and twenty clergymen, the major part of whom have been educated at my own expense, afford a substantial proof that I have not neglected my spiritual functions, or the care of souls under my charge; and if that be not sufficient, I can produce satisfactory documents to prove that I have expended, since I have been in this Province, no less than thirteen thousand pounds of my own private means, beside what I received from other quarters, in building churches, chapels, presbyteries and school-houses, in rearing young men for the Church, and in promoting general education. With a full knowledge of these facts, established beyond the possibility of a contradiction, my accusers can have but little regard for the truth, when they tax me with neglecting my spiritual functions and the care of souls. The framers of the address to His Excellency knew perfectly well that I never had, or enjoyed, a situation, or place of profit or emolument, except the salary which my Sovereign was pleased to bestow upon me, in reward of forty-two years faithful service to my country."

The conduct of Father O'Grady was the more inexplicable in that Bishop Macdonell had always treated him with consideration and respect and had reposed in him a more than ordinary degree of confidence. He made him a Vicar General and entrusted him with many difficult and delicate missions, little suspecting the sort of treatment he was to receive in return. But the Bishop has long been justly accorded a high place among the makers of Upper Canada, while the unhappy priest is now well nigh forgotten. But we turn to happier themes.

New Missions.

As if to console the Bishop for the sore trials through which he had passed, a great impetus to religion occurred about this time. As the Province became opened up, and priests were forthcoming, many new parishes sprang into existence, and the consolations of religion were placed within reach of the Catholic settlers. Stations which hitherto had enjoyed but the occasional visit of a priest now received pastors of their own.

This was the case in 1833 and 1834 with Cobourg, Port Hope, Dundas, Guelph, St. Thomas, London, St. Catharines, and other places. Father Dempsey was given charge of Cobourg and Port Hope, Father John Cassidy of Dundas and Guelph, while Father Daniel Downie looked after St. Thomas and London.*

The first church erected in Guelph was commenced by Father Cullen, who succeeded Father Campion, as missionary in the Western district. This would be about 1832 or 1833.† It was completed by Father John Cassidy, who was the first priest to reside in the village. It was at first named St. Patrick's,‡ and was a frame structure, which did duty for many years, being destroyed by fire about the year 1844. It was replaced by the stone church of St. Bartholomew in 1845. Father Cassidy remained until 1837, when he was replaced by Father Thomas Gibney, who was parish priest until 1846, when, on returning from a sick call, he was thrown from his carriage and received injuries from which he died soon after.§

Dundas was united with Guelph until 1838, when Father John Fox was installed. In Dr. Rolph's "Canada and the West Indies" (1836) the Catholic church is described as "an interesting object, with its white spire surmounted by the holy symbol of the Christian faith."

In St. Thomas, Father Cullen obtained from a settler (Archibald McNeil) three acres of land in the east end of the village, to be held and used for a church and burying-ground.‖ This is the site of the present church. The first church was built in 1830, and was a small frame structure, afterwards used as a school house. It was under the invocation of St. George, and continued in use until the erection of the present Church of the Holy Angels. On the retirement of Father Downie, Father J. M. Burke took charge and remained until 1838, being succeeded by Father M. R. Mills for a brief space, and he by Father James O'Flynn, who presided until 1842.

---

* Rev. J. M. Coffey's "Historical Sketch of London Diocese." The "Quebec Almanac" gives Rev. James Berinett, or Bennett, as in charge of St. Thomas and London in 1834 and 1835, and Rev. J. Keegan in 1836 and 1837.

† "Annals of the Town of Guelph," 1877.

‡ Bouchette's "British Dominions in North America."

§ Besides St. Bartholomew's Church in Guelph, Father Gibney built churches at Goderich, Irishtown and Stratford. See "The Catholic," 1841.

‖ "St. Thomas Journal."

The first church built in London was on the corner of Richmond street and Maple avenue. It was a primitive structure of logs with an earthen floor, and was dedicated by Father Downie in 1834. The fortunes of London continued to be bound up with St. Thomas until 1845, when Father Mills, formerly at St. Thomas, was placed in charge of the Townships of London and Westminster.*

Until the year 1838 the Catholics of St. Catharines were dependent upon the priest at Niagara for the consolations of religion. In that year Father J. M. Burke took up his residence among them, and probably built the frame church which was burned down in 1842.

The priest who succeeded Father Dempsey in Cobourg was Father Alexander Kiernan, who built the first church, a frame building, "subscribed to by Christians of all denominations." Sheriff Ruttan and Hon. Zachariah Burnham donated the ground and gave $60 cash. Father Kiernan also received from Mr. Charles Clark, an Anglican, a gift of $50 and the site for a church in the village of Bond Head, Clark Township.† In 1834 and 1835, Father Fitzmorris was in charge of the missions on the River Trent, and Father Patrick Foley of those on the Thames.

An Interesting Event.

A great stir was created in York in 1834 by the conversion of Hon. John Elmsley to the Catholic faith. Mr. Elmsley was a son of Chief Justice Elmsley, and nephew, in consequence, to Peter Elmsley of Oxford, the celebrated classical critic and editor. He was born at "Elmsley House," the site of the present Government House, corner of King and Simcoe streets, and during his earlier career served the Crown in various capacities. In 1830 he was called to the Executive Council of Upper Canada, which dignity, however, he resigned in 1833 owing to his inability, as he said, to act independently there. The immediate occasion of his conversion was the reading of Abbe Travern's (later Bishop of Strasbourg) "Commentary on the sixth chapter of St. John's Gospel." He had hitherto been an active and zealous member of the Church of England, and his withdrawal from that communion gave great offence to its chief pastor

---

* "Historical Sketch of the Diocese of London," 1885.
† "The Catholic," Dec. 22nd, 1841.

in York, the Venerable Archdeacon Strachan. Owing to the prominent position Mr. Elmsley occupied in the Province he felt it his duty to make public his reasons for the momentous step he had taken, and this he did by publishing an edition of the pamphlet which had so greatly influenced him, with comments thereon of his own. This he circulated broadcast through the Province gratis. A spirited controversy ensued. Dr. Strachan, taking alarm lest Mr. Elmsley's conversion might influence others, made the event the text of a sermon from the pulpit of St. James church, and followed it up by a pamphlet on the "Errors of Romanism." Then came an edition of Blanco White's "Poor Man's Preservative Against Popery," no doubt considered unanswerable by the bellicose Archdeacon. But he was not suffered to have it all his own way. Bishop Macdonell, then residing at York, was not disposed to interfere in the controversy, but not so his Vicar. The "smoke of battle was scented afar" at Kingston, and Father W. P. Macdonald girded on his armour. In an incredibly short space of time he had written and published "Remarks on Doctor Strachan's Pamphlet Against the Catholic Doctrine of Christ's Body and Blood in the Eucharist," which pamphlet practically settled the controversy, being immeasurably the ablest and most effective that appeared. It is an admirable summary, drawn from Scripture and the Fathers, of Catholic teaching on the subject of which it treats.*

Mr. Elmsley proved the sincerity of his conversion by the ardour with which he threw himself into the practice of his new-found faith. He became a great benefactor of the Church† and took an active part in every good work. His death occurred in 1865, in the 64th year of his age.

1835 TO 1838.

The years 1835 and 1836 were signalized by the rise of parishes or missions at Waterloo, Penetanguishene, Cornwall, and Raleigh on Lake Erie. Of the former, Father J. B. Wirriats was the first pastor, being succeeded by Father Peter Schneider in 1838. The first priest in recent times to reside at Penetanguishene was Father J. B. Proulx, whose stalwart

---

* There appeared also another Catholic pamphlet entitled: "Husenbeth's Defence of the Catholic Church: with a preface by a **Catholic Layman of Upper Canada**," Toronto, 1834. The author is not known.

† The ground on which **St. Michael's College and St. Joseph's Convent** now stand was the gift of Mr. Elmsley. The Basilian Fathers have erected a tablet to his memory in St. Basil's Church.

frame was so long conspicuous in the Diocese of Toronto. He, as already mentioned, took up his residence there in 1835,* but in 1838 removed to Manitoulin Island, and was succeeded by Father Amable Charest. Previous to 1834 Cornwall had been part of the parish of St. Andrew's, but in that year Father James Bennett took up his residence in the town. The first church (a wooden building) had been built in 1829 or 1830, and it continued to do duty until the erection of the brick church in 1855 or 1856. Father Bennett continued as pastor until 1842.† Father J. B. Morin, who first resided in the township of Raleigh (1835), continued in charge during Bishop Macdonell's lifetime.

During the years 1836 and 1838 Bishop Macdonell issued several pastoral addresses, not only to his own flock, but to the inhabitants of the Province at large. In one of these, addressed more especially to Protestants, he says: "I address my Protestant as well as my Catholic friends because I feel assured that during the long period of four-and-forty years that my intercourse with some of you, and two-and-thirty years with others, has subsisted, no man will say that in promoting your temporal interest I ever made any difference between Catholic and Protestant; and indeed it would be both unjust and ungrateful in me if I did, for I have found Protestants upon all occasions as ready to meet my wishes and second my efforts to promote the public good as the Catholics themselves: and it is with no small gratification that I here acknowledge having received from Orangemen unequivocal and substantial proofs of disinterested friendship and generosity of heart."

To his own Catholic countrymen he said: "When a Prime Minister of England (Mr. Addington) in 1802 expressed to me his reluctance to permit Scotch Highlanders to emigrate to the Canadas, from his apprehension that the hold the parent state had of the Canadas was too slender to be permanent, I took the liberty of assuring him that the most effectual way to render that hold strong and permanent was to encourage and facilitate the emigration of Scotch Highlanders and Irish Catholics into these colonies."

---

* Lots 116 and 117 in 2nd concession, east side of Penetanguishene road in Township of Tiny, were obtained by grant from the Government on Feb. 3rd, 1834.

† Judge Pringle's "Lunenburg."

And lastly to Irish Catholics, for whom he had ever exhibited a paternal regard, he had this to say:* "Your loyalty and general good conduct, my friends, have obtained for you the approbation and confidence of Government, notwithstanding the attempt that was made to create a general prejudice and raise an alarm in the Province on the arrival of the first batch of Irish Catholic emigrants in the settlement of Perth. They were reported as riotous, mutinous and what-not. An application was made for military force to put them down, and this report was sent to the Home Government. Being at the time on the Continent, the Colonial Minister, Earl Bathurst, wrote to me to hasten my return to Canada, as the Irish Catholic emigrants were getting quite unruly. On coming to London and calling at the Colonial Office I assured Lord Bathurst that if fair play were given to the Irish Catholics and justice done to them I would pledge my life their conduct would be as loyal and as orderly as that of any of His Majesty's subjects. Mr. Wilmot Horton, the Under-Secretary, who happened to be in the office at the time, requested that I would give him that assurance in writing in order to take it to the Council, which was just going to sit. Yes, my friends, I pledged my life for your good conduct— and during the period of fifteen years which have elapsed since that pledge was given I have had no cause to regret the confidence I placed in your honour and your loyalty."

The years 1837 and 1838 were marked by the "Rebellion" in Upper Canada. "In 1836," says Chevalier Macdonell, "Bishop Macdonell foresaw the coming storm and considered it the duty of every citizen to exert the utmost efforts to prevent the interests of justice and order from falling into unworthy hands. He issued an address to the freeholders of Stormont and Glengarry, enjoining them, in plain and forcible language, to elect representatives of sound and loyal principles, who would have the real good of their country at heart, and not allow themselves to be misled by the political schemers who were endeavoring to drive the Province into rebellion against the legally constituted authority. It must not, however, be supposed that because the Bishop was such a strenuous advocate of law and order he acted with slavish party attachment, or that he was unaware

---

* In a letter to his Vicar General in 1830 he wrote : " What a pity we could not prevail on some of the noble-hearted and heroic daughters of St. Patrick to cross the Atlantic and communicate a spark of the love of God and holy zeal for the religion of Christ which filled their own hearts to the hard and selfish mind of some of our Canadians of both Provinces."

of the many abuses which then weighed upon the country, impoverished its resources and checked its progress. On the contrary, he acknowledged these evils, but, at the same time, he maintained with reason that they were foreign to, and not inherent in, the Constitution; that they could be safely and permanently removed by constitutional means alone; and that rebellion, so far from redressing these grievances, would only confirm, and perhaps aggravate them a hundredfold." But the " Rebellion" belongs to the domain of civil history, and we refer to it only incidentally. As the Bishop predicted, it ended in ignominious failure, while the evils of which the country complained were in due time removed by constitutional means. At Kingston in 1835 the Catholic clergy had a disagreeable duty to perform. Von Shoultz and others of the "invaders" who had effected a landing near Prescott, only to be taken prisoners and condemned to death, were Catholics, and it fell to the lot of Fathers Angus Macdonell and P. Dollard to prepare them for the end. It will be remembered that at his trial Von Shoultz was defended by a then rising young lawyer who was destined in time to become Prime Minister of Canada and one of the most famous men of his day—John A. Macdonald.

Ordained priest at Valladolid, on the 16th of February, 1787, Bishop Macdonell celebrated his jubilee on the 16th of February, 1837. The ceremony took place in the parish church at St. Raphael in presence of more than two thousand persons. The gentlemen of the Seminary at Montreal expressed a desire that the ceremony should be performed in the magnificent parish church (Notre Dame) of that city, but the Bishop found it more in accordance with his own feelings, as it certainly was more gratifying to his own people, among whom he had laboured for upwards of thirty years, to celebrate this joyful event among them. The Bishop of Montreal and many of his clergy desired to be present, but were prevented by the severity of the weather. Nineteen priests, however, assisted at the ceremony and all the prominent gentlemen of the District, besides many from a distance were present. The Bishop addressed his countrymen before Mass in Gaelic, their native tongue; he called to their recollection the destitute state in which he found their mission, and indeed the whole Province in regard to religion, on his arrival in the country in 1804, there being no clergy, no churches, no presbyteries, or schools; and what rendered the labour of a missionary more arduous, no roads. His pastoral labours were not confined to the County of Glengarry; they extended from one end of the Province to the other, and for many years he had no fellow-labourer to assist him within a distance of seven hundred miles. Under such overwhelming difficulties, he had much reason to acknowledge and thank the merciful Providence of Almighty God for making him, although unworthy, the humble instrument of procuring for them the many temporal and spiritual advantages which they at present enjoy. In conclusion, as this might be the last opportunity he should have of appearing before them in this world, Bishop Macdonell begged their forgiveness for any bad example he had given them and for any neglect or omission of his duty during his ministry among them for so many years; trusting much to their prayers and supplications to the Throne of Mercy on his behalf, to enable him to prepare his long and fearful accounts against the great and awful day of reckoning, which, in the course of nature, could not be far distant; and he promised them that he would never cease to offer up his unworthy prayers for their spiritual and temporal welfare.* Tears flowed from the eyes of the Bishop and his hearers during this affecting discourse. After Mass, the ceremony concluded with an impressive sermon by Vicar General Macdonald.

The long cherished desire of Bishop Macdonell to found and endow a seminary for the education of his clergy was put into practical effect in 1837. He obtained a charter from the Legislature, and set aside a piece of land in Kingston on which to erect a building. At a meeting convened at his residence it was resolved that he should proceed to England, accompanied by Father Angus Macdonell and Dr. Thomas Rolph, for the purpose of collecting funds wherewith to carry out his project.

The corner stone of the college was laid on June 11th, 1838, Bishop Macdonell officiating, assisted by his coadjutor, Mgr. Gaulin, Vicar General Angus Macdonell and others of his clergy. At the Bishop's request Dr. Thomas Rolph delivered an address, saying, among other things, that it was the anxious desire of the Bishop that a priesthood should be raised in the Province, fearing God, attached to the institutions of the country, and using their assiduous efforts to maintain its integrity; that until such an institution was founded, the Bishop could not be as responsible for his clergy as he could wish to be. "Such," says Chevalier Macdonell, "was

---

* Chevalier Macdonell's "Reminiscences," p. 30.

the commencement of Regiopolis College. Sad to say the prosperous career so fondly anticipated by the learned orator has not yet dawned upon it. Its present condition we all know ; its future, time alone can show."

STATISTICS.

Notwithstanding his great age Bishop Macdonell did not slacken in his zeal for the Church, or in his efforts to place within reach of the humblest and most isolated settlers in the Province the means of fulfilling their duties as good Catholics. He had the consolation of knowing that the small band of devoted priests whom he had to second his efforts at the beginning of his episcopate had so multiplied that, on leaving for Europe in 1839, there were no less than 34 scattered through the Province, from the Ottawa River to the Detroit. No less than eight missions had sprung into existence in 1838 and 1839. A priest (Father P. Lefebvre) had taken up his residence at L'Orignal, on the Ottawa ; at Amherstburg, in the West, Father Augustin Vervais had been placed in charge ; while in what is now the Archdiocese of Toronto, parishes had been established at the Gore of Toronto (Father Eugene O'Reilly), at Adjala (Father H. Fitzpatrick), and on Lake Simcoe (Father John Cassidy). Father Proulx had gone to live amongst the Indians on Manitoulin Island, leaving Father Charest in charge of Penetanguishene ; and at Hamilton, Vicar General Macdonald had become the first resident priest. A church had been built some years before. In Toronto (the name York had been discontinued in 1834), St. Paul's was still the only Catholic church, though it had ceased to afford sufficient accommodation for the rapidly increasing Catholic population of the city and vicinity. Father Patrick McDonagh had been its pastor since 1833, and for a time he had as assistant Father Murth Lawlor (or Lalor), who, however, was transferred to Picton about 1838. Unfortunately we have no means of estimating the Catholic population of the Province at the beginning of Bishop Macdonell's episcopate or towards its close. The official census, though it gives the religious statistics of the other Provinces of Canada, fails to do so in the case of Upper Canada until the year 1842. We are, accordingly, left entirely to conjecture. Dr. Thomas Rolph, in his valuable work on "Canada and the West Indies," frequently quoted in the course of this narrative, gives the Catholic census for 1834, but fails to say whence his information is derived. His figures are as follows :

Statistics.

EASTERN DISTRICT.

Mission of St. Raphael .... 4,765.
Mission of St. Andrew .... 3,587.

OTTAWA DISTRICT.

Mission of Longeuil .... 2,554.

JOHNSTOWN DISTRICT.

Mission of Prescott and Brockville .... 1,522.

BATHURST DISTRICT.

Mission of Bytown .... 3,221.
Mission of Perth .... 3,643.

MIDLAND DISTRICT.

Mission of Kingston .... 4,163.

HALLOWELL DISTRICT.

Mission of Belleville .... 1,135.

NEWCASTLE DISTRICT.

Mission of Peterborough .... 3,584.

HOME DISTRICT.

Mission of Toronto .... 3,240.
Mission of Adjala .... 2,356.
Mission of the Townships of Toronto and Trafalgar .... 785.
Mission of Penetanguishene .... 856.

GORE DISTRICT.

Mission of Guelph and Dundas .... 1,537.

NIAGARA DISTRICT.

Mission of Niagara .... 2,040.

LONDON DISTRICT.

Mission of London and St. Thomas .... 3,536.

WESTERN DISTRICT.

Mission of the River Thames .... 2,600.
Mission of Sandwich .... 4,724.
Mission of Amherstburg .... 2,580.

Total 52,428

The total population of the Province in the same year, as given in the official census, was 321,145. In 1840 the population of the Province had increased to 432,159; the city of Toronto to 13,092; and it is certain the Catholic population increased in the same period at a proportionate ratio.

In 1834, according to Dr. Rolph, there were 34 churches (Catholic) in Upper Canada, viz.: two each in the missions of St. Raphael, St. Andrew, Longeuil, Prescott, Bytown, Peterborough, Toronto, Adjala, Guelph, Niagara, London, and the River Thames; one each in the missions of Perth, Sandwich and Amherstburg; three in Kingston mission, and four in that of Belleville. In the missions of Toronto and Trafalgar Townships, and in Penetanguishene, there does not at that time appear to have been any church. There are no statistics of churches in 1839 and 1840; but, judging from the number of new parishes and missions established in the interval, the increase must have been considerable.

Catholics had also begun to take an active part in the public affairs of the Province, and had established for themselves, as was fitting, an enviable reputation as an industrious, law-abiding people. Major Dunlop, a well-known character in the Province, writing in 1832, has referred to the Irish Catholics as "by far the easiest conciliated of any emigrants who come to the Province." The same writer's tribute to the Catholic clergy is worthy of being reproduced here. He is arguing that a share of the Clergy Reserves should be given to the Catholics, and goes on to say:

"An elder of the Kirk, and bred in the most orthodox part of Scotland, I came to this country strongly prejudiced against Catholicism and its ministers; but experience has shown me that these prejudices were unjust. I expected to find both priests and people as violently opposed to the British Government here as at home—I found them the strongest supporters of the Constitution. I had been taught to believe that a Catholic priest was a hypocritical knave, who ruled his misguided followers for his own selfish purposes—I have found them a moral and zealous clergy, more strict in their attention to their parochial duties than any body of clergy I ever met in any part of the world, and not a bit more intolerant than their clerical brethren of any other sect."*

In addition to the grants already mentioned, Bishop Macdonell had secured from the Government, lands in trust for churches, etc., at Fenelon,

---

* "Statistical Sketches of Upper Canada." London: 1832.

1826; Toronto Gore, 1834; Adjala, 1834; Township of Harwick (Town of Chatham), 1834; Trent, 1836; Tyendenaga, 1836; Toronto, on the late Military Reserve (now occupied by St. Mary's Church and Presbytery), 1837; Township of London, 1837; on the River St. Clair, in the Township of Moore, 1838. He had also secured several money grants towards the erection of churches and schools throughout his diocese. The Church of England, however, had the lion's share of Government support. Between the years 1789 and 1833, 23,905 acres of public lands had been set apart by the Crown as glebes to clergymen. Of these the Church of England received 22,345 acres, the Church of Scotland 1,160, while only 400 acres fell to the Catholic Church.

To the Bishop's wisdom and foresight in thus providing for future generations, we are in this, as in other matters, deeply indebted. His reward is in the stately fabric which the Church in Ontario has now grown to be.

Bishop Macdonell's Death and Burial.

Before proceeding to Europe with his colleagues, as arranged in 1837, Bishop Macdonell was tendered a banquet by the Celtic Society of Upper Canada. The affair took place at Carmino's Hotel, Kingston, and was largely attended, not only by leading Catholics but by most of the prominent men of the city of all denominations and by the officers of the garrison. It served to show in what estimation he was held by the leading men of the day. A few weeks afterwards he sailed from Kingston on the steamboat "Dolphin," and in due time landed at Liverpool (Aug. 1st, 1839), proceeding from thence to London, where he communicated with the Colonial Office regarding emigration and other matters. In October he went to Ireland, with the intention of being present at a great dinner given to the Catholic Prelates at Cork, but being delayed in the journey he did not arrive in time. Nevertheless he visited several of the Bishops; and being unable, in the West of Ireland, to obtain any other conveyance than a jaunting car, he was exposed during an entire day to a drizzling rain, which exposure brought on an attack of inflammation of the lungs. He was laid up at Carlow College, and afterwards with the Jesuit Fathers at Clongowes Wood, but recovered sufficiently to proceed to Dublin, where he was again indisposed. On recovering, he visited the Catholic Primate at Armagh, and from thence accepted the invitation of the Earl of Gosford (formerly Governor-General of Canada) to visit him at Gosford Castle, near Armagh, where, under the roof of that kind-hearted nobleman, he appeared to have entirely recovered his strength. He shortly afterwards proceeded to Scotland, arriving at Dumfries on Jan. 11th, 1840. What followed we learn from a letter to Lord Gosford by Rev. William Reid, parish priest at that town, whose guest the Bishop had become the day following his arrival.* Having been all night on the road, Father Reid writes, the Bishop was very much fatigued, but, on the morning of the 12th, insisted on saying Mass, being, however, almost exhausted by the effort. After breakfasting he became quite a new man; and, with the exception of one short attack of difficulty in breathing, continued apparently in excellent health and spirits until the night of the 14th, when, about 4 o'clock a.m., he called his servant, told him to bring his respirator, for he felt difficulty in breathing, to put on a fire and to put the bedclothes closer to his back. Father Reid and a physician were immediately summoned, and the former, who came instantly, seeing how ill the Bishop was, administered to him without delay the last rites of the Church. He was still in life, but spoke not another word, and when the doctor arrived, had just breathed his last, "without a struggle," says Father Reid, "without pain, and without the least agony."

The body was put into a leaden coffin, and, with the advice of Bishop Carruthers, sent to Edinburgh, where Bishop Gillis,† Coadjutor to the Vicar Apostolic of the Eastern District of Scotland, in recognition of the late prelate's illustrious services to the Catholic Highlanders, resolved that he should be buried with honour. The funeral service took place in St. Mary's Cathedral on January 25th, and was performed with extraordinary pomp. Bishops Carruthers and Gillis of Edinburgh, Murdoch of Glasgow, and Scott of Greenock, together with a great number of priests, assisted at

---

* Lord Gosford, on receiving tidings of the sad event about to be related, had written anxiously to Father Reid for particulars. I regret that space forbids the publication in full of the latter's reply. There is a copy in the archives of St. Mary's College, Montreal. Father Reid had been a fellow-student of the Bishop's at Valladolid.

† Bishop Gillis was a Canadian by birth, having first seen the light in Montreal on April 7th, 1802. He received his early education under the Sulpician Fathers in that city, and, when fourteen years of age, removed with his father to Scotland. He was the founder of St. Margaret's Convent, Edinburgh, the first conventual institution established in Scotland since the so-called Reformation. He died in 1864. See "History of St. Margaret's Convent," Edinburgh, 1886. Another native Canadian who, as an ecclesiastic, rose to great distinction abroad, was the late Vicar-Capitular of the Diocese of Hexham and Newcastle, England, Mgr. Consitt, who was born at Clifton, Upper Canada, in 1819. He was the author of a "Life of St. Cuthbert," and other important works. He died in 1887.—R.I.P. See "Catholic Weekly Review," April, 1888.

the ceremonies, which were witnessed by a large congregation met to do honor to their distinguished countryman. The sermon was preached by Bishop Murdoch of Glasgow, who dwelt on the exalted character of his deceased brother, and adverted to his zeal and perseverance in furthering the interests of the Catholic faith, both in his native land and in Upper Canada. At the conclusion of the ceremonies the body was removed to St. Margaret's Convent and placed in the vaults beneath the chapel, pending such arrangements as should be made for its removal to Canada.

The news of Bishop Macdonell's death was received with the greatest sorrow in Upper Canada. He had been so long identified with the Province, and had taken such an active part in all that pertained to its development and prosperity, that it was felt on all sides that a great light had been extinguished. Lord Gosford, a former Governor General, but voiced the popular sentiment when he wrote: "Both on public as well as private grounds his loss must be deeply deplored—to Canada indeed irreparable, and at a moment, too, when the knowledge, experience, integrity and philanthropy which he so pre-eminently possessed, were so greatly needed in the settlement of its affairs, that country can scarcely expect to find his like again. I had the happiness and satisfaction of knowing him intimately—in honesty of purpose, in spotless integrity, manly-mindedness, and in benevolence of feeling, he was not to be surpassed."*

At Kingston a Solemn Requiem Mass was sung by Bishop Gaulin for the repose of the deceased's soul. It was attended by all the priests of the Province as well as several from the United States. Vicar-General Macdonald, one of the late Bishop's oldest and most valued friends, preached the funeral sermon.

Although Bishop Macdonell's successors in the See of Kingston always cherished the intention of bringing his remains to Canada, this was not effected until 1861, when Bishop Horan visited Edinburgh, and by the co-operation of Bishop Gillis, then Vicar-Apostolic, accomplished his mission. He returned to Canada in June of that year, bringing the remains with him. They were placed in the vaults of Notre Dame Church, Montreal, where they remained until October, when they were transferred

---

* Archives of St. Mary's College. An impartial estimate of Bishop Macdonell's career appeared at the time in the "British Whig" of Kingston. It is reprinted in Chevalier Macdonell's "Reminiscences," p. 42.

to Kingston. The ceremonies in connection with the re-interment were of the most solemn character. Among those who assisted were the Archbishop of Quebec, the Bishops of St. Hyacinthe, Three Rivers and Ottawa; and among laymen, Hon. (now Sir) Alexander Campbell, James Morton, M.P., and the Mayor of Kingston. A company of Rifles formed a guard of honor. After Solemn Requiem Mass, and a sermon by Father Bentley of Montreal Seminary, the remains of the great Bishop and Patriot were committed to their last resting place beneath the Cathedral, in the midst of the people he had loved so well in life.*

But one event more in connection with Bishop Macdonell remains to be chronicled. He had been the means of establishing the Highland Society in Canada, and had ever taken a deep interest in its proceedings. On his death, therefore, it was felt that some action should be taken to perpetuate his memory. Accordingly, in 1843, there was erected, with befitting ceremonies, in the parish church of St. Raphael, a marble tablet bearing this inscription:

ON THE 18TH OF JUNE, 1843,

THE HIGHLAND SOCIETY OF CANADA ERECTED THIS TABLET

TO THE MEMORY OF THE

HONORABLE AND RIGHT REVEREND ALEXANDER MACDONELL,

BISHOP OF KINGSTON,

BORN 1760† — DIED 1840.

THOUGH DEAD, HE STILL LIVES IN THE HEARTS OF HIS COUNTRYMEN.

CRITICAL NOTE.—The various sources from which the foregoing narrative has been derived have to some extent been indicated in the text and in foot notes. The reader who wishes to pursue the subject further will find abundant material touching the earlier period in the printed works there cited, and in such books as Abbe Ferland's Life of Bishop Plessis and Abbe Faillon's History of the French Colony in America; and, from a non-Catholic standpoint, in the many books in English on early Canadian history. There is, however, a lamentable scarcity of material, printed or in manuscript, touching the period covered by Bishop Macdonell's episco-

---

* In September a solemn Requiem Mass for the repose of Bishop Macdonell's soul had been celebrated in St. Michael's Cathedral, Toronto, Father Northgraves being the celebrant.

† There is evidence to show that the Bishop was born on the 17th July, 1762. When a man has long occupied a prominent position, people are naturally inclined to overestimate his age; thus a Scotch periodical, in announcing the Bishop's death, assigned to him 100 years. It seems that his age was 77 years and almost 6 months.".—Chevalier Macdonell.

pate—1819 to 1840. The private papers of that prelate have been lost, and the most diligent enquiries have thus far failed to find the least trace of them. Were they forthcoming, a flood of light would be thrown upon the early history of the Church in Upper Canada. Among printed books, Chevalier Macdonell's Reminiscences will be found of great interest in the study of one of the most picturesque figures in the annals of the Province. Dr. Rolph's Statistical Account of Upper Canada (Dundas, 1836), which, besides being the work of a noted Catholic layman, is also interesting as being among the earliest printed books in the Province. Father Macdonald's periodical, "The Catholic" (Kingston, 1830), is valuable, and so are the later volumes of "The Mirror" (first published at Toronto, 1837). The earlier volumes yielded but scanty results. Finally, the Archives of St. Mary's College, Montreal, are rich in the materials of Canadian ecclesiastical history. Through the kindness of Rev. Father Jones, S. J., the writer has been permitted to avail himself of them.

ADDENDA.

The following extract from the "Bratish Whig" of Kingston, 1840, already referred to, will be read with interest in connection with the foregoing:

"Of the individuals who have passed away from us during the last twenty-five years, and who have taken an interest in the advancement and prosperity of Canada West, no one probably has won for himself in so great a degree the esteem of all classes of his fellow-citizens than has Bishop Macdonell. Arriving in Canada at an early period of the present century, at a time when toil, privations and difficulties inseparable from life in a new country awaited the zealous missionary as well as the hardy emigrant, he devoted himself in a noble spirit of self-sacrifice, and with untiring energy, to the duties of his sacred calling, to the amelioration of the condition of those entrusted to his spiritual care. In him they found a friend and counselor; to them he endeared himself through his unbounded benevolence and greatness of soul. Moving among all classes and creeds with a mind unbiased by religious prejudices, taking an interest in all that tended to develop the resources or aided the general prosperity of the country, he acquired a popularity still memorable, and obtained over the minds of his fellow-citizens an influence only equalled by their esteem and respect for him. The ripe scholar, the polished gentleman, the learned divine, his many estimable qualities recommended him to the notice of the Court of Rome; and he was elevated to the dignity of a Bishop of the Catholic Church. The position made no change in the man: he remained still the zealous missionary, the indefatigable pastor. His loyalty to the British Crown was never surpassed; when the interests of the Empire were either assailed or jeopardized on this continent he stood forth their bold advocate; by word and deed he proved how sincere was his attachment to British institutions, and infused into the hearts of his fellow-countrymen and others an equal enthusiasm for their preservation and maintenance. Indeed, his noble conduct on several occasions tended so much to the preservation of loyalty that it drew from the highest authorities repeated expressions of thanks and gratitude. As a member of the Legislative Council of Upper Canada (to which he was called by Sir John

Colborne on Oct. 12th, 1836, his active mind, strengthened by experience acquired by constant association with all classes, enabled him to suggest many things most beneficial to the best interests of the country, and the peace and harmony of its inhabitants."

Of a like character is the estimate of Bishop Macdonell to be found in Mr. H. J. Morgan's "Biographies of Celebrated Canadians":

"In every relation of life, as subject, relative and friend, he was a model of everything valuable. To his Sovereign he brought the warm and hearty homage of a sincere, enthusiastic, unconditional allegiance, and the most invincible, uncompromising loyalty; as prelate, he was kind, attentive and devoted to the interests, welfare and happiness of his clergy; as a relative his attachment was unbounded, and his death created an aching void to hundreds of sorrowing relatives whom he counseled by his advice, assisted with his means, and protected by his influence; as a friend, he was sincere, enthusiastic and unchangeable in his attachments. Such, indeed, was the liberality of his views and the inexpressible benignity of his disposition, that all creeds and classes united in admiration of his character, respect for him, and congregated together to bid him farewell as he left the shores of the St. Lawrence on that voyage which proved but the prelude to that long and last one, from which there is no return."

THE LIFE AND TIMES OF THE RIGHT REV. MICHAEL POWER, D.D.

FIRST BISHOP OF TORONTO.

BY

H. F. McINTOSH, Esq.,

CORRESPONDING MEMBER OF THE AMERICAN CATHOLIC HISTORICAL SOCIETY
OF PHILADELPHIA.

The Right Rev. Michael Power, D.D.
BORN AT HALIFAX, N.S., OCTOBER 17th, 1804
DIED AT TORONTO, OCTOBER 1st, 1847

CHAPTER IV.

1841-1847.

LIFE AND TIMES OF BISHOP POWER.

Bishop Gaulin—Diocese of Kingston divided—Diocese of Toronto—Bishop Power—The First Diocesan Synod—The Clergy—The Coming of the Jesuits—Notable Events—St. Michael's Cathedral—Pastorals—Death of Gregory XVI., and Accession of Pius IX.—The Bishop visits Europe—The Typhus—Death of Bishop Power.

"Greater love than this no man hath, that a man lay down his life for his friends."

WITH the death of Bishop Macdonell the scope of our history narrows to the Western half of the Province. True, more than a year was yet to elapse ere the division of the Diocese should take place, but the interval is marked by no event, save one, which need here be recorded.

By right of succession Mgr. Gaulin became Bishop of Kingston on the demise of Bishop Macdonell. He took formal possession of the See on Passion Sunday, 1840, and, while his health lasted, discharged the functions of his office with zeal and discretion. The many good works instituted by his predecessor were continued by him, chief among which may be mentioned the erection of Regiopolis College, which, in due time, opened its doors to aspirants to the priesthood and to other young men in quest of higher education. He also set on foot a project for the erection of a new Cathedral, the corner stone of which was laid in September, 1843.

But the event for which his episcopate was chiefly remarkable was the division of his Diocese. Feeling his health giving way, he applied to the Holy See to be relieved of a portion of his vast charge, or, failing that, for the appointment of a coadjutor, naming at the same time for the latter office, Very Rev. Michael Power, Vicar General of the Diocese of Montreal. He was so far successful in his representations, that not only did the division of his Diocese take place, but he received a coadjutor as well, not in the person of Father Power, but in that of Rev. Patrick Phelan, formerly a Sulpician priest of Montreal, and later, parish priest at Bytown, who, on Aug. 20th, 1843, was consecrated Bishop of Carrhae, with right of succession to Kingston. From the first, Bishop Phelan, owing to the precarious state of Bishop Gaulin's health, undertook the greater part of the diocesan work; and when, through utter prostration, the latter retired to his native Province for much-needed rest, Bishop Phelan became administrator. Bishop Gaulin never returned alive to his See, his physical condition being such as would not permit him to resume the burdens of the episcopate. He died at St. Philomene, on May 8th, 1857; and, on the 13th of the same month, his remains were brought to Kingston and interred beneath the cathedral. Bishop Phelan succeeded to the title, but survived his predecessor only one month. He died on June 6th, and was likewise laid to rest in the vaults of St. Mary's Cathedral. "His loss," says his biographer,* "has been deeply deplored, and his obsequies were kept with marked devotion. Indefatigable in all the duties of a good pastor and faithful Bishop, his memory will not die, but will be kept in eternal recollection."†

Diocese of Kingston Divided.

The division of the Diocese of Kingston had been under consideration even during Bishop Macdonell's lifetime. The rapid development of the Province and the constant accessions to the Catholic population by immigration, had put it out of the power of one Bishop to properly oversee so extensive a diocese, and it is probable that Bishop Macdonell had intended, on finishing his business in Scotland, to proceed to Rome, and there to lay the matter before the Holy See. His unexpected death intervened; but on Bishop Gaulin's accession to the See of Kingston, that prelate being then in poor health, the necessity of the division of the diocese became more than ever apparent, and formed the subject of extensive correspondence

---

* "Life of Rt. Rev. Patrick Phelan:" Kingston, 1862.
† The subsequent Bishops of Kingston were Rt. Rev. E. J. Horan, 1858-75 ; Rt. Rev. John O'Brien, 1875-9; Most Rev. J. V. Cleary, 1880-9, when, on the erection of Kingston into a Metropolitan See, he became Archbishop. The best days of the old diocese have been renewed under his vigorous and enlightened rule.

between the several members of the Canadian hierarchy.* In 1841 Bishop Bourget of Montreal visited Europe. Before his departure he wrote to Bishop Gaulin, expressing his willingness, should that prelate so desire, to lay the matter before the Propaganda, and to use his influence in furthering the end in view. To this Bishop Gaulin joyfully acceded, and to his brother prelate he entrusted a letter to Pope Gregory XVI., setting forth fully the state of affairs and praying for relief from a portion of the burdens which, in his weak state, weighed so heavily upon him. Mgr. Bourget left for Europe in June, 1841, accompanied by his Vicar General, Father Michael Power. After visiting London and Paris they proceeded to Rome, and, at the first opportunity, the Bishop submitted to the Holy Father the affair of the Diocese of Kingston. The Pope was much impressed with the account of the state of religion in that distant portion of the Christian World and readily acquiesced in the measure proposed to him. He promised Mgr. Bourget that the matter would be carefully considered, and action taken as speedily as circumstances would permit. With this assurance the Bishop left Rome and returned to Paris, whence Father Power had preceded him, having stolen away from the Eternal City in the hope of escaping the burden of the episcopate which, as he had become aware, was being sought for him. September found the two ecclesiastics in London, with the object of interviewing the Colonial Office with regard to the proposed changes in Upper Canada. Being requested to submit their proposals in writing, Father Power, as Vicar General, addressed a letter to the Secretary, Lord Stanley, setting forth in detail the reasons for the erection of a new diocese. "Our Bishop's wish," he wrote, "is to ascertain whether there should be any objection on the part of Her Majesty's Government, if the proper ecclesiastical authorities thought fit to divide into two distinct Sees, the Diocese of Kingston, in that part of Canada heretofore known as the Province of Upper Canada. The motive for asking this division is the absolute impossibility of the whole of the existing Diocese being properly governed by one Bishop. Your Lordship is perfectly aware of the great extent of that part of Canada and its increasing population; thousands of emigrants from the Mother Country are coming in, and in all probability will continue to proceed to that part of Her Majesty's Dominions for a number of years to come. It therefore becomes urgent that a

---

* Copies of this correspondence are preserved in the Archives of the Archdiocese of Toronto.

new See be immediately erected at the other extremity of the Province for the purpose of providing more effectually for the spiritual wants of those who are actually settled in that part of Canada, as well as for the new settlers who may arrive hereafter."* In reply, Lord Stanley, through his Secretary, stated that he could not undertake to fix a date when the matter would be decided, as the legal advisers of the Crown would first have to be consulted. Verbal assurance must, however, have been given to the effect that no objection would be offered to the proposed measure, as official sanction was not given until September, 1842, when the Diocese of Toronto was already nearly nine months old. Having concluded their business in London and Paris, Mgr. Bourget and his companion returned to Canada.

The Diocese of Toronto.

By a bull of Pope Gregory XVI., dated under the Fisherman's Ring, Dec. 17th, 1841, the division of the Diocese of Kingston was effected, and all that portion of the Province lying west of the District of Newcastle was erected into a separate diocese.† On the same day Very Rev. Michael Power was named the first Bishop, with permission to choose the city and title of his See. On January 9th following he received faculties, and Bishop Gaulin was directed to attend to his consecration and installation with all convenient speed.

Father Power was the unanimous choice of the Canadian episcopacy. Archbishop Signay of Quebec, Bishops Bourget and Gaulin, and the clergy of the two dioceses of Montreal and Kingston, had all addressed strong recommendations to the Holy See in his behalf; and Pope Gregory XVI., recognizing in this concordant testimony that which tended to the best interests of the Church in Upper Canada, was graciously pleased to comply. Father Power, on the other hand, was not anxious for the dignity, having, as already related, hurried away from Rome in the hope of escaping it; and now that the appointment was actually made, he sought by every means in his power to have it set aside. On April 10th he addressed a strong letter to his Bishop, pleading his unworthiness for so high and responsible an office. But this humble estimate of himself did not find an echo in the

---

* Very Rev. M. Power to Lord Stanley. Archives of the Archdiocese of Toronto, vol. i., p. 11.
† The limits of the Diocese were officialy defined as follows: West of Newcastle, from Lake Ontario to Lake Muskoka; from thence by a line directed North-west through Lakes Moon and Muskoka to Western branch of Two Rivers, emptying into the Ottawa; all West of that, including Lake Superior, districts.

hearts of others. He was recognized on all sides as the man best fitted by his wisdom, firmness and piety for the great work of founding a new diocese; and finding, therefore, that all his importunities to be passed over were of no avail, the good priest bowed to the yoke and prepared for the arduous work that lay before him. Bishop Bourget on his part recognized the great loss he would sustain by the departure from his diocese of so good and zealous a priest. Writing to Bishop Gaulin he said : " The subject whom you ask of me appears the best prepared for the important ministry about to be conferred upon him. Although I have great need of his services I shall part with him with a good heart because the greatest good of the Church is concerned."*

Having accepted the office, Father Power, in conformity with the privilege extended to him, chose Toronto as his Episcopal See. He recognized in that city not only the most populous community in the Province at that time, but also the great metropolis of the future, the centre of wealth and influence, the home of culture and the fine arts.

Bishop Power's consecration took place in the parish church at La-prairie, on May 8th (Octave of the Ascension), 1842. The officiating prelate was Bishop Gaulin, who was assisted by Bishops Bourget of Montreal and Turgeon of Sydime (coadjutor to the Archbishop of Quebec), and by many of the clergy of the Diocese of Montreal. The ceremony was witnessed by a vast concourse of people, who, while they rejoiced over the elevation of their beloved pastor to a higher dignity, yet their joy was not unmixed with tears at the thought that he was leaving them forever.

On the day of his consecration the new Bishop addressed a Pastoral letter to the clergy and laity of his Diocese, in the course of which he said : " The common father of all Christians, Gregory XVI., having taken into serious consideration the vast extent of territory heretofore placed under the jurisdiction of our Venerable Brother, the Right Rev. Bishop of Kingston, has been pleased to erect the whole of the more western portion of Canada into a separate and distinct bishoprick ; and by apostolical letters bearing date the seventeenth day of last December, and addressed to us, he has likewise been graciously pleased to nominate and appoint us the first Bishop of the newly erected Diocese and immediate suffragan of the Holy

---

* Archives, vol. i., p. 2.

Roman See. We were at the same time authorized, by letters of the same date, to make choice of the most suitable and convenient place in our Diocese for our future residence. We have in consequence determined, with the advice and approbation of our Episcopal Brethren, to take our title from the city of Toronto, and there to establish our Episcopal See. Most willingly would we have declined the responsibility of so high and so awful a dignity, and last year while residing in the Eternal City, we made the strongest representations that the choice should fall upon some one more capable of fulfilling the duties of the episcopal charge: for we had frequently present to our mind the expressions of that great light of the Church, St. John Chrysostom: 'that those who are raised to that office require a great soul and much courage; that they stand in need of a thousand eyes on every side; that whilst they undertake to convert others, they may not suffer themselves to be perverted.' But feeling that all further resistance on our part would be unsuccessful, we finally yielded to the desire of the Sovereign Pontiff and consented to take upon ourselves the yoke of the Lord, by receiving episcopal consecration. After our acceptance our first thought was to cast ourselves in spirit at the feet of the great Prince of Shepherds and Chief Pastor of souls, to beg of Him to grant us strength generously to bear our burden, and bestow upon us a portion of His divine grace, according to the measure of the giving of Christ. For, although deeply conscious of our inability to fulfill the obligations of the high office to which we have been raised, we are nevertheless consoled with the assurance that the Providence of Almighty God frequently makes use of instruments apparently the most inadequate to accomplish its divine purposes; for we are informed by the Holy Spirit of God, that the foolish things of the world hath God chosen that He may confound the wise: and the weak that he may confound the strong: and the things that are base and contemptible and the things that are not; that no flesh should glory in His sight."*

On May 9th the Bishop formally named as his Secretary, Rev. John J. Hay, a former student of the Propaganda, whom he raised to the priesthood on the 21st of the same month.† On the 10th he named Father W. P. Macdonald of Hamilton as his Vicar General.

---

* Archives, vol. i., pp. 12-13.
† At the same time he ordained three other priests, three deacons and one sub-deacon. The priests were Revs. C. Cassidy, L. Turcot and M. J. Timlin.—" The Catholic," June 1st, 1842.

On June 25th Bishop Power, accompanied by Bishop Gaulin, arrived in Toronto. The two prelates were met at the wharf by a large number of Catholic citizens and escorted to the residence of the pastor of St. Paul's, Rev. W. P. McDonagh. On the following day (Sunday, June 26th) Bishop Power was formally installed into the charge of his Diocese. At the appointed hour, a procession of about 1,500 men and boys formed in order at the church and proceeded to Father McDonagh's residence, where the Bulls constituting Mgr. Power Bishop of Toronto were read and duly acknowledged by Bishop Gaulin. The procession then re-formed, and accompanied by the two prelates, returned to the church, where the new Bishop feelingly addressed the people, and bespoke their earnest co-operation in the arduous labors that awaited him. The whole day, says a contemporary, was passed in solemnity. After Vespers, at which the Bishops assisted, a sermon was preached by Rev. Father Thomas Wilson, a Dominican from Zanesville, Ohio.*

BISHOP POWER.

It may be said with truth that Toronto was blessed in its first Bishop. In the person of Bishop Power were united the piety of the recluse, the zeal and capacity of the missionary, and, as the event proved, the patience and courage of the martyr—a happy combination only to be found in its perfect development in the ranks of the Catholic clergy. He was a native of Halifax, Nova Scotia, where he first saw the light on October 17th, 1804. His father, William Power, was captain and owner of a vessel which sailed regularly between Halifax and St. John's, Newfoundland. His mother was noted all her life for her piety and devotion to her husband and children, and from her the future Bishop imbibed that simple, child-like faith in God and devotion to the Blessed Virgin which were two of his strongest characteristics. When only twelve years of age, by the advice of Bishop Burke, who even at that early age discerned in him the marks of a true vocation, he was sent to Montreal, where he entered the Seminary of St. Sulpice, and under the Fathers of that institution made rapid progress in his studies. His theological studies were subsequently pursued, partly in the same institution and partly at the Seminary of Quebec. On Aug. 17th, 1827, being then in his 23rd year, he was ordained priest at Montreal

---

* Father Wilson was at one time Provincial of the Dominican Order in Ohio and Kentucky. See Dr. John Gilmary Shea's "History of the Catholic Church in the United States," vol. iii.

by Bishop Dubois* and was immediately thereafter appointed to the mission at Drummondville, Lower Canada, where he remained until 1831, when he was placed in charge of all the missions on both sides of the Ottawa as far as Bytown. After two years service in that capacity, he was, in 1833, made curé of St. Martine, in the county of Beauharnois, and labored there with great success until 1839. In the latter year he was removed to the important parish of Laprairie, and was made Vicar General of the Diocese of Montreal, continuing as such until his elevation to the episcopacy in 1842. A noteworthy incident in his pastorate at Laprairie was his generous and hospitable treatment of the Fathers of the Society of Jesus, who, in the early part of 1842, had come to Montreal on the invitation of Bishop Lartigue, to resume those missionary labors which, in times past, had been the glory of the Canadian Church. It was the design of Bishop Bourget, who had succeeded Mgr. Lartigue, to place these Fathers in charge of Chambly College, but unexpected obstacles having intervened to prevent this, he was, for the moment, in a quandary how to provide for them. In this dilemma Father Power suggested that they should be installed provisionally at Laprairie, and the Bishop having at once acquiesced, he went to a great deal of trouble and expense in making suitable preparations for their reception. By his glowing accounts of the past history of the Jesuits in Canada he so inflamed the warm-hearted French Canadians that they were impatient to receive the Fathers in their midst, and begged the Bishop to make them their pastors when Father Power should have taken his departure for Toronto. Accordingly, the Jesuits became regularly installed at Laprairie, and Father Power's part in bringing about that consummation is to this day remembered with gratitude by the Society.†

In addition to his ordinary parochial duties at Laprairie, which in themselves were by no means light, Father Power acted as chaplain to the Catholic soldiers in the garrison. His services in this capacity were formally recognized by the military authorities, and by the Government.‡

His departure from Laprairie was the occasion of great sorrow and regret, not only on the part of his own flock, but by all classes of the community. The "Montreal Gazette" (May 20th, 1842), in the course of

---

* Tanguay's "Repertoire General du Clerge Canadien." Mgr. Dubois was Bishop of New York.
† Archives of St. Mary's College, Montreal.
‡ Canadian Archives, Series C, vol. lxx., p. 19.

an editorial with reference to his consecration and approaching departure, thus spoke of him: " His loyalty to the Sovereign has always been distinguished by manly integrity and unswerving zeal, as those who know his endeavors to quell an unprovoked rebellion, and to control the passions of a misguided people can testify. While discharging with truth and fidelity the duties of his own station, he lived on uniform terms of friendship and good neighborhood with every denomination of Christians, however different from his own, and not only gained the esteem of Protestants, but of their clergy, with many of whom he is associated in the true spirit of a gentleman, and on a footing of genuine Christian liberality and good-will. Wherever he goes, Bishop Power, we are sure, will carry those feelings and sentiments along with him; and we cannot refrain from congratulating those over whose religious duties he has been chosen to preside, upon their good fortune in being instructed and directed by a prelate who, while he will maintain the integrity of his sacred office untinged by bigotry or superstition, cannot fail to indicate the truly British virtues of inflexible loyalty, charity and hospitality."

The First Diocesan Synod.

In taking up his residence in Toronto, Bishop Power found himself face to face with difficulties of no ordinary kind. His diocese covered an immense territory, and the members of his flock in many sections were inadequately, if at all, supplied with the means of fulfilling their duty as true children of the Church. In his own episcopal city, now grown to be a thriving community of about thirteen thousand inhabitants, the Catholics numbered about three thousand, with but one priest to minister to their spiritual requirements. St. Paul's was the only church in the city, and, on the Bishop's advent, it became, for the time being, his Cathedral.

As a first step towards the proper organization of his Diocese, Bishop Power summoned a Synod of his clergy. It met in the month of October in St. Paul's church, being preceded by a spiritual retreat of five days, conducted by Father Peter Chazelle, S. J., one of the six Jesuits who, in the month of June preceding, had arrived in Montreal from Kentucky.* Father Chazelle had formerly been rector of St. Mary's College in that State, and had a wide reputation as a preacher and director. He was

---
* The other five were: Fathers Felix Martin, Remi Tellier, Paul Luiset, Joseph Hanipaux and Dominic Duranquet. Tanguay's " Repertoire General," pp. 212-13.

assisted at the retreat by Father Louis Boué, a secular priest who had come to Canada with the Jesuits. The Synod was opened and presided over by the Bishop in person, and was attended by sixteen priests, whose names and stations were as follows:

Very Rev. W. P. Macdonald, V. G., Hamilton; Rev. M. R. Mills, Brantford, Indiana and Dumfries; James O'Flynn, Dundas, Oakville and Trafalgar; James Bennet, Tecumseth and Adjala; Edward Gordon, Niagara and Niagara Falls; Patrick O'Dwyer, London and St. Thomas; Eugene O'Rielly, Toronto and Albion; J. B. Proulx, Manitoulin and the Upper Lakes; Michael McDonnell, Maidstone and Rochester; Thomas Gibney, Guelph and Stratford; Peter Schneider, Waterloo, Wilmot and Goderich; James Quinlan, Newmarket and Barrie; Amable Charest, Penetanguishene; W. P. McDonagh, Stephen Fergus, and J. J. Hay (Secretary of the Diocese), Toronto. The only absentees were Very Rev. Æneas Macdonell, V. G., Sandwich; Revs. J. B. Morin, Raleigh; and Augustine Vervais, Amherstburg, who, from legitimate causes, were unable to attend. On the first day Bishop Power celebrated Pontifical Mass, Father Chazelle, S.J., being Deacon, Father Proulx, Sub-Deacon, and Father Charest, Assistant Priest. This was followed by the profession of faith of the clergy present, and by the other formulas usual on such occasions. The second day was signalized by the celebration of Mass for the repose of the souls of the late Bishop Macdonell and the deceased clergy of the Diocese; and on the third day, being Sunday, Mass was celebrated in honor of the Most Pure Heart of Mary. The Synod was brought to a close by the celebration of a Mass of thanksgiving to the Holy Ghost, at which the Bishop pontificated, after which a *Te Deum* was sung and a sermon preached by Father Mills. At Vespers, Vicar General Macdonald preached an eloquent sermon, which was followed by Benediction of the Blessed Sacrament.

Two events of the Synod call for special mention. The first in order is the consecration of the Diocese to the Sacred Heart, which took place with ceremonies of the most solemn and impressive character. To that act of devotion, prompted by the Bishop's piety, it will perhaps never be given us to know just how much of the subsequent prosperity of the Diocese is due.

The second event is the project of establishing a college at Sandwich which should be the centre of the Indian missions. It was the Bishop's design to entrust the carrying out of this project to the Jesuit Fathers, but his early death intervened, and it was not until 1857 that the scheme was realized. The Jesuits retained charge of the college for only two years, when, on the advent of Bishop Pinsonneault, they withdrew and that prelate placed it in charge of the Basilian Fathers from Annonay, France, who, after conducting it for a short time, also withdrew, but resumed control under Bishop Walsh, and have ever since conducted it, as well as its sister institution at Toronto (St. Michael's College), with marked ability.

The effect of the Synod was to place the Diocese on a firm footing, and to provide for the proper organization of the parishes. The statutes adopted were chiefly directed to this end, and they bear the impress of Bishop Power's executive and administrative ability. They were such as much older dioceses had not at the time the advantage of possessing.

On September 15th, formal advice had been received from Sir Charles Bagot, then Governor General, to the effect that the Colonial Secretary had communicated to him Her Majesty's authority for recognizing Mgr. Power in his official character as Roman Catholic Bishop of Toronto. The reader will recollect that when in England in 1841, Bishop (then Father) Power had, as Vicar General of the Diocese of Montreal, written to Lord Stanley to ascertain if there would be any objection on the part of Her Majesty's Government to the erection of a new diocese in Western Canada.

In entering, therefore, upon the second year of his episcopate, the Bishop had the gratification of knowing that he occupied a satisfactory position with respect to the civil as well as to the ecclesiastical authorities.

THE CLERGY.

Of the priests who assisted at this Synod it may be interesting, as well as being in keeping with the plan and scope of this work, to give such meagre biographical details as I have been able to glean from the Archives of the Diocese, and from periodicals and other publications of the time. Some of them have already been noticed in the preceding chapter, to which the reader is referred.

Father Michael Robert Mills came to the Diocese from Dublin, where he had labored for some years with great fruit under Archbishop Murray. It is said he was formerly an Anglican clergyman and a graduate of the

University of Oxford. He was certainly a fine scholar and preacher, and his services in the latter capacity were in constant demand at church openings, the laying of corner stones and other notable occasions. He went to London in 1843, and was for some time chaplain to the garrison there. He subsequently became a Trappist, and in that austere community died a holy death.

Father W. P. McDonagh came from the Archdiocese of Tuam in Ireland. He was sent to Canada by Archbishop O'Kelly to collect funds towards the erection of a new cathedral, and on the invitation of Bishop Macdonell decided to remain here. His first station was at York, where he succeeded Father O'Grady. He afterwards went to St. Catharines, where he earned the thanks of his ecclesiastical superiors and of the civil authorities by practically putting an end to faction fights among the laborers on the Welland Canal. He built a church at St. Catharines in 1844 which cost seventeen thousand dollars. He died at Douro, in the county of Northumberland, some years later.

Father Thomas Gibney, whose pastorate at Guelph has already been referred to, was a native of County Meath, Ireland, whence he came to Canada about 1835 or 1836, and was shortly afterwards ordained priest. Guelph was his first station in Upper Canada, and he ended his days there in 1846, as already related. He was a pious, zealous man, and was much respected by all classes of the community.

Father Michael McDonnell came from the Diocese of Limerick in 1840, and was placed in charge of the mission at Maidstone and Rochester. He retired from the Diocese in 1844.

Father J. B. Proulx, born at Lachine in 1808, was ordained at Montreal on July 26th, 1835, and was first stationed at Laprarie, opposite Montreal.* On coming to Upper Canada he was sent by Bishop Macdonell to work among the Indians at Penetanguishene, and afterwards on Manitoulin Island. In 1846 he was given charge of the parish at Oshawa, and in 1858 came to Toronto. His later career is fresh in the memory of all.

Father Amable Charest was a native of St. Anne de la Perade, in the Province of Quebec, where he was born in 1807. He was raised to the

* Abbe Tanguay's "Repertoire General du Clerge Canadien."

priesthood in Glengarry in 1837, and was sent immediately to Penetanguishene to take up the work so well begun by Father Proulx. Here he remained for many years, and in 1854 returned to his native Province.

Father Patrick O'Dwyer was born in 1802 in the Archdiocese of Cashel, Ireland. On becoming a priest in 1833 he came to Canada, and labored successively at Quebec, St. Dunstan, Beauport, and Grosse Isle. He came to Upper Canada in 1837,* and after some years removed to the United States and settled at Cincinnati.

Father John James Hay, already referred to as Secretary of the Diocese, was born in the County of Glengarry on June 24th, 1818. His theological studies were pursued in the Seminary of St. Raphael, and subsequently at the Propaganda, Rome. He was ordained priest at Montreal on May 21st, 1842, having, a few days previously, been named by Bishop Power (who ordained him) Secretary for the new Diocese of Toronto. The wisdom of this appointment was more than justified by the exemplary manner in which Father Hay discharged the duties of the office. Almost all the early records of the Diocese are in his handwriting, and the neatness and circumspection in which they were kept prove him to have been a model secretary. In 1846 he became first Archdeacon of the Diocese, and was twice administrator, first during Bishop Power's absence in Europe in the early part of 1847, and later, jointly with Father Carroll, on the Bishop's death in the Fall of the same year. He survived the Bishop less than two years, his death occurring on Feb. 19th, 1849, in the 31st year of his age, to the sorrow and regret of the whole community. He was buried in St. Michael's Cathedral, where a handsome marble tablet marks his last resting place. Father Hay was a model priest, and his early death deprived the Diocese of one who had, to all appearances, a career of usefulness and distinction before him.

Of Fathers James Quinlan and Stephen Fergus all that can be ascertained is that the former was ordained in 1834 by the Bishop of Waterford, and that he left Ireland in 1837, and that the latter came from the Archdiocese of Tuam.†

Father James Bennett, who was in charge of Tecumseth and Adjala in

---

* Abbé Tanguay's " Repertoire General."
† Archives of the Archdiocese of Toronto, vol. i., pp. 30-39.

1842, was transferred to Whitby in June, 1843, but did not long survive the change. He died at Kingston in Sept., 1843, and is buried there.*

Of Fathers O'Flynn, Schneider, O'Reilly, Morin and Vervais, the Archives of the Archdiocese make no mention beyond the entry of their faculties. They are remembered by the older people as zealous and devoted priests, who, having finished their labors in this world, now sleep the sleep of the just.

The Coming of the Jesuits.

On Nov. 12th, Bishop Power made formal application to Very Rev. Father Roothaan, General of the Society of Jesus, for priests of that Society to aid him in the missions of his Diocese. In the course of a long and interesting† letter he dwelt with enthusiasm on the past history of the Jesuit missions in Canada; on the patient zeal and heroic fortitude of those early missionaries who had traversed the inmost recesses of the continent in the hope of winning the untutored savages to Christianity and to civilization; and with special emphasis did he call to mind the intrepid Brebœuf and his companions, who had watered with their blood the soil of what is now the Archdiocese of Toronto. The Bishop had always been an ardent admirer of the Society of Jesus. He had, on the advent of its sons at Montreal, proved their staunch friend, and had begun the labors of his own Diocese by summoning one of them to conduct the first Diocesan Retreat, and to contribute his knowledge and his experience to the councils of his first Synod, and now he sought to enlist their services permanently in the work upon which he had entered.

In the course of his letter to Father Roothaan he gives some very interesting information about the Diocese. The total number of Catholics within its limits he placed at about fifty thousand, mostly Europeans and their descendants, with here and there a settlement of Christian Indians. This number was being constantly augmented by the arrival of Irish immigrants and a few Catholics of other nationalities, who were attracted by the promising field which Upper Canada, or Canada West as it was now very generally called, then presented. This rapid increase in his flock necessitated also an increase in the ranks of his clergy, and with the

---

* Archives, vol. i., p. 50.
† Archives, vol. i., pp. 33-4.

meagre resources at his disposal, and in the face of other difficulties incidental to a new diocese, he naturally turned to Father Roothaan (whom he had visited when in Europe in 1841) for aid. It was his desire that the Jesuits should take up the thread of their ancient missions in the territory bordering on Georgian Bay, on Manitoulin Island, and along the north shore of Lakes Huron and Superior; and he also contemplated, as already stated, the foundation of a College which should be entrusted to their care.

He then goes on to say that on his recent visit to the northern portion of his Diocese he had found one mission of about 600 Indians, all of whom were Catholics. In another colony of 6,500 Indians, there were 2,500 Catholics, and of the others, many showed a disposition to embrace Christianity. He had himself baptized 62 infidels, of whom 38 were adults, one a chief of the tribe, and the missionary (Father Prouls) had in a short time baptized 40 children. At the same time the Bishop had conferred Confirmation upon 100 Indians who had been prepared for the Sacrament by Father Prouls. The great drawback which he had found to the conversion of the poor people was the presence among them of sectaries, who, though they met with but indifferent success, yet managed, by a free use of money and presents, to produce a certain external conformity.

Bishop Power's appeal to Father Roothaan met with a favorable response. In July, 1843, Fathers Peter Point and John Peter Chone came to the Diocese and were, the month following, placed in charge of the Parish of the Assumption at Sandwich, where, with other Fathers of their Society, they continued to reside until 1859, when, on the transfer of Bishop Pinsonneault's See from London to Sandwich, they relinquished charge of that mission. Of Father Point, a writer in "L'Etendard"[*] in 1884 thus speaks: "The Jesuits, on coming to Sandwich, had at their head a man who, besides a rare administrative talent, was possessed of ardent zeal, a rare gift of speech, and was blessed with the heart of an apostle—Father Peter Point." The labors of these Fathers at Sandwich were singularly fruitful, and their departure was an occasion of deep regret to every member of the parish, from the highest to the lowest. The new church commenced by Father Macdonell, V.G., was completed by them and dedicated in 1846, and, as already recorded, they founded the College of the Assumption in 1857.

---

[*] "Catholic Record," May 31st, 1884, cited in Father Coffey's "City and Diocese of London," 1885

Besides the mission at Sandwich, the Jesuit Fathers had at one time charge also of Chatham and of Wilmot (now the village of New Germany), in the County of Waterloo. In the year 1853 they were installed by Bishop de Charbonell to the pastoral care of Guelph, where they have ever since continued to reside, to the great advantage of religion and education. This, with the exception of the Lake Superior and Georgian Bay missions, is the only parish in Ontario now under their care.

It was in the year 1846 that the Jesuits arrived in Penetanguishene to resume their labors amongst the Indians on the Upper Lakes.* Fathers Dominic Daranquet and J. P. Chone were the pioneers, and they were followed by others not less devoted than themselves who literally turned their backs upon civilization for the sake of the Red Man. The labors of these Fathers recall to mind the missions of the seventeenth century in the same locality, the soil of which had been consecrated by the blood of martyrs. At the present time the Jesuit Fathers have under their charge missions at Port Arthur, North Bay, Sault Ste. Marie, Fort William, Manitowaning, Garden River, Wikwemikong and Sudbury, all in the Diocese of Peterborough. They have had phenomenal success with the Indians, who regard them with a love and trust truly filial in its character.

Notable Events.

On Nov. 22nd, 1842, the devotion of the Way of the Cross was erected in St. Paul's Church, Toronto, being the first church in the Diocese so favored. The next to receive a similar favor was the church of St. Vincent de Paul, Niagara, on Dec. 13th, 1844.

On March 10th, 1843, the Bishops of Canada† addressed a joint letter to the Directors of the Hudson's Bay Company, on the subject of the sale of liquor to the Indians. The havoc caused by this dangerous traffic was great and widespread, and had, perhaps, more to do with the degradation of the native races of America than all other causes combined. The Bishops' letter implored the governing body of that ancient and powerful corporation to stay the ruin being brought upon the Indians by the indis-

---

* An interesting account of this parish was read by the present pastor, Father Laboreau, at the meeting of the Canadian Institute at that place in the summer of 1891.

† The Bishops who affixed their signatures to this letter were Archbishop Signay and Bishop Turgeon, Quebec; Bishops Bourget, Montreal; Gaulin, Kingston; and Power, Toronto.

criminate sale of intoxicating liquors, and to take such measures as would confine the traffic within safe limits. The evil has never been altogether overcome, but it was no doubt due to the combined influence of the Catholic Bishops that some mitigation of it was subsequently brought about.

In May of this year there came to the Diocese Father John Carroll. This priest, a native of Queen's County, Ireland, came to America while very young, and pursued his studies at Halifax, N.S., where he was ordained by Bishop Burke, whose nephew he was.* During his subsequent residence in Halifax he was instrumental in securing the abolition of the Test Act, the provisions of which excluded Catholics from public offices.† He afterwards labored in the Dioceses of Quebec and Charlottetown, P.E.I., his exeat from the latter being dated Aug. 17th, 1832.‡ On his advent at Toronto, Bishop Power made him a Vicar General, and on the death of the Bishop he, jointly with Archdeacon Hay, became Administrator of the Diocese, and on the death of the latter in 1849, acted alone in that capacity until the arrival of Bishop de Charbonnel. During his administration the clergy of the Diocese presented to the Governor General, the Rt. Hon. Earl of Elgin and Kincardine, an address of sympathy on occasion of certain violent attacks made upon his Excellency's conduct of his high office. On Father Carroll's resignation of the Administratorship, when a successor to Bishop Power had been appointed, he was made the recipient of an address and testimonial by the Catholics of Toronto. He subsequently went to the United States and died at Chicago in 1889, the oldest priest in America, lacking only four years of being a centenarian. He is said to have been a near relative of the celebrated Charles Carroll of Carrollton, one of the signers of the Declaration of Independence, whom he frequently visited at his ancestral home in Virginia.

Fathers Peter Connolly, Hugh Fitzpatrick, P. S. Sanderl, William McIntosh, Francis Prendergast and Charles Kileen also came to the Diocese in the year 1843. Father Connolly came from the Diocese of Boston, but did not remain long here, leaving again in 1844. Father Fitzpatrick, who had been with Bishop Gaulin in Kingston, also left in

---

* Baltimore "Catholic Mirror," June 29th, 1889.
† "The Church of England in Nova Scotia": N.Y., 1891.
‡ Archives, vol. i., p. 47.

1844, and Father Sanderl was a Redemptorist, who, on leaving the Diocese again about 1853, went on a pilgrimage to Jerusalem.* No particulars are now obtainable about Father McIntosh, who was a talented young priest and very promising. He was assistant to Father Macdonald at Hamilton. Father Prendergast came from the Archdiocese of Tuam. Father Kileen, who came from Cincinnatti, was ordained by Bishop Power.

In September Bishop Power visited the Western portion of his Diocese.† To the Catholics of Amherstburg, Sandwich and Tilbury, he addressed pastoral letters, commending their fidelity to their several pastors, their zeal and charity in every good work, and urging them to further efforts for the advancement of religion and the education and religious training of their children.

On July 12th, 1844, the Sovereign Pontiff issued a Bull, erecting all the Dioceses of Canada into one Ecclesiastical Province, with Quebec as the Metropolitan See. The reader will remember that when, in 1819, the then reigning Pontiff, Pius VII., raised Quebec to this dignity, exception was taken to the measure by the British Government; and in deference thereto, Bishop Plessis had obtained from the Holy Father permission to defer the assumption of the archiepiscopal title until such time as a change should take place in the attitude of the civil authorities. This change had long since come to pass, and, in 1841, negotiations had been opened between the Canadian Bishops and the Holy See towards the erection of an Ecclesiastical Province and the consequent assumption by the Archbishop of Quebec of his proper title and dignity. By Apostolical Letters, Pope Gregory XVI. had now made this an accomplished fact, and the event was an occasion of great joy to the Church in Canada.

Bishop Power, in his pastoral address announcing it, said: "We invite you, brethren, to return heartfelt thanks to Almighty God for this new manifestation of His divine favor to His Church in Canada, and from which we may hope to derive many signal blessings and important advantages. Let us pray that this complete ecclesiastical organization may tend to the more rapid progress of the Catholic faith, bind together

---

* He is mentioned in De Courcy's "Catholic Church in the United States," Dr. Shea's translation, N.Y., 1857.

† The Bishop's first pastoral visit was to Penetanguishene and Manitoulin Island in August, 1842. Being unable to proceed as far as Sault Ste. Marie, he sent Father Proulx in his stead, making him the bearer of a letter to the Catholics of that settlement. Archives, vol. i., p. 21.

more firmly all the members of the Church, afford to her now well-established hierarchy the means of laboring together in more perfect unity of design, and by the united efforts of her first Pastors, of infusing new vigor and fresh energy to the most remote and most infant portions of the Catholic Church in this Province."*

On March 25th, 1845, the Legislative Assembly of the Province of Canada issued Letters of Incorporation to the Bishops of Toronto and Kingston, empowering them to acquire and possess property for eleemosynary, ecclesiastical and educational purposes, and in general to exercise such powers as are common to bodies corporate. The Act also extended the same powers to other dioceses that might in the future come into existence in the Province.

St. Michael's Cathedral.

From the beginning of his episcopate Bishop Power had felt the need of a suitable Cathedral Church. The Catholic population, keeping pace with the expansion of the city, had long since outgrown St. Paul's; and, with the march of the city westward, it became necessary to provide for those who resided at a distance from the old church, which had been built in the days when Toronto was but a hamlet on the banks of the Don. One of the Bishop's first cares, therefore, on coming to the city, was to secure a suitable site for his projected Cathedral, and with this in view he instituted a weekly penny collection at St. Paul's, as the nucleus of a building fund. He finally succeeded in purchasing the block of land on Church street, on which the Cathedral, Palace and Loretto Convent now stand. It was owned by Hon. Peter McGill of Montreal, and had formerly been used as a market garden. The price paid for the property was £1,800, which sum Bishop Power advanced out of his own private means.† The Bishop was adversely criticized by some people for having fixed on a site lying so much on the outskirts of the city, but it took but a few years to demonstrate the wisdom of his choice. What then lay on the outskirts is now in the very heart of the city, and, at Toronto's present rate of progress, it is, perhaps, only a question of years when it may be found expedient to erect a new and larger Cathedral much further west and north.

* Archives, vol. i., pp. 72-3.
† " Life of Archbishop Lynch," by H. C. McKeown: 1886.

The excavation for the new Cathedral was begun on April 7th, 1845. On that day a large force of men, who gave their services for the occasion gratuitously, assembled with their teams, and in an incredibly short space of time the work was done. Building operations began immediately and progressed so rapidly that on May 8th the corner-stone was laid by the Bishop in person, assisted by Fathers Macdonald, V. G., McDonagh, Gordon, O'Reilly, O'Dwyer, Timlin, Carroll, Hay, Quinlan and Nightingale.* It was an ambitious design in the state of things at that time to enter upon an undertaking of such magnitude; but Bishop Power was a man of faith, and confided thoroughly in the generosity of his flock. Nor was this confidence misplaced, for his efforts were nobly seconded at every turn; and Bishop, priests and people being thus united, the fair form of St. Michael's Cathedral gradually rose from the soil and gave to the world another example of Catholic faith and generosity. Unfortunately Bishop Power did not live to see this great work completed, but at his death he left it so far advanced, that within a year thereafter (Sept. 29th, 1848) it was solemnly dedicated to the service of Almighty God by his Lordship Bishop Bourget of Montreal, assisted by the Bishops of Kingston, Bytown and Martyropolis.

Concurrently with the Cathedral was erected St. Michael's Palace, which has ever since been the official residence of the Bishops and Archbishops of Toronto. It was blessed on Dec. 7th, 1846.

PASTORALS.

Bishop Power's pastorals are twelve in number, dating from the letter he addressed to his people from Laprairie prior to taking possession of his See. They all bear the impress of a strong individuality, and are characterized by a sweet and ardent piety, and a heartfelt affection for those committed to his care. Some of them have already been enumerated in the foregoing pages, and consequently do not call for further mention.

He was accustomed to address his flock at each recurring Lent, and it is in these letters especially that we get a glimpse of the saintliness of his character. In that of 1844 he announced the establishment in his Diocese of the Association of the Propagation of the Faith, which he describes as

---

*Father William Nightingale came from London, England. He was subsequently in Guiana, South America, then in New York. He remained in Toronto less than a year. Archives, vol. i, p. 77.

" one of the most admirable institutions and greatest works of mercy of modern times."

"We should not forget," he wrote, "that we have not fulfilled our duty towards our neighbour if we confine our charity and our solicitude to those with whom we live; for the divine light of revelation shows us a brother, a friend in every member of the human race, and the order of the Lord is that each man should take care of his neighbour. It teaches us, moreover, that all men, without exception, are our neighbours and should be dear to us; for all men form but one family in Adam and in Jesus Christ. We, therefore, stand indebted to those who have not yet received the precious gift of faith, who, in the energetic words of Holy Scripture, are seated in darkness and in the shadow of death, and who would, perhaps, have made a better use of this inestimable blessing than we have done. Let us, therefore, cheerfully contribute to the good work and bestow our mite on those truly evangelical men who sacrifice all the comforts of this world, their repose, their health, their liberty, and who are even ready to lay down their lives for the propagation of the Faith."* Little did he realize that in this last clause he was portraying his own glorious end.

Of the Bishop's pastorals on the death of Pope Gregory XVI., and the election of Pius IX., and of that on the famine and distress in Ireland in 1847, I shall have occasion to speak later on. His last, dated just two months before his death, was to promulgate the Jubilee proclaimed by Pius IX. on the occasion of his elevation to the Papal Throne.

Death of Gregory XVI. and Accession of Pius IX.

On June 1st, 1846, His Holiness Pope Gregory XVI. entered into rest. In announcing the melancholy intelligence to his people Bishop Power wrote :

"It is with feelings of no ordinary grief that we make known to you that it has pleased Almighty God to withdraw from this world, after a life of great labors and eminent piety, the Supreme Pastor of His Church, and the Father of all the faithful, Gregory XVI., who departed this life, full of years and of merits, in the capital of the Christian world, on Monday, the first day of June. From what we know of the burning zeal and spotless life

---

* Archives, vol. i., pp. 56-9.

of this excellent and well-beloved Pontiff, we have every reason to hope that he has already received at the hands of a merciful God the fullness of the reward promised to the good and faithful steward, who had not neglected but improved the many talents committed to his care. But, beloved brethren, the judgments of God are very severe; we, therefore, most earnestly invite you to join with all the children of the Church, and to beg fervently of the Almighty (if He has not already glorified His servant) to listen, in his behalf, to the voice of the Church, now praying throughout the world, through the merits of Jesus Christ, whose Vicar he was upon earth, to hasten the moment when he who was our High Priest may be graciously admitted to a place of light, of refreshment, and of everlasting peace."

The interregnum between the death of Gregory XVI. and the election of a successor was one of the shortest in the annals of the Church. Sixteen days only had elapsed when it was made known to the world that his Eminence Cardinal Mastai Ferretti had been duly and canonically raised to the Supreme Pontificate, and had ascended the Throne of Peter under the title of Pius IX. To enter into details of this most memorable event is not within the scope of this history, but in common with the rest of the Catholic world the event itself was personal to every member of the Diocese. "How consoling," wrote the Bishop to his people, "for us to witness, in the midst of all the trials and tribulations of our Holy Mother the Church, the continued fulfilment of the eternal promises of Christ, and to behold, notwithstanding the convulsions and revolutions of states and empires, and in defiance of all the changes of the oldest institutions of the world, the wonderful stability of that Divine Structure founded on a rock, against which the powers of Hell shall never prevail!"

THE BISHOP VISITS EUROPE.

In order to obtain additional priests for his diocese, as well as to seek assistance in the building of his Cathedral, Bishop Power visited Europe in January, 1847. In announcing his coming departure to his people, he besought their earnest prayers for the success of his mission and for his own safe return; he urged them to renewed efforts for the completion of the sacred edifice which had been so auspiciously begun; and he committed the care of the Diocese during his absence to his Vicar General and Archdeacon, Fathers Macdonald and Hay.

The number of priests at his disposal was altogether inadequate to the wants of the Diocese. They were twenty-five in number, an increase of seven since his first arrival in Toronto, their names and parishes being as follows:* Fathers W. P. Macdonald and John O'Reilly, Hamilton; P. Point and J. A. Menet, S.J.'s, Sandwich; James Jaffray, Maidstone; M. Duranquet, S.J., Walpole Island; J. J. Chone and J. Hanipaux, S.J.'s, Manitoulin Island; J. B. Pedelupe, S.J., St. Mary's Falls; P. J. Beaupre, S.J.,† Amherstburg; J. B. Morin, East Tilbury; M. R. Mills, St. Thomas and London; James Quinlan, Brantford; P. Schneider, Goderich; Simon Sanderl, Wilmot and Guelph; Wm. McIntosh, Indiana; P. O'Dwyer, Dundas; W. P. McDonagh, St. Catharines; E. Gordon, Niagara; E. O'Reilly, Gore of Toronto; J. B. Proulx, Newmarket; A. Charest, Penetanguishene; and J. J. Hay, J. D. Ryan and T. T. Kirwan (Pastor of St. Paul's), Toronto. Some of these remained in the Diocese but a short time; the connection of others with it or with dioceses subsequently cut off from it, was life-long. Prominent among these was Father John O'Reilly, then curate to Father Macdonald, who, as Dean of the Diocese of Hamilton, died at Dundas in 1884. Father O'Reilly had been ordained by Bishop Power in 1846, and was immediately thereafter sent to Hamilton, and then to Dundas. When the fever broke out in 1847, the Bishop recalled him to Toronto, where for four weeks he laboured incessantly in the immigrant sheds, administering the sacraments to as many as forty-five in a day. At the end of that time he was himself prostrated with the disease, but, notwithstanding, continued his priestly labors until quite exhausted.' On his recovery he returned to Dundas, where he ministered for the rest of his life, loved and respected by all who knew him.

Bishop Power remained in Europe for nearly six months. He spent some time in Rome, and had several audiences with the Holy Father, in the last of which, on the eve of his departure, he received in person from the hand of Pius IX. his Encyclical Letter on the state of affairs in Ireland. From London he addressed a short Pastoral Letter to his flock, transmitting to them this weighty document of the Father of the Faithful, whose paternal heart went out in sympathetic sorrow to the suffering poor in that unhappy country. Bishop Power had himself witnessed the terrible distress to which the Irish people were reduced at this memorable period, having

* Canadian Mercantile Almanac: Niagara and Toronto, 1847.
† Not mentioned in Tanguay's "Repertoire General."

spent some weeks in their midst; and the heart-rending scenes with which he was there brought face to face so wrought upon his sensitive and compassionate nature as to impart to his countenance thereafter an habitual sadness of expression.

The affliction from which the peasantry of Ireland at this time suffered was the grim spectre, famine. The failure of the potato crop, their staple article of food, had plunged them without warning, and therefore without preparation, into a season of the direst and most terrible distress, which not even the elaborate machinery of modern philanthropy was able adequately to alleviate. The Government, though tardily, made some effort to avert the impending calamity, and private charity did nobly; but misgovernment and absentee landlordism had already done their work, and in spite of every effort to the contrary the poor people by the thousand perished on the roadside like dogs, and found a pauper's grave under the green sod of their well-beloved but grievously afflicted land.

The patience and resignation which the people of Ireland exhibited in this fearful crisis won for them the admiration of the civilized world. "There is," said a writer in the Dublin "Evening Post," "no more extraordinary fact connected with the deplorable condition of this country than the patience with which our poor people endure their sufferings. They have been taught by their admirable pastors the duty of submission, and they have exhibited to the world an example for which, perhaps, there is no parallel in ancient or modern times. In reply to expressions of commiseration, the starving peasant would exclaim: 'Welcome be the will of God.'"

When in Ireland Bishop Power made arrangements with the Loretto Community to send a colony of their Nuns to Toronto, to assist in the work of Catholic education. Accordingly, in September, five members of the order arrived here, and were joyfully received by the people. Owing to the death of the Bishop which occurred within a month from their arrival, the poor Sisters were left "fatherless" and unprovided for; but the charity of the Catholics of Toronto came to their aid, and their difficulties being tided over, they embarked on that career of usefulness which has conferred such inestimable benefits upon the city and Province.

The Typhus.

Following in the wake of the famine in Ireland came fever and pestilence. Those who had escaped death in the one form were soon called upon to confront it in another; and, in the light of subsequent events, theirs was perhaps the happier lot who, in the first months of the famine, succumbed to its fearful ravages. They were at least spared the horrifying spectacle to which the succeeding pestilence reduced their unhappy countrymen.

Much has been written in late years on the subject of absentee landlordism in general and on the landlordism of Ireland in particular. It is not my intention to enter upon a discussion of the subject, which would be altogether out of place here. But it is impossible altogether to avoid it in narrating events which were going on in Ireland at the time of which I write, and which had a very direct effect upon the course of Catholic affairs in Canada. The efforts made by the British Government to mitigate the distress, and the heroic charity of individuals, have already been referred to, but never did the landlords of Ireland appear in a less enviable light than during this period of national humiliation. Honorable exceptions there no doubt were, but as a class, the one thing which seemed to concern those to whom the people had a right to look for help and sympathy was how best they might rid themselves of so uncomfortable a burden. The poor-houses were already crowded to excess, and hence no avenue of relief was available in that quarter, but there lay a vast new country far across the ocean which seemed to offer a convenient dumping-ground for the starving creatures whose piteous appeals for a crust of bread were anything but music in the landlord's ear. The embarkation of shipload after shipload of aged and infirm, of helpless widows with large families, and of those whose constitutions had been enfeebled by previous sickness and destitution was the result. It was not the young, able-bodied laborer who was thus sought to be got rid of, but, in nine cases out of ten, just such persons as described; and as the United States Government had but recently passed stringent laws against the landing of penniless emigrants on its shores, the tide naturally turned towards Canada. The people on their part, seeing no prospect of relief from this desperate state of affairs in Ireland, and misled by the promises of assistance to be given them on their arrival at Quebec,*

---

* These promises were never fulfilled, perhaps were never intended to be. For instance: "upwards of two thousand persons," says Mr. J. M. O'Leary, "were shipped by the agents of Lord Palmerston

eagerly grasped at the specious offers held out to them, and consequently the opening months of 1847 witnessed a spectacle which, thank God, is as rare as it is melancholy. "The quays of Dublin," says a contemporary writer, "resemble the halting-place of an eastern caravan. Crowds of emigrants, with their separate allotments of baggage, cover every available spot. The greater number are conveyed to Liverpool, but many shipped directly from this port. Two vessels sailed last week with a full complement, and two more, in which nearly 1,200 passengers are booked, will sail on Tuesday next. A Dublin agent has gone to Liverpool to charter vessels for the conveyance of 1,300 families from one Irish estate, the expenses to be partly borne by the landlord and tenant."*

In this way close on 100,000 emigrants quitted Ireland for the British Colonies in America during the first six months of 1847. Meanwhile, what was passing in Canada? The Canadian Government, forewarned by its medical officials, had established a quarantine station at Grosse Isle in the Gulf of St. Lawrence, and, in anticipation of considerable sickness among the emigrants, had made somewhat extensive preparations for their reception and treatment. But they greatly under-estimated the task that lay before them. The constitutions of the emigrants, enfeebled by the famine through which they had passed, and the accommodation provided for them on board ship being miserably insufficient for animals, far less human beings, the mortality amongst them on the voyage over was appalling. Fever and dysentery broke out a few days after leaving port, and there being no adequate medical attendance to relieve the stricken, there was in most cases nothing left for them but to die. Out of 2,782 emigrants who left Ireland in seven vessels which reached Grosse Isle between the 14th and 21st of May, 184 had died on the voyage, and a large proportion of the survivors had contracted the dread disease, the typhus. Mr. Stephen De Vere, a nephew of Lord Monteagle, who had heroically submitted himself to the privations of a steerage passage for the purpose of learning by actual experience the real condition of the emigrant, thus describes what he saw:

"Before the emigrant has been a week† at sea, he is an altered man.

from his Irish estates, who not only promised them clothing, but assured them that his Lordship's agent at Quebec, where there was no such person, had been instructed to pay them from £2 to £5 each family according to their number."—"Catholic Record," April 9th, 1892.

* Cited by Mr. J. M. O'Leary in the "Catholic Record," April 9th, 1892. The whole melancholy story is very ably and fully told by Mr. O'Leary in this and following numbers of the "Record."

† The vessel on which Mr. De Vere embarked was two months on the voyage out.

How can it be otherwise? Hundreds of poor people, men, women and children of all ages, from the driveling idiot of ninety to the babe just born, huddled together without light, without air, wallowing in filth, and breathing a fetid atmosphere, sick in body and despair at heart; the fevered patients lying between the sound in sleeping places so narrow as almost to deny them the power of indulging, by a change of position, the natural restlessness of the disease; by their agonized ravings disturbing those around and predisposing them, through the effects of the imagination, to imbibe the contagion; living without food or medicine, except as administered by the hand of casual charity; dying without the voice of spiritual consolation, and buried in the deep without the rites of the Church."*

And was the condition of the unfortunate people any better at Grosse Isle? Somewhat, doubtless, but the preparations made by the Government were entirely inadequate to the exigencies of the occasion. The only accommodation for emigrants on the island was the hospital sheds of 1832 and 1834 (the cholera years), and the new one erected in May of this year. These were soon crowded to overflowing; and as other vessels arrived, only the dangerously ill were permitted to land, and the many others who had the disease in various stages were kept on board until further accommodation could be provided. Recourse was then had to marquees and bell-tents, but only when public opinion had forced the Government to take further action in the matter.

But I have not space to go further into details of the sad story. Vessels continued to arrive and to discharge their pestilential freight on the inhospitable isle. During all that summer the energies of the small staff of physicians and clergymen were taxed to the utmost capacity, and all they could do was to ease and console the bedside of the dying as their limited strength would allow. In all 90,150 emigrants landed at Quebec in the year 1847. There had died on the voyage 5,282, and in quarantine 3,389, a total of nearly nine thousand victims to long years of misgovernment and oppression in holy yet unhappy Ireland. And year after year, as the blue waters of the noble St. Lawrence sweep past the lonely isle, bearing on its peaceful bosom the floating palaces which carry a constant stream of pleasure-seekers between the old and the new worlds, how few are aware, or if aware, ever give a passing thought to the innocent castaways who,

---

* "Catholic Record," April 9th, 1892.

beneath the sod of Grosse Isle, sleep their last long sleep until the great day when they shall be summoned into rest and peace eternal.

Death of Bishop Power.

What, the reader may ask, has the foregoing to do with the Diocese of Toronto? We shall see. Those who passed the inspection of the quarantine officers and were allowed to proceed up the river to Montreal and to Upper Canada, carried with them the seeds of the pestilence and scattered them far and wide. The fever broke out simultaneously in many places and added victims by the hundred to the already vast total on board ship and at Grosse Isle. Over seven hundred died at Quebec; 3,330 (these are the official figures) at Point St. Charles, Montreal; 130 at Lachine, and 3,048 at various points in Ontario, not including Toronto.* At Toronto the mortality was very great also (863), and Bishop Power's clergy were entirely unequal to the responsibility thus thrust upon them, though they worked heroically day and night to console and succor the sick and the dying. The priests residing at Toronto were Fathers Hay and Kirwan; but, owing to the already precarious state of the former's health, the work devolved almost entirely upon the latter, until Father John O'Reilly was summoned from Dundas to assist him. Father Carroll also came from Niagara to lend a helping hand; and these three were constant in their attendance at the immigrant sheds, in the hospital, and in the homes where the disease had penetrated. One by one they sank under the work from sheer fatigue, or themselves succumbed to the fever; the Bishop was then left almost alone, to battle as best he could with the difficulties of the situation. Father Carroll was able, in some measure, to assist him, but the Bishop for some days bore the brunt of the work. Then came a call at midnight that a poor woman lay dying at the immigrant sheds, and asked for succour. There being no one else to answer to the call, the Bishop, recognizing in the poorest and most helpless of the Irish immigrants a member of his flock, placed the Bread of Life in his bosom and went out into the night to fortify a soul for its last journey. He fulfilled his mission, but, as it proved, at the cost of his own precious life. It is said that as he came out of the pestilential abode, he raised his hands and his eyes to Heaven, and, in a voice of deep emotion exclaimed: "My God! what

---

* In all there perished during this miserable year on the voyage and in Canada, 16,825 out of 97,953 emigrants.

crimes England has to answer for!" The next day symptoms of the dread malady exhibited themselves and rapidly developed into a malignant case, which in a few days terminated fatally.

When it became known in the city that Bishop Power was dead expressions of the most heartfelt sorrow were heard on every side, and the occasion and manner of his death called forth the respect and admiration of the entire community. The "British Colonist," the leading newspaper of the day, referring to the sad event, said: "It is not for us to pronounce his eulogy. The sorrow of his flock; the regret of the community, the members of which have learned to appreciate his exertions to promote peace and brotherly love among us; the tears that moisten the cheeks of many persons not within the pale of his Church, to whom we have spoken of his untimely decease, are the best evidences of the loss sustained in his death. May it be our lot to see a successor appointed to the episcopate whom all may learn to love as well."

The Bishop's death occurred on the first of October. On the 5th his remains were conveyed to their last resting place beneath the new Cathedral. As that edifice was not yet roofed in, the funeral cortege first proceeded to St. Paul's Church, where the solemn services for the dead were performed and the people allowed to pay their last tribute of respect to the departed.* As an additional evidence of the respect in which Bishop Power was held by others than the members of his own flock, it may be stated that the shops on the line of the funeral procession, with one or two exceptions, were closed, and that thousands thronged to witness the mournful spectacle.

Some years afterwards a movement to erect a memorial of Bishop Power was set on foot in Toronto. In calling attention to the matter a correspondent of "The Mirror" (Dec. 3rd, 1858) wrote: "Supported by that pure charity which animated the Apostles, the saintly Bishop Power might be seen traversing the almost deserted streets of Toronto to afford the last solemnities to the soul of a departing immigrant. No hovel was too mean, no fever shed too loathsome to bar his entrance or thwart him from his purpose, which was the greater glory of God and the salvation of

---

* A funeral service for Bishop Power was held also in St. Mary's Cathedral, Halifax—his native city. A Requiem Mass was celebrated by Very Rev. Father Connolly, Father Hannan being deacon, and Father Phelan sub-deacon. It is worthy of remark that the two first named became subsequently Archbishops of Halifax.

immortal souls. But he fell in the performance of his sacred duties; he yielded up his life a martyr to the sufferings of our countrymen. Yet still his remains lie cold and unhonored in St. Michael's Cathedral; no monument is there to tell the traveller of the glories of the past; no lasting tribute of your thankfulness for the greatest of benefits. He is gone; the silent earth has closed over him, and with it, it seems to me, the memory of his heroic deeds is buried in oblivion. But such, I am sure, cannot be the case. It is almost impossible for Irishmen to recall the memories of the frightful calamity without a feeling of the deepest veneration for the first Bishop of Toronto and his exalted virtues. If your minds be dead to his great sacrifice, then let him rest unhonored and unnamed; if not, let some outward mark of respect be paid to his untiring zeal and energy."

The outcome of this movement was the handsome marble tablet which now adorns the chancel of the Cathedral, and which bears the following inscription:

IN MEMORIAM.
ILL.MI ET REVERENDMI MICHAELIS POWER,
Primi Episcopi Torontini.
In Civitate Halifaxiensi, N. S., natus est.
Sacerdos ordinatus in Diœcesi Marianopolitana.
Cum magno animarum fructu laboravit.
Creatus est Episcopus in Ecclesia Laprairie,
Die viii. Maii, 1842.
Fundamenta hujusce Cathedralis die viii. Maii, 1845, jecit.
Post multos labores pro Christo susceptos morbum lethalem contraxit
in visitandis aegrotantibus lue infectis, et,
Ecclesiæ sacramentis munitus Spiritum Deo reddidit ætatis suæ 43, A.D. 1847.
Cujus ossa prope altare majus in cryptis religiose servantur.

There stood also another tablet directly over the Bishop's place of sepulture bearing an English inscription, but this was removed during the recent alterations. It may be well to append it also. It read as follows:

UNDERNEATH LIE THE REMAINS OF
RIGHT REV. DR. MICHAEL POWER,
BORN IN HALIFAX, N. S.
CONSECRATED
FIRST BISHOP OF TORONTO ON THE 8TH OF MAY, 1842.

HE LAID DOWN HIS LIFE FOR HIS FLOCK ON THE 1ST OF OCTOBER, 1847,
BEING THE 42ND OF HIS AGE. R. I. P.

Little remains to be added to the history of this period. Bishop Power's best eulogy is in the simple, unadorned story of his useful life and holy death. His residence in Toronto was too short, perhaps, to enable him to bring to fruition the many projects he had in view for the advancement of religion in the Diocese; but it was at least long enough to allow him to lay a firm and sure foundation, upon which his successors have raised a glorious and enduring structure. The Diocese came into his hands raw material: he drew together its widely scattered missions and formed them into a concordant whole, in constant communication with the fountain-head at Toronto. He personally visited the members of his flock, even in the most remote sections, and by his paternal solicitude for their welfare, temporal as well as spiritual, caused them to feel that in him they had a Bishop who was truly a father to his people. His constant endeavour was to gather around him a band of zealous and devoted priests, who would second his efforts at every turn, working with him and with his people for the growth and advancement of the Catholic faith in this country, then just emerging from primeval solitude, and offering unequal advantages to the long oppressed children of his race who could here pursue their way in the peaceful enjoyment of their religion and the undisputed possession of their homes. Under his wise direction much was accomplished towards this end; and looking back from this last decade of the century to review the progress of fifty years, we can, with grateful hearts, acknowledge that in Bishop Power the Diocese had a wise and prudent founder to whom we are indebted for many of the blessings we now enjoy.

But his richest gifts to us are his holy memory and his honoured name, which should ever be cherished as among the most valued of our possessions. Of him may be used with equal truth the words applied to the great pioneer Bishop of the neighboring Republic: "The scrutiny of history in our day recognizes the high estimate of his personal virtues, his purity, meekness, prudence, and his providential work in moulding the diverse elements in the Province into an organized church. His administrative ability stands out in high relief when we view the results produced by others who, unacquainted with the country, rashly promised themselves to cover the land with the blossoms of peace, but raised only harvests of thorns."*

No words can more fittingly close this chapter than those with which it is begun: "Greater love than this no man hath, that a man lay down his life for his friends."

---

* "Life and Times of Archbishop Carroll," by John Gilmary Shea. New York, 1888.

CRITICAL NOTE.—Unlike the period embraced within the preceding chapter, the historian or the student of the life and episcopate of Bishop Power has abundant manuscript material to work upon, though the foregoing may be said to be the first published work on the subject. Bishop Power, besides being conspicuous as a man of action, was also of studious and methodical habits; and he caused to be set down in writing every fact of any consequence, and carefully preserved every document of importance which related to the Diocese. The result is that the student of history is placed under a deep debt of gratitude to him for these commendable precautions. Little, therefore, need be added for the information of those who may desire to go deeper into the subject, the printed authorities, as in the case of the former chapter, being fully indicated in the text and foot notes. There is, however, a short sketch of the Bishop in the initial number of "The Irish Canadian" which has been made use of; and I cannot forbear again calling attention to the able and complete account of the melancholy events of 1847 which Mr. James M. O'Leary of Ottawa has published recently in the "Catholic Record." It is to be hoped he may be induced to republish it in a more permanent form.

THE LIFE AND TIMES OF THE

RIGHT REV. ARMAND FRANCIS MARIE, COMTE DE CHARBONNEL,

SECOND BISHOP OF TORONTO,

BY

REV. JOHN R. TEEFY, B.A., C.S.B.,

SUPERIOR OF ST. MICHAEL'S COLLEGE, TORONTO

The Right Rev. Armand Francis Marie, Comte de Charbonnel,

Second Bishop of Toronto.

BORN AT MONISTROL-SUR-LOIRE, FRANCE, DECEMBER 1st, 1802

DIED AT CREST, FRANCE, MARCH 29th, 1891

CHAPTER V.

1850-1859.

THE LIFE AND TIMES OF BISHOP DE CHARBONNEL.

Family—Ordination and Entry to St. Sulpice—Coming to America—Services Among the Fever Patients—Bishop of Toronto—Separate Schools—Return to France—Propagation of the Faith—Archbishop of Sozopolis.

> "Whose remembrance yet
> Lives in men's eyes ; and will to ears and tongues
> Be theme and hearing ever."—Cym., Act iii., Sc. 1.

IT was reserved for France, so closely connected with the earlier history of this country, and so renowned for the missionary spirit of her children, to give Toronto its second bishop in the person of Armand Francis Marie, Comte de Charbonnel. He belonged to an old and illustrious family numbering amongst its ancestry many a member who had, at the point of the sword and with his blood, inscribed his name in chivalry's golden records. During the second crusade (1147-1149) John de Charbonnel had received from his sovereign, Louis VII. of France, his title of Count for services rendered Church and country. In the fifteenth century the descendants of this John de Charbonnel, originally from the old Province of Vivarais, which corresponds to the department of Ardeche, settled not far away in the Haute Loire. Here they acquired by marriage several castles and a baronetcy in Yssingeaux, still a flourishing town. St. Francis of Sales was a kinsman of the family.

The Bishop's father was John Baptist de Charbonnel, his full title being Comte de Charbonnel, Baron of Saussac, Lord of Bets, Flachats and Camblaire. It was he who in 1791 had saved the two daughters of Louis XV. and aunts of Louis XVI. by securing their escape from France. He married in 1789 Mary Claudine di Pradier, daughter of the Marquis D'Agrain, first President of the Parliament of Dijon, during the war of the French revolution. The second son of this marriage was Armand Francis

Marie, the subject of our sketch, born near Monistrol-sur-Loire on the first of December, 1802.

At the age of nine he was sent to college at Montbrison (Loire), and the following year to Annonay, where he continued his classical studies with brilliant success. Wishing to devote himself to the priesthood, he entered the Seminary of St. Sulpice in Paris for the course of philosophy and theology. Here he so distinguished himself that at the age of twenty (1822) he was offered a professorship of philosophy.

The following year, when about to enter upon his sub-deaconship, he was earnestly requested by his father to abandon the ecclesiastical state and become head of the family. He refused, saying that if he abandoned what his superiors deemed to be his true vocation, far from being the support and honor of his name, he would be its disgrace, and he would furthermore risk his eternal salvation by not corresponding to a call from God.

His ordination as priest took place in 1825. His rank and talent immediately brought him into notice ; he was appointed almoner to the Duchess of Berry in memory of the loyal courage of his father. But the honor signified by the choice of a sovereign, the glory attached to the exalted functions, the prospects held out for the future, were no temptation to the young Abbe, who had already trampled high earthly dignities under foot. His soul needed a more active and trying life to satisfy his zeal and spirit of sacrifice. " The grace which God gave me," he used to say afterwards, " of declining this favor, was in my eyes, after that of holy orders, the greatest of my life."

ENTRY TO THE SULPITIANS.

Father de Charbonnel entered the Society of St. Sulpice* and was sent to Lyons in 1826, where he was professor of dogmatic theology and Holy Scripture, and afterwards treasurer. At Lyons in 1833, during a revolt of working men, he saved by his energy and persuasive eloquence the Grand Seminary from pillage and the government troops from a severe encounter. For this signal service he was offered a cross of the Legion of Honor, which he steadfastly refused.

---

* Amongst his companions in the novitiate were the late Archbishop Purcell of Cincinnati, the Rev. Fathers Quiblier, Biblandele and Baile, who, except the first named, in turn became Superiors of the Sulpitians in Montreal.

The following year his health obliged him to rest. It being restored, he was sent to the Grand Seminary of Versailles, where he remained two years, and afterwards to that of Bordeaux. Here he took the resolution of coming to America. It is very difficult to assign the true reason which determined the Abbe de Charbonnel to this important step. He was a very successful teacher; his learning, his quick, lively eloquence, his great spirit of faith, his charming originality, were remembered at Lyons and Bordeaux for forty years. Cardinal Donnet, who had been at college with him at Annonay, wished to make him his vicar general, or at least to give him the superiorship of his Grand Seminary in place of M. Hamon. His wish to escape these and all other honors may have been one factor in his resolution; but judging by the energy which he afterwards displayed, a greater factor was his desire for harder work in the vast missionary fields of America. Not only was there continual intercourse between the Sulpitians of France and their American houses at Montreal and Baltimore, but the immediate predecessor of Mgr. Donnet was Cardinal Cheverus. He was the first Bishop of Boston, whence he was called in 1823 to France to the See of Montauban until 1826, at which date he was made Archbishop of Bordeaux. As his death took place in 1836, the year before the Abbe de Charbonnel was stationed in this city, the subject of our sketch must have heard directly from the zealous prelate, or from those with whom he had but lately spoken, of the growing church beyond the sea. Accordingly he determined to leave his country and give himself heart and soul to more apostolic work than was afforded in any educational institution.

Departure for America.

He left France for Canada in 1839. After remaining at Montreal for some time, where his eloquent sermons soon attracted attention, he went to Baltimore for the purpose of studying English, and returned to Montreal about the year 1842. The episcopal dignity still pursued him. Before he had been three months in the country, the Governor-General, Lord Sydenham, asked him to accept the mitre in some English colony. He replied with his usual vivacity: "If I had wished to be bishop I would not have left France." In 1844 Mgr. Blanc, Archbishop of New Orleans, besought him to be his coadjutor *cum jure successionis*. The suffragans of the New Orleans province petitioned the Holy See upon the same subject; but the missionary was inexorable. Father de Charbonnel's distate for the episcopate may be gathered from the following extracts of letters written after his consecration :

To Father Point, Sandwich, dated Toronto, September 25, 1850: "May you be blessed, you and yours, with the heart of one who rather would be a Jesuit than Bishop, and pray for him as, according to the Litanies, for those in their agony, *ora pro me*."

To the same Father Point, S.J.: "Why can I not fill the vacancies with the sons of St. Ignatius, and after the last stroke become one myself? You would choose rather to be only a simple and modest religious, and I also, dear Father; let us unite our two acts of obedience in the Divine Heart, source of all obedience, and there let us embrace each other as two brothers who help each other to carry their crosses."

To Mgr. Gaulin, Bishop of Kingston, dated Oct. 12, 1850: "Monseigneur—I do not know how to excuse myself to you for not having written sooner; it is not, however, through bad will, still less to avenge myself for the fact that you are one of the principal causes of the position in which I find myself. If there is a diocese of Toronto in the Church, and if there is a poor Bishop whom people call the Bishop of Toronto, it is to the Bishop of Kingston he owes it. If you had kept all the diocese which ceased to belong to you by division there would neither have been first or second Bishop of Toronto. I cannot but admire the zeal which made you divide your diocese, but nevertheless from it I have become what I am, as the good Father Larkin expresses it : the one of all the bishops in the vast world who needs compassion most."

The Fever Amongst the Irish.

The Abbe de Charbonnel remained in Montreal until 1846, the year of the dreadful fever amongst the Irish immigrants. Broken in health and heart these poor people had come out to this country in ship loads, only to find a grave where they had hoped to build a home. Even to-day in Montreal the traveller may see hard by the waters of the swift St. Lawrence the cairn marking the spot where thousands of these victims lie buried. Many of their children found a parent's love and a parent's roof amongst the charitable French Canadians. What part the saintly Father de Charbonnel took in all this, his care of the dying, of those that were left behind, and still more

> "That best portion of a good man's life,
> His little, nameless, unremembered acts
> Of kindness and of love,"

none but the historian of heaven knoweth. The sadness of that time is bitter—the circumstances which drove the exiles from home and those under which they entered this country, and the half-hearted manner they were cared for by the Government, and the wholesale slaughter which the pestilence made amongst them—all these may be forgiven but can never be forgotten. The ministers of religion did their utmost; their zeal remains in grateful memory. And none labored more devotedly than the apostolic Father de Charbonnel. Heeding no danger he was continually in the fever sheds, with heavenly consolation for the dying and earthly charity for those who were spared. While many of his comrades in the priesthood fell at their post, he, trusting to his strong constitution, labored on. But at last the plague overtook him; he was stricken down with the fever and brought to the very edge of the grave. His vigor served him—he recovered, and on becoming convalescent he went to France for the sake of his health.

The following year (1848) the electors of the Haute-Loire wished him to enter the national assembly in place of his brother, Louis, who had been killed at the barricades in the Faubourg St. Antoine at Paris in the month of August, 1848. The Abbe declined the honor, preferring the professional chair which he occupied once more in the Grand Seminary of Aix in Provence.

The Bishop of Toronto.

About this time the see of Toronto had become vacant by the death of its first bishop, Dr. Power. Father John Larkin,* who had refused the same mitre in 1841, was named in 1848. In fact the Bulls had arrived, but he positively declined the honor. Then the choice fell upon the Abbe de Charbonnel, who, from a retreat which he had preached in 1845, was already favorably known to the priests of the diocese. In a consistory held at Rome, March 15, 1850, he was preconized Bishop of Toronto. The Bulls reaching him April 18th, he immediately quitted Aix for the purpose

---

* Father Larkin was a native of Newcastle, England. On coming to Canada he became a Sulpitian and taught in Montreal Seminary. He subsequently entered the Society of Jesus in Kentucky and became one of the foremost members of the order.

of pleading the cause of his humility before the Supreme Pontiff. The Pope, Pius IX., would not take a refusal, and as an encouragement promised to consecrate Dr. de Charbonnel with his own hands. The ceremony took place in the Sistine Chapel on May 26th, 1850, in presence of a large assembly, amongst whom were the French Ambassador and the General of the French troops at Rome. As a souvenir of consecration the Holy Father presented the Bishop with a well filled purse and a chasuble of gold cloth upon which were embroidered the Papal arms. In addition to these His Holiness offered him his choice between a fine ciborium and a rich chalice. His Lordship chose the ciborium; then taking the chalice in the other hand, he turned towards Pius IX., saying: "*Quid retribuam Domino pro omnibus quae retribuit mihi;*" and finishing the quotation said: "*Calicem salutaris accipiam et nomen Domini invocabo.*" ("I shall take the chalice of salvation and call upon the name of the Lord.") The Pope, with a smile, appreciated the ready answer, and the Bishop withdrew, happy possessor of all three. A few days afterwards he quitted Rome to travel through France in the interests of his diocese; and while he is on his way to the scene of his labors, let us cast a glance at religion in Toronto.

Nearly three years had passed since the death of Mgr. Power. During the first part of this interregnum Archdeacon Hay was administrator; he dying in 1849, the Very Rev. John Carroll was placed in charge. There were in the diocese 28 priests, from Oshawa on the East to Sandwich on the West, and as far North as the Manitoulin Island and Sault Ste. Marie. Within the present limits of the diocese the following is the list of priests: City of Toronto, Very Rev. J. J. Hay and Rev. T. Kirwan; County of York, Rev. J. B. Proulx; Whitby District, Rev. E. Smith; Adjala, Rev. M. R. Mills; Penetanguishene, Rev. A. Charest; Niagara, Rev. J. Carroll; St. Catharines, Rev. W. P. McDonagh. This leaves 22 for the present dioceses of Hamilton and London, the most flourishing missions being those of the French on the West. Outside of the cities of Toronto and Hamilton there could not be said to be a single resident priest. Those who are put down for a certain place, as Dean Kirwan for London in 1850, and Father Proulx for Oshawa, had such a vast extent of country to visit that their duty was everywhere and their home nowhere.

The following, taken from the Provincial Census, is the population which these handful of workmen had to serve:

Toronto Diocese (present limits) 1850:

City	7,940
Country	22,004
Total	29,944

Hamilton and London Dioceses:

City of Hamilton	3,981
City of London	1,179
Country	42,101
Total	47,261
Grand Total	77,205

The districts of Manitoulin Island and Sault Ste. Marie are not included in this table. Making an approximation, the population would be 80,000.

There were not many clerical changes at this period. A resident priest was placed at London in 1849, and the following year Ingersoll and Dundas were opened.

Institutions there were none. There were poor and infirm, but charity had not as yet built them a home. The only religious in the city were the Ladies of Loretto. Coming just as Bishop Power was on his death-bed, with only one priest, or at most two, in the city, and these overtaxed by the calls which the fever made upon them, this pioneer community was most severely tried. They have outlived these difficulties; and their history is as edifying for their zeal and success in the work of education as for their patience in their early suffering.

Owing both to the unsettled state of the law and the scattered population, Catholic schools were few in number and poor in prospect. The following is the number for the Province:

Year	No.
1848	32
1849	31
1850	46

From a "Statement furnished the City Board of Trustees" in 1852 we find that there were in the Catholic Schools of Toronto 706 pupils under the care of 12 teachers, of whom two were Sisters of Loretto, and five were Christian Brothers.

At this time there were only two Catholic churches in Toronto, the Cathedral and St. Paul's. The interior of the former was quite unadorned. With plain windows and white walls the dazzling light presented a very unpleasant glare, and stood in strange contrast to its appearance after Canon Filbert had employed his art upon it. At the time of which we write there was no tower, no sacristy. The altar stood a little forward of its present position, with a passage on either side leading to small galleries. An immense picture of the Last Supper formed a reredos to the main altar, which was in fact the only one. It was consecrated on Sept. 29, 1848, by Bishop Bourget of Montreal, Bishop Phelan of Kingston preaching the sermon. As canon law forbids the consecration of a church in debt, that of the Cathedral ($57,600) was assumed by the late Hon. John Elmsley and the late S. G. Lynn, Esq.

From the history of the different missions it will be seen that in 1850 there were very few churches outside the city. The log hut of the early settler served the purpose; or, sometimes

> "A crucifix fastened
> High on the trunk of a tree * * * * *
> Looked with its agonized face on the multitude kneeling beneath it
> This was their rural chapel."

When the word reached them that the priest had come, the faithful gathered from far and near. With tear-stained cheek and swelling breast they worshiped at that humble shrine and strengthened their soul with the Bread of heaven. Their lot was hard: their life was simple. In that simplicity they left to succeeding generations the faith which they had transplanted from saintly soil. If the Church has since lost numbers of its children in this country it is due, not so much to the character of the pioneers themselves, as to the want of organization and instruction. To effect the one and impart the other was under the then existing circumstances impossible. Few if any priests had accompanied the different bodies of immigrants, and those who were already here were not numerous enough. The settlers themselves were too scattered to have that regularity and frequency of attendance so necessary to sustain faith and piety.

Arrival in Toronto.

Such was the state of the diocese when Mgr. de Charbonnel, after a brief sojourn in France, entered Toronto Sept. 21st, 1850, as its ecclesiastical head. He was accompanied by Mgr. Prince, Coadjutor Bishop of Montreal, one Basilian priest (Father Molony), and three students. The following day, Sunday, he took formal possession of the See, and (as he writes) " the debt with which it is burthened," the full amount of which was $70,000. We are indebted to " The Mirror" of Sept. 27th, 1850, for a report :

"The newly installed Bishop officiated. Rev. Mr. Marcoux was assistant priest. Messrs. Tellier, S.J., and Villeneuve were deacons of honor; and Messrs. Schneider and Proulx were deacon and sub-deacon of the Mass. The Bishop preached in the evening upon the duties of the Good Shepherd. He began by hoping that they would excuse his imperfect English, when he assured them that he warmly represented to His Holiness the Pope how utterly unfit he was for the position, that he only accepted it upon the express command of the Holy Father. He spoke of his labors in Montreal amongst the Irish immigrants. He had caught, he continued, the fever during that memorable year and was lying upon what was considered his death-bed. But that providence, whose invisible hand directs and governs all things, had otherwise decreed; and through its controlling will he stood then before them as their Chief Pastor, ready at all times to risk everything, to sacrifice everything, even life itself, if necessary, for the welfare of the flock committed to his care. In proof of his entire devotion to their services he assured them that he had made over the whole of his paternal estate in France to assist in liquidating the debt contracted for the building of the magnificent Cathedral in which they were, and for such other religious purposes as the Diocese mostly stood in need of, without so much as reserving a single farthing for his own private use. He concluded by promising to visit them all; but he wanted especially to see the poor, to cheer, to console, and if possible to relieve them. He wished to be a friend and father to them all, and he hoped with God's blessing to act the part of the Good Shepherd with benefit to their eternal salvation and his own."

Such was the zeal and devotion with which the saintly Bishop entered upon his onerous duties. What were the results of his first year's labors may be judged from his report to Rome, written at Baltimore :

"Thanks to God, and the zeal of five disinterested priests who live with me under an easy rule, things are going better.

"I have striven to overcome my repugnance to preach in English, the only language necessary for me, preaching every week, and often two or three times, and more particularly in Lent.

"The ceremonies and instructions fill our Cathedral at Vespers as well as at the High Mass.

"I have visited a portion of the Catholics of the city, going from house to house, seeking the lost sheep; a certain number have returned to the pasture of our holy church; but all is not perfect. I intend to have a mission given as soon as I shall have a sufficient number of workmen.

"I am expecting Capuchins, Oblates from Marseilles, Marists from Lyons and Basilians from Viviers. The founder of the first, Louis della Vagna,* a Genoese, has stopped at London to assist his Eminence Cardinal Wiseman.

"I have already sixteen Fathers of the Society of Jesus, who render me all kinds of consolation by their fervor and zeal. I have one of them (Father Tellier) who is my confessor and that of all the priests in Toronto, by their own choice.

"I have asked for five Brothers of the De La Salle Institute in order to open Catholic schools.

"I hope to have soon some Sisters of Charity called the Sisters of St. Joseph, or the non-cloistered Sisters of the Visitation of St. Francis de Sales. In the meantime we have established two benevolent Societies, one for men and the other for women, whose alms added to our own resources make an annual total of fourteen or fifteen hundred dollars for our poor.

"The rich amongst the Catholics of the city are most edifying, and several render me all kinds of services. Two Englishmen, converts from Anglicanism, have saved the whole Catholic establishment in Toronto by giving all their fortune as security. I should be happy, Mgr., if the Holy See would grant a mark of satisfaction to those two fervent Christians, the

---

* This saintly priest eventually came to Toronto in the Spring of 1856 and was placed in charge of St. Mary's Church. See an interesting sketch by Mr. H. F. McIntosh.

Hon. Captain John Elmsley, and Mr. S. G. Lynn, Merchant. They resemble, body and soul, those Angles of whom St. Gregory remarked, when he saw them for sale in the market place at Rome, that they would soon come to be called Angels. Captain Elmsley has gone to sea in order to gain money and help his Bishop, from which I was not able to dissuade him. He has also given me some land which I have already offered to the Rev. Jesuit Fathers in order to induce them to establish themselves.

"By the generosity of Toronto, of the Propagation of the Faith, of my relatives and friends, I have already paid $14,000 of my debts. I am availing myself of the vacancy in the see of Baltimore,* where I worked some time, to come here and receive gifts from my friends and establish purses for my diocese in the Grand and Little Seminaries of Baltimore, which are excellent."

In the Spring after his arrival he issued the following pastoral inviting the Catholics of the Diocese to contribute towards the liquidation of the Cathedral debt:

"Dearly Beloved Brethren: When our illustrious predecessor was questioned where he would find means for building the Cathedral of Toronto, he answered, 'In the hearts, faith, piety and devotedness of our poor but generous people.'

"Relying upon that sure and inexhaustible source, nine months before his glorious death he invited all of you, by the most impressive motives, to contribute towards his great undertaking, which, said he, could be completed or paid for only through the zealous co-operation of the city and whole diocese of Toronto. 'Let every one (pastoral address of the 29th of December, 1846) give with a good heart whatever he can spare, and this noble pile will soon stand before all as a monument of your zeal for the glory of the House of God. If any one should be unable to contribute at once let him treasure up daily, weekly and monthly, whatever he purposes to give for his mother church. We would be very sorry to place any bounds to your liberality; but there are none that have been in this favored Province for a short time who cannot contribute at least five shillings towards this sacred edifice. Your faith teaches you that God leaves no

---

* It was in the interval between the death of Archbishop Ecclestone and the consecration of Archbishop Francis Patrick Kenrick.

good work unrewarded, and that therefore by your contributions you will prepare abundant blessings for yourselves, for your children, and for your children's children for generations to come.'

"Your first Bishop's heroic charity, dearly beloved brethren, made him give his life for you, before you gave him your contributions; I say for you, Catholics of the Diocese, as well as for those of Toronto, because when, during the raging typhus of 1847, he was pressed not to expose himself but to send for some country missionaries. 'No!' was his reply. 'My missionaries will not send for me on such occasions—let every one—let me be at my post!'

"It is in the name of that magnanimous Pontiff, dearly beloved brethren, that we, his unworthy successor, come now to beg of you what you would give him for his Cathedral, were he to come from Heaven to receive himself your generosities.

"On our arrival we found a debt of £11,216 11s. Owing to the unparalleled liberality of Toronto, combined with our exertions, blessed by Pius IX., we have diminished the debt by £2,500, and destined the interest of the same to our contemplated schools.

"Dearly beloved brethren, be proud, as I am, of our brethren of Toronto; at the end of October last, they gave us in cash for our debt £160. During November thirteen hundred of them subscribed £1,300, to be paid within twelve months, and have paid for their first instalment upwards of £250, besides the £23 given every Sunday either at the door of the Church or at the Offertory, and £163 as a Christmas gift.

"Who could believe all this done in four months by a congregation of six or seven thousand, amongst whom so many are late immigrants in distress? Catholics of the diocese! I am sure you will imitate the nobleness of Toronto; and you—ever very liberal even to foreigners—will not have the blame of sending abroad your own Bishop for the purpose of begging on behalf of so rich a Province. Yes! We will pay the debt of our Cathedral! The House of God shall cease to be the property of men; and we pledge ourselves (besides offering up weekly, and on the 29th day of September in each year, the Holy Sacrifice for St. Michael's benefactors) to apply the interest of such amount as you may please to contribute towards the liquidation of the debt, in enriching your numerous and always increasing missions with new and select missionaries.

"Unless the Clergy exert themselves, 'as they are bound to do,' wrote our predecessor, 'the people will not take the interest that they should do in the Cathedral.' But, far from any such danger, thank God, we have already received substantial proofs of the zealous and liberal co-operation of our venerated co-laborers. Moreover, we have been obliged to moderate the excessive contributions of some of them.

"Wherefore, according to the direction of your late Bishop, in each mission let a committee be formed, composed of the clergymen and two or three laymen, who will receive donations and subscriptions for the Cathedral at stated times, and send every sum of £5 to us, or to Mr. Maurice Scollard at the Bank of Upper Canada, in Toronto, with the names and donations of the subscribers, that they may be published successively in the columns of the 'The Mirror,' to which journal we are already very much indebted for many valuable services.

"This letter shall be read in all the Churches and Stations, throughout the Diocese, on the Sundays immediately after Easter and on the Sunday previous to our visitation, during which we will have the pleasure of reading from the altar the list of the subscriptions of our benefactors.

"Pray for your Bishop, dearly beloved brethren; he wants it much more than money; and may the Almighty pour down His blessings on your spiritual and temporal concerns! Amen

"Toronto, March 25th, 1851."

The zeal and devotion of the earnest Bishop were already bearing fruit in the spiritual, the educational, and the material order of the diocese.

On May 1st, 1851, the five Christian Brothers referred to in the report were installed by Brother Patrick, who afterwards became Assistant Superior of the Order in Paris. These devoted sons of the Blessed De La Salle have, to the advantage of growing generations, ever since been in charge of the Toronto Separate Schools.

In October of the same year four Sisters of St. Joseph came from Philadelphia to take charge of the poor. This was the mustard seed of charity which, grown to a goodly tree, has now spread its branches over the four dioceses of Toronto, Hamilton, London and Peterborough—the first of those saintly handmaids of religion who, in the schools, orphanages and hospitals, have done such noble work in the various occupations of corporal and spiritual mercy. Their interesting history will be found in another chapter of this volume. Sufficient will it be here to quote concerning them from Bishop de Charbonnel's second report to Rome, dated Baltimore, May 18th, 1852. He writes: "My Sisters of Charity have a happy success, and we have been able to found a branch in the second city of the Diocese, Hamilton. Those of Toronto have charge of 55 orphans, visit the sick, help the poor."

The House of Providence.

It was not until 1856 that Bishop de Charbonnel undertook the building of the House of Providence, for which delay he apologizes in his pastoral: "Had we not found a debt of £12,000, with a yearly interest of £700, to be liquidated when we arrived amongst you, dear brethren; had it not been our first duty to build a college, a female academy, and make provision for religious education, an indispensable foundation of all good, immigrants in distress would have been the principal object of our devotedness."

"Be not astonished," he continues, "dear brethren at those special feelings of our heart towards emigrants; we ourself, an emigrant's son, whose parents and relations received in the greatest distress the kindest hospitality in Germany and England; and our tender mother was so kind towards the companions of her adversity in the land of exile, that she sold a part of her fine dress to support a starving octogenarian emigrant.

"Besides giving a little comfort to poor emigrants in our House of Providence, could we not therein also attend some special cases of sickness and gather up some more orphans? We supported 30 of them a few years ago; we support now 80, and had we more room we might receive a hundred more.

"Another motive for increasing our houses of beneficence is that indigence, idleness, mendicancy, intemperance, and all immoralities, are too often sisters living together; therefore, to suppress, or at least to diminish these domestic and social disorders, which will be one of the main objects of the House of Providence, is one of the best works of moralization; and this want is so much felt that one of our members, dear brethren, has already subscribed £200, and several others have made generous offers for the same purpose.

"A personal reason for us to found that House of Providence is our long desire to die in a house of the kind; as soon as our Holy Father, our supreme master upon earth, will give his consent to our withdrawal from the government of this diocese, we will resign St. Michael's House into other hands, to make of your House of Providence our resting place. There, emigrant, poor, old and infirm, we will be the chaplain, the servant, the friend, the father of all the suffering or afflicted inmates of that house of your benevolence, and so we will prepare ourselves for that happy death promised to the merciful—mercy, happiness and glory."

Erection of the Dioceses of Hamilton and London.

The last paragraph speaks clearly the zealous but heavy-hearted Bishop's mind upon one point, his continued aversion for the episcopate and his desire for retiring. As early as the second year after his consecration we find him making strong representations to Rome upon the necessity of accepting his resignation, or at least of granting an auxiliary who by language would be more in touch with the people. In 1853 he had succeeded in having a very strong appeal, if not command, made to an eminent Sulpitian* of Montreal, to be associated with him as Coadjutor Bishop. It was Bishop de Charbonnel's intention for one to remain in Toronto, while the other was to reside at Hamilton. He suggested that on account of Hamilton's central position it should be raised to an archbishopric. Through the humility of the priest referred to, the plan was a failure. His Lordship therefore asked that two new Sees be erected, one at Hamilton, the other at London. To this effect the Council of Quebec, on June 3rd, 1854, petitioned the Holy See; and the following year the Council again pressed its prayer most urgently. The prelates plead the great necessity of priests. "In the division of Hamilton," they write, "there is one mission of more than 15,000 Catholics where there are only two priests. The Rural Dean of London could not succeed in four years in getting any help for his vast mission." The necessities of schools, worship, instruction, discipline, were all laid before the Propaganda with such force that the prayer was readily

---

* The late venerable Father Dowd.

granted and the bulls issued establishing the two Sees of Hamilton and
London. The Rt. Rev. John Farrell of Peterborough was consecrated
Bishop of Hamilton on May 11th, 1856, by Mgr. de Charbonnel; and the
Rt. Rev. Peter Adolphe Pinsonneault was consecrated at Montreal, the
18th of the same month, Bishop of London.

It was for the accomplishment of this great work that the Bishops of
Canada in Council at Quebec gave Dr. de Charbonnel the title of " Father
and founder of the ecclesiastical province of Toronto," and wrote to Pius
IX. " that his works were prodigious and they struck everyone with
astonishment."

All important as the erection of these two Sees was, it by no means
absorbed the attention of the zealous Bishop, whose work of establishing
the Sisters of St. Joseph in this diocese was the last we noticed. In
August, 1852, four Basilians, with the Very Rev. Father Soulerin as
Superior, arrived at Toronto, to begin a Catholic College. No work was so
dear to the heart of Bishop de Charbonnel as that of education, and
especially the proper formation of young men for the holy priesthood. He
writes May 30th, 1853:—" I have received from Providence 15 workmen
whom I deem good and some excellent. Of these last are five Basilian
priests,* who direct my rising Seminary. I have bought some adjacent
land and built an addition to the episcopal residence† at a price of $9,600.
I have already thirty students, who give hope, and of whom four will soon
be studying logic. I have six others in theology at Montreal, one at
Quebec, one at All Hallows, with whom the different Superiors are well
satisfied; so that in a few years, *si Deus incrementum dat* (if God give the
increase), we shall have missionaries, children of the soil, well called and
formed to the ecclesiastical spirit, learning and discipline.

SEPARATE SCHOOLS.

Another kindred subject was the perplexing and serious question of
Separate Schools. From Bishop de Charbonnel's residence in Montreal
for several years he was quite conversant with the state of education in
Lower Canada, as well as with the struggles which the Upper Canadian

---

* The fifth was Father Molony, who had come out with the Bishop on his first arrival in Toronto.
† The old St. Vincent Chapel.

Catholics were maintaining on behalf of Separate Schools. When, therefore, upon his arrival as Bishop of Toronto, he found the Act of 1850 ready to be put into force he knew the ground upon which he stood and the task which lay before him. At the close of the first year of his episcopate he wrote to Rome upon the subject: "I purpose to neglect nothing to assure the success of this vital question." He certainly kept his resolution with the courage of his ancestral crusaders. "In season and out of season," "in good repute and evil repute;" amidst the insults of mobs and the calumniating misrepresentations of more insidious foes; now in council with his fellow-bishops, now single-handed, Bishop de Charbonnel fought the fight for the conscience of his people. He petitioned the political authorities; he commanded his own subjects; he appealed to the religious faith of every Catholic member of the House of Parliament and to the justice of every fair-minded Upper Canadian. His whole episcopate was one continual struggle against an autocratic Superintendent, against wily politicians and against popular bigotry upon this vital subject. The success he achieved was not all that could be desired; but, considering the circumstances, it was a great deal. To explain his stand upon the subject we quote at length from a letter written to Dr. Ryerson, Chief Superintendent of Education, dated May 1st, 1852:

"I read secondly in the correspondence of that great Archbishop whom the whole Church lamented, the mediator between Ireland and England, the Dove of Dublin. In Ireland it was required that in all the schools for the education of the poor, the Bible, without notes, should be read in the presence of all the pupils of all the schools, and that the catechism and all books of that kind should be excluded. Is not this the case in our mixed schools? 'These regulations (continues the incomparable Dr. Murray) our Bishop resisted and endeavored most earnestly to withdraw the Catholic pupils from the schools of that kind. That a remedy might be provided for this most wretched state of things, our Government, strongly urged by me, and others, at length decided to establish another system of educating the poor, which would be more acceptable to the Catholics.'

"Suffer me then, Mr. Superintendent, to obey God rather than man, and to resist, as did the loyal and conciliating Archbishop, your unhappy school system, strive to rescue from it my dear children, and to remedy this great scourge by urging our Government to give us a system which will be acceptable to us—a system which shall not render the condition of the Irish here worse than it is in Ireland—a system worthy of American or Canadian liberalism, so much wanted in this world, unless Upper Canada prefers to continue, what I cannot, in strict logic, call anything but a cruel and disguised persecution.

"I have said, that if the catechism were sufficiently taught in the family or by the pastor, so rare in this large Diocese, and if the mixed schools were exclusively for secular instruction, and without danger to our Catholics, in regard to masters, books and companions, the Catholic Hierarchy might tolerate it, as I have done in certain localities, after having made due inquiry.

"Otherwise, in default of these conditions, it is forbidden to our faithful to send their children to these schools, on pain of the refusal of the Sacraments; because the soul and heaven above everything; because the foot, the hand, the eye, occasions of sin, ought to be sacrificed to salvation; because, finally, Jesus Christ has confided the mission of instruction which has civilized the world to no others than the Apostles and their successors to the end of time.

"It is their right, so sacred and inalienable, that every wise and paternal christian governor has made laws respecting instruction only in perfect harmony with the teaching Church—the Bishops united to their supreme and universal Head; and this right is so inviolable that of late, as well as in former times, in France, in Belgium, in Prussia, in Austria, as in Ireland, the Bishops, with the Pope, have done everything to overthrow or modify every school or university system opposed to the mission given by Jesus Christ to His sacred college.

"'Go therefore teach all nations, and preach to every creature (St. Mark), teaching them to observe all things whatsoever I have commanded you, and lo, I am with you even to the end of the world.' (St. Matthew.) 'He that believeth shall be saved, and he that believeth not shall be condemned.'" (St. Mark).

THE PROGRESS OF THE DIOCESE.

While the educational struggle was a continual anxiety to Dr. De Charbonnel he still had energy to give to the material order of the diocese, which steadily advanced. New churches were built, new parishes formed. In the city, St. Mary's Church on Bathurst street was erected in 1851; and, after being served from the Cathedral for a few years, had a resident pastor for the first time in 1854. St. Basil's parish was started for the northern portion, when the Basilian Fathers removed to their property on St. Joseph street in 1856; St. Patrick's parish was the last established in the city under Bishop de Charbonnel. The country kept pace. Barrie in 1855 started a distinguished roll of zealous pastors with Father Jamot, afterwards Bishop of Peterborough, while Brock could boast of having as its first pastor no less a person than the present Archbishop of Toronto. The following year Orillia was opened with Father Synnot as parish priest.

The returns for 1859 give 33 priests in the diocese. Adjala was divided into two parishes; Streetsville and Fort Erie were also formed. The state of the Cathedral debt may be gathered from the following extract of a letter written by Bishop de Charbonnel to the President of the Propagation of the Faith at Lyons, France, dated Quebec, May 28th, 1855: "I hasten therefore to tell you that, thanks to the gifts of the Propagation of the Faith, the debt with which the Church had burthened me is nearly altogether extinct, and to repeat to you in my gratitude that without some unforeseen misfortune I hope to spare you funds in favor of some Bishop poorer than I am."

In this same report his Lordship tells us that there were three Conferences of the St. Vincent de Paul Society, and that he celebrated the Definition of the Immaculate Conception during the first three Sundays of February with all the pomp of which they were capable. The Atlantic cable was not then laid; so that it was some time after the definition when the news was announced in Toronto.

The state of the diocese and its vast extent kept Bishop de Charbonnel always on the move. During the first two years of his episcopate he did not pass a dozen Sundays at home. In May, 1851, he was at Baltimore collecting; and shortly after at Quebec attending the first Provincial Council. The following year his Lordship was again at Baltimore at the

Plenary Council of the American Church. In 1854, at the request of Bishop Spalding, he preached a retreat to the Clergy of Louisville, Kentucky. There he met for the first time his countryman, Father Bruyere, whom he afterwards induced to come to Toronto, and whom, in 1857, he made his Vicar-General. In 1855, in company with Archbishop Hughes of New York, and Bishop McKinnon of Arichat, Nova Scotia, Bishop de Charbonnel assisted at the opening of the new Cathedral at St. John's, Newfoundland, when he consecrated one of the altars. He visited Rome twice, first in 1856 and again in 1857.

Concerning the visitation of his own diocese, his Lordship writes: "My health permits me to travel and collect continually in the diocese; while at the same time I preach, hear confessions, confirm, officiate, inspect; and my expenses of house, table, clothes, travel, are reduced to almost nothing. I travel alone and by ways as economical as they are incommodious; but all that is nothing in comparison with the pleasure of liquidating the debt put upon me; of founding and ameliorating useful institutions, all in keeping a state of health which is almost scandalous; another would be sick unto death—the worst news and business have not yet deprived me of three minutes' sleep when I throw myself upon my couch, nor a mouthful when I go to table; and however, I drink only water and milk. There is something more; it is, that if I could laugh in English as well as I can in French my gaiety would be excessive."

His Lordship Resigns and Returns to France.

Through all this growth of religion, while others admired, one alone was never satisfied—Bishop de Charbonnel himself. In his own eyes he was but a useless servant. It mattered not that his zeal and self-denial had freed the diocese from debt, had started and fostered much-needed institutions; that his prudence and judgment of character had peopled the country with a new generation of earnest priests; and that his courage had remained undaunted in the great battle of religious education. In his own sight all this was nothing. It was not enough that he had been freed from two-thirds of his diocese; he longed for a coadjutor more kindred to his people, who would free him still more. To the first steps which his Lordship took for this purpose before the Holy See, Pius IX. replied: "I have received only praise of your administration." The Pope sent the Bishop to make a retreat at St. Eusebius that he might content himself with remaining Bishop of Toronto. He obeyed and returned to his See, but only to renew his prayer more earnestly the following year (1858). This time it was granted; Father Lynch, President of the College of the Holy Angels, Niagara Falls, was chosen and consecrated coadjutor, Nov. 20th, 1859. On the feast of the Purification, Feb. 2nd, 1860, Bishop de Charbonnel performed for the last time his episcopal functions in Toronto by consecrating the High Altar in St. Michael's Cathedral. Two addresses were presented his Lordship, one on behalf of the Clergy by the Rev. Father Walsh, now Archbishop Walsh; the other on behalf of the laity. In a few days he started for Europe. He resigned his See April 26th, 1860, when he was named Bishop of Sozopolis.

Later the same year there might have been seen at the novitiate of the Capuchin Monastery of Auguste (Alma) in the Roman Province, a novice as remarkable for his fervor as he was distinguished for his age and dignity. It was Bishop de Charbonnel. Thither had his love of poverty and sacrifice attracted him. At the close of his novitiate he returned to France and took up his residence at Lyons. Honors which he had avoided with such care and laid aside with such self-denial, still pursued him in his monastic retreat. He was offered one of the Sees of Algeria, which he refused. He consecrated the rest of his life to preaching and to the conducting of retreats. But the work of his predilection, to which he gave his whole soul, was the Propagation of the Faith. His simple evangelical word, original in its expression and spoken with the ardor of an apostolic heart, produced the most wonderful results of generous devotion both in town and country. His success caused the two central councils of the Association to ask the Supreme Pontiff that Mgr. de Charbonnel should be entrusted with the mission of preaching everywhere in favor of the Propagation of the Faith. "None," wrote the Presidents, "have the work more at heart or understand so well the means of spreading it by preaching. Undoubtedly very few possess in so high a degree the art of drawing the multitudes, and very few see their words followed by more consoling results." Accordingly Cardinal Barnabo, through the Superior General of the Capuchins, imposed this work upon Bishop de Charbonnel, and recommended all Ordinaries to treat with the greatest respect a Bishop "who had deserved most excellently of the Catholic religion." (*De Catholica religione optime meritum.*)

Not long after his return to France he was appointed Auxiliary to Cardinal Bonald, Archbishop of Lyons, whom he represented at the Vatican Council. His time was very much occupied with the various episcopal functions. But this did not prevent him undertaking and performing much more. In fact he seemed to multiply his works, as he advanced in age. More than fifty ecclesiastical retreats, besides those given to religious communities, missions in parishes, confirmation in six different dioceses, ordinations for years at Lyons and Annonay, were the works of supererogation of this indefatigable laborer. To those who represented that so much was not compatible with his age and dignity he replied: "We shall rest in heaven; here below we must work for the good Master."

Upon one of these occasions, when he was in Paris at the Church of St. Roch, a collection for the Irish, who were suffering from famine at the time, was taken up, in which Lady McMahon was deeply interested. The venerable Bishop de Charbonnel, in his generosity, took off his pectoral cross, and threw it into the plate, exclaiming: "I am but a poor Capuchin: I have nothing; but I cannot forget my Irish people of Montreal and Toronto—I give my cross." The following day the cross was returned to him, having been redeemed at a high price.

It must not, however, be supposed that Bishop de Charbonnel was merely an active minister of religion, mighty in word and work. He was especially a man of God, a man of deep interior spirit, indefatigably devoted to the work of his own perfection, as edifying by the simplicity of his manners as by the austerity of his life and the practice of those virtues which form saintly priests. Many are the stories of his humility, while his spirit of mortification rendered his house by no means pleasant to such as did not feel called to lead a severe monastic life. His love of poverty is shown in the following anecdote: a friend met his Lordship in a third-class railway carriage, and enquired how it was that a gentleman of his rank and years travelled third class. "Because," was the characteristic reply, "there is no fourth class." Of undoubted talent, and still more exalted virtue, he was a bishop of the primitive Church; and, like them, he has left his mark wherever he passed. The clergy of France, the immigrants of Montreal, the people of Toronto, still bear the fruits of his cultured learning, his zealous charity and his indefatigable labors.

Archbishop of Sozopolis.

He had been away from Canada about ten years when Toronto was raised to an archdiocese, and in 1880 Archbishop Lynch of Toronto, Bishops Walsh of London, Crinnon of Hamilton, and Jamot of the Northern Vicariate,* petitioned the Pope that His Holiness would give Mgr. de Charbonnel some special mark of satisfaction " for the signal services he had rendered the Church both in Canada and France by raising him to the rank of Archbishop." Cardinal Caverot, Archbishop of Lyons, associated himself to the plan in very warm terms, deeming it a debt of gratitude which he and his people owed to this venerable prelate. The petition was granted. On Dec. 16th, 1880, His Holiness, Leo XIII., issued a decree, ordering that Mgr. Armand Francis Marie de Charbonnel, Bishop of Sozopolis, shall enjoy the hierarchical degree, title and honor of Archbishop of Sozopolis and the title of Archbishop, so that henceforth he shall be called Archbishop—Bishop of Sozopolis.

The honor he then received neither turned him away from his work nor exalted him in his own eyes. It was only in 1883, when his failing strength prevented him undergoing the fatigue of preaching and administering, that he gave up any portion of his labors and withdrew to La Roch, not far from Lyons. He afterwards retired to a small Capuchin monastery at Crest, a small town in the Department of Drome, for the purpose, as he used to say himself, of making by prayer and austerity a more immediate preparation for eternity. He kept on working, and it was only at the age of eighty-five that he wrote most affectionately and mournfully to the Superior of the Basilians at Annonay that he could never go to ordain any more members of that family he loved so well. But if he could not go abroad he could do something at home ; so he used to hear confessions in the monastery. Quietly his life passed on like the slow ebb of a placid sea, or the calm sunset of a long summer day. The end came and found him still at work. On Holy Saturday, when he had spent several hours in the confessional, he was taken ill, and on the following day, Easter Sunday, March 29th, 1891, the soul of this venerable, saintly prelate passed to its reward for the long and useful life worn out in the glory of God and the salvation of his neighbour.

On the Wednesday following the funeral service, at which the Bishop of Valence presided, was held in the parish church at Crest. The Cardinal

---

* The Diocese of Kingston was vacant at the time.

of Lyons was represented at the obsequies. All that was mortal of the great, apostolic Bishop de Charbonnel was then placed in the vault of the Capuchin Convent of Crest. His grave is there; but his monument is in our very midst; and his memory is in benediction.

ADDENDA.

We subjoin a short sketch of the late venerable Monsignore Bruyere, the latter part of whose career was spent in London, but whose name will ever be closely associated with that of Dr. de Charbonnel as Bishop of Toronto, not only because of the close friendship which existed between them, but especially for the active part which the Monsignore took in the defence and cause of religion during his residence in Toronto.

Jean Marie Bruyere was born at Chezelles, a pretty village situated on the Rhone in the south of France, not far from the great city of Lyons. He received Holy Orders in 1830, and ten years after, volunteered his sacerdotal services to the American mission, of the labours and sacrifices of which he had heard through the renown of his saintly countryman, Bishop Flaget, the apostle and pioneer prelate of Kentucky. When in 1840 Father Bruyere arrived at Louisville, Kentucky, he was appointed professor of dogmatic theology in the College of Bardstown. At this time, Father Martin John Spalding, afterwards Bishop of Louisville, and later still Archbishop of Baltimore, was pastor of the Cathedral of Bardstown. Between them a cordial intimacy sprang up, so that when elevated to the episcopate Bishop Spalding urgently invited Father Bruyere to take charge of the Cathedral of Louisville, which the latter accepted in 1848. From Louisville he came to Toronto in 1854, and was placed in charge of St. Michael's Cathedral, where " by his unfeigned piety, his devotion to duty, his condescension and kindness he commanded the respect and admiration of all classes." His celebrated controversy with the Chief Superintendent of Education upon the Catholic School Question attracted widespread attention and proved him to be a most vigorous writer and valiant champion of religious freedom.

In 1857 he was appointed Vicar-General by the following letter from Bishop de Charbonnel, who at the time was in Rome: " Very Rev. and

Dear Sir—In consideration of your services, particularly in the cause of Catholic education, or rather to speak a more apostolic language, in order that you may more effectually serve the Church, be pleased to accept the titles of Vicar-General of the Diocese of Toronto, and of Administrator of the same in case of death, with all faculties, which, for the due performance of these two-fold duties, and by the authority of the Holy See, we can and do confer upon you."

After the retirement of Bishop de Charbonnel from the See of Toronto, at the urgent request of Bishop Pinsonneault, and with the consent of his Ordinary, Father Bruyere went to the London Diocese, continuing his work of zeal in the capacity of Vicar-General and rector of the Cathedral of Sandwich. Besides the parochial duties incumbent upon him, from which he never relaxed, he was often deputed to fulfill difficult tasks of a diplomatic character, which he never failed to accomplish to the best interests of all concerned.

Shortly after the arrival of Dr. Walsh as Bishop he continued the good priest in his office and dignity. When his Lordship changed the See to London Father Bruyere accompanied him, and for over twenty years continued there the faithful exercise of his priestly functions and the holy practice of his priestly virtues, so exemplary, so eminent and so manifold. In all his relations with his brother priests he was most courteous and condescending, while towards episcopal authority he was a model of loyalty and obedience. Without being ascetic he was a man of great piety, faith and prayer. He was the first to enter the Church for his meditation in the morning, and the last to leave his post in the confessional at night. His charities were of that nature which does not permit the left hand to know what the right hand doeth. Sixty years of service, with no extravagance of living, no luxury, with only a few books, not enough saved to bury him! Such was the result of his labors.

While on a visit to Rome Bishop Walsh obtained from the Holy Father, Pius IX., the elevation of Vicar-General Bruyere to the Roman Prelature. The decree reads as follows: "Beloved Son—Health and Apostolic Benediction. We are aware of your merits, so consonant with the excellence and dignity of an ecclesiastical person, that we are induced to confer upon you an honor which will be an evidence of our paternal affection for you. Wherefore we absolve you from all ecclesiastical censures, which would be an obstacle in this matter, if you have incurred any, and by these letters, by our Apostolic authority, we choose, appoint and declare you to be a Monsignore of this city, that is to say, our domestic prelate. Therefore, beloved son, you may freely and lawfully wear the robe and cape commonly called *Manteletta*, of violet color, and outside of the Roman Court, the Rochet; and by the same authority, and in virtue of these presents, we grant to you the enjoyment of all the rights, faculties, indults, privileges, prerogatives and precedencies which our other domestic prelates use and enjoy, and which they are, or will be, entitled to use and enjoy, all other Apostolic constitutions and decrees to the contrary notwithstanding.

" Dated at Rome at St. Peter's under the seal of the Fisherman, 12th December, 1876, in the thirty-first year of our Pontificate."

Monsignore Bruyere lived to enjoy this well-deserved token of his Bishop's respect and friendship for a little over eleven years, when he died at the patriarchal age of ninety-two on Feb. 13th, 1888. His name, like the names of his countrymen, Bishops Flaget, de Charbonnel, Jamot, will ever be found amongst the apostles and missionaries of this Western Continent.*

---

* This account of Monsignore Bruyere is substantially taken from "The Catholic Record," London, Ontario.

THE LIFE AND TIMES OF THE MOST REV. JOHN JOSEPH LYNCH,

ARCHBISHOP OF TORONTO,

BY

THE HON. T. W. ANGLIN,

EX-SPEAKER OF THE HOUSE OF COMMONS.

THE MOST REV. JOHN JOSEPH LYNCH,
First Archbishop of Toronto.

BORN AT CLONES, COUNTY MONAGHAN, IRELAND, FEBRUARY 6th, 1816
DIED AT TORONTO, MAY 14th, 1888.

CHAPTER VI.

1859-1888.

THE LIFE AND TIMES OF ARCHBISHOP LYNCH.

Birth and Education—Missionary Career—College of the Holy Angels—Bishop of Toronto—Archbishop—Silver Jubilee—Death.

> "And, to add greater honours to his age
> Than man could give him, he died,
> Fearing God."—KING HENRY VIII., Act iv. Sc. 2.

ALTHOUGH Catholicity had made such wonderful progress in Upper Canada while Bishop Power and Bishop de Charbonnel governed the Diocese of Toronto, the condition of the Church in this Province was still in many respects unsatisfactory. The religious institutions founded by those Bishops were yet in their infancy and required infinite care and constant effort to sustain and develop them; others were required and must be established as soon as possible. The number of priests was far too small, and to increase their number was very difficult. The churches, few in number, were nearly all mere temporary structures, scarcely sufficient to shelter those who could assemble in them. In many districts the Catholics were so few in number, so scattered, and so poor, as to be unable to erect even the most humble chapels. These districts a priest seldom visited, unless when called to administer the last Sacraments to the dying. To hear Mass and approach the Sacraments were blessings which the Catholics so situated could enjoy only on rare occasions and at long intervals. The priests, overburdened with the other labors of their ministry, could not even in the cities and towns attend sufficiently to the religious instruction and training of Catholic children. In country districts Catholic children had little opportunity of learning any more of their religion than their parents, sometimes ignorant, generally exhausted by excessive labour, could impart; and knowledge, strength of mind and the most robust faith were there required to resist the malarious influence of the anti-Catholic atmosphere in which they lived. Bigotry, prejudice and intolerance were rampant, and rendered the condition of many Catholic families almost intolerable; and the majority, hoping that the Common School would prove the grave of Catholicity, opposed every amendment of the School Law which the Catholics demanded.

It was evident that if Catholicity was not to suffer serious losses in the conflict in which all human powers and influences were arrayed against it, the successor of Bishop de Charbonnel must be a man of great ability, of great learning, eloquent, full of zeal, full of energy, self-sacrificing, pious, prudent, practical, conciliatory and courageous; one whose devotion to duty and simplicity of life all good men must admire; one to whom, because of his learning, his earnestness, his moderation and his charity, the fiercest fanatic must listen with respect. Providence, which orders all things wisely, had prepared such a man for the position.

Birth and Education.

John Joseph Lynch was born near Clones, in the County of Monaghan, Ireland, in the year 1816. Owing largely to the influence of his mother, of whom he always spoke with loving reverence, he, at a very early age, was filled with a desire to become a priest, and to devote his life to the propagation of the faith in infidel lands, or to the service of those of his fellow countrymen in America, who, for want of priests, were unable to practise their religion. The purity of his life, his piety, the regularity with which he received the sacraments, and his earnest devotion to the Blessed Virgin, proved that he was indeed called by God, and that he was true to his vocation. He received his early education at a school in Lucan taught by a graduate of the Dublin University, and he was there distinguished for his bright intellect and his attention to his studies. When seventeen years of age he went to the Academy of St. Joseph at Clondalkin, where he spent a year and a half, and in 1835 he entered the College of the Lazarists at Castleknock, established a short time previously. There he studied diligently for two years. Those who knew him in after life will not be surprised to learn that he excelled in logic, and that he was the most active member of the Literary Club of the College, which he founded. His ability to govern even then manifested itself, and he was made Prefect of the boys. He finished the collegiate course at Castleknock in 1837; and having then determined to join the Lazarist Order—the Congregation of the Priests of the Mission—he was sent to the Seminary of St. Lazare, Paris, the first postulant from the College at Castleknock. There he spent three years earnestly striving to prepare for the work of the Foreign Missions, in which he hoped to be engaged, and devoting every hour which he could spare from the regular work of his class to the study of history, sacred and profane, for which the fine library of the Seminary afforded special facilities. In due time he received minor orders and sub-deaconship from Mgr. Affre, the Archbishop of Paris, who a few years afterwards was killed at the barricades, a martyr of charity. His superiors soon after determined that he should return to Ireland, there to be ordained priest, and take part in the work in which the Lazarists were engaged. Longing for the realization of the wishes and hopes of his boyhood and youth, he begged that he should rather be sent on a Mission to the heathens, or allowed to work in any of the countries in which Irish Catholics were so much in need of priests. His superiors thought the work then to be done in Ireland of great importance; and with that profound respect for authority for which he was so distinguished throughout his whole life, he submitted to their decision and returned to Castleknock. In June, 1843, he was ordained deacon and priest at Maynooth by Dr. Murray, Archbishop of Dublin, and on the feast of Corpus Christi he celebrated his first Mass, at which his father and mother and brother and sisters assisted.

Missionary Career.

Father Lynch, full of zeal and energy, devoted himself earnestly to the laborious and exhausting work of the Missions. He took especial delight in instructing the young, expounding to them in simple language the great truths of Christianity, enkindling their enthusiasm, strengthening their faith with knowledge, and preparing them to resist successfully the temptations which many of them, he knew, must encounter.

In this work he was engaged until 1846, when Bishop Odin, himself a Lazarist, who had been appointed Vicar Apostolic of Texas, went to Ireland to look for priests who would aid him in the cultivation of that vast field of missionary work and enterprise. Father Lynch he found eager to accept his invitation; and his superiors, urged by the Bishop, who represented the deplorable condition of the country entrusted to his care, reluctantly gave their assent. He took passage for New Orleans in company with Father Fitzgerald, another Lazarist, who was also destined for the Texas mission. They landed in that city on June 29, 1847, and were kindly received by the Archbishop, Mgr. Blanc. Having obtained passage in a small steamer employed in carrying U. S. soldiers from New Orleans to Vera Cruz for service in the Mexican War, which had begun a short time before, they reached Galveston early in July and proceeded thence, accompanied by Bishop Odin, to Houston. This was to be their head-quarters for some time.

Texas was at that time sparsely settled. The population was to be found, as in this country in its earlier days, along the banks of the rivers. The total number of Catholics was supposed to be about ten thousand. Some were Mexicans, but the majority were Irish; and of these not a few were as fervent in their faith as when they trod the green hills of holy Ireland, and strove earnestly to transmit the faith to their children. But in many the want of priest and sacrifice and sacrament, and the Protestant influences by which they were surrounded, had chilled or paralysed the faith, so that it could scarcely be regarded as any longer living; and the children of such Catholics, if nothing were done to save them, would almost certainly become Protestants. Of those whose parents had never taken the trouble to teach them what Catholicity is, several were avowed Methodists or Baptists.

Father Lynch and Father Fitzgerald were the first priests who had ever been regularly stationed at Houston, which was but the centre of their operations. As soon as they were fairly settled there, and the necessary preparations were made, Father Lynch, on horse-back, with huge saddle-bags, in which were packed vestments and the other requisites for the Holy Sacrifice, and such changes of linen and other underclothing as were absolutely necessary, set out to look for Catholics wherever they might be found and to carry to them the consolations of religion. He was courteously and even kindly received everywhere. Wherever he found any Catholics he gave instructions, heard confessions, said Mass, gave Holy Communion to those who made due preparation, blessed marriages and baptized children. The Catholic churches of any description were very few and he usually heard confessions and said Mass in private houses, or in barns when the houses were not large enough. He preached in hotels, courthouses, and wherever he could get an audience. In Austin, the capital of the State, there was no Catholic Church. In the morning he said Mass in the house of a Catholic ; but in the evening the Legislative Chambers were placed at his disposal, and the Governor and several other Protestants were among the congregation. Indeed Protestants, many of whom had never seen a priest, moved by curiosity, crowded to hear him. Amongst those generally regarded as Protestants were some Catholics, who sought to be reconciled to the Church, pleading in excuse for their cowardly conduct that as there were no priests in the country and the Protestants were intensely prejudiced against Catholics, they thought it best to say nothing about their religion. All this involved constant and severe labor ; but the fatigue, hardships and exposure to intense heat and fierce storms which he had to undergo in searching for the Catholics who lived in remote settlements, and sometimes far from any settlement, were more exhausting and dangerous to health. Frequently, after a long day's journey, either because he had lost his way or had miscalculated the distance, he was compelled to sleep on the ground, with his saddle as a pillow, fortunate if no storm burst over the place where he lay. Sometimes, after riding all day in a drenching rain-storm, night overtook him far from any human habitation. He loved to tell of the many instances in which, while thus wandering, he was providentially led to the dwellings of Catholics, of whom he had not heard. More than once he was thus brought to the bedside of the dying in time to administer the last sacraments.

The satisfaction which he must have felt in reviving the faith of the indifferent and tepid, in bringing the consolations of religion to those in danger of death, and in the manifestations of joy and delight with which he was received by those who remained steadfast amidst trials and temptations must have done much to conteract the effect of the privations, sufferings and excessive fatigue to which he was so often exposed ; and when the weather was fine, and his daily journeys not too long, he imagined that he was even stronger and in better health than at any previous period of his life. He had even learned to prefer sleeping out of doors in fine weather when the alternative was spending the night in the stifling atmosphere of a badly kept bed-room in a Texas inn. But soon after his return to Houston in the fall of 1847 he was attacked by a fever which brought him to the point of death. He recovered, but he had not regained his strength when it became necessary for him to resume his labors, as the services of his assistant, Father Fitzgerald, were urgently required in another district. Excessive fatigue brought on a relapse, and again he seemed to be in danger of death. This attack of fever was followed by an attack of ague, which proved so debilitating that he was unable to discharge any of his duties. Bishop Odin took him to Galveston, hoping that change of air and careful nursing would restore his health; but when, after some months, there appeared to be no improvement, he accepted the invitation of Archbishop Blanc to spend some time in New Orleans. There he regained his strength so far as to be able to say Mass and hear Confessions occasionally, and to attend the invalid soldiers sent from the seat of war in Mexico to the Military Hospital near the city. But the fever still clung to him, often prostrating his strength completely, and on the approach of summer it was decided that he must proceed farther north. Accordingly in March he went to a Lazarist College in Missouri known as St. Mary's of the Barrens, which has given many zealous bishops and devoted priests to the Church. Having recovered his health and strength sufficiently, he was appointed President of the College. In this position, for which his qualities of mind and his experience at Castleknock and at St. Lazare seemed peculiarly to fit him, he was eminently successful. He introduced, as far as practicable, the system and discipline of the old Benedictine monasteries. His duties as President did not occupy all his time, nor did the most careful attention to those duties satisfy his zeal for the glory of God and the salvation of souls, and he frequently engaged in missionary work. In 1849 he was elected by the Lazarists in America to attend the general assembly of the Order which was held in Paris in that year. When the work of the assembly was done he visited Rome and had an interview with the Holy Father, Pope Pius the Ninth, who granted an indulgence to the students of St. Mary's to be obtained as often as they studied in presence of the Statue of the Blessed Virgin, which was placed in the study hall when the office of Prefect was abolished. Before he returned to America he made a brief visit to his family in Ireland. He loved to relate that soon after he reached home his pious mother said to him: "I am delighted to see you, but I did not ask for this blessing. I always invoke the assistance of the Blessed Virgin in anything I ask from God, and I always obtain it. I did not ask that you should come and see me. I was afraid to ask that, lest my prayer should be granted and I should thus be the means of taking you from your duties to God and to your people." It is no wonder that the son of such a mother was, during his whole life, remarkable for his simple, child-like faith, his spirit of self-denial and self-sacrifice, and his devotion to duty.

He was President of St. Mary's for seven years. It seemed that he had found the place in which he could be most useful, and that the rest of his life would be devoted to the work in which he was so successful. But this was not the will of God. He had partly recovered his strength, but the position of the College was so unhealthy that it was found necessary soon after to abandon it; and Father Lynch, in his zeal for God's service, disregarded the dictates of the most ordinary prudence. Exposure and excessive work brought on paralysis of the side. The attack for a time threatened to prove fatal, and from its effects he never fully recovered. It was obviously necessary that he should leave St. Mary's and seek farther north a place not scourged by fever and ague.

COLLEGE OF THE HOLY ANGELS.

In what he called "a discourse" delivered in November, 1881, Dr. Lynch stated that when he was a little boy a picture of Niagara Falls made a wonderful impression on him. "He gazed on it again and again with astonishment and delight, and raising his heart to God he anxiously enquired if there were Catholics living round the place where they could so well adore God, the Creator of heaven and earth and of all things. This image, this thought, this enquiry pursued him until he beheld multitudes of Catholics around the Falls with their temples of true worship, and with a College and Seminary to train up priests who would offer up the most holy sacrifice of the new law, and give honor and praise to God for ever and ever. This is the work of God: the conception came from Him, and the means and the perfection of the work." In the course of time he met Bishop Timon, then Bishop of Buffalo, who spoke of having Niagara Falls in his Diocese, and he asked: "Were there Catholics around it, and had they a Church?" "There are a few Catholics," was the reply; "but there is no church. Come to us and we shall have a church and a Seminary also." At that time it seemed to all who knew him that the education and training of young men for the priesthood was his especial vocation, and that it should be his life work. The invitation was renewed at intervals; and when in 1855 Father Lynch, having been again elected to represent the American Lazarists at a general assembly in Paris, obtained from the Superior General leave to accept the Bishop's invitation, the day-dream of his boyhood seemed to be fulfilled.

The establishment of the Seminary of Our Lady of the Angels was not without many and serious difficulties, and the beginnings were small. It was difficult to procure a suitable site, and difficult to get money sufficient to pay for the land required and for the buildings which must be erected. While the efforts to overcome these difficulties were made, Father Lynch devoted himself to the arduous work of giving Missions, and hardships, privations and overwork again brought on an attack of chills and fever. He had scarcely recovered from this when he returned to work, and again he was prostrated by sickness. When giving a retreat to young men in the Buffalo Cathedral he had an attack of erisypelas of a most dangerous character. All these difficulties were overcome by the help of Providence. A magnificent site within fifteen minutes drive of the Falls was secured for the Seminary. A priest, who had prayed for months that God would direct him how to use ten thousand dollars which was at his disposal, was led to bestow it upon Father Lynch for the Seminary; other donations were received; Father Lynch recovered his health, and a number of pious, intelligent youths presented themselves as candidates for the ministry. The grandeur and sublime beauty of the place inspired professors and students and did much to create a profundity of feeling and an elevation of thought, strengthening the purpose and purifying the aspirations of those who wished to devote their life to the service of God in religion. In the discourse to which we have referred Dr. Lynch said: "It was a delight on festival days to cross over to the island of Niagara Falls, and there to sing the Magnificat and other canticles in praise of God and His Blessed Mother. The scene was grand and the chant soul-stirring. Before us was the mighty cataract, with clouds of incense arising at Nature's high altar. The booming of the falling torrents was a solemn bass to the vocal praise of a few Catholic boys with pure hearts and noble intentions and resolves to serve that God who speaks in the voice of many waters." Of the total number of students during the first twenty-five years of the Seminary's existence it is estimated that three hundred became priests. The number ordained in the Seminary during that period was two hundred and fifty. What, as Dr. Lynch said in his discourse, must at first have appeared "the wild project of a penniless enthusiast" soon proved to be the work of wisdom which, under Providence, relies on the zeal and self-sacrificing spirit of the Catholic priesthood and the faith and generosity of the Catholic people.

When the success of the Seminary was assured Father Lynch, who saw the hopes, the aspirations, the longings of his boyhood thus realized, might well have thought that this place, to which Providence had led him by paths so long, so difficult, and apparently so devious, was to be his permanent abode ; that here he would for the rest of his life do, in obedience to God's will, the work for which he was by many deemed to be especially destined. But he had not yet reached the goal. We see now—what he could not have known then—that he was still undergoing preparation, spiritual and intellectual, for the work, more important for the glory of God and for the salvation of souls, in which he was so long to be engaged.

It has been already stated that Bishop de Charbonnel, on a visit to the Irish College at Paris, first heard of Father Lynch and of the establishment of the Seminary of the Holy Angels from Father McNamara of the Irish College in that city. Father McNamara spoke so highly of his fellow-student that the Bishop, as he afterwards related, said to himself: " I have found my coadjutor." On his return to Canada the Bishop called on Father Lynch and invited him to preach a retreat to the nuns of St. Joseph's, Toronto, and afterwards to give a mission in St. Michael's Cathedral. This was in the summer of 1858. The Bishop, finding that he possessed the great qualities which Father McNamara had so enthusiastically described, besought the Pope to give him the assistance of Father Lynch in the work which had become too heavy for him to perform unaided. Of this the Bishop, perhaps fearing another disappointment, said nothing ; and when, in September, 1859, Father Lynch received the Bulls appointing him coadjutor Bishop with the right of succession, he was so surprised that he could not for some time determine what he ought to do. He loved the work in which he was then engaged, and the Seminary still required all that his piety, his learning, his experience and his zeal could do for it to ensure its success. He dreaded the turmoil, the excitement, the life of continued effort and struggle to which he was now called, and in his humility he shrank from undertaking the dread responsibilities of the Episcopate. He prayed for God's guidance ; he sought the advice of many friends. Forced to the conclusion that it was the will of God, he at length consented to take up the heavy burden which God's Vicegerent thought fit to impose upon him, and on the 20th of November he was consecrated in St. Michael's Cathedral by the Bishop of Toronto, assisted by Bishop Farrell of Hamilton and Bishop Timon of Buffalo.

BISHOP OF TORONTO.

When, in the following April, Bishop de Charbonnel's resignation was accepted, Dr. Lynch became Bishop of Toronto. The difficulties with which he found himself surrounded might almost be regarded as appalling—difficulties from within and difficulties from without. The want of priests too often leads to apathy on the part of the people, and to a spirit of insubordination which sometimes assumes the mask of religious zeal. Bishop de Charbonnel had done all in his power to supply the want of priests. He had induced several saintly ecclesiastics to come from France to his assistance, some of whom remain with us to this day, edifying their flocks by their piety and their devotion to God's service. But in the whole diocese, when Dr. Lynch became Bishop, there were only thirty-six priests, including the four Basilian Fathers in charge of St. Michael's College. Of the thirty-six, four returned to France with Bishop de Charbonnel, and others soon after. As in other parts of America, vocations to the priesthood were few, and to procure a sufficient number of priests required much time and patient efforts. Bishop Lynch took to his own house and himself taught such young men as seemed to possess the dispositions which should distinguish the candidates for Holy Orders. The churches numbered forty-three, but with few exceptions these were small and rudely constructed. The convents and other Catholic institutions were doing much good, but were still in their feeble infancy. The policy of Bishop Lynch, as enunciated by himself, was "to build on the foundations which his predecessor had laid, and to follow his blessed example." To inflame the spirit of Catholicity wherever it was smouldering, to awaken it where dormant, to strengthen it where it was weak, was an imperative duty, and until this was done little else could be accomplished. The Bishop, as soon as possible, visited every part of the Diocese, giving retreats followed by the Forty Hours' Devotion, preaching, teaching, administering Confirmation, promoting the establishment or improvement of Catholic schools, and doing all that could be done in the way of reorganization with the very limited means at his disposal. In all this he was zealously and ably seconded by his priests, who, animated by his example and guided by his wisdom, shared his energy and enthusiasm. He fully understood the importance of teaching Catholics, and as far as may be Protestants also, what Catholic doctrine is and what men must do to be saved; and in most cases he found that it was absolutely necessary to prepare for such instructions by showing that the Church does not teach the doctrines falsely ascribed to her by her enemies. In language studiously plain and simple, yet penetrating and profoundly eloquent, he dispelled errors, refuted calumnies and proclaimed the glorious truths which the Catholic Church, faithful to her divine commission, teaches always and everywhere. Up to the close of his life crowds, Protestants and Catholics, flocked to St. Michael's to hear his sermons and lectures, ever beautiful in their simplicity and effective because they were earnest, clear, comprehensive and thorough. How much these did to dispel the clouds of misbelief, to mollify the fierce bigotry and bitter prejudices which darkened the moral atmosphere of Toronto and other parts of Ontario in his early days, and to create that better feeling which of late has begun to prevail amongst the educated and well disposed it would be difficult to estimate, as it would be impossible to tell how much they did amongst Catholics to revive faith and enkindle devotion, to strengthen the weak, confirm the wavering and bring souls to God.

In 1862 Bishop Lynch visited Rome on the invitation of Pope Pius IX. to attend the canonization of the Martyrs of Japan. His Holiness had a very vivid recollection of the College President whose modes of instruction and ideas of discipline he so much admired. On his way back he visited Ireland and saw much of the country and of the condition to which the people were reduced. He spoke on this occasion at a great meeting held in the Rotunda, Dublin, at which Archbishop Hughes of New York also spoke. Both exhorted the people to continue the peaceable constitutional agitation for Home Rule in which they were engaged, and thus to obtain the changes in the land laws and the freedom to strive for the industrial development so essential to their welfare. In 1863 Bishop Lynch held his first diocesan synod, and submitted for its approval a code of rules adapted to the wants and circumstances of the diocese and thoroughly in harmony with the general laws of the Church. In 1865 he addressed a letter to the Bishops and Clergy of Ireland which attracted much attention at the time. He described in strong and earnest language "the evils of a wholesale emigration of an impoverished people." Left without guidance, deprived of the wholesome influences which had sustained their fathers in trials and temptations, living where they seldom heard Mass or saw a priest, or buried in the most wretched quarters of the great cities where irreligion and vice were rampant, many, he declared with sorrow, were sunk in social and moral degradation. It was asserted, and with too much truth, that millions were thus lost to the Church and to God. He wrote similar letters afterwards, but it was not easy to find or suggest an effectual remedy for evils so frightful. The poverty which drove the Irish people from home prevented any organization of their emigration, and so destitute were the great majority when they landed on this continent that they must accept employment of any kind wherever it could be got.

In September, 1869, Bishop Lynch, in obedience to the summons of the Sovereign Pontiff, left Toronto to attend the Vatican Council. On his way to the Eternal City he visited the Lazarists at their home in Paris, and afterwards visited the Capuchins at Lyons, where he passed some days with his saintly predecessor, Bishop de Charbonnel. He arrived in Rome five days before the formal opening of the Council on December 8th, the Feast of the Immaculate Conception. In this, the greatest, grandest and most important assemblage that the world had witnessed for centuries, amongst the 720 bishops and the other dignitaries who, at the call of the successor of St. Peter, had gathered from all quarters of the world, the most illustrious men of all the nations and peoples on whom God has bestowed the great gift of the Faith, and who have been true to their vocation, the Bishop of Toronto held a position of which his children in the Faith might well be proud.

Archbishop of Toronto.

All Upper Canada and the country stretching thence towards the setting sun was at one time part of the Diocese of Quebec. The great Province of Ontario was still a portion of the ecclesiastical Province of Quebec. For many obvious reasons it had for some time been deemed desirable to erect an independent Province in Ontario, of which Toronto should be the Metropolitan See. The growth and progress of the Church in Ontario had been such as to justify this creation and render it desirable. The presence of the Canadian Bishops in Rome afforded the opportunity of consulting them all without the delays which so often attend on correspondence. On March 15th Dr. Lynch was appointed Archbishop; on the 20th of the same month he appeared before the Consistory to " postulate for the

Pallium" in person; and on the 25th, the Feast of the Annunciation, he received the Pallium from the hands of Cardinal Antonelli in the Pope's private chapel. At the next meeting of the Council he was conducted by his venerable predecessor, Bishop de Charbonnel, to the place assigned to him amongst the Archbishops. Of the Archbishops and Bishops from British America, only the Archbishop of Toronto and the Archbishop of Halifax spoke in the Council on the great question of the Infallibility of the Pope. Dr. Lynch spoke earnestly in support of the proposal that the dogma should be immediately defined, but he suggested some amendments in the wording of the resolution proposed for adoption.

The Council was not permitted to complete its work. The outbreak of one of those terrible wars which have so transformed the face of Europe within a few years, rendered an adjournment necessary. But it was not adjourned until, by the definition of the dogma, the Church was prepared to encounter more vigorously and promptly the perils with which she was threatened.

Of the seven hundred and twenty-five Bishops who attended at the Council six had been students in the little College at Castleknock at the same time. At the Council they represented all these quarters of the globe. They were Dr. McCabe of Ardagh (Ireland); Dr. Finnelly (Vicar Apostolic), Madras; Dr. Grimley, Cape of Good Hope; Dr. Feehan of Nashville (now Archbishop of Chicago); Dr. Moran of Dunedin (Australia), and Dr. Lynch of Toronto.

On his return to Toronto the Archbishop was welcomed in a manner becoming his high character and the dignity of the great position to which he had been elevated. The first Council of the new ecclesiastical Province was held at Toronto in 1873, and was attended by Bishop Walsh of London, Bishop Crinnon of Hamilton, Bishop O'Brien of Kingston, and the Archbishop, who, of course, presided.

In 1879 the Archbishop again went to Rome to pay his decennial visit *ad limina Apostolorum*. He again visited Ireland in that year, making, as before, careful observations and diligent enquiries into the condition of the people. In the interviews he had with the Duke of Manchester, who was then Lord Lieutenant of Ireland, and with Sir Stafford Northcote (Lord Iddersleigh), a member of the Imperial Cabinet, he strongly urged that the only certain remedy for the evils, about the existence of which there was no question, was Home Rule. It was on this occasion that he was presented at a levee held by the Prince of Wales on behalf of the Queen. This was the first appearance of a Catholic prelate at the English Court since the reign of James II. The formal recognition of the rank and dignity of a Catholic Archbishop by the Sovereign may, he thought, do something for the promotion of Catholicity, which he had always so much at heart.

When the growth of the population in the Northwestern part of the Archdiocese rendered a division necessary Father Jamot, who had served years as Vicar General in Toronto, was, on the recommendation of the Archbishop, appointed Vicar Apostolic of all the district on the Canadian side of Lake Superior, and was consecrated Bishop of Sarepta, *in partibus infidelium*, in the Church of Our Lady of the Sacred Heart at Issonden, France, on February 24th, 1874. A few years after, the creation of a new diocese to the eastward of Toronto became necessary, and in July, 1882, on the recommendation of the Archbishop, who, with the approval of the Suffragan Bishops, visited Rome for the purpose, the diocese of Peterboro' was created and Dr. Jamot was appointed its Bishop, retaining for the time the administration of the Vicariate in the far west. On the 21st of September Bishop Jamot was duly installed in the new See.

In the summer of this year the Archbishop had a severe attack of erysipelas. His recovery was for some time extremely doubtful, and he never became completely free from its debilitating effects. It was fortunate that he had some time before secured the services of Dr. O'Mahony, Bishop of Eudocia, *in partibus infidelium*, as assistant Bishop. The ability, eloquence, energy and zeal of Dr. O'Mahony did all that was possible to supply the want which the prolonged illness of the Archbishop created.

These are but the mile-stones which marked the career of the great Archbishop and the progress which the Church made in this Province while he was Bishop and Archbishop of Toronto. He worked incessantly, indefatigably, in season and out of season. His whole life was devoted to the service of God and of the Church. His every thought and word and act were directed to the one great purpose. The pleasures of the world he seemed utterly to disregard. He lived with the most frugal economy. The merely personal expenses of any respectable mechanic were probably greater than those of the Archbishop; but no well-founded appeal to his charity or his patriotism was ever made in vain. He never sought to do by a few spasmodic efforts what he knew must be accomplished by patient effort, long sustained; and so the great institutions which are now the glory of the Archdiocese and the pride of the Catholic people rose gradually and steadily from their small beginnings, almost imperceptibly attaining their present grandeur and importance. Whatever seemed necessary for the salvation of souls he endeavored to do; whatever appeared to be most urgent he strove most earnestly to accomplish. He neglected nothing; he forgot nothing. Difficulties did not abate his resolution nor delays chill his ardour in the service of those entrusted to his care. The sermons he preached, the lectures he delivered, the pastorals and the letters on Irish and Catholic questions which he wrote, would, if collected, fill many volumes, and yet not the smallest of his pastoral duties was ever neglected or postponed. He was able to do so much work because he worked so many hours every day of his life; because he worked so earnestly and with such a profound sense of responsibility; and because his object in all he did was to serve God and do his duty. And his labours were so successful because he always strove to do what was right and said what was true.

Mr. McKeown, in his life of Archbishop Lynch, published in 1886, says: " The amount of labour performed by his Grace since first taking possession of his See has been something enormous. He has repeatedly visited all portions of his diocese. He has preached, confirmed, ordained priests, consecrated bishops, assisted at Councils, and has many times borne the inconvenience of an ocean voyage to visit Rome in connection with the affairs of his vast and important charge. From the day the mitre was placed upon his head to the present he has never spent an idle hour. Age has not impaired his activity nor affected his zeal. He is as anxious for the welfare of the Church and as zealous for the salvation of souls to-day as he was when, as a young priest, he braved the hardships of a missionary life in Texas. His health, though greatly enfeebled in the many serious attacks he has suffered from disease and the ravages incurred by hardships and overwork, still permits him to do good service in the cause of religion by the indomitable will of its possessor. Although at an age when most men would rather be relieved from the labour of preaching, the Archbishop preaches more frequently than any of his priests. His lectures upon Catholic doctrine and belief always attract large audiences; and it is not an infrequent sight to see the vast and spacious Cathedral filled from the altar to the doors with eager auditors composed in a large measure of Protestants.

Indeed a large number of educated and cultured non-Catholics make it a point of regularly attending his Grace's discourses, and many have been by these means brought into the Church. It is always exceedingly difficult to estimate the value and effects of purely spiritual work. Proselytes indeed may be numbered, but who could venture to number the souls in which faith was rekindled and the love of religion was revived by those efforts of the Archbishop; or to tell how often the wavering were strengthened, the tepid and indifferent were awakened to a sense of duty, the weak and erring were brought back to the ways of virtue and piety. Of the millions who were driven from Europe and cast upon the shores of America about the middle of this century, very many were poorly equipped for the great spiritual struggle in which they were forced to engage; and it would be no slight praise of any Bishop to say that during this transition period, this period of severe trials and many tribulations, few or none were lost to the Church in his diocese."

The spirit manifested at the Separate School Board, even in recent years, shows how serious were the dangers through which the Archbishop guided his flock with safety. Nowhere perhaps were the dangers and difficulties which beset Catholicity greater or more formidable; nowhere were they more bravely confronted; nowhere were they more successfully overcome. The storm of bigotry and hatred which raged round his predecessor lost none of its fury when Dr. Lynch became Archbishop; but, met with unyielding firmness and Christian moderation by argument and appeals to reason, it lost much of its force. The intelligent and well-disposed were first reached, and they often, without intending it, exercised a wholesome influence over the ignorant and violent. The intolerance begotten of fanaticism and ignorance still prevails all too widely, still loves to indulge in offensive language and offensive demonstrations, and exercises a malignant influence on public affairs; but it is no longer as fierce and violent as it was when Dr. Lynch became Bishop of Toronto. This change is due largely to the firm, conciliatory conduct of the Catholics, the great majority of whom have admirably exemplified, as business men and workmen, as fathers of families and as citizens, the truth, the excellence and the ennobling principles of their faith; but much is due also to the spread of knowledge and the growth of better feelings amongst Protestants, to which the lectures of the Archbishop materially contributed.

When Dr. Lynch became Bishop of Toronto the excitement caused by the discussion of the Separate School question was at its height. Bigotry and intolerance were at white heat. To continue the agitation for Catholic rights under such circumstances and to carry it to a successful issue was a task of great difficulty, and the brunt of the conflict must necessarily be borne by the Bishop of Toronto. Abuse, threats and violence Dr. Lynch met with firmness and a calm dignity, which won the respect of the bitterest foes of the Church. Misrepresentation and calumny gave him opportunities for those appeals to common sense, and to the love of truth and justice, which in time produced such remarkable effects. It was evident from the very beginning that under his guidance the Catholic cause was gaining ground. An account of the immediate circumstances which brought about a legislative settlement of the long-pending and vexed School Question in 1863, as well as of the various amendments of the Separate School Act passed since that time, will be found in another chapter. The passage of the Separate School Act in 1863 was followed by a lull in the fierce sectarian tempest which had raged so long. But when, some years afterwards, Archbishop Lynch objected to having those Catholic children, who still attended public schools, forced to use Scott's Marmion in the study of English poetry, a fierce cry arose, proving that the feeling of hostility to Catholic education, so universal at one time, was still widespread and powerful. Happily the results of the elections which it was hoped could be carried by such means proved that intelligence, good sense, sound ideas of justice and right and kind feeling are now so widely diffused that efforts to gain power and place by appeals of that kind will probably never again be successful.

For that better knowledge of what Catholicity is, and what Catholics who live up to the principles and precepts of their religion must be; for the more liberal spirit and the more kindly feelings which now prevail, the Province and its people, Protestant and Catholic, English, Scotch, French, Irish and German, are much indebted to the wisdom and prudence and untiring, incessant efforts of Archbishop Lynch.

The growth of Catholicity rendered it necessary to transfer to other portions of God's vineyard some of the priests on whose counsel and co-operation the Archbishop was wont chiefly to rely. He was forced to give Dr. Walsh to the diocese of Sandwich, now the diocese of London, and the success which crowned the labours of that prelate, the magnificent cathedral which he gave to London, the numerous spacious and handsome churches built throughout that diocese, the increase in the number of priests and of religious institutions, and above all the increase of fervor and piety amongst the Catholic people, prove how wise was the choice and how great was the sacrifice. Vicar General Jamot, one of the most earnest, zealous, energetic and devoted of priests, he afterwards gave to the diocese of Peterborough. Of the thirty-six priests who welcomed Dr. Lynch on his coming to the diocese, only ten remained in the Archdiocese when the Archbishop celebrated his Silver Jubilee. And amongst the young men whom he raised to the priesthood, death was ever so busy that the number of priests increased slowly.

Mr. McKeown, in his admirable biography of the Archbishop, says of the work accomplished in the diocese during these years: " In 1859 there were in the diocese forty-three churches. At present there are seventy-one churches in all. St. Michael's Cathedral has been finished, the tower and spire completed, and altogether about $40,000 have been spent upon it within the last twenty-five years. Of institutions of learning there are the St. Michael's College; the De La Salle Institute, conducted by the Brothers of the Christian Schools; the Convents of St. Joseph and Loretto; the Monastery of Our Lady of Mount Carmel at the Niagara Falls, and also the fine Convent of the Loretto Nuns at the same place. This last named Order has also established Convents in Toronto, Hamilton, Stratford, Lindsay, Guelph and Belleville. The Convent in Lindsay, built under the personal supervision of the late lamented Father Stafford was one of the finest educational buildings in the country. The Sisters of St. Joseph have also, in addition to their fine institutions in Toronto established others in several towns and cities of Ontario, and have in the city of St. Catharines by far the finest building for educational purposes in the place. The community of St. Joseph have opened a Convent under the name of Notre Dame Institute in Toronto, where such young ladies as come to Toronto for the purpose of attending the Provincial Normal School may obtain board at reasonable rates and be protected from the dangers to which young women from the country are more or less exposed in the boarding houses of a large city like Toronto. This noble community, in addition to teaching the girls of the Separate Schools, also take charge of the St. Nicholas Home, a boarding house established for the accommodation of the working boys of the city. The Sisters of St. Joseph also direct the House of Providence, a charitable institution for the aged and infirm.

"Orphans and destitute children, especially those in danger of becoming vicious and depraved, are also received in the House of Providence. The boys are sent to the beautiful Orphanage at Sunnyside, one of the grandest memorials of Dr. Lynch's administration; the girls are still cared for in the House of Providence. The Convent of the Precious Blood, the nuns of which spend their lives in prayer and holy contemplation and in labor, was founded in those years, and like all the other religious institutions, has grown despite difficulties and discouragements.

"The inscriptions on some of the shields with which St. Michael's Cathedral was adorned on the occasion of the Silver Jubilee, furnish perhaps the best epitome of the principal events in his administration of the diocese.

> Loretto Convent, established in 1862.
> St. Joseph's Convent, established in 1863.
> St. Michael's tower and spire built in 1865.
> Loretto Abbey, Wellington Place, extended in 1867.
> St. Nicholas Home, established in 1869.
> Attended Ecumenical Council in 1890.
> De La Salle Institute, established in 1871.
> Consecrated Bishop O'Brien, Kingston, in 1873.
> Consecrated Bishop Crinnon, Hamilton, in 1874.
> Consecrated Archbishop Taschereau, Quebec, in 1874.
> Convent of the Precious Blood, established in 1874.
> Magdalen Asylum, established in 1875.
> Convents of St. Joseph, established in St. Catharines, Thorold, Barrie and Oshawa.
> — Forty Parish Churches and thirty Presbyteries established.
> Seventy Priests ordained for the Diocese.
> St. John's Grove and House established.

To these should be added the Church of our Lady of Lourdes, the memorial of the Archbishop's Jubilee. And the beautiful new Churches of St. Mary and St. Paul, Toronto, deserve especial mention.

For those who, immersed in such occupations and burdened with great responsibilities, think only of all that has yet to be done, of the difficulties to be overcome, the wants to be supplied, the good to be accomplished, time flies rapidly. The twenty-fifth anniversary of his consecration must have come upon Dr. Lynch almost by surprise, but he prepared to celebrate it with due solemnity. Then were the deep affection and heartfelt reverence of his flock, and the esteem and respect of the people of Toronto of all denominations fully manifested. The Archbishop, who had attended the Council at Baltimore as a guest, was accompanied on his return by the Archbishop of Philadelphia, the Bishops of Buffalo, of Burlington, Vt., of Harrisburg, Pa., of Ogdensburg, N.Y., of Cleveland, O., of Savanna, Ga., of Albany, N.Y., of Brooklyn, N.Y., of Detroit Mich., of Little Rock, Ark., of Newark, N.J. The Catholic Societies wearing their regalia, carrying their banners, and preceded by bands of music, and the other Catholics of the city in carriages and on foot, went to the railway station to welcome the Archbishop and his guests. The streets along the line of the procession were crowded by citizens of all races and creeds, and of every class, who joined heartily in the welcome. Amid the cheering of the multitudes, the music of the bands, the joyous clangour of bells, and the glare of numberless fireworks, the prelates were escorted to St. Michael's Cathedral, which was beautifully decorated and brilliantly illuminated. Amongst those who welcomed the American Bishops at the railway station, or united with them in the thanksgiving at the Cathedral, were the Archbishop of Quebec, the Archbishop of Halifax, the Bishops of Montreal, Ottawa, St. Hyacinthe, St. John, N.B., Kingston, London, Hamilton, Peterborough, and Eudocia, the Vicar Apostolic of Pontiac, and a large number of the most eminent of the Clergy of all the Provinces. The Cathedral could not contain a fourth of the multitude who sought admission. The ceremony of the next day was grand and impressive beyond description. The sermon, preached by the eloquent Archbishop of Philadelphia, was a magnificent utterance of the thankfulness and the pious emotions of the vast congregation and of the thousands who in vain sought even standing room. As evidence of the strength and general prevalence of the good-will and friendly feeling which the Archbishop ever sought to create and foster, and of the respect and esteem in which he was then held by all classes, it may be well to state that the Lieutenant-Governor of the Province, Hon. J. B. Robinson (and Mrs. Robinson), and the Mayor of Toronto, Mr. Boswell, attended officially, sitting in the seats set apart for them, and that of those who were so fortunate as to obtain admission to the Church, a large proportion were Protestants. After Mass, addresses were presented by the Clergy of the

Archdiocese, and by the Catholic laity of the several parishes. Each was accompanied by a "testimonial of the love and esteem enshrined in the hearts" of the Catholic people.

The religious ceremony was followed in the evening by a banquet at the Rossin House, to which, besides the Archbishops, Bishops and Priests who had crowded the Cathedral Sanctuary in the forenoon, and a number of prominent Catholics, several representative Protestants were invited. The Archbishops and Bishops who spoke at this banquet dwelt mainly on the services Dr. Lynch had rendered to the Church. Bishop Loughlin, of Brooklyn, said he "had known His Grace before he was raised to the Episcopacy. His Grace had been a great worker for his Divine Master, and he had done a great deal to advance religion. The speaker was at his Consecration twenty-five years ago, and all who witnessed his manner of living since that time would say that he had been loyal to his country, and loyal to his God ever since he took charge of this See." Archbishop Ryan, of Philadelphia said: "For over thirty years I have known your Archbishop. I knew him in Missouri, the scene of his missionary labors, and have marked his career ever since, always with the greatest gratification and pride in my old friend of thirty years ago." Archbishop (now Cardinal) Taschereau, of Quebec, said he "had come here a long distance after a long voyage from Europe, to show his gratitude to the Archbishop of Toronto, who was his Consecrator." Archbishop O'Brien, of Halifax, said that "down by the sea they were glad that this celebration was taking place, and in congratulating his Grace he spoke for many." Bishop Ryan, of Buffalo, "was glad to see that Archbishop Lynch had been so justly honored. He had done a great deal in the way of harmonizing the Society in which his lot had been cast." The Bishops of the Province, in like manner, bore testimony to the value of the services which the Archbishop had rendered to religion. The Protestant dignitaries who spoke bore testimony to the immense services his Grace had rendered to Society, dispelling prejudice and creating a spirit of harmony where strife and animosity had long prevailed. Lieutenant-Governor Robinson, in proposing the health of the Archbishop said: "The interesting ceremonies of this day are brought to a fitting conclusion in this sociable and hospitable gathering. As I looked upon this scene I could not but think it an evidence of the generous spirit of an Irishman—the doing of one who was unwilling that this, one of the greatest days of his life, should pass without the presence of his friends,

Protestant and Catholic alike, to share with him the remembrance of this day twenty-five years ago. Few of us, perhaps none, can expect to equal the grace and magnitude of the hospitality which has called us here to-night; but there is one thing Protestants and Catholics alike may well try to emulate—the noble and liberal spirit which has prompted it. . . . The Archbishop of Toronto, in the discharge of his great duties, has preached the gospel of peace, good-will and mutual respect." Mayor Boswell made a few remarks, commenting with expressions of pleasure upon the good feeling which existed between all classes of the community. He congratulated the Archbishop upon his broad-mindedness. Hon. O. Mowat, Premier of Ontario, said: " I have been delighted, sir, with the observations you have made to-night. I share with all my heart in the sentiments you have expressed regarding the desirability of harmony amongst all classes of the community. I rejoice to know that there is so much good feeling between the Protestants and Roman Catholics of my Province. There never was a time when there was so much unity between the two great sections of the community as at this moment. . . . I apprehend, sir, that not a little of this feeling is due to your Grace. During the twenty-five years you have lived amongst us in your high position, we have learned to know something about you. We know that amongst your own people you are loved and admired, and that you deserve to be. We have learned also the esteem and respect which are due to your character. We have found you, sir, to be a man of the most gentle nature, of most kindly disposition, of most generous character. We have found you always interested in whatever was for the benefit of the poor and suffering. We have found you anxious to promote what you considered to be for the public advantage, and while we Protestants cannot join in the religious congratulations you have received this day, we can, at all events, congratulate our Catholic fellow-citizens upon having such an Archbishop as you are. . . . The good feeling which prevails amongst us is manifested in many ways. . . . I am glad to have this opportunity of expressing the great esteem and respect with which the Protestants of this country regard you." Archbishop Lynch's own views and feelings on this subject were admirably expressed in the speech in which he replied to the toast proposed by the Lieutenant Governor. He said: " I rejoice very much indeed at the good, kindly feeling which exists amongst, I may say, the *élite* of Toronto of all nationalities and all creeds. We are here as brothers on this earth of ours, not to harm one another, but to honor and reverence and respect one another, and especially to respect the conscientious feelings of our neighbors. I would have a very poor opinion of a man who would not love a friend because he was of another way of thinking. We should not allow our politics or our religion to interfere with our friendships. Friendship is too holy a thing to be interfered with by outside-world considerations. Hence I say that our friends are of no particular politics. They are our friends, and that is quite enough."

The testimonials presented on this occasion the Archbishop devoted to the erection of the Church of Our Lady of Lourdes, to whom he had a particular devotion. This beautiful little church will serve, as he intended, as a memorial of his Silver Jubilee, and of the growth and progress of Catholicity in the archdiocese while governed by him. It was not necessary to keep alive his name and his memory, which are enshrined in the hearts of a grateful people.

The Archbishop's health was remarkably good at the time of his jubilee, and he continued to work with zeal as fervent as ever and with renewed activity. He preached and lectured and wrote more frequently and earnestly, and attended carefully to his multifarious duties, never neglecting even the least important. It seemed that a life so useful, so valuable to those over whom he had charge, and to others, would be prolonged for many years. But such was not God's holy will. He died unexpectedly a martyr to duty, and his death was a fit crowning of a life which had been all devoted to the service of God and the good of his fellow men.

On Sunday, May 6th, 1888, he preached in St. Michael's Cathedral, and was apparently as strong and vigorous as he had been at any time for years. On the forenoon of Tuesday, May 8th, although he felt unwell, he left Toronto to attend a conference of the clergy at St. Catharines. On the way to St. Catharines he accidentally received a slight wetting, and this almost immediately aggravated his illness. So unwell was he on Wednesday that several of the priests urged him either to remain at St. Catharines and call in medical assistance or to return at once to Toronto for the purpose. But he had made an appointment to give Confirmation at Merritton on Thursday, and he would not, because of an illness which he did not think dangerous, disappoint the children and their parents who had made preparation for his visit. After the close of the Conference on Wednesday, he proceeded to

Merritton and there, although suffering much from the illness which had made rapid progress, he confirmed all the children who were prepared for the reception of that great Sacrament. His work having been done he hastened back to Toronto. Arriving there late on Thursday night he drove to St. John's Grove, where he had chiefly resided for several years. The physicians, who were summoned as soon as possible, found that he was suffering from congestion of the lungs, which had made such progress that his recovery was impossible. One who was in attendance at his death-bed writes: " His indomitable courage never for an instant failed him. He heard calmly the decision of the physicians, provided for the administration of the diocese, made a slight addition to his will, and then asked that the last Sacraments should be administered to him. They were administered by the Right Reverend T. O'Mahony, Bishop of Eudocia, *in partibus infidelium*, his Auxiliary, in presence of Very Reverend F. P. Rooney and Very Reverend J. M. Laurent, his Vicars-General, of Very Reverend J. J. McCann, Dean, and Reverend J. F. McBride, his Secretary. A few hours after his heart began to fail, and at one a.m. on Saturday, May 12th, 1888, the great Archbishop passed to his eternal rest so calmly that those who watched by his couch scarcely knew when he departed." On the following day the triumphant festival of the Ascension was celebrated with becoming pomp in St. Michael's Cathedral, but its heavily draped pulpit proclaimed to the vast congregation that its Archbishop was no more. Vicar-General Laurent made the usual announcements, and with the affecting simplicity and sublime tenderness that the Church deals with all its children, it was noticed that when the faithful were asked to pray for the souls of those in the parish who died during the week, amongst others there was mentioned the name of John Joseph Lynch.

The news of the Archbishop's death took the public by surprise, and all sections of the community were profoundly moved. The expressions of esteem for his loss were universal and earnest, and all joined in paying respect to his memory. On the day of his funeral the chancel of St. Michael's was crowded with Bishops and Priests, who had come from many quarters to manifest the esteem in which he was held, and to take part in the solemn Sacrifice, the pious prayers and the mournful and impressive ceremonies with which the Church consigns the mortal remains of her prelates to the tomb. From the time of his death until Monday evening the dead Archbishop lay in the parlor in St. John's Grove. The body was then removed to the Cathedral, followed by an immense procession, and laid in the grave on Wednesday following. It was the wish of the deceased prelate that his body should not be interred within the Cathedral, but in a plot of earth on its north side, so that those who visited might recite a prayer over his grave. At the Requiem Mass His Eminence Cardinal Taschereau officiated and there were present the Archbishops of Montreal and Ottawa, and a great number of Bishops and ecclesiastical dignitaries. The Right Reverend Bishop Ryan preached an appropriate eulogium on the occasion. The Government of the Province, the Council of the City of Toronto, and other public bodies, were represented at the funeral, and the great church, the surrounding grounds and the street, were densely crowded by Catholics, who wished to give expression to their feelings of sorrow for their spiritual father, and of loving affection and reverence for the great pastor who had lived and died in their service and God's; and by Protestants, who thus manifested their esteem and respect for him who, fulfilling all the duties of his exalted position, had rendered such great services to the whole community. The influence for good, which he wielded during his administration of the Archdiocese, the memory of his many virtues will do much to perpetuate.

The Archbishop's will, which is a very brief document, gives further evidence of his entire unselfishness and of his thorough devotion to the service of God's Church and God's people. Poor, it says, he came to the Archdiocese, and poor he left it. From the revenues he had never taken for his own use more than sufficient to cover the cost of his very frugal living and other unavoidable expenses, and at his death the utmost value of all the personal property at his disposal was but a few hundred dollars. This he left to his successor to be used in the service of the Church, with the exception of a small sum to be paid for Masses for the repose of his soul and a small amount to be paid by way of annuity to an aged relative.*

---

* When the Archbishop's will was proved it was found that his estate amounted to less than five hundred dollars—not enough to pay his funeral expenses. He left no debts.

The following is the text of his will :

In the name of the Most Holy and Undivided Trinity, Amen.

This is the last Will and Testament of me, John Joseph Lynch, Archbishop of Toronto, Assistant at the Pontifical Throne, &c.

I do hereby protest that I die in the profession of the Holy Roman Catholic and Apostolic Church, and I herewith send to his Holiness Leo XIII., the successor of St. Peter, my last act of homage and veneration and ask his Apostolic benediction.

The ecclesiastical affairs of the See of Toronto, on the demise of Archbishop Lynch, were entrusted to Vicar-General Rooney and Vicar-General Laurent, pending the appointment of a successor. This was not accomplished for some time, when the present Archbishop, the Most Rev. John Walsh, D.D., formerly Bishop of London, was elevated to the Metropolitan rank. A sketch of his life and labors, so far as they have gone, has already been placed before the reader at the beginning of this volume. This chapter therefore completes the history of the prelates of the Archdiocese of Toronto up to the present time.

I commend my soul to the mercy of God, and I direct that my body be buried in the manner and according to the directions given to my Executors.

I came poor to the Diocese and poor I am leaving it, not having appropriated anything of the revenues beyond my necessary expenses.

I hereby declare that all lands and tenements, goods, chattels, moneys and property of every kind and nature soever, and wherever situate, shall become the property of my successor when he shall be appointed by the Holy See.

I appoint the Right Reverend Bishop O'Mahony, Auxiliary of the Archbishop, and the Very Reverend Father Rooney, Vicar General, both of this City, to be the Executors of this my last Will and Testament, and I direct them to have two hundred Masses said for the repose of my soul.

I revoke all former wills made by me heretofore at any time.

Dated at Toronto, this 13th day of March, in the year of our Lord 1883.

        Signed,   JOHN JOSEPH LYNCH, Arp., Toronto.

Signed, published and declared, by the said Testator as and for his last Will and Testament, in the presence of us present at the same time, who in his presence and at his request have hereunto signed our names as witnesses.

    Signed,   D. A. O'SULLIVAN, Barrister-at-Law.
    Signed,   CHARLES J. O'HAGERTY, R.C.C.
    Signed,   J. H. CAMERON, M.B.

In consideration of having left all my personal property to my successor in the Diocese of Toronto, I direct him to pay to my sister, Mrs. Eliza McDonald, care of Thos. O'Callaghan, Dundalk, Ireland, the sum of one hundred dollars per year as long as she lives, and if necessary this is to form a Codicil to my will executed 13th March, 1883.

    Signed,   JOHN JOSEPH LYNCH,
                             Archbp. of Toronto.

Signed in the presence of two witnesses, present at the same time

    D. A. O'SULLIVAN.   CHARLES J. O'HAGERTY, R.C.C.

THE RELIGIOUS COMMUNITIES.

BY

REV. JOHN R. TEEFY, B.A., C.S.B.,

SUPERIOR OF ST. MICHAEL'S COLLEGE, TORONTO.

VERY REVEREND CHARLES VINCENT, V.G.,

Provincial of the Community of St. Basil.

BORN AT VALLONS, FRANCE, JUNE 30, 1828.
DIED AT TORONTO, NOVEMBER 1, 1890.

CHAPTER VII.

THE RELIGIOUS COMMUNITIES AND THEIR WORK.

The Basilians—Father Soulerin—Father Vincent—The Christian Brothers—The Sisters of Loretto—The Sisters of St. Joseph—The House of Providence—The Nuns of the Precious Blood—The Sisters of the Good Shepherd.

It is fair to this history, as it will undoubtedly be interesting to our readers, that a special chapter be given to the religious communities, whose works are so monumental and so closely connected with the progress of religion in this portion of the Lord's vineyard. The zealous prelates of the diocese, recognizing its wants, have all in turn called to their aid first one society and then another, until education and charity are very well provided for. Under the care of these men and women, institutions have been built up which have become the pride of all concerned. There are the Christian Brothers and three religious communities of priests, the Basilians, the Carmelites, and the Redemptorists, while the following communities of Sisters are established here, viz: the Sisters of Loretto, St. Joseph, the Precious Blood, and the Good Shepherd.

The object of the Carmelites and Redemptorists being to give missions and preach retreats, a brief sketch of them is given in connection with the two parishes of which they have charge, viz: Niagara Falls, on the Canadian side, and St. Patrick's Church in the City of Toronto.

SECTION I.

THE BASILIANS.

From an earlier chapter in this volume it will be seen that Dr. de Charbonnel, who received his classical education in one of the houses of this community, introduced it into his diocese. And avoiding repetitions we open this section with a short history of the Congregation of St. Basil.

At the close of the last century two disastrous events threatened ruin to the formation of the French clergy, the suppression of the Jesuits and the

Reign of Terror. To counterbalance the former several small associations of priests were formed, having for their object the early education of candidates for the priesthood; but the latter swept like a hurricane over the fair land of France, destroying the sheltered homes of clerical learning and well nigh sweeping all marks of religion into the depths of frantic unbelief and legitimized persecution, which has not ceased even to this day. It was under such auspices that the Basilian community had its beginning. In 1800 Mgr. d'Aviau, Archbishop of Vienne, a town south of Lyons, desiring to recruit subjects for the priesthood, opened for young men a refuge where a few could devote themselves to study and the carrying out of their pious ambition. Three priests, seconding his wishes, began at St. Symphorien, in the mountains of Vivarais, to teach the rudiments of Latin to young peasants. The following year the establishment, endowed by the Government with the title of secondary school, numbered more than a hundred students. In 1802 the school was moved to Annonay, the most important town of the Department of Vivarais. Here, advancing with the authorization of the Empire, its numbers swelled to four hundred. In 1822, upon the advice of Mgr. Brulley, Bishop of Mende and administrator of the Diocese of Viviers, the professors of the College of Annonay formed a pious association, binding themselves by a simple promise to consecrate their life to the teaching of youth. The association formed at that time, although somewhat varied and modified, remains the same. As early as 1837 Pope Gregory XVI. pronounced by a decree the Institute of the Priests of St. Basil worthy of praise: "*Institutum Societatis sacerdotum a sancto Basilio laudandum.*" Taking a further step at the suggestion of Mgr. Guibert, Bishop of Viviers, and afterwards Archbishop of Paris, the members of the Society applied to Rome for their establishment as a community bound by the religious vows of poverty, chastity, obedience and stability. At length, on November 23, 1863, Pius IX., of holy memory, issued a decree approving and confirming the "pious Institute." Such is a very brief sketch of a small community whose work is as important and successful in the new world as it is in the old. To its history in the new world let us now devote a short space.

The foundation of the provincial house in Toronto in 1852 has already been noted, and we take them up again, fairly established with the late venerable Father Soulerin as Superior, and a staff consisting of Fathers Maloney, Malbos, Vincent and Flannery. The last two were at that time ecclesiastics in minor orders. Of this pioneer band Father Flannery is the only survivor. Born in the County of Tipperary, Ireland, he was sent for his education to the Basilian Fathers, amongst whom he had friends. And when an English colony was started, as might be expected, he came with it. Some years after his ordination as priest, which took place in 1853, he withdrew from College work and was attached to the Archdiocese of Toronto. This field he also changed for London, where he has for a long time been the respected pastor of the city of St. Thomas. Here, still hale and hearty, with happy recollections of times long gone by and companions now passed away, when friends gather around, he tells of the early days of St. Michael's College and the students who have since risen to distinction. A man of fine literary taste, rich in humor and imagination, with a vein of poetry which he has cultivated with success, Father Flannery was admirably fitted for a professor's chair. And although he gave up teaching he never abandoned the cultivation of his natural talent for literature: being for a long time editor of the "Catholic Record" of London and the "Catholic Weekly Review" of Toronto.

On June the 29th, of the present year, in recognition of Father Flannery's literary attainments and the services he had by his pen rendered religion, the University of Georgetown, District of Columbia, which is under the care of the Society of Jesus, conferred upon him the honorary title of Doctor of Divinity.

Father Soulerin.

There are few names with sweeter memories to those who knew him than the name and memory of the saintly and revered Father Soulerin, first Superior of St. Michael's College.

He was born near Largentiere, a small town in the South of France, in the year 1807. He received his education amongst the Basilian Fathers, whom, after its completion, he joined in their work of zeal. At the request of the Bishop of Grenoble he accepted, in 1828, the professorship of Philosophy in the Seminary of that important diocese. After a residence here of two years he was appointed professor of Rhetoric in the College of Feysin, Isere. This establishment being suppressed in 1849, the Abbe Soulerin was made Director of Studies in the College of Annonay. When Bishop de Charbonnel applied to the Superior General of the Basilians to open a College in

Toronto, Father Soulerin was sent, in 1852, as Superior. The Institution opened in one of the houses on Queen street opposite the present Metropolitan Methodist Church; but it was moved to a wing of St. Michael's Palace, which had been especially built for the purpose, and which was afterwards known as St. Vincent's Chapel. Here boys who are now Bishops of God's Church learned the elements of their classics; for it numbers amongst its earliest students Bishops Denis O'Connor of London, Richard A. O'Connor of Peterborough, and T. J. Dowling of Hamilton. These and others, like Vicar-General Heenan and Father Ferguson, are amongst the honoured names of those who sat on the early forms of the College. In September, 1855, the corner stone of the present building of St. Michael's College on St. Joseph street was laid, and the work of teaching began in it the following September. Since that time the following additions to the building, which terminated then at the second door to the east: In 1865 the main building was extended to the eastern wing, which was added in 1872. In 1877 the Sanctuary of St. Basil's Church was built, and in 1886 the Church was extended in front and the tower erected.

Returning to Father Soulerin: he continued, with zeal and prudence, the management of the College until May, 1865, when he was elected Superior-General of the Community of St. Basil. This required his removal to France. He had been made Vicar-General by Bishop de Charbonnel, and was twice administrator of the Diocese during his Lordship's absence. His extensive learning, his deep humility and simple piety won for him the esteem and confidence of his equals, the love and respect of all his confreres and students.

After governing the community for fourteen years with the same care as had characterized him in America, Father Soulerin rendered his soul to God in November, 1879.

FATHER VINCENT.

Father Soulerin's successor was Charles Vincent, who was Superior for twenty-one years, from 1865 to 1886, and who, so lately departed, still lingers in the hearts of all that knew him. A man of great simplicity, of quick, practical judgment and deep insight into character, and coming to this country while young, he was well fitted to take charge of an educational institution which had a large field for usefulness and a bright future before

St Michael's College.

it. Under him the growth of the College advanced steadily; the number of students increased and the building enlarged. In 1881 the College was affiliated to the University of Toronto upon a basis similar to that of several of the Catholics of England and Ireland with the London University. All the teaching, or as much of it as the College authorities find convenient, may be done in the College; while all the examinations upon mental and moral science are upon the matters taught in St. Michael's College.*

Father Vincent was born at Vallons, in the Department of Ardeche, France, June 30th, 1828. His education was begun in the College of Aubinas, and completed in the College of Annonay, where he joined the Basilian Community. He had only minor orders when he came to America, but was ordained priest on May 22nd, 1853, in the Chapel of Loretto Convent, then situated on Simcoe street, in the building which for many years past has been used for the offices of the Attorney General of the Province.

In 1870, at the request of Bishop Walsh of London, the Basilian Fathers started a College at Sandwich, entitled Assumption College, with the Rev. Denis O'Connor, C.S.B., as Superior. When Dr. O'Connor was raised to the episcopate he was succeeded by the Rev. Daniel Cushing, C.S.B., who still presides over it, to its continual success and progress.

On May 22nd, 1878, the Silver Jubilee of Father Vincent's priesthood was celebrated with a great outburst of enthusiasm and affection on the part of the old students and friends of the College. Archbishop Lynch, to show his appreciation of him, made him his Vicar-General, which honor was also conferred upon him by the present Archbishop of Toronto, soon after his Grace came to the city.

In 1886, feeling that he had long enough held the reins, and that his strength was giving way, he asked to be relieved of the Superiorship of the College, while he was to retain the Provincialship of the Community. His request was granted, and Father Daniel Cushing, at the time Director of Studies in Assumption College, Sandwich, was appointed Superior of St. Michael's College. Father Vincent continued to reside in the College. His health growing very feeble in 1890, he resigned his provincialship. Soon

---

* The following is the Statute of the University Senate: "In the honor department of Mental and Moral Philosophy of the fourth year the Senate shall institute two distinct examinations on the two systems of Philosophy taught in the confederating arts colleges."

In the second and third years all the examinations are under the direction of the Colleges.

afterwards a cold brought on an attack of jaundice and dropsy, which, after a lingering illness, carried him off on the 1st of November, 1890. Strange coincidence, his funeral took place on his feast, St. Charles' Day, November 4th; and many an old student, who so often had come to rejoice with him on that day, now came to pay his last respect to his memory and offer prayer for his soul.

In the Provincialship Father Vincent was succeeded by the Very Rev. Victor Marijon, who also is from the Department of Ardeche, France, who is the present zealous and pious Provincial of the Basilians.

After three years Father Cushing, resigned the Superiorship of the College, and was succeeded, in 1889, by the writer of this sketch.

It would be impossible to enumerate the many ecclesiastical and other professional men of the country and of the neighboring republic who have passed through St. Michael's College. Besides the Bishops of Hamilton, Peterborough, and London, already mentioned, there are the two Vicars-General* of Toronto, Vicar-General Heenan of the Diocese of Hamilton, two of the Deans† of Toronto, Archdeacon Campbell, Father McEvay, Rector of the Cathedral of Hamilton; Father Rudkins, Chancellor of the Diocese of Peterborough; Father Quinlivan of St. Patrick's, Montreal; Father Conroy, Chancellor of the Ogdensburg Diocese; and many others whose talents, burnished by the Basilian Fathers, are in the service of the Great Master, to the honor of their teachers and the sanctification of souls.

SECTION II.

THE CHRISTIAN BROTHERS.

This Community, whose proper title is "Brothers of the Christian Schools," was founded by a French priest, the Blessed Abbe Jean Baptiste De La Salle, an intimate friend of M. Nyel of Rouen, who drew his attention to the subject of education, the importance of which his tenderest charity and keen perception fully appreciated. He resigned his preferment, renounced his private fortune, and gave himself up to the work of forming these teachers into a

---

* Very Rev. F. P. Rooney and Very Rev. J. J. McCann.
† Very Rev. Dean Harris and Very Rev. Dean Cassidy.

community by giving them rules and the title which they bear to this day. The teaching was to be gratuitous. He insisted that Latin should be no longer an obligatory subject, but that the basis of their teaching, after the catechism, should be their own language. He required that the Brothers, who bound themselves by vow to devote their lives to teaching in the schools, and wore the religious habit, should be and should remain laymen equally with the professors and assistant teachers employed under them. For the training of the Brothers the Founder instituted a Novitiate; and for the professors, &c., a Normal school. Founded at Rheims in 1686, this appears to have been the first training school for primary teachers in Europe. The Blessed De La Salle lived to see his community established in many of the principal towns of France. Since his death, which took place on the 7th of April, 1719, it has not only survived the many shocks given society in France by revolution, but it has spread through various other countries. According to the statistics of 1891 the Brothers had under their charge 1,750 schools, attended by 314,133 scholars, of whom 289,000 were receiving gratuitous instruction. There were 13,262 Brothers and 5,000 Professors employed in teaching. At the same date the Novices numbered 3,897.

The Christian Brothers were first brought to Toronto in May, 1851, by Bishop de Charbonnel. Brother Patrick, who afterwards became one of the Assistants to the Superior General of the whole Order, and whose death took place a year or so ago, introduced and established them in Toronto. St. Michael's School was the first opened, and in September of the same year, two classes were started in St. Paul's Church. St. Patrick's School followed in 1853 in a red brick building on the eastern side of St. Patrick's Market. It consisted of four classes, two taught by the Brothers and two by the Sisters of Loretto. In the same year a school-house containing three rooms was built for St. Paul's Parish on the corner of Power and Queen streets. St. Mary's School, Bathurst street, was opened about 1854. These schools have since been either very much enlarged, or replaced by new and splendid buildings erected to supply the increasing demands of the various parishes. The school for St. Paul's parish, built some twelve years ago, is a handsome, commodious building; St. Mary's has also been very much enlarged and renovated; St. Helen's of Brockton has just completed a second magnificent building for a school; St. Basil's parish has two, one on St. Vincent street and the other on Yonge street, near the Catholic Cemetery. There are not Brothers in all these;

but they have grown with the growth of Catholicity. Brother Patrick was succeeded by Brother Hugh, who first opened the Academy of the De La Salle in 1863 on Jarvis street, which was intended for those who wished an advanced education in commercial subjects, as well as for those who purposed entering afterwards upon a classical course preparatory to philosophy and theology. The Academy proving very successful, it was determined to establish an institution which would stand to the separate schools of Toronto as the collegiate institutes do to the public schools. The Bank of Upper Canada, on the corner of George and Duke streets, was secured. By a strange turn of events, the land upon which the Bank stood was but reverting, if not to its original, at least to a very kindred, purpose—it having been donated by the Government to Bishop Macdonell for a church and afterwards exchanged by his Lordship for ten acres outside of the city. The pupils of the Academy were transferred to the Bank on the 17th of March, 1870. In 1871 the energetic Brother Arnold, who was then at the head of the Institute, built a large addition to the old building. The property is now vested in the separate school board, who also provided for the Collegiate Institute work for girls by placing them under the care of the Sisters of St. Joseph.

Brother Arnold, who was the third Superior of Toronto, removed to Montreal, where he still continues the self-sacrificing work of education. To him succeeded Brother Tobias, under whose energy and government the Community of Toronto has grown into a separate province, which step was taken May 26th, 1888, when the houses of Ontario were separated from the District of Montreal. On December 27th, 1890, the Ontario novitiate was opened at the De La Salle Institute. It comprises three departments, viz : a preparatory and a senior novitiate and a scholasticate, the first under Brother Sulpicius, late Director of the Community of St. Catharines; the second under Brother Halward, who for many years had been Director of the Community of Kingston; and the third under Bro. Edward, former Director of St. Patrick's Lyceum, Ottawa.

The new District of Toronto has already shown prosperity and development. Early in 1890 a new house was opened at Renfrew, and in the same year the Brothers took charge of St. Helen's school, Brockton. In 1891 his Lordship Bishop Dowling, of Hamilton, established a house of the Community in that city. These houses and that of St. Catharines, founded in 1876, are the outgrowth of the zeal and devotion of an earnest and successful teaching religious order. It would be out of place here to pass any eulogy or do anything more than sketch their establishment and progress in the Diocese. Their rule—a severe one—standing through two hundred years, is a proof of its wisdom, stability and excellence; their religious life is a guarantee that they are teachers of something more than mere book learning, and gives them an insight into character which enables them to exercise a powerful influence in directing the mind and moulding the character of those under their charge.[*]

SECTION III.

THE SISTERS OF LORETTO.

The effect of religious persecution is very strikingly evident in England, where the comparatively faithful few suffered and endured heroically, suffered, not alone the swift death which gave them the martyr's palm and crown, but endured the slow, agonizing torture, the weary prison, exile from home and country, in fine, the deprivation of all things earthly rather than separate from the love of Christ.

The spirit of these noble sufferers for conscience sake is aptly expressed in the answer given by Sir Thomas More to the Duke of Norfolk. When the Lord Chancellor made his final decision to stand upon his principles the Duke told him of his danger, saying: "By the Mass, Master More, it is perilous striving with princes; the anger of a prince brings death." "Is that all, my Lord?" said More; "then the difference between you and me is this—that I shall die to-day, and you to-morrow."

It is to this same age of persecution that the children of Mary's Institute look for their spiritual ancestry; it is there they find the foundation-stones and first pillars of their Congregation. During the troubled era of James I. and his successors certain noble ladies, actuated by a spirit of zeal and self-sacrifice, left England, sought refuge on the Continent, and finally established themselves in Bavaria. Here they realized the two-fold object of their self-imposed exile—the peaceful exercise of their holy religion, and the laudable work of providing for young English girls a place of Catholic education where they might be thoroughly trained for the contest

[*] This account of the Christian Brothers is taken largely from the Life of Archbishop Lynch by H. C. McKeown, Esq.

which awaited them in their native land. The history of their early vicissitudes, recorded elsewhere,* belongs not, properly speaking, to these pages; but the arduous beginnings deserve at least a passing notice, if only to mark how the Canadian Mission resembled the parent Institute in that dominant characteristic of all works on which God has set His seal.

The Institute, in its early days, had houses in the principal cities of Europe; but Munich, Bavaria, is regarded as the cradle of the Congregation. Here the "English ladies" found warm and constant friends in the persons of the Elector, Maximilian I., and his wife, Elizabeth. The Electoral family never wavered in its friendship towards them, and Maximilian Emmanuel (grandson of Maximilian I.), Duke of both Bavarias and Prince Elector of the Sacred Roman Empire, was among the first to petition the Holy See for the confirmation of the Rules of the Institute of the Blessed Virgin Mary. It was during the administration of Anna Barbara Babthorpe, Superior-General, that this petition was granted by His Holiness, Pope Clement XI., who, on the 13th of June, 1703, issued a brief containing the apostolic approval of the Rules of the Institute. Thus the Rules were confirmed without the Community being approved. From the year 1703, then, until late in the nineteenth century the "English Virgins" stood in an exceptional and anomalous position among congregations of simple vows. Their rule had been approved, while to the Institute itself such approval was wanting; it was evident, owing to its antiquity alone, that it did not possess an advantage enjoyed by kindred congregations of more modern origin. Very earnestly, therefore, did the Superior of the York Convent, Rev. Mother Juliana Martin, hope and pray that so desirable an object might be attained. She did not, however, see her way towards proceeding actively in the matter until, in 1876, Father John Morris, of the Society of Jesus, one of the best friends of the Institute, took the case in hand, and so skilfully directed it, that to him, under God, its successful issue must be mainly attributed. In September, 1876, a petition was addressed by the Superior and Community of the York Convent to his Holiness, Pope Pius IX. of blessed memory, begging the favor of apostolic approbation and confirmation of the Institute. The petition was accompanied by commendatory letters from the Bishop of Beverley, the Right Rev. Dr. Cornthwaite, and the Bishop of Rodiopolis, Vicar-Apostolic of Patna, the ecclesiastical Superior of some of

* Life of Mary Ward, by Mary C. E. Chambers; St. Mary's Convent, York, edited by H. J. Coleridge, S.J.; Mrs. Ball: a biography, by William Hutch, D.D.; Mother Frances Teresa Ball, by H. J. Coleridge, S.J.

the houses of the Institute established in India, and which were filiations of Rathfarnham. With a readiness and promptitude which excited general surprise, the Holy Father, by a decree of the Sacred Congregation of the Propaganda, dated February 15th, 1877, granted his solemn approbation and confirmation of the Institute.

Returning to the earlier history, we find that the permanent establishment of the Institute in York was mainly effected, under Almighty God, by Sir Thomas Gascoigne. Through his benefactions the Superior, Mrs. Redingfield, was enabled to purchase, on the 5th of Nov., 1686, a house and garden at Micklegate Bar, on the site of the present convent, which the Institute of Mary has occupied uninterruptedly ever since. Here went on a quick, hidden work which effected more than can be told for the preservation of the Catholic faith in the country through the apparently hopeless years of penal persecution. This convent became a favorite place of female education, and has just claims on our affectionate veneration; it deserves well of the Catholic world if no other work had been accomplished within its walls than the training of two such noble souls as Frances Ball and Mary Aikenhead. Here Frances Ball spent five years of her girlhood; hither when assured of her vocation to the cloister, she came, at the express wish of Dr. Murray, the great Archbishop of Dublin, to be thoroughly trained in the traditions and principles of the spiritual life. Here she passed seven years of probation and preparation, returning with two companions to Dublin in 1821, to plant at Rathfarnham, " under the shadow of the saving Cross," the Irish offshoot of the Institute, in speaking of which our late Holy Father, Pius IX., said: " I know it well—it is a fruitful branch of a noble tree."

Reverend Mother Ball called the first house of the Institute in Ireland "Loretto Abbey," from Loretto, the celebrated Italian shrine. The other houses of the Institute of the Blessed Virgin Mary are called "Loretto Convents," from the parent house at Rathfarnham; from the houses the name has passed, almost unconsciously, to the inmates, who are generally known as "Loretto Nuns."

At the present date the Institute has more than one hundred and fifty houses in different parts of the world—Bavaria, Prussia, Austria, the Tyrol, Hungary, Italy, Spain, Turkey, England, Ireland, India, America, Australia,

South Africa, and the Mauritius. Of these about fifty are filiations of the Irish Branch of the Institute.

Upon his appointment to the Episcopal See of Toronto the Right Rev. Dr. Power visited Ireland, and obtained from Mrs. Ball a promise that, as soon as he should have made the necessary preparations for their reception, she would send him some members of the Institute to conduct the superior education of the female portion of his flock. It was not until 1847 that the design was carried out. In that year, on the Feast of Our Lady of the Snow, August the 5th, four professed nuns and one novice set out from Kingstown to proceed to America by way of Liverpool. These were Sisters M. Teresa Dease, M. Bonaventure Phelan, M. Gertrude Fleming, and Reverend Mother Ignatia Hutchinson, whom Mrs. Ball had appointed Superior of the little band of missionaries.

They reached Liverpool on the 6th of August and immediately proceeded to the Convent of Mercy, where they received a most cordial welcome from the Superior, Mrs. White. Here they had the pleasure of an introduction to the celebrated Father Gentili, who addressed them in a few words which were admirably calculated to impress them with a high sense of the dignity which God had conferred on them in calling them to labor in the foreign missions.

The voyage to America, which was made in the sailing vessel " Garrick," proved far from comfortable to the little band of religious women owing to the rough manners and language of some on board. After a passage of six weeks they reached New York and thence started for their new home in Toronto, where they arrived on September 16th, 1847.

On landing the embarrassment of the poor nuns was very great. They knew not where to go, and were too timid to ask. And when at last they succeeded in reaching the Bishop's residence, it was only to meet a father upon whom death had thrown its terrible shadow. His Lordship could not hide his anxiety, which was increased by the arrival of these poor Sisters at a time when the very city was a plague-house, and his own home a hospital, and the few priests near him stricken with the fever. But his zeal did not forsake him; and he who had stood by the bed of sickness until he was about to be prostrated by it, installed these chosen children of our Blessed

Mother, who had come so far to serve him, in their new home on Duke street.

They were welcomed by a few of the leading Catholics of Toronto, whose names have long been cherished and remembered with gratitude by the Community. Amongst them we select the well known promoter of every Catholic cause in Toronto, the Hon. John Elmsley, and Mr. Lynn, the latter of whom is bound to the history of Loretto Convent by his eldest daughter, Charlotte, who was the first member of the Blessed Virgin's Sodality in the Canadian schools, and one of the first postulants in the Sisterhood, and, since the death of Mother Teresa, Superior of the American branch of the "Loretto Nuns."

We now resume the recital of the early history. The death of the venerable Bishop Power prostrated Mother Mary Ignatia and her companions; but with true religious virtue and faith they bowed themselves under the hand of God.

Father Paré was now sent with kind offers of service on the part of the Bishop of Montreal. Another devoted friend was Father Harkin, who was chaplain, confessor, and indeed class-master.

Taking advantage of the Christmas vacation the nuns made their eight days' annual retreat, which they had been unable to do at the usual time. During that retreat, Sisters M. Bonaventure and Gertrude showed symptoms of the disease which was to bring them, after terrible suffering, to an early grave.

The Sisters who taught in the poor school, which was a long distance from the Convent, were obliged to walk there every day in winter through unusually deep snow. On reaching the school their clothes were often almost saturated, and in this condition they taught and labored till five in the afternoon, when they returned home, scarcely able to see their way through the clouds of snow. One morning, it is related, the cold was so intense that on suddenly entering the school-room, heated by the crowd of little ones, one of the Sisters, overpowered by the change of temperature, fell, to all appearance, lifeless. Help was sought, but when it arrived the courageous religious had already arisen and was presiding over one hundred and fifty pupils. Sister Mary Gertrude had charge of this school, and Almighty God so permitted it that, notwithstanding her state of suffering from a swelling in her knee, by which her foot was also affected, she continued to walk to and from the school every day, each step causing her intense agony. At last she was obliged to relinquish her labors amongst the poor, whom she so much loved; nevertheless, in the true spirit of her vocation, she desired to work, and continued to be of much use to the Community at home. It was an admirable lesson to see Sister M. Gertrude enlivening by her cheerful presence the hours of recreation, while the pain she endured from her swollen and gangrened foot never for an instant left her. The wildest and most unmanageable pupils were subdued by her firm, yet gentle manner, and knowing something of her great sufferings they revered her as a saint.

While Sister Mary Gertrude was enduring her severe tortures, disease had carried off Sister Mary Bonaventure, who died on the 11th of April, 1849. Three days after her death Rev. Mother Ball, as if by inspiration, asked two of the Community in Ireland to come to the relief of the Canadian Colony. They accepted: Sister Joachim Murray, who still lives, loved with deep affection by all her old pupils and revered by all who know her, and a lay Sister, Sister Ita Cummins.

The Community was still further tried when Sister Gertrude had to have her leg amputated, but to little purpose. She lingered in patience and suffering until Christmas of 1850, when she died a saintly death. To her memory the following tribute is paid by one of the Community who knew her: "So edifying was this Sister that the memory of her virtues remained long after she had been withdrawn from this passing world." But the heaviest loss was yet to come when the Superior, Mother Ignatia, was called to her eternal reward on the 9th of March, 1851. "Nature and grace combined to her adornment, as the purity of her soul seemed reflected on her beautiful countenance. Her career was brief, but well fitted to prepare her for the happy close which ended her life of trial and suffering in Canada."*

Mother Teresa Dease, being chosen to succeed as Superior, assumed the duties of her office under depressing circumstances. The Community consisted of only three professed choir sisters, two novices and two lay sisters. The pupils were few, and the house inconvenient. But they found one comfort in their confessor, the Rev. Father Tellier, S.J. His holy example, his

---

* Notes by one of Mother Ignatia's spiritual children.

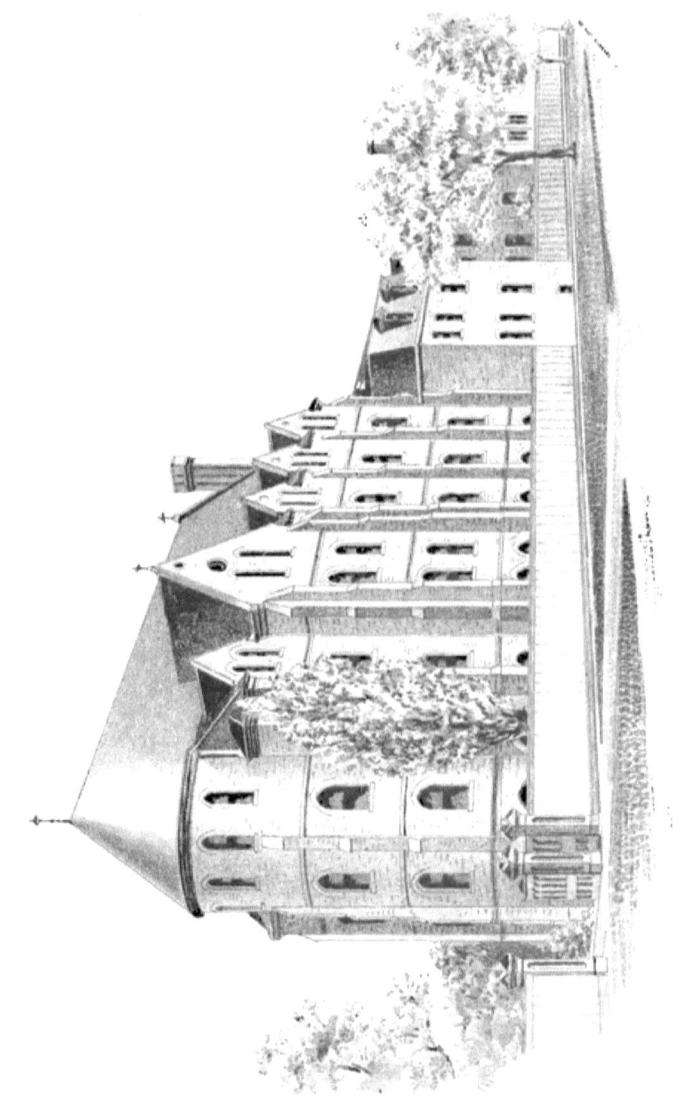

Loretto Abbey

fatherly advice and his regular attendance, proved a consolation and support to the rising Community.

Bishop de Charbonnel wrote to the Archbishop of Dublin, setting forth the misery in which the poor Sisters were situated, and appealing for more volunteers. "Most Rev. Lord," he concludes, "I earnestly beg your Grace the favor of obtaining from the mother house of our venerable Sisters whatever you can in their behalf. They are the children of Ireland and a glory to their country; they were your spiritual daughters before becoming mine; they have made the most generous sacrifice; they have suffered heroically; they are sinking under the hardships of their situation."

Towards the close of 1851 the Bishop's letter produced fruit, when Sisters M. Purification Oulchan and M. Berchmans Lalor came to the help of the Canadian mission. The following year the Sisters moved to a convent on Bathurst street, which had been built for them—not particularly comfortable or imposing, but healthy and commodious. And the change soon made itself felt. In 1853 the Community had so far increased in numbers that five were sent to open a house in Brantford, which place was, a few years afterwards, changed for London, where they had better opportunities for promoting the object of the Institute. When Bishop Farrell took charge of Hamilton he offered the Sisters of Loretto a house in Guelph. They readily accepted and took possession in June, 1856. The house in Guelph proved so successful that during the first few years of its existence no fewer than thirty-four of the pupils became members of the Community.

The Community now steadily advanced: a house was opened at Belleville in 1857; another at Niagara Falls, on the Canadian side, in 1861. In 1870 the latter had flourished so well that the foundation stone of a magnificent building was laid, which is to-day a beautiful work of art amidst the most beautiful surroundings of nature. Then, in 1865, a charming site in Hamilton having been purchased, Mt. St. Mary's was opened under the protection of "Mater Admirabilis."

Returning to the mother-house, we find them changing the convent on Bathurst street for a much better one on Bond street, which in turn soon became too small, so prosperously did things advance. At last, in 1867, through the kind services of the present Archbishop of Toronto, then Vicar-

General of the Diocese and pastor of St. Mary's Church, the property known as "Lyndhurst" was purchased; and from September 8th, 1867, what had been a most fashionable house of the world was thenceforth to be a religious house of education, and known to many of our readers as Loretto Abbey.

In 1874 a branch was started at Lindsay, which has since been closed. A house was founded in 1878 at Stratford; and in 1880 a new field of labor was opened up at Joliet, a city of Illinois, not far from Chicago. An idea of the good which the Institute is doing in that western city can best be formed from the fact that there are 200 pupils in its Academy and about 700 in the two parochial schools of which the Sisters have charge.

The following are the statistics of the schools and academies, as far as available:

SEPARATE SCHOOLS.	PUPILS.	ACADEMIES.	PUPILS.
Stratford	250	Stratford	72
Guelph	300	Guelph	83
Hamilton	160	Hamilton	125
Joliet	670	Joliet	200
Belleville	230	Belleville	60
Niagara Falls	100	Niagara Falls	85
De La Salle		Loretto Abbey	200
Brockton		Bond street	140
Winchester street		Wellesley Place	100

MOTHER M. TERESA DEASE.

We close this section with a sketch of the late reverend Mother Mary Teresa Dease, written by a member of her community. We deem it a fitting tribute to the memory of one whose hidden life, as religious and superior, for so many years was a model to her sisters, a guide to her pupils, and an edification to the Church in this country.

"Reverend Mother Mary Teresa Ellen Dease," inscribed on a tomb near the pretty little cemetery of Loretto Convent, Niagara Falls, is a simple and striking epitaph that arrests the attention of even the casual visitor to this quiet home of the dead. This epitaph contains only three words: "Mother, Model, Guide"—simple, indeed, but most eloquent and truthful return of love and loyalty from devoted children to the cherished memory of their revered and lamented reverend Mother, Mary Teresa Ellen

Dease, for forty years (1851-1889) the Superior of the Sisters of Loretto in Canada.

The many foundations, convents, educational and religious works that have been briefly outlined in the foregoing sketch of the Loretto Institute in Canada, all remain as monuments to Mother Teresa's memory. But the simple words inscribed on her tomb tell the secret of her life's success, and are the surest pledge that her work shall live in the lives of those to whom she was Mother, Model and Guide.

The history of Catholicity in the Archdiocese of Toronto would not be complete without a few words on the life and character of Rev. Mother Mary Teresa. This remarkable woman had all the qualities that win admiration, success and esteem in any walk of life. Bishop de Charbonnel, second Bishop of Toronto, a man of wide experience, deep discernment, and cautious opinion, said that Rev. Mother Teresa was the most perfect type of the lady and religious he had ever met. She possessed all the advantages of family and birth, all the graces of high breeding, all the charming attractions of personal beauty, the most winning sweetness, combined with a rare dignity and repose of manner—everything, in fine, that goes to secure highest social success, while her brilliant and solid intellectual gifts would have easily led up to literary fame. But her success was to be found in the service of God, and her fame to be a model to her children of Loretto.

Ellen Dease was born of distinguished family in the county of Meath, Ireland, on May 7th, 1821. The best blood of Nugents, O'Reillys and Deases flowed in her veins. The late illustrious Count Nugent of Austria was her near kinsman. Her cousin, the Very Rev. Edmund O'Reilly Dease, to whom Mother Teresa bore striking resemblance, was many years Provincial of the Society of Jesus in Ireland. He was a man of surpassing gifts of mind and heart, and was acknowledged to be the greatest English theologian of his time, beloved by his Jesuit brethren for his simple, sweet and most amiable character. Indeed, those who knew both well said Father O'Reilly and Mother Mary Teresa were exceedingly alike in mind and heart, as well as in personal appearance. The members of Ellen Dease's own immediate family were distinguished for talent and piety, as well as for noble work in the cause of God and His Church. Her elder sister, Anna Maria, was a religious of the Institute of Loretto in Ireland,

and died in the odor of sanctity at Loretto Convent, Fermoy, in 1878, having been Superior for 25 years. The example of her sister's life in Loretto might have had some influence, under God, in deciding Ellen's vocation.

It is one of the most striking things in the life of Mother Teresa that little is known of her early years, for she never talked about herself. We learn, however, that after careful home training under attentive private tutors, she completed her education in the best schools of Dublin; and, in answer to the call of the Master, left home, and family, and friends, joyously gave up all that the world holds dear, and on the 16th of January, 1845, entered the novitiate at Loretto Abbey, Rathfarnham, near Dublin, to consecrate her life to God. The distinguished Rev. Mother Ball was then Superior of Loretto. Her quick intuition and keen spiritual discernment soon discovered in her postulant a pearl of great price, a chosen soul, destined to do great things for God. From the very beginning of her religious life, Ellen Dease put into daily practice the divine principle she afterwards gave her children as their religious motto—"*In silentio et spe fortitudo vestra.*" "In silence and hope be your strength."

On the 15th of October, 1845, Miss Dease received, with the usual solemnity, the religious name of Mary Teresa, which she bore with such honor for 44 years; and on the 3rd of August, 1847, Sister Mary Teresa was solemnly professed. This profession completed her preparation; for just two days after, she, with five other Nuns, was chosen for the mission to Canada. The story of their coming, of their early struggles, disappointments and sufferings, has been already told. Very little of her privations was ever heard from Mary Teresa. Her strength was indeed in silence and hope, and never was such strength more needed than in the beginnings of the little Community of Loretto in Canada. When the first Superior of this valiant band, Mother Mary Ignatia Hutchinson, was called to her reward in 1851, Sister M. Teresa was chosen to take her place. The world wants statistics as proofs of successful work. It has these statistics of Mother Teresa's success in the brief history of the Institute of Loretto in Canada given above. The summary is eleven first-class educational institutions directed by teachers who have received the highest testimonials of excellence and competency, and whose pupils have often given public proof of the best intellectual and moral training. What the world does not stop to consider is the silent power that established these Institutions, and the wisdom from above that fashioned and formed to strength and efficiency those who direct them so well.

The great mind that planned in silence, the brave heart that worked on in hope, were known only to God, and to those who see in faith the strength of God beneath the surface of things that appear. The ministers of God know how to admire the great soul of Mother Mary Teresa, and how to appreciate the spiritual influence of her silent power and action. Three distinguished prelates of Toronto had ample opportunity of studying her character. We have heard the testimony of Bishop de Charbonnel. Seeing the wonderful formative influence Mother Teresa exercised over her children, the late lamented Archbishop Lynch said, " that holy woman has infused her spirit into the whole Community."

But perhaps no one living had better opportunities and power of judging the true character of Mother Mary Teresa than the present illustrious Archbishop Walsh. As a young priest at St. Mary's, Toronto, he was chaplain and spiritual director of the Community; and his interest in everything connected with the welfare and progress of the Institute increased with years, and is now made perfect in the kindest paternal care. What impressed him most in the character of Mother Teresa was her profound and practical reverence for everything holy and divine. And what was particularly striking in this great reverence was that Mother Teresa had a deep sacred respect for souls, for the secrets of hearts, and for every human being. Her strong and lively faith beheld Christ in every Christian, and saw the Creator in every soul made to the image of God.

But, after all, it was only her children who could know Mother Teresa as she was. They saw the great, bright, broad mind in her every word and work. They knew the security they had in giving most sacred confidence to her wise and prudent keeping, and how safely they could trust to her holy guidance. But especially did the children of her love feel the beating of that great heart of hers, always ready with the word of comfort, encouragement and gentle praise. Mother, indeed, was she in the reverent and tender care she had for the least of her children—model and guide in following to the letter the rule she would have her children observe.

As Mother, Model and Guide, may she continue to live in those she has left to complete her work.

SECTION IV.

THE SISTERS OF ST. JOSEPH.

The foundation of the "Congregation of the Sisters of St. Joseph" dates back to the year 1650. Under Divine Providence, its founders were the saintly Mgr. de Maupas, Bishop of Le Puy, France, and Rev. Jean Paul Medaille, of the Society of Jesus.

In his missionary labors, Father Medaille had met many pious young women, who, besides having in view their own sanctification, were anxious to devote themselves to the works of charity in the service of their neighbor. He was pleased with their pious desires, and suggested to Bishop de Maupas the establishment of the "Sisters of St. Joseph." That eminent prelate, calling to mind the original idea of St. Francis de Sales, warmly approved of the suggestion of Father Medaille.

In establishing the Order of the Visitation, St. Francis de Sales intended it to be a Congregation of women who, in addition to self-perfection, should undertake the visitation of the sick and poor, and, in general, all those duties that tend to advance the spiritual and temporal welfare of their neighbor. Though the saintly founder finally yielded to the force of arguments in favor of a cloistered community, his first design was happily realized a few years later, in the establishment of the "Congregation of the Sisters of St. Joseph," an Order uniting, as it does, a life of contemplation with the active works of charity and education.

In compliance with the Bishop's desire, Father Medaille assembled these pious young women in the house of Madame de Joux, a devout widow of Le Puy. In 1650, on the feast of St. Teresa (Oct. 15), the Bishop placed the Female Orphan Asylum under the charge of the little Community. After exhorting them to the two-fold exercise of charity—the love of God and the love of their neighbor—he invested them with the religious habit, placed them under the protection of St. Joseph, and ordered that henceforth they should be called the "Congregation of the Sisters of St. Joseph."

These first founders then set about drawing up rules which would assure the stability of the new society. They were decided on little by little, the foundation being those first written by St. Francis de Sales for the Order of the Visitation, and which Bishop de Maupas called the best guarantee for the future of the new Institute. Father Medaille added thereto some regulations of St. Ignatius, especially in regard to the vows which were to impose the same obligations as the simple vows pronounced at the close of the novitiate in the Society of Jesus.

By an episcopal ordinance, dated March 10, 1651, Bishop de Maupas solemnly confirmed the establishment of the new Institute; he founded several houses of the Congregation in his own diocese, and throughout his life manifested the greatest zeal for its advancement. His successors continued to promote the good work, the civil power gave its sanction, and Louis XIV. confirmed by letters patent the establishment of the Congregation.

Gradually the Order spread through the adjoining parts of France. Its members were employed in various ways; the education of the young; the care of the orphan, the sick and the infirm; the charge of hospitals, and the visitation of the poor—such were, up to the time of the French revolution, the principal works which claimed their attention.

But the fatal year of 1789 brought many miseries to the church in France, and not the least among them was the forced suppression of religious Communities. The convents of the Sisters of St. Joseph were taken possession of in the name of the Commune, and the members obliged to seek, as best they could, some place of shelter. The Superior, Rev. Mother St. John Fontbonne, found a refuge in the home of her parents. Here she was joined by two other sisters, and together they performed the religious exercises of the Community. Being, at length discovered, they were loaded with chains, and dragged to the prison of St. Didier, there to await the death sentence. Many other members of the Community were thrown into the same prison, and Mother St. John proved herself an heroic mother to her companions by constantly encouraging them to suffer with fortitude and resignation. On a certain day they were to be guillotined for refusing to take the prescribed oath: morning came and found them in readiness, but the sudden fall of Robespierre the night before brought them pardon and liberty. Though these courageous souls were not privileged to die for the faith, the names of Sisters of St. Joseph are not wanting on the list of the martyrs of the revolutionary period.

As soon as peace was restored to the Church, Mother St. John endeavored to reorganize the Community. This proved to be no serious task; the restoration of their property was refused, and a spirit hostile to religious orders prevailed among the people. But after years of patient sufferings and ardent supplications, Mother St. John was called to the city of St. Etienne to transform a pious association there established into a new Congregation of the Sisters of St. Joseph. The Archbishop of Lyons, Most Rev. Dr. Fesch, strongly approved of restoring the Order by means of this association, composed, as it was, of young girls and former members of religious communities. This was accordingly done in 1808, and shortly after, the Sisters were able to resume the religious habit, reopen their convents, schools and asylums. And in a truly wonderful manner did the Order increase; the Government gave its authorization in 1812, and henceforth new foundations were made, not only in France, but in many other European countries. A few years later, and we trace the Congregation to the shores of India and America.

The mother-house of the Sisters had, in the meantime, been established in Lyons, and from this centre radiated the various colonies of the Community that supplied "the foreign missions." The Sisters of St. Joseph first came to America in the year 1836. They were but six in number, and came to the diocese of St. Louis, Missouri, at the request of the late Bishop Rosati. Among these missionaries were two nieces of Rev. Mother St. John Fontbonne, already mentioned as the second foundress of the Community. One of these, Mother Delphine Fontbonne, was placed in charge of the first convent opened in America, that of Carondelet, in the suburbs of St. Louis. Soon after she was appointed Superior of a convent and novitiate opened in Philadelphia.

In the year 1851 the late revered Bishop de Charbonnel passed through that city on his return from a visit to Baltimore. He had felt that his episcopal city of Toronto stood in pressing need of a community that would instruct the young, visit the sick and the poor, and take care of orphan children. The family of Fontbonne* in France being favorably known to Bishop de Charbonnel, he entreated Rt. Rev. Dr. Kenrick, Bishop of Philadelphia, to send Mother Delphine, with some of her religious, to make a foundation in

---

* The Bishop's father, Count de Charbonnel, had greatly assisted Mother St. John Fontbonne in re-organizing the Community after the French Revolution.

his diocese. Permission being given, Mother Delphine arrived in Toronto Oct. 7, 1851. She was accompanied by Sister M. Martha, from the novitiate of St. Louis; Sister M. Alphonsus, and Sister M. Bernard,* from the novitiate of Philadelphia. On their arrival in Toronto, the Sisters were entrusted with the care of an Orphan Asylum situated on Jarvis street, (formerly Nelson). A novitiate for the new foundation was soon opened, and in it many pious souls sought seclusion from the world. In the following year, 1852, the Separate Schools were placed under the direction of the Sisters; and though difficulties presented themselves, owing to poverty on the one hand and bigotry on the other, the classes were well attended. Gratifying results soon rewarded the labors of the Sisters. The orphans were well provided for; the children prepared for the worthy reception of the Sacraments without detriment to their progress in secular learning; sinners were reclaimed; prisoners visited and instructed; the sick and the dying consoled.

In April, 1852, at the request of the Very Rev. E. Gordon, V.G., three Sisters were sent to Hamilton to take charge of an Orphan Asylum there. For over four years the establishment remained a mission house of the Toronto Novitiate; but with the formation of Hamilton Diocese the branch became a parent stem, from which, in turn, other missions have successively sprung. In addition to various charitable institutions, the Sisters conduct many of the parochial schools throughout the diocese of Hamilton.

In June, 1854, the Sisters removed to their Convent on Power street, which they had in the meantime been enabled to erect. In the Orphan Asylum a sufficient number remained to attend to its various duties. The new Convent was blessed and the first Mass celebrated by the late Very Rev. Father Gordon, V.G., on the feast of the Visitation. In September of the following year, 1855, the first boarding school for young ladies was opened in St. Paul's parish. The little Community, rapidly increasing, soon extended its sphere of usefulness. In less than five years' time it numbered five different houses—three within the city limits, and two in other parts of the diocese.

* The only survivor of these four missionaries is Mother M. Bernard Dinan, the venerable Superior of the "Sacred Heart Orphan Asylum," Sunnyside, Toronto. For over forty-two years she has borne the sweet yoke of her Divine Master, and faithfully served Him in some of the most responsible offices of the Community.

But God, whose designs are all-wise and inscrutable, willed to impress the sign of the Cross on the humble Community blessed with so prosperous a beginning. It pleased Him to call to Himself Rev. Mother Delphine, and to crown her virtuous life with a happy and edifying death.

Towards the close of the year 1855 a fever-stricken patient was admitted unawares into the Sisters' Orphan Asylum. Rapidly the contagion spread among the inmates; and in attending them, no fewer than nine Sisters contracted the disease. Their devoted Superior, Rev. Mother Delphine, though overwhelmed with grief, was untiring in her attention on her beloved children. But when God requires the sacrifice maternal tenderness and unremitting care are unavailing. After witnessing the edifying death of two of her Sisters she herself was stricken with the disease; and on the 7th of February, 1856, she was numbered among "the faithful departed." Having in life been a holy example to her dear spiritual children, she taught them in her last moments how a true religious should prepare to meet her crucified Spouse.

Rarely has a Superior been more tenderly venerated, more deeply lamented. The sorrow of her sisters, assembled around her death-bed, was in proportion to the affection they bore their saintly mother, whose cherished name still lives in the hearts of her spiritual children; and to-day, after a lapse of well nigh thirty-seven years, the sacrifices she made, the virtues she practised, are frequently recounted for the edification and example of the young religious.

In a letter written by Bishop de Charbonnel to the Director of the Grand Seminary of Lyons, France, the sad news was conveyed to Mother Delphine's brother, Rev. J. Fontbonne. His Lordship pays the deceased Superior the following tribute :

" My Dear Friend—It will be easier for you than for me to find the Abbe Fontbonne, formerly a missionary in America, and at present stationed in the diocese of Lyons, somewhere about Verrieres, if I am not mistaken.

" It is my sad duty to announce to him that his sister, Mother Delphine Fontbonne, Foundress and Superior of the Religious of St. Joseph in Canada, entered into her reward, February 7, 1856, one hour after midday, holily fortified with all the rites of the Church, and surrounded by the most devoted attentions.

"This excellent and worthy niece of the saintly Mother St. John had, in five years, established in Toronto, a Novitiate, an Orphan Asylum, a House of Providence, which affords to the poor every spiritual and temporal succor, and several other houses in the diocese. Endowed with great wisdom and experience, this holy Superior enforced the rule with sweetness and firmness. Her judgment was solid, her mind clear and penetrating, her prudence enlightened and far-seeing. She was laborious, energetic, active and provident.

"At the age of twenty-one she was appointed Superior of the first colony of Sisters sent from France to St. Louis, Mo., and now she is dead at the early age of forty-two.

"Her robust health promised her a long life, but she has fallen a victim to her charity while attending some of her sisters and novices stricken with fever.

"Will you be kind enough to transmit this communication to her reverend brother, and inform also the Rev. Superior General of the Mother House at Lyons, that the suffrages of the Community may be given to our dear deceased Sister, although I feel assured she has entered into beatitude.

"I hope when I go to Europe to be able to get a considerable number of sisters and novices. We have work here for a hundred if we could get them. . . . . The religious are called to do an immense good here; and, as I sometimes tell them, they can do everything but give absolution; they can, however, give instead perfect contrition and charity."

The obsequies of Rev. Mother Delphine, at which Bishop de Charbonnel officiated, were celebrated on the 9th of February, with a religious solemnity worthy of her who was lamented. It was indeed an edifying and most affecting sight to witness the whole Community, then forty-eight in number, paying a last public tribute of veneration to their dear departed Mother. And it would seem that her petitions in heaven were more powerful than her prayers on earth had been: after her death the epidemic that had done such fatal work entirely ceased, and her remaining spiritual children, guided by a wise and prudent Superior, Rev. Mother Teresa, were spared to continue their various charitable undertakings.

One of the most important of these was the management of the House of Providence.

In the course of a few years the Community was again in a prosperous condition; many fervent subjects had been received, several new houses of the Congregation opened, and the pupils of both the parochial and the boarding schools constantly on the increase.

The convent erected on Power street in 1854 soon proved too small to serve the triple purpose of mother house, novitiate and academy. It was, therefore, considered necessary to erect a convent that would afford ample accommodation to the steadily increasing Community. But lacking as they did all earthly resources, the Sisters could only appeal with childlike confidence to Him who promises a hundred fold, even in this life, to those who leave all for His sake. Though not in a desirable locality, the ground adjoining the House of Providence was at the disposal of the Sisters, in case they wished to build thereon. This they reluctantly decided to do, fearing that nothing better would offer itself. Stones for the foundation were accordingly drawn and other preparations made for beginning the work in the spring of 1862. But Divine Providence willed otherwise. A novena of adoration was begun by the Community in order to learn, if possible, the holy will of God in their important undertaking, and in answer to it their faith and piety were rewarded. In February, 1862, the Hon. John Elmsley heard, through the good Basilian Fathers, of the difficulties under which the Sisters labored, and generously donated them two acres of the land known as the "Clover Hill Estate."

The erection of St. Joseph's Convent and Academy was immediately begun, and in August, 1863, the building was completed. It was blessed on the Feast of the Assumption, the first Mass being celebrated by the late Archbishop Lynch, who delivered a fatherly and most pathetic discourse to the assembled Sisters. Several additions have since been made to the main building, the principal being the new eastern wing, erected in 1883, and specially devoted to academic purposes.

The Community had, in the mean time, succeeded in purchasing a number of adjoining lots; these, in addition to the land donated, form the spacious square known as "St. Joseph's Place."

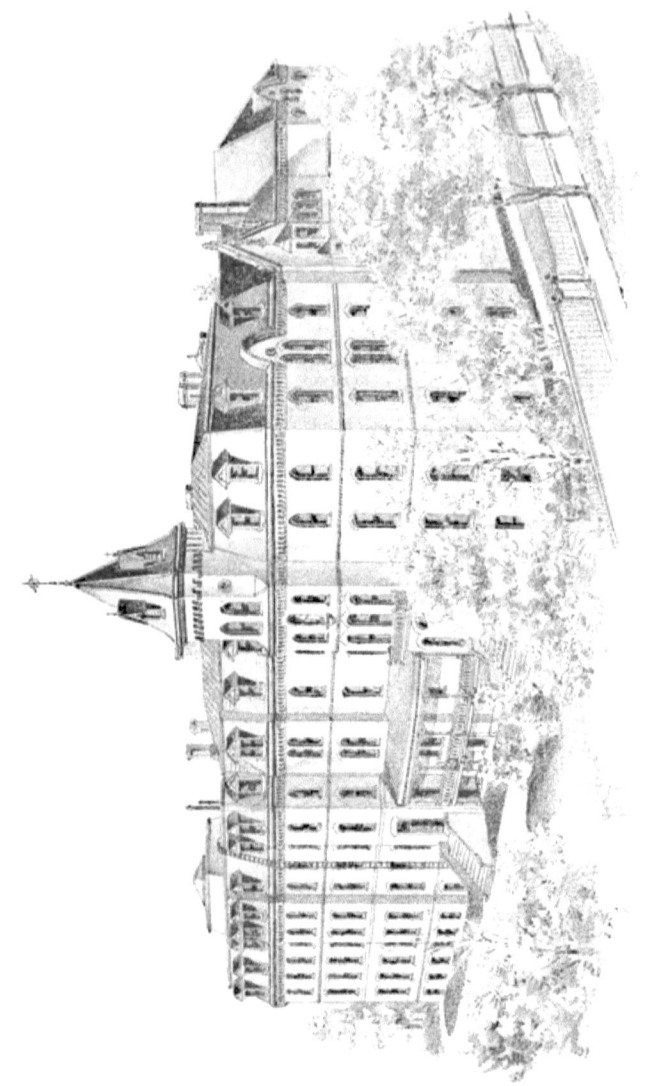

St Joseph's Convent.

As previously stated, the Sisters were given charge of the parochial schools in the city as early as 1852, the first under their direction being St. Patrick's school, then situated on Queen street. In the following year a school was opened in St. Paul's parish, two Sisters being placed in charge. Gradually the number of parochial schools increased, till at present (1892) there are under the direction of the Sisters of St. Joseph in Toronto and its immediate vicinity forty-four classes with a daily average attendance of over two thousand two hundred pupils.

The high classes for girls of the Separate schools are taught by the Sisters of St. Joseph. To the curriculum of studies, formerly identical with that of collegiate institutes, have lately been added phonography, type-writing, and a thorough commercial course. The pupils qualify for third and second class teacher certificates, and the success attending their efforts at the various departmental examinations proves that the work of preparation is carefully and thoroughly done. In addition to the Separate schools, the Sisters in St. Mary's parish conduct a private day-school for young ladies and a class for junior boys. In September, 1890, the Sisters removed into their new "St. Mary's Convent" on Bathurst street, a large and cheerful building.

Several new and important missions had in the mean time been opened. In December, 1856, at the request of Very Rev. Dean Grattan, three Sisters were sent to St. Catharines to take charge of the parochial schools. With the growth and prosperity of the town the number of classes gradually increased; as did also the attendance in the select school opened for young ladies in 1870. The Sisters were, therefore, encouraged to provide more ample accommodation, and as a consequence they erected, in 1874, St. Joseph's Convent and Academy, one of the most imposing edifices in the city of St. Catharines. In January, 1858, four Sisters were sent to Barrie at the request of Rev. Father Jamot, afterwards Bishop of Peterborough. In November of the same year, in response to the appeal of Rev. Father Proulx, the mission of Oshawa was opened; and in August, 1875, four Sisters were sent to Thorold to open a branch house of the Community. The permanent establishment of the Sisters of St. Joseph in this town is principally owing to the endeavors of the zealous pastor, Rev. T. Sullivan.

In all these different missions the Sisters take charge of the parochial schools, conduct music classes, visit the sick and poor, and attend to the religious training of the children entrusted to their care.

The next mission was opened in London in December, 1868. At the request of Rt. Rev. Dr. Walsh, now Archbishop of Toronto, five Sisters were sent to take charge of an Orphan Asylum. The little Community remained subject to the mother house in Toronto until December, 1871. On receiving letters of obedience from Most Rev. Archbishop Lynch, the Sisters in London were constituted into a regular diocesan Community; a novitiate was at once opened and in a short time mission houses were established throughout the diocese. In addition to the care of the sick and poor, the Sisters are engaged in conducting both parochial and select schools.

At the request of the late revered Bishop Jamot, who had a previous knowledge of the work of the Sisters in the Archdiocese of Toronto, a colony of five Sisters was sent to Port Arthur in August, 1881. They took charge of the parochial schools, conducted music classes, and undertook such works of mercy as the exigencies of the place required. In an addition built to their convent in 1883 the Sisters were induced to open a temporary hospital. The following year the erection of "St. Joseph's Hospital" was begun, and rapidly pushed on to completion. Though under Government control, the Sisters have retained the direct management of this great work of charity.

In September, 1883, at the request of Rt. Rev. Bishop Jamot, four Sisters were sent to take charge of the parochial schools in Cobourg. The pupils increasing in numbers, additional Sisters were soon required. A private class for young ladies was also opened in the convent building; but being found a matter of much inconvenience, it was closed after a short time.

In the vicinity of Port Arthur is situated the Indian village of Fort William. In the summer of 1884, in answer to the request of Bishop Jamot, four Sisters went from Toronto to take charge of the school for Indian girls, who are kept as boarders in the Convent. They are either orphans or children whose homes are at too great a distance from the school to allow them to attend it regularly. Besides the ordinary work of the class room the pupils are taught sewing, knitting, and all kinds of housework, somewhat after the manner of an industrial school.

The diocesan organization of the Sisters of St. Joseph in the diocese of Peterborough is of recent date. By the wish of their ecclesiastical Superiors the Sisters remained subject to the mother house in Toronto for nine years, the final separation taking place in June, 1890. The mother house or novitiate of the diocese is in Lindsay; and though but a short time opened, many fervent subjects have embraced therein the humble and laborious life of religious. To the direction of the Sisters the girls' classes of the parochial schools in Lindsay are entrusted.

In the neighboring town of Peterborough the fine new "Hospital of St. Joseph" is under the care of the Sisters. This charitable institution is open to all classes and creeds; and, apparently, sectarian differences do not hinder a large number from seeking admission. Many additional requests for new foundations from the mother house in Toronto have been regretfully refused, owing to the limited number of subjects to meet the demand.

Sacred Heart Orphan Asylum, Sunnyside.

It has already been noticed that an Orphan Asylum was intrusted to the care of the Sisters of St. Joseph on their arrival in Toronto in 1851. This home for the homeless was founded by that great and good man, Hon. John Elmsley, under the auspices of the saintly Bishop de Charbonnel. Until his Lordship's charitable design of opening a House of Providence was realized in 1857, the Asylum supplied, as far as possible the long felt want of such an institution. In 1859 the orphans were transferred from the Asylum on Jarvis street to the House of Providence, in which separate apartments were fitted up for their accommodation. But after the lapse of a few years it was considered necessary to secure a separate building for the children and leave the House of Providence for what it was originally intended—a home for the sick, the incurable and the aged poor. With a view, therefore, to opening a branch institute of the House of Providence, the Sunnyside property was purchased in 1881. This property, situated near the junction of Queen street and High Park, had previously been in the temporary possession of the Sisters. In 1876 the charitable owner, Mr. H. Speid, offered to the Superior of the House of Providence the free use of the house and grounds for the space of three years, with the expressed wish that the residence should be used as an orphanage. He generously extended the time for two years longer, and then offered the property at a very reasonable price. In June, 1881, his Lordship Bishop O'Mahony, with the approval of Archbishop Lynch, made the purchase for the sum of $9,500.

The Sisters again obtained possession and in a comparatively short time they removed the infant children to their new home, leaving, for the time being, the larger ones in the House of Providence. But that institution becoming overcrowded, it was considered advisable to erect an addition to the Sunnyside building for the better accommodation of the orphan boys. The corner-stone of the new institute was laid on the feast of the Nativity of Our Lady, 1884, by his Grace Archbishop Lynch; and on the feast of St. Teresa, October 15, 1885, the orphan boys, to the number of one hundred and thirty, were transferred to the new Asylum at Sunnyside. The change has proved a highly beneficial one— the picturesque and healthful surroundings, the out-door exercises, the large and cheerful class rooms, have each and all contributed to elevate the moral and physical well-being of these homeless boys.

With so pleasing an experience, the Sisters next endeavored to improve the temporal welfare of the orphangirls, who had, in the mean time, remained in the House of Providence. In the Spring of 1890 it was decided by the Community, with the approbation of his Grace Archbishop Walsh, to erect a second addition to the Sunnyside Institute for the accommodation of the orphan girls. The first sod was turned on the 27th of April, 1890, the feast of the Patronage of St. Joseph, and in August, 1891, the entire building was complete. On the 8th of September following one hundred and twenty orphan girls were removed to the "Sacred Heart Orphan Asylum," the name by which the institute is at present known. Children are left at the House of Providence till old enough to enter the class room. On the 24th of the same month Archbishop Walsh dedicated the new "Chapel of St. Joseph," and "Sacred Heart Orphan Asylum." In doing so, his Grace delivered a most eloquent and pathetic discourse; he eulogized the good work in which the Sisters were engaged, and showed that in taking care of the poor and the homeless they were doing the work our Divine Lord began on earth.

In the new portion of the building, also, the class room, dormitories, refectories and play rooms are large, airy and well lighted, and every arrangement seems designedly made to benefit "God's poor little ones." In addition to class work the girls are taught sewing, knitting and various other household duties; the boys being occupied at the same time in tailoring, knitting, gardening and other useful employments. The registered attendance of children averages about two hundred and seventy, though the institution has ample accommodation for nearly four hundred inmates.

St. Nicholas Institute.

The St. Nicholas Institute was founded in 1869 by the late distinguished prelate, Archbishop Lynch. He conceived the charitable design of opening a house for working boys wherein they would be protected from evil society, and experience at the same time the comforts of a home. The building is connected with the Convent of the Sisters of St. Joseph on Lombard street. These good religious have the general management of the institute, while a trustworthy man has the immediate superintendence of the boys. These average in number about fifty, and are in general well conducted and honorable. In course of time many of them have greatly improved their condition in life, and have thus happily realized the anticipations of the illustrious founder.

Notre Dame Institute.

In April, 1871, the Notre Dame Institute was founded by the late Archbishop Lynch. Knowing that many respectable Catholic girls came to the city to attend the Normal School, fill positions in stores, learn trades, etc., he determined to secure them a comfortable boarding house under the control of a Religious Order. For this purpose the building on Jarvis street, formerly used as an Orphan Asylum, was fitted up, a large addition built, and the institution placed in charge of the Sisters of St. Joseph. So well did the establishment succeed, that in the course of a few years it was found necessary to secure a more commodious building.

The new Institute on Bond street, to which the Sisters removed in 1885, is well adapted to the needs of the occupants. It is in a more desirable locality, and within easy reach of churches, schools, and the business portion of the city.

This building situated on Bond street had once been employed as a Baptist Church. It was purchased by Archbishop Lynch and turned into a public hall. The Sisters of St. Joseph then bought it, and completely changing the interior, turned it to the purpose for which Notre Dame had been established.

Within the last few months the purpose of the house has again been changed, and Notre Dame has been converted into a Catholic Hospital under the charge of the Sisters of St. Joseph.

House of Providence, Toronto.

The largest charitable institution in the city of Toronto, if not in the Province, is that known as the House of Providence, situated in the east end of the city. It is an imposing edifice, the main building being 130 feet by 60 feet and four stories high, and is situated in a very desirable locality.

Under God, the House of Providence owes its origin to the charitable zeal and wise forethought of the late Monseigneur de Charbonnel, that truly good man, whose heart was ever responsive to the appeal of the suffering poor, and whose mind was tireless in its efforts to assuage their miseries.

The laudable work undertaken by his predecessor was assiduously carried on by the late lamented and much revered Archbishop Lynch, and to his wonderful energy and whole-souled charity may be attributed many of the spiritual and temporal blessings now enjoyed by its inmates.

The object of its establishment, together with the projected plan of maintenance, probably suggested to the holy founder of the institution the name "House of Providence," so aptly applied. Since its foundation in 1857, it has been a refuge and a comfortable home to thousands of sick, infirm, destitute and forsaken, who otherwise would have been thrown on a cold world.

A special interposition of Providence seems, too, to have contributed to the success and support of the establishment. At the time of its commencement the spirit of bigotry prevailing in Toronto was very strong, and was manifested in an attempt to destroy the new building by a modern "Gunpowder Plot." An early discovery of the design, however, happily led to it being frustrated. Many interesting circumstances are still related by the older members and by friends of the Community, to show the truly providential manner in which the institution, in its earlier days, was often relieved and its inmates succored at a time when prospects looked anything but encouraging.

In the year 1857, while the building was yet under course of construction and almost destitute of furniture, it was opened under the direction and management of the Sisters of St. Joseph.

A number of sick and destitute were its first inmates; and, though accommodations were meagre and sources of maintenance uncertain, the

HOUSE OF PROVIDENCE, POWER STREET.

Sisters were not discouraged, but went bravely on in their divine mission, sometimes going from door to door soliciting alms to procure the necessaries of life for God's poor and needy who were given to their care.

In the year 1859 a number of orphan children who, since 1851, had been under the charge of the Sisters on Jarvis street, were removed to the House of Providence, and a portion of the building was set aside for their accommodation, as their late asylum was not large enough for the constantly increasing numbers. From that time until 1885, when Sunnyside Home was prepared for the orphan boys, the two institutions were combined, being under the same roof and the same management.

The orphan girls remained at the House of Providence until September of last year (1891), when, Sunnyside Home having been suitably enlarged, they too were removed there. With the exception of children under four years, who still occupy the first flat, the House of Providence is now filled with the sick, the aged and the incurables, for whose benefit it was originally intended. The poor old men occupy detached buildings, except the incurables, who have just been removed to the large school rooms lately vacated by the orphan girls.

The growth of the House of Providence has kept pace with that of the city, and with the ever increasing demands made upon such institutions; but though the building has been enlarged to almost four times its original size, it is at present filled to its utmost capacity, having about five hundred and thirty inmates—including thirty Sisters in charge.

In the course of about ten years from the date of foundation, the building had become so over-crowded that, from time to time, many deserving poor had to be denied admittance; but owing to limited resources and the struggling of the Sisters to meet current and necessary expenses, all thought of enlarging the building was reluctantly set aside until Christmas, 1872.

While several charitable ladies were devoting at that festive season their means and time to the poor, they noticed with pain how the Superior was obliged, on account of the crowded state of the house, to close God's door against the suffering members of Christ. Explanations followed; a public meeting was called; a list opened, and five thousand dollars were subscribed forthwith. The Catholics throughout the city were appealed to, and responded with their usual generosity. Indeed it would be unfair not to notice the charity of all citizens when it was ever a question of the House of Providence. The rich have given of their abundance, and the poor have added their mite. It would not do for a book like this to name or distinguish any—better for them that their names be written in the Book of Life.

The new wing, a large building 140 feet by 55 feet, was completed at the close of 1874, at a cost of $35,600; and in January, 1875, was blessed by his Grace Archbishop Lynch. An increase in the Government grant at that particular time, obtained through the influence of the Hon. C. F. Fraser, was indeed most opportune. In an amendment to the "Charity Aid Act," a clause was introduced awarding a certain sum towards the support of each inmate in the different charitable institutions, instead of giving indiscriminately, as had been done heretofore. This obviously just and wise measure was long and strenuously opposed by an anti-Catholic faction of the Government, who complained of its being "an appropriation of public funds to sectarian purposes;" but notwithstanding this opposition justice prevailed, and instead of the pittance formerly granted, the House of Providence received the next year from Government the very liberal sum of $3,298.54, and the Orphan Asylum $1,593.88; making a total of $4,892.42, as compared with the grant of $1,500 of the previous year. By the adjustment of this grant seven cents a day was allowed for each inmate of the House of Providence, and two cents a day for each inmate of the Orphan Asylum.

In order to show the fairness and the justice of this measure we make a few quotations. In his report on "Charities" to the Lieutenant-Governor in Council, the Inspector, Mr. Langmuir, made the following remarks: "These figures appear to prove that, in the past, this large institution, the House of Providence, has not received from the Government, anything like what it deserved for the work it has performed."

Four years previously, in 1871, the Grand Jury reported as follows: "The Grand Jury this day visited the House of Providence, in which there were 360 inmates. They found the House scrupulously clean and evidently well managed, and they fully concur with the opinion of the last Grand Jury, that the Government grant of $960 per annum is quite disproportionate to the magnitude and work of the establishment."

There being no proper accommodation for the inmates to hear Mass, it was deemed necessary to build a chapel, which was done in the year 1881. This new building afforded further accommodation, so much needed, on the ground floor and basement. The latter had been originally intended for the incurable men, but on account of the great numbers of sick poor who daily and weekly sought admittance, they were destined, until the present year, to be deprived of it.

We quote from a circular of Archbishop Lynch, in reference to the annual statement of the House of Providence:

"Nothing short of an almost miraculous interposition of Providence could have enabled the good Sisters presiding over the institution, with the slender resources at their disposal, to shelter, feed and clothe so many (530) poor whom God has adopted as His own children; to supply medicine to the sick, and even to provide coffins for those whom God has called to Himself. The intelligence and patience, above all, the industry and self-sacrifice exhibited by the poor Sisters in the management of the establishment are beyond all praise. Every hand that can be employed is trained to industry. The making and mending of clothes, washing, cooking and baking are done in the House. By industry such as this salaries to servants are saved, and the Sisters are able to support, at a cost of less than fifty dollars a year, persons who, in Government establishments, would cost three or four times that amount. From this it will be seen how worthy so noble an institution as the House of Providence is of the support of the kind-hearted people; and those who contributed towards it, according to their means, will not hear addressed to them on the great Day of Judgment the reproach of our Blessed Lord: 'I was hungry and you gave me not to eat; naked and you clothed me not; homeless and you took me not in.'

"The expenditure last year ($31,600) was increased by the erection of a new roof on the main building, and payments of debts on the chapel and adjoining buildings. These costly repairs were not undertaken for the sake of embellishment, but because they were absolutely necessary. Desirable as ornaments are, the good Sisters would not think of sacrificing for them funds so much needed by the destitute orphans and sick poor, whose welfare, both spiritual and temporal, they so dearly prize."

On another occasion his Grace wrote: "The good Sisters have all the trouble and anxiety of collecting funds and managing so large an institution, and suffer a great deal mentally and bodily; but they act as the servants of Jesus Christ, and their confidence in His mercy is justified."

The Archbishop made frequent visits to the House of Providence; and, with his usual paternal kindness and condescension, would walk around the sick wards to speak words of comfort and encouragement to the suffering patients and feeble old people.

Besides the care and anxiety his Grace always took in the spiritual interests of God's poor and lowly, he showed an equal solicitude in alleviating their temporal wants. For many years he had agitated an increase of Government grant for the incurables in the House, and in 1885 succeeded in obtaining it. The year following he addressed a pastoral to the patrons and benefactors of the House; of which he writes in these terms: "We are happy to say that the Government, on the report of the visiting physicians, and on the recommendation of Hon. Mr. Christie, has allotted three large wards in the House as a home for incurables, and has granted the daily allowance (15 cents each) which is given to the incurable Hospital of the city. This will prove a very great help, and has been fairly merited. The House of Providence has recently been visited by his Honor the Lieutenant Governor and several members of Parliament, and more recently by his Worship the Mayor, and many of the Aldermen. Every part of the House, from the kitchen to the upper dormitories, was inspected. All were surprised at the extent, the cleanliness, and the good order, evidently not expecting to see so much good in operation. His Honor the Lieutenant Governor made the following report: 'The Lieutenant Governor has great pleasure in recording for himself and for those by whom he is accompanied the great satisfaction with which they have viewed the excellent institution, which speaks volumes for the care, order, practical charity and skill with which it is conducted.'

"His Worship the Mayor also wrote : ' I have felt great pleasure in observing the care and kindness which are noticeable in the House ; also the perfect order and cleanliness of the institution.'

" Many similar records may be seen in the visitors' book, as several distinguished persons have from time to time since its establishment honored the House by their visits. Among these may be mentioned Her Royal Highness Princess Louise, and each newly appointed Governor-General, his Eminence Cardinal Taschereau, besides prelates and clergy from all parts."

The House of Providence depends for its support mainly on the voluntary contributions of the charitable citizens of Toronto and the Archdiocese, supplemented by the grant before mentioned from the Ontario Government, and another from the city, which latter has steadily increased from $100 to $3,000, the grant of the present year. It is, besides, occasionally assisted by donations from municipalities and bequests of private individuals.

As its door is open to all classes and creeds, Protestants have at all times been very liberal in their contributions, and especially has this been the case on the occasion of the Sisters' annual collecting tour through the city in the fall. An annual pic-nic held on the Queen's Birthday is another source of revenue ; and citizens testify, by their attendance in great numbers, their appreciation of the good work and their interest in its success.

A few years ago the Sisters were accorded the privilege of making an annual collection in the month of November in the various Catholic churches of the city, the proceeds of which are apportioned to the House of Providence and Sunnyside Orphan Asylum. The Sisters also collect among the farmers in the Winter season flour, meat, butter, wool, clothing, etc., all of which goes to lessen the monetary expenses of the House.

In this somewhat lengthy sketch we have endeavored to give to the public an outline of the foundation and history of one of Toronto's oldest and most noted benevolent institutions; also to set before them some information as regards its aims, the nature of the work it performs, and its character in general. Crude and imperfect though it be, it will not, we hope, be devoid of interest to those actively or otherwise employed in the grand and God-like work of Christian charity.

Continuing under the patronage of the great St. Joseph—the silent saint of the Catholic Church—we trust that its future may be productive of the same beneficent results as its past, and that it may always rank foremost among institutions of its kind in America.

SECTION V.

THE SISTERS OF THE PRECIOUS BLOOD.

One of the most important works in the Church is the hidden work of prayer. And in no age have there been wanting chosen children of Christ's Spouse who have been led to devote their life and energies to contemplation and to the reparation of the injuries and insults which sin offers to the outraged majesty of God. In such an atmosphere have grown up many of the most fragrant flowers of the Saints—the Catharines, the Gertrudes and the Teresas—whose virtues and fervor have been an odor of sweetness to the whole Church. Most, if not nearly all of these Communities were founded in Europe. But Canada may pride itself in having established one, having for its specific object the adoration of the most Precious Blood.

In 1861 Mgr. Joseph Larocque, Bishop of St. Hyacinthe in the Province of Quebec, decided, after mature consideration, to follow the promptings of divine grace which were very evidently manifested in the person of Miss Aurelie Caouette, a young lady of his cathedral city. While still at the convent of Notre Dame Miss Caouette was wonderfully attracted to devotion towards the most Precious Blood. The special favors which she received, and the supernatural evidence of God's will determined the saintly Mgr. Larocque to enter upon the arduous task of establishing a contemplative Community whose particular purpose would be to honor the Precious Blood of our Divine Lord, and by their life of prayer and penance make atonement for the insults which sin offers that great price of our redemption.

Accordingly, on the Feast of the Exaltation of the Holy Cross, September the 14th, 1861, the pioneers of the Community, four in number, met in Miss Caouette's house, where holy Mass was celebrated. Of this little band only two remain, the foundress, who took for her name in religion Sister Catharine Aurelie of the Precious Blood, and her cousin, Euphrasia Caouette, whose name in religion is Mother St. Joseph, and who has been Superior of the house in Toronto ever since its foundation. The young religious began with more zeal than prudence. The penances which these innocent souls imposed upon themselves, the entire child-like trust they placed in God, and the fervor with which they performed all the religious exercises, were more to be admired than imitated. However, in due course of time the saintly prudence of Mgr. Larocque tempered their zeal, and experience taught the sisters themselves that if they wished their Community to have any stability, to take its rank amongst the religious institutes of the Church, they must moderate their ardor and not follow their own guidance. A strict but careful rule was little by little drawn up, which has since, with some modifications, been conditionally approved by the Holy See.

In 1864 Archbishop Lynch first conceived the idea of introducing the Sisters of the Precious Blood into his diocese, " in order," as he expressed it to the Sisters themselves, " to help him to bring down the blessings of God upon those souls which were the object of his solicitude." But it was not until 1869 that this wish was accomplished. The community was too few, too young and too poor to stand division. But on the Feast of the Nativity of the Blessed Virgin, September 8th, 1869, the Convent of the Precious Blood was founded in Toronto by five choir sisters and one lay sister chosen from the St. Hyacinthe Monastery. Of these only one remains to tell the story of their early trials and sufferings, the revered Superior, Mother St. Joseph, who still governs her house with the zeal and prudence of a true religious, who has seen the little home of St. Hyacinthe spread until it numbers to-day seven flourishing houses and nearly two hundred sisters in all. The early chapter of the Community's history in Toronto is one of poverty and hardship. They at first were settled in the old Loretto Convent on Bathurst street. In 1872 they moved to the corner of St. Joseph and St. Vincent streets, opposite St. Michael's College. This house in turn became too small, and a larger one was purchased farther west on St. Joseph street. But no private residence is very suitable for a religious family. And this was the case with the Sisters of the Precious Blood in Toronto. The Sisters increasing in number, the building was too small; and, what was of more serious consideration, they could not carry out their rule, which required that they should be cloistered and entirely secluded from the world. For some time the health of the Sisters was so seriously affected by the crowded state of the house that a change was of vital importance to the continuance of the Community. Accordingly a large addition was made to the Convent, the corner stone of which was laid by his Grace Archbishop Walsh, May 28th, 1891; and now that it is completed, the Sisters enjoy all the accommodation for their life and rule according to the directions of the Institute. The cost of the improvements is about $24,000.

In the basement are latticed waiting rooms for visitors, refectories for ladies making lengthened visits, kitchen and laundry. The greater part of the ground floor is occupied by the chapel, which is divided into two sections—one for the nuns and one for the public. The novitiate is also on this floor. The first floor above is devoted to Community rooms, parlors, and rooms for ladies who wish to spend some days in retreat. The whole of the second floor is devoted to cells for nuns, of which there are twenty-seven. The furnishings throughout are neat, but simple and severe, and in perfect keeping with the unostentatious piety and mortification of the Sisters of the Precious Blood.

Their life consists chiefly in prayer. They recite every day the divine office, rising at midnight to chant matins and lauds. Special days of fast and abstinence are ordered every week by the rule, and severe penances are practised by these holy souls, who, unknown to the world, present themselves as holocausts to the Precious Blood of our Divine Saviour. Suffering and silent prayer were His lot upon earth; they yearn to imitate Him and to obtain for His Precious Blood a more abundant harvest of souls. What good these holy sisters do none but the angels know; they are, however, faithful guardians upon earth of our spiritual interests. We need them in these days of an unspiritual people, and it is one of God's choicest blessings upon this Diocese that a house of this Community has been established herein.

We feel that no historical notice of the Sisters of the Precious Blood would be complete without a word concerning one who has been to them much more than ordinary benefactress. If this Community is established in Toronto upon anything like a firm basis, it is due to the zeal, the prudence and devotion of Miss Mary Hoskin. Not only did this charitable lady bring the Community out of its lowest state of poverty and enable it to buy the property on the corner of St. Joseph and St. Vincent streets, but the Sisters owe their fine new home to her energy and care. Miss Hoskin is of an English family, sister of one of the leading lawyers in this city, and is a convert to the faith. Since her mother's death, some years ago, she lives in the Convent of the Precious Blood, to whose interests she devotes her life with most deserved success.

SECTION VI.

THE SISTERS OF OUR LADY OF CHARITY OF REFUGE.

The more abandoned a soul is the more does it become an object of that divine charity which ever seeks the lost and strives to raise the fallen. And of all abandoned souls none is more pitiable than those of unfortunate women. Betrayed by false friends, condemned by the world and ostracized by society, they have too often perished in their misery or been a scandal to thousands. But from the time when the Master of all took one such by the hand and, raising her up from degradation, made her the model of all penitent souls, there have always been communities of women specially devoted to the work of reforming their sex. Of one of these we have the good fortune of possessing a house in the city of Toronto. The title of the Community is the Order of Our Lady of Charity of Refuge, which was founded by the venerable Father John Eudes at Caen in France in the year 1641. It is modelled upon the Community of nuns established by St. Augustine, whose rules were in substance adopted by the saintly priest when founding them. They received approbation from Pope Alexander VII. in 1666, from Innocent XI. in 1681, and from Benedict XIV. in 1741, who put a final seal upon the constitutions and statutes of the Order, which had been revised at the General Assembly of the Community held at Caen in 1734.

The end of the Institute is to labor for the salvation of souls, for which purpose the nuns, in addition to the usual vows of poverty, obedience and chastity, bind themselves by a fourth vow to spend their life in the instruction of those who voluntarily place themselves under their care to reform and do penance. The rule also allows the Sisters to educate children for preservation from a life which, by its surroundings, might be an occasion of sin. The Community, a strictly cloistered one, is composed of choir, lay, and out-door sisters the last named being principally employed in the care of the apartments outside the enclosure and in transacting the business of the monastery. There are houses of the Community in many of the European countries as well as in America.

This order, at the request of the late saintly and charitable Archbishop Lynch, established a house in Toronto in 1875, under the title of "Monastery of our Lady of Charity." The founder, Mother St. Jerome, Tourneux, professed in the Convent at Rennes, had come from France to Buffalo, N.Y., as Superior of the Good Shepherd Convent there in 1855. Thence she went to Ottawa, where she established a convent in 1866. Here she remained until 1875, when, accompanied by Sister Mary of St. Joseph Raiche as assistant and two other choir sisters, one lay and one out-door sister, she arrived in Toronto on the 11th of September. They were most heartily welcomed by Archbishop Lynch, who remarked that for eleven years he had been asking for a house of their Community, and now he thanked God they had come at last.

On the feast of St Teresa, the 15th of October, the day from which the foundation dates, Archbishop Lynch assisted by Vicar-General Rooney, blessed the altar and chapel.

As with the other communities of the diocese, the early years of these devoted religious were marked by poverty, self-denial and hardship. At first occupying that building which is closely connected with three out of the four Communities of Sisters in the city, viz: the Bathurst street Loretto Convent, they moved to a property known as West Lodge pleasure grounds. On the 13th of July, 1879, the Sisters, with nineteen inmates, took possession of their new home. Their next step was to purchase four adjoining lots for a sum of sixteen hundred dollars ($1,600). Then, in

1879, they built a house for the "children," the name by which the penitents are called, which enabled them to carry out the rule requiring the children to be entirely separated from the Community. This was thoroughly carried out, when a handsome and more commodious house was erected, the corner stone of which was laid on the 30th of September, 1888, by the Very Rev. Father Rooney, at that time Administrator of the Diocese. This new Monastery was solemnly blessed by his Grace Archbishop Walsh on the 12th of December, 1889.

The Community numbers twenty-seven professed sisters and eight novices. At present, these have charge of seventy-five penitents. They are divided into three classes: firstly, the young girls; secondly, the aged and infirm; and lastly, the class of perseverance, or of St. Magdalene, consisting of those who wish to remain all their life. After several years of trial, in which they must give proofs of solid virtue, they are permitted to bind themselves by promise to remain all their life within the enclosure. They wear a special habit and have particular devotions and a rule of their own; they are not, however, allowed to become members of the Community.

In 1879 Mother Mary of St. Aloysius Schottmuller, who had founded the Monastery at Pittsburgh, was elected Superior in place of Mother St. Jerome, which office she still holds, to the welfare and success of all concerned.

SECTION VII.
THE SISTERS OF THE HOLY CROSS.

This Community, which has charge of St. Raphael's Academy, Sainte Croix in the County of Simcoe, was overlooked in the general list of the religious at the introduction of this chapter on account of the distant situation of its house and the purely local character of its work.

In 1885 the late Father Michel, then pastor of Sainte Croix parish, invited these good Sisters from Montreal to teach the English and French languages in the Separate schools of his parish, and to take charge of an Academy which he had built. Notwithstanding many other demands from various quarters upon the Sisters, they readily complied. Six Sisters, coming at the close of the year 1885, opened the select school on January 7th, 1886. They have an average of ninety pupils at the Separate school and of thirty at the Convent.

The Institute originated at Le Mans, France, some fifty years ago through the zeal of Father Antoine Basile Moreau, who had previously founded the Fathers of the Holy Cross and the Brothers of St. Joseph. The three Orders are chiefly devoted to the instruction of youth. Shortly after its establishment branch houses were started in the United States and Canada. The Indiana branch became, twenty-five years ago, independent of France; and this example was afterwards followed by the Canadian branch, which has its mother house at St. Laurent, near Montreal.

SUPPLEMENT.

CHARITABLE ORGANIZATIONS.

I.

THE ST. VINCENT DE PAUL SOCIETY.

Although this Society lays no claim to the rank of a religious community, still the work it does is so kindred to that of the Communities that no more suitable place than the present chapter could be found wherein to record its history and work in the Diocese.

The principle of this most deserving Society is thus laid down by Frederick Ozonam, its chief founder: "It is for the members to maintain themselves strong in the Catholic faith, and propagate it amongst others by the practice of charity."

The first Conference of Charity of the Society of St. Vincent de Paul in Toronto, and in the Province of Ontario, was founded on the 10th of November, 1850, by seven Catholic gentlemen, of whom but one survives, the venerable Chevalier Macdonell, President of the Particular Council of the city. The other names were: G. M. Muir, T. Hayes, C. Robertson, D. K. Feehan, and S. G. Lynn. A Conference was formed under the title of "The Conference of Charity of Our Lady of Toronto," with the following officers:

President,	G. M. MUIR.
Vice-President,	T. HAYES.
Secretary,	W J MACDONELL.
Treasurer,	CHARLES ROBERTSON.
Assistant Secretary,	D K. FEEHAN.
Assistant Treasurer,	S. G. LYNN.

His Lordship Bishop de Charbonnel, being present during a portion of the meeting, was requested by the President to grant them his approbation, and "that he would do them the favor of accepting the title of Patron of their Society in this Diocese." The Bishop expressed himself "satisfied with the object of the Society, of which he much approved, and stated that when in France he had been an honorary member of one of the Conferences. In the course of an instruction which he addressed to the Conference, his Lordship earnestly recommended the practice of abnegation of self, of humility, of union among the members of the Society, a careful selection of candidates for admission as members, on which the success of the Society would greatly depend, together with Christian prudence and a cautious avoidance of giving unnecessary publicity to the acts of charity performed by them."

The school house on Stanley (Lombard) street was offered and accepted for the meetings, which, it was agreed, should be held every Sunday after Vespers. A room in the rear of the premises of the Vice-President, T. Hayes, Esq., was given for the safe keeping of their stores and provisions.

After a collection, which amounted to one pound five shillings and three half pence, the meeting was closed with prayer.

Thus was started in the Sacristy of St. Joseph's Chapel, St. Michael's Cathedral, the Society which, during the past forty years and more, has done through the city so much hidden good and practised so much unostentatious charity.

The President, Mr. George Manly Muir, who was a clerk in the Legislative Assembly, changed his residence, the following year, 1851, to Quebec, where he was appointed President of the Particular Council in 1859. In 1866 Mr. Muir became President of the Superior Council of Canada—which position he held until about a year before his death, which took place on the 8th of July, 1882. His name was held in veneration by the early members of the Conference he founded, and his words of wisdom and charity were deeply cherished when he addressed them from his higher position.

The Conference of Our Lady continued to increase in resources, numbers and works, so that at the end of two years it was deemed expedient to establish a new conference in the east end of the city. But as it is too long for the purpose of this sketch to trace fully the growth of the Society, the following extracts from the Report for Toronto, read at the general meeting, July 20, 1890, give the date of establishment of each Conference and the different Presidents:

"The Conference of our Lady was aggregated on the 6th of January, 1851 the first President being, as already stated, Chevalier G. M. Muir. His successors have been: W. J. Macdonell, John Wallis, Charles Robertson, Patrick Hughes, Patrick Curran and E. F. Wheaton.

"The Conference of St. Paul was aggregated on December 19th, 1853, under the presidency of D. K. Feehan, succeeded by William Paterson, J. G. Moylan and J. J. Mallon.

"The Conference of St. Mary was aggregated on the 13th June, 1854. The Presidents have been James McMahon, James Nolan, Thomas Barry, Patrick Cosgrave, Francis Rush and Martin Burns.

"The Conference of St. Basil was aggregated on the 31st of October, 1859, under the Presidency of the Hon. John Elmsley, succeeded by Charles Robertson, Richard Baigent, Remy Elmsley, M. O'Donnell and J. J. Murphy.

"The Conference of St. Patrick was aggregated on the 29th of February, 1864 Presidents: James Nolan, Martin Murphy and William Burns.

"The Conference of St. Peter was aggregated on the 23rd May, 1887. Presidents: Michael Ryan, Samuel Dunbar and John Rodgers.

"The Conference of the Sacred Heart (French Canadian) was aggregated on the 6th of November, 1889—President, P. Jobin.

"The Conference of Our Lady of Lourdes was aggregated on the 6th of November, 1889—Patrick Hughes, President.

"A Conference exists in St. Helen's, Brockton, which has not yet been aggregated to the Society."

A Conference also exists in St. Joseph's parish, Leslieville, which has not yet been aggregated to the Society.

The following extract is taken from the Report of the Superior Council of Canada for 1891. Reviewing the work done in Toronto, the report says: "The Conferences of this city, over and above the ordinary works of the

Society, pay great attention to visiting the poor in the hospitals, and have for the purpose a special committee, with officers to look after them and see to the collection of funds for their assistance. And how much good consequently do they not do among the suffering members of Jesus Christ, as well as among those who are expiating their misdeeds against society! By means of visits, prayer books, rosaries, and good books, they inspire the one with patience and the other with the resolutions to lead better lives. But if they minister to the sick and to those in prison, they also labor to moralize the poor by means of libraries. Several conferences have their libraries, containing a large number of volumes, which they annually increase. Thus the St. Basil Conference possesses 1013 volumes. The Librarian acknowledges receipts to the amount of $40.47, and an outlay of $40.27 ; 64 volumes were added during 1890, and 886 books were loaned during the year.

"The St. Patrick's Conference has to-day 916 volumes on its shelves. The receipts of its library were $55.32, and the outlay $37.11."

We give the following table showing the work done by the Society during the various years mentioned:

YEAR	No. of Conferences.	No. of Members.	Receipts for the Year.	No. of Persons Relieved.
1878*	3		$3,329	
1889	8	245	3,046	1,033
1890	8	248	1,939	1,012

The Constitutions of the Society require that when there are two or more Conferences in a town they shall be united under a particular Council, which is designed for the direction and supervision of the works and measures which interest all the Conferences. The Particular Council of Toronto was established on February 26th, 1854, with Chevalier W. J. Macdonell as President, who still holds this important position. The Chevalier sat at the cradle of the St. Vincent de Paul Society in this city; he has ever since taken the deepest interest in its steady growth and its

* This was the first year in which the annual report was printed.

untold works of charity. By education, rank and character he was admirably fitted for the chair which he has so long occupied, and he gave himself up to the work which it entailed with a devotion which has produced excellent fruit both in the spirit animating the Society and the good which it has done.

CHEVALIER W. J. MACDONELL,
Knight of the Holy Sepulchre.

William John Macdonell, who comes of a Scotch family, was born at Boston in the State of Massachusetts, on November 14th, 1814. He received his preliminary education in Boston High School, and completed it in Montreal College with the Sulpicians, where he acquired a thorough knowledge of the French language. In his early business life he was engaged at Kingston as forwarding Commissioner. When, afterwards, he came to Toronto he was Manager of several banking and loan institutions, being for ten years President of the Toronto Savings Bank and ten more its Manager. He was for many years a member of St. Andrew's Society.

He held the distinguished position of French vice-consul for twenty-six years, and resigned through ill health. In recognition of his long services the French Government conferred upon him the Cross of the Legion of Honor. Some few years ago he was also signally honored by the Holy Father, who, through the intervention of the Patriarch of Jerusalem, created him a Knight of the Holy Sepulchre, so that his title is Chevalier Macdonell.

We have briefly outlined the career of one whose fatherly care of the St. Vincent de Paul Society well deserved more than a passing notice. Mr. Macdonell is a man of wonderful memory, of deep piety and great charity— one of those souls who are in the world, yet not of the world, and who are becoming rarer by reason of the spirit of the age.

The Chevalier, having a great taste for literature, gathered in the course of his long career one of the finest private libraries in Toronto. Amongst these valuable works, in company with the great writers of the past, he used to spend his leisure hours, and cultivate his mind with a learning which was both varied in its subjects and deep in its research. Mr. Macdonell has generously donated his library to St. Michael's College, where it is preserved and known as "The Macdonell Library."

Taking up the account of the Particular Council, we give its officers as at present constituted:

President,	CHEVALIER W. J. MACDONELL.
Vice-President,	J. J. MURPHY.
Secretary,	ALEXANDER MACDONELL.
Assistant Secretary,	JAMES RYAN.
Treasurer,	H. T. KELLY.
Assistant Treasurer,	M. MEYER.

In July, 1884, a special Board consisting of such members as should be appointed was established for the purpose of visiting the hospitals and prisons. The duties were to visit the sick and supply as far as possible religious and interesting reading, as well as clothing when required. In order to place the Board in a position to carry on the work more efficiently his Grace Archbishop Walsh kindly granted an annual collection in all the Churches of the city—"Hospital Sunday." The following figures will give an idea of the articles distributed, but cannot convey any notion of the sympathy afforded and the consolation bestowed: Prayer Books, 245; Beads, 252; Scapulars, Crucifixes, &c. The members of the Board* are:

President,	PATRICK HYNES.
Vice-President,	MARTIN BURNS.
Secretary,	E. A. CULLERTON.
Treasurer and Librarian,	J. J. MURPHY.

Outside of the city there are conferences of the St. Vincent de Paul Society at Collingwood, organized in 1874; Orillia, organized in 1885; Newmarket, organized several years ago; and St. Catharines, organized in 1885.

* This list is from the Report of 1890.

II.

THE LADY VISITORS TO THE HOSPITAL.

This work, after calling attention to the Hospital Board of the St. Vincent de Paul Society, cannot be passed by unnoticed. The work is of a kindred nature. When the St. Vincent de Paul Society appointed its Committee of Hospital Visitation a difficulty was found in regard to the female patients. The Board waited upon the late Archbishop Lynch to propose the advisability of forming a Society of Ladies who would undertake the work of looking after the spiritual interests of these sufferers. Accordingly in May, 1885, a society was established with Mrs. B. B. Hughes as President; and to this good lady's direction the efficiency of this deserving association is largely due. The other officers are:

Secretary,	MISS MARY FOY.
Treasurer,	MISS MARY HOSKIN.
Librarian,	MISS MARY CASSIDY.

The Society is formed of members from the parishes of St. Michael, St. Paul, St. Basil, St. Patrick, and Our Lady of Lourdes. Each parish takes a month for visiting. Its meetings are held the first Monday of every month. The fees are made up of an annual subscription of one dollar from the members, and a share in the "Hospital Sunday" mentioned above.

SEPARATE SCHOOL LAW

AND

THE SEPARATE SCHOOLS OF THE ARCHDIOCESE.

BY

JAMES F. WHITE, Esq.,

INSPECTOR OF SEPARATE SCHOOLS

REV. BRO. TOBIAS,
PROVINCIAL OF THE CHRISTIAN BROTHERS

CHAPTER VIII.

SEPARATE SCHOOLS.

Early Legislation—Acts of 1841, 1853, 1855, 1863—Separate School Law of Ontario under the British North America Act—Recent Legislation—Separate Schools of the Archdiocese.

AT the time of the Union, Quebec already had a system of Separate schools, and both Provinces had devoted to secondary education relatively greater attention than to primary, so that consequently the latter was not generally in a flourishing condition. The first Parliament under the new constitution passed a School Act, applicable alike to both sections of the Province, providing for Separate or Dissentient schools in each, and largely increasing the grants for elementary education. In regard to Separate schools, the chief features were that the religious minority might collectively signify their dissent in writing, stating the names of the persons chosen as trustees, who should have the same rights and duties as those elected for Common schools. Taxes were levied uniformly on all, and, with the legislative grant, were divided between the two classes of schools in proportion to the number of their supporters. Separate schools were not authorized in towns and cities; but, in lieu of this, a joint Board of Catholics and Protestants, in equal numbers, controlled all urban schools. They were empowered to license teachers, to select text-books and regulate the course of study, and to visit and examine all classes. If it were arranged that certain of these schools should be attended only by Catholics and others only by Protestants, then the Catholic committee was to have exclusive control over these Catholic schools, and the Protestants over their own. But, where mixed schools prevailed, there should be no distinct committees. This measure was introduced as much at the request of the Protestants of Lower Canada as to benefit the religious minority here, and was passed with little if any opposition. The first rural Catholic Separate school established under this law was in the township of Kingston; but not many were organized for the first two or three years. A short trial proved that, with such different conditions in the two parts of the Province, one School Act would not work harmoniously. Accordingly a new law was passed in 1843, applicable to Ontario alone. This recognized and extended the principle of Separate schools, permitting them either in town or in country, and to Catholics or to Protestants, upon the application in writing of ten residents. But Catholics could demand such a school only when the Common school teacher was a Protestant, and Protestants had a like choice if the teacher were a Catholic. These schools received their share of the legislative grant according to average attendance, and were subject to like laws and regulations with Common schools.

Meanwhile Dr. Ryerson, who had been appointed Chief Superintendent of Education for Upper Canada, and had spent some time in examining the school systems of Europe and the United States, published an elaborate report on elementary education as the result of his investigations. He advocated the taxation of all property for school support, the establishing of Normal and Model schools, the appointing of District Superintendents, and insisted that every Protestant had the right to have his child use the Bible as a text-book. To aid him there was appointed a Council of Public Instruction, having representatives of the chief religious denominations. Bishop Power having consented to act was named Chairman. An Act framed by Dr. Ryerson, and based on his report, was passed in 1846. In regard to Separate schools its provisions were identical with those of the preceding measure. But in the following year a new school bill became law, giving Boards of trustees in cities and towns power to determine the character of the schools, whether "denominational or mixed." This restored matters to nearly the same position as they were in by the Act of 1841, but without the safeguard that one-half the Board should be Catholic. Evidently it was intended to suppress, if possible, all urban Separate schools, since they could be established only at the pleasure of a Common school Board. Naturally Catholics complained loudly at being thus deprived of their then existing rights. At the same time opponents of Dr. Ryerson's views fiercely assailed his Common School Act through the press and in Parliament. Finally a new measure was, without due consideration, passed through the

House in 1849. It contained no provisions for Separate schools in any form, but forbade the use of the Bible as a text-book. Upon the advice of some of his Ministry, the Governor suspended the operation of the bill, and in the following year another regulation framed by Dr. Ryerson was enacted. Upon the petition of the Catholics, headed by Rev. J. Carroll, Administrator of Toronto, most of their former rights were restored to Separate school supporters. The Act made it the *duty* of the Board, upon the application in writing of twelve residents, to authorize the establishment of one or more Separate schools, for "Protestants, Catholics or colored people," to prescribe the limits for such schools and to arrange for the first election of their trustees. But, as before, Catholics could have a Separate school only when the teacher of the Common school was a Protestant, and *vice versa*. Though this permitted greater freedom than former Acts and was to that extent a welcome concession, a few years' working convinced clergy and people that its provisions were still too restricted. As an instance, when the Catholics of Toronto applied to have a second school they were refused on the ground that the statute allowed but one in a municipality. This objection having been sustained in Court, a "Short Act" was introduced in 1851, restoring the right to have a Separate school in each ward, or in two or more wards united, as the applicants might judge expedient.

At that time taxes were levied alike on the supporters of Common and Separate schools, and, along with the government grant, were divided between them in proportion to their average attendance. The Act defined the "school fund" to consist of the legislative grant and at least an equal sum raised by local assessment. But some Boards interpreted this to mean that, if they raised an amount larger than the Government grant, Separate schools would not be entitled to share in such overplus. The Protestants of Chatham, deciding to erect a new school building costing £1,200, levied for this purpose a tax on all property indiscriminately. To this the Separate school supporters submitted, thinking they would receive their due share; but the Board refused to give them any portion of this surplus money or to allow them the use of any part of the building. The Catholics complained of this great injustice, and Bishop de Charbonnel laid the matter before Dr. Ryerson. He protested also against the use in mixed schools of anti-Catholic text-books, and against Catholic pupils being compelled in some places to assist at Protestant prayers or religious exercises. The Chief Superintendent attempted to defend this unjust taxing of Catholics on the rather sophistical plea that they might afterwards join these Common schools; and he threatened that, if the Separate school agitation were continued, all Catholic teachers in the Common schools would be dismissed.

Acting together the Catholics again petitioned the Government for relief from an imperfect and unjust school law. The Bishops conjointly addressed a memorial to the Governor protesting against their people being forced to support the Common school system as, one "conducive to indifferentism and often to aversion for religion," and asking that Separate school supporters be relieved from contributing to the building or maintenance of Common schools. They also requested to know from the Ministry, from some of whom they had received promises of relief, whether they intended incorporating into the new school bill the amendments indispensable for securing the rights of Catholics. In reply Bishop de Charbonnel received early in 1853 this assurance from Attorney General Richards : " I hope that the provisions of the Bill will be such as to prevent future dispute and difference. As I said before to you personally, I have endeavored to give to the Separate schools in Upper Canada the same rights and powers as the Dissentient schools in Lower Canada have."

But, despite these protests of good will and equal rights, the Government declined to make more than a nominal improvement in the law, as a powerful agitation against Catholic claims had arisen in the country. Heretofore all Separate school measures had passed with the consent of both sides of the House and in general without any division. But now a new party had arisen with the avowed object of abolishing Separate schools. Dissenting ministers preached against them, and a section of the press denounced them in no measured terms. The schools were described as supported by Protestant money, and inflammatory appeals were made not to allow Catholic doctrine to be inculcated in schools assisted by the state.

About 1851 Catholic Institutes were first organized in Ontario, one of their chief objects being to further the interests of Separate schools. At a meeting of the Toronto society early in 1853, presided over by Bishop de Charbonnel, a resolution was passed pledging the Institute " to oppose by all constitutional means the re-election of the present Ministry, and of any of their supporters, if at the next session of the Provincial Parliament full justice is not done to the Catholics of Western Canada with reference to the free working of their Separate schools." Directed by these Institutes, petitions were widely circulated and largely signed; as many as 18,000 names being sent to the Government, 2,000 of which came from Toronto. When these petitions were presented, the Hon. Mr. Hincks, leader of the Reform Government, in the course of the discussion paid a high tribute to the moderation which Bishop de Charbonnel had always shown on the school question. The bill of this session known as " The Supplementary School Act" was satisfactory as originally introduced; but through changes made in committee it became of little service.

The Act of 1855.

In 1854 all the Bishops of Canada met in the Second Ecclesiastical Council of Quebec and issued a highly important pastoral on education. They say: "We beseech you, dearly beloved brethren, if you feel the slightest solicitude for the salvation of your children, do not expose them to enter those schools where they will be taught to call into question the most positive dogmas of revelation." At the same meeting they memorialized the Governor-General, Lord Elgin: " We do not ask exclusive privileges; we demand simply and solely that the law which regulates Separate schools on behalf of Protestants in Lower Canada, should be extended to the Catholics of Upper Canada."

Meanwhile a general election was held, and the whole Catholic body, headed by their Bishops, took an active part in the contest to protect their cherished rights. Party lines were for the time laid aside, and a solid Catholic vote given to those candidates who were ready to redress their grievances. As a consequence, a majority favorable to their demands were returned. Petitions asking for a fair recognition of their educational rights were signed by Catholics in thousands. The three Bishops of Upper Canada issued a comparative table showing in what respects the Catholic minority here were at a disadvantage as compared with the position of the Protestants in Quebec, and framed a Bill embodying the changes sought from the Government. The chief demands were: (1) The placing of Separate schools for everything under one official, not opposed to the system; (2) But one trustee for each ward and one Board in towns and cities; (3) Free circumscription of sections; (4) That three heads of families, not twelve as now required, might establish a school;

(5) A share in all taxes and municipal funds in the ratio of population; (6) That trustees should license teachers till they secure a Catholic Normal School; (7) That having once joined a Separate school, the supporter be relieved of making an annual declaration; (8) That they be freed from contributing to Common school libraries or buildings.

The Bishops had received assurances from the new Ministry that they were most anxious to meet their views and to allow Catholics to educate their youth in their own way. Bishop Phelan, with the approval of the other Bishops of Upper Canada, wrote to Hon. John A. Macdonald, Attorney General, West: "I trust you will not be prevented from doing us justice by allowing us the same rights and privileges for our Separate schools as are allowed the Protestants of Lower Canada. If this be done at the present session we will have no reason to complain, and the odium thrown upon you for being controlled by Dr. Ryerson will be effectually removed. If on the contrary the voice of our opponent upon the question of Separate schools is more attended to and respected than the voice of the Catholic Bishops, the Clergy and nearly 200,000 of her Majesty's loyal Catholic subjects claiming justice for the education of their youth, surely the Ministry that refuses us such rights cannot blame us for being displeased with them, and consequently for being determined to use every constitutional means in our power to prevent their future return to Parliament."

Finally Hon. Mr. Morin, who had expressed his determination to obtain equal rights for his co-religionists here, or resign his seat in the Cabinet, drew up, at the request of his colleagues, a bill which was just and satisfactory. Being raised to the bench he entrusted the measure to Attorney General Macdonald, who owed his election largely to Catholics, and who expressed his desire to give them full justice. But Mr. Macdonald, thinking it would be safer in the hands of an Irish Catholic, passed it to Hon. L. T. Drummond. The latter prepared a bill greatly inferior to that of Mr. Morin, which, however, upon the protest of the Bishop he promised to amend. But, as the session was nearing an end without the measure being introduced, Dr. de Charbonnel hastened to Quebec to watch over the interests of his people. At last it was brought up in the Council by Col. Taché; and immediately afterward in the Assembly by Mr. Macdonald, and passed its second reading with but some unimportant amendments which tended rather to its improvement. The friends of the measure then relaxed their efforts and most of them left the Capital, amongst others Bishop de Charbonnel, "thanking God that after seven years of severe struggling, equal rights were secured at last!" On the last night of the session it came up for the third reading under charge of Mr. Drummond, who with the large majority at his back could have carried it through without a single change. But in committee George Brown moved amendments which he said were of a trifling character, and the Government suffered change after change till at last the liberal nature of the act was completely destroyed. Immediately on the passing of the bill, information was telegraphed to Toronto, and, not knowing the deception that had been practised, the Bishop thanked the Government for having passed the measure. But, when the truth was known, nothing could exceed the indignation felt and shown by the friends of Catholic education upon finding how they had been cajoled and deceived. The Bishop forwarded to the Governor his resignation as a member of the Council of Public Instruction, declaring that it was an insult to prefer, as the Government had, on a question solely affecting the Catholic people, the advice of Dr. Ryerson, a Methodist minister, to that of the heads of their Church; and protesting against the conduct of Mr. Drummond and others on the last night of the session.

This measure was not of course wholly bad; it conferred several important advantages: (1) Catholics were no longer required to appeal to the Common school Board, a presumably unfriendly body, for authority to establish their schools; (2) Separate schools could be organized even when the Common school teacher was a Catholic; (3) Trustees for Separate schools were placed on the same footing as those for Common schools; (4) It allowed a Catholic tenant of a Protestant landlord to support a Separate school; (5) The list of supporters with the amount subscribed was required but once a year instead of twice as formerly; (6) The legislative grant was now received direct from the Chief Superintendent, not through the local inspectors.

But while these changes were certainly of benefit to the schools, the Act yet fell far short of a full measure of justice. The chief grievances complained of, and those from which Quebec Protestants were free, were: (1) Exclusion from the municipal assessment for school purposes; (2) Requiring an annual notification; (3) Contributing to Common school buildings and libraries; (4) Receiving no share of public school moneys except the legislative grant; (5) Preventing Catholics from supporting a school in a neighboring section. This last restriction was one of great severity, for it allowed in general only weak sections in rural districts where, with a scattered population, it was usually impossible to establish a strong school within the boundaries of the Common school section. Municipal Councils and Common school Boards, to whom Catholics had previously to apply before legally establishing a Separate school, frequently took more than a fair advantage of their powers by alleging all sorts of irregularities or mere pretexts as a plea for not granting them a proper share of the school fund. In general, great difficulty was experienced in the endeavor to collect taxes under the Act, so that in Toronto, with a population of two thousand Catholic ratepayers, the Separate schools were unjustly deprived of the taxes of eight hundred. In consequence, the trustees decided to throw themselves upon the voluntary support of the people and made collections at the church doors.

The first sections of the law of 1855 repealed all the provisions of previous Acts and contained no clause perpetuating any Separate school already established. It provided simply for the establishment of new school corporations. As first introduced the bill granted the same privilege to Episcopalians, Jews, colored persons, &c., the intention being that any denomination might have its own Separate schools. It also contained at first, a highly important clause adopted from the measure proposed by the Bishops, requiring that "all the provisions of this Act and generally all the words and expressions thereof, shall receive such large, beneficial and liberal construction as will best secure the attainment of the objects thereof, and the enforcement of its enactments, according to their true intent, spirit and meaning."

Soon, letters appeared from different parts of the country protesting against the hardships of the Act and demanding a new measure, since Catholics in some cases were yet taxed twice. Thus the campaign opened anew; and, instead of the matter having been settled by the Coalition Government, it was left in a more complicated and difficult form than ever.

In December of the same year Bishop de Charbonnel published a letter pointing out the advantages and the defects of the school law, and advising the course to be pursued to obtain a more equitable enactment: (1) "To require from any new candidate for Parliament a pledge to support Separate schools in Upper Canada as enjoyed by the Protestants in Quebec. (2) To oppose, by all constitutional means, the election of any member who has voted or acted against that support. If our active co-operation might be of any service in any constituency of our Diocese, ... We would give it most willingly within the measure of our ability and without any human consideration. (3) To make the necessary declaration before the first of February," etc. Again in his Lenten pastoral he strongly exhorts Catholic electors to use their votes and influence in favor of Separate schools, and he enjoins parents that they are under obligation to make sacrifices necessary to secure such schools rather than incur the danger of sending their children to mixed schools.

At the opening of the session of 1856 an amendment to the Act of the previous year, which had authorized the double taxing of Catholics, was introduced by the Toronto member, Mr. Bowes, as the Ministry, fearing their Orange supporters, declined to make it a Government measure. No opposition was anticipated to such a just and equitable clause, but, to the surprise of all, a Ministerial amendment was moved that the law was satisfactory as it then stood. This was defeated. George Brown moved a resolution to abolish all Separate schools in Upper Canada, asserting that they were demanded only by the clergy and that the laity did not favor them. In reply, Mr. Felton, a Protestant member from Lower Canada, stated that he had no faith in the sincerity of the broad Protestant principles of Mr. Brown, who dealt largely in appeals to the passions and ill feelings of different sects, hoping thereby to mount to power. He believed that the Protestants of Upper Canada were not of the same opinion as Mr. Brown, since the highest authority of the Church of England here had recently expressed views entirely opposite. He proposed an amendment to confer on Catholics in Upper Canada the same privileges as were enjoyed by the Protestants of Quebec. The outcome of the debate was that nothing was done, the question being given a hoist.

It is impossible in a sketch like the present to do anything more than merely note the various battles of this great campaign. In the general elections of 1857 Catholics obtained from prominent Conservatives assurances of relief on the school question. But, though the Government had a good working majority, it did nothing to fulfil its promises.

Then came the question of the Clergy Reserves. Dr. Ryerson advised the municipalities to devote the money to establish school libraries. Father Bruyere objected to the proposal on the ground that the official list of books from which township libraries were to be selected was, on account of its sectarian bias, unfair towards Catholics. A warm and celebrated controversy ensued. Dr. Ryerson alleged that Dr. Power, the first Bishop of Toronto, was favorable to the Common school system. But letters of Dr. Power to the Hon. John Elmsley were quoted proving the contrary. Bishop Pinsonneault of London, writing to congratulate Father Bruyere on his able defence of Catholic education, declared that both Bishops Macdonell and Power, far from favoring mixed education, had merely tolerated what they then could not prevent, and that they had labored most faithfully to establish thoroughly Catholic schools wherever circumstances permitted.

In 1859 Dr. Lynch was consecrated Bishop, and Dr. de Charbonnel retired to France. Although the latter had not secured all that he desired still he had gained a great deal. His zealous successor continued the fight.

Early in the session of 1860 Mr. R. W. Scott, member for Ottawa, introduced a bill to improve the condition of Separate schools. The chief changes proposed were : (1) Five heads of families instead of twelve might organize a school ; (2) The one notification given by a supporter on joining to be sufficient without annual renewal ; (3) Trustees should be relieved from making their returns of attendance under oath, thus placing them in the same position as Common school trustees ; (4) Allowing the supporters of rural schools to form their own sections, and to have a union of adjoining sections. These would all be important concessions, particularly the last, as heretofore it had been found very difficult to establish strong rural schools.

The third reading of this bill fell on the morning the House was to be prorogued. When it came up the Hon. George Brown arose and announced that, though the measure might have a majority ten times as great, he would not permit it to become law. His intention was to speak against time until the Governor should arrive. He gained his point, sealed the fate of the bill, and prevented justice being done.

Early in the session of 1861 Mr. Scott introduced a nearly similar measure, which never reached its second reading.

In April 1862 Mr. Scott once more brought his bill before the House. It was changed somewhat from the former measures, and particularly in the following points: (1) Trustees should have power to grant certificates; (2) Notice of support to be given on or before March 1st; (3) A school should not share in the Government grant unless the average attendance reached at least fifteen; (4) Roman Catholic clergymen should be *ex-officio* members of Separate school Boards within their respective missions; (5) The holidays for Common schools not to be binding on Separate schools, but the trustees to prescribe such vacations as they see fit, provided the teaching days did not exceed a certain number each half year; (6) The Education Department to enforce no rules for the management of such schools, and not to interfere with their text-books.

The bill was referred to a Committee of the House and was understood to have the support of the Ministry, the second reading being carried by a vote of 93 to 13. But, though its prospects appeared so favorable, it again happened that a single member was able to prevent justice being done. Mr. Ferguson, Deputy Grand Master of the Orangemen, expressed his determination to speak hour after hour, and, if need be, day after day, to enforce the withdrawal of the bill. However unpalatable this display of unreasonable opposition to what the majority considered a just measure, there was no course but to abandon it for a time, or delay indefinitely the business of the session.

Soon afterwards the Coalition Government was defeated on the Militia Bill, and a Liberal Ministry succeeded to office, with John Sandfield McDonald and L. V. Sicotte as leaders for Upper and Lower Canada respectively. At the formation of the Cabinet the question of Separate schools was discussed, and it was agreed that a satisfactory bill should be carried the following session. On going to their constituents for re-election, members of the Ministry repeated this declaration. It was, however, not to be a Government measure, but left to a private member. This open guarantee of fair play was unquestionably the best course for the ministers to pursue, as it tended to disarm unreasonable opposition and allay groundless fears.

About this time the Anglicans began anew an agitation to have their claims recognized, as they had for some years been maintaining a system of Separate schools while contributing also to Common schools. They had already petitioned Parliament eight or nine times, but their Bishop attributed the failures to the fact of their being insufficiently supported. They now resolved to demand that, when any denomination should at their own expense erect school houses within cities or towns, the Government should extend to such denomination the provisions of the Separate School Act.

The Act of 1863.

In March, 1863, Mr. Scott once more introduced his bill. This was the perfected work of three years, embodying certain changes suggested by the Bishops and trustees, and accepted as satisfactory by Dr. Ryerson, who had objected to his former bills. In moving the second reading, Mr. Scott said that he sought for his co-religionists only the rights to which they were entitled, but with no desire to interfere with the Common school system.

The chief objection urged against this measure was, that other denominations would have the same rights as Catholics to demand such concessions, and the granting of them would break up the Common schools. But it must have been evident, even to those who were raising this objection, that as the Catholic Church, guided by its prelates, had been the only denomination which, with unanimity and persistence, demanded Separate schools, so Catholics alone would feel conscientiously obliged to maintain them. With them it was a question of faith and religious principle, with which no temporal expediency could interfere.

The principal amendments proposed were : (1) That trustees should be empowered to grant certificates to the teachers ; (2) That a Separate school should be open at least six months in the year and have an average of fifteen or more pupils to entitle it to share in the legislative grant ; (3) That these schools should not receive any part of the Clergy Reserves when devoted to school purposes. These amendments were all lost. Mr. Scott moved that teachers for Separate schools should obtain their certificates in the same manner as Common school teachers generally, "provided that persons qualified by law as teachers either in Upper or Lower Canada shall be considered qualified teachers for the purposes of this act." This was a most important point, as it ensured a proper standard of qualification for secular teachers, while permitting the employment of religious orders without further examination ; it was duly adopted.

Few measures, having arrayed against them so many and such powerful influences, had ever been carried through the House with such large majorities on every division. On the second reading it passed by 80 to 22, being supported by a majority of 14 from Upper Canada, and by all the Lower Canadian followers of the Government except one. The vote on the third reading was 76 to 31, there being but three Catholic members from Upper Canada. This time there was not a majority from Upper Canada, and some opponents of the measure raised the question of double majority, as the proposal affected the interests of only one section of the Province, and it should have a clear majority from that section to become law. But this principle had not been strictly observed for some time, and John S. McDonald deciding to call for the yeas and nays, the bill passed on the division, and he was sustained in his course. In the Upper House the majority on every reading was yet larger than in the Assembly. The Act was finally sanctioned on May 5th, 1863, to take effect from December 31st of the same year.

Thus, after a brave struggle of more than twenty years, the Catholics of Upper Canada had at last obtained a fair measure of the educational freedom to which they were so justly entitled. The almost incessant agitation on this question had been the cause of bitter sectarian disputes and much discontent, but no previous attempt at solution could be considered satisfactory. It is difficult to see the consistency of opposition that, while accepting the principle of Separate schools in agreeing to maintain them as then existing, would yet oppose all attempts at their improvement, which, without being unfair to Protestants, would be a great relief to Catholics. But the elections of the same year gave an assurance that the agitation in the country against the measure had practically ceased, for but one member pledged to repeal the Act was elected. To the untiring zeal and perseverance with which Mr. Scott battled for true toleration and recognition of just rights in education, is attributable in no small degree the triumph of this measure in the House, and the Catholics of Ontario owe him consequently a deep debt of gratitude.

The following utterance of " The Canadian Freeman " of March 19th, 1863, shows how Catholics at that time viewed the measure as to its finality : " We regard the slight concessions contained in Mr. Scott's bill only in the light of an instalment of our legitimate demands. Sooner or later the whole debt must be acknowledged and paid. We stand upon the broad and liberal basis of the Constitution, and demand for our co-religionists in Western Canada the same rights and advantages as are enjoyed by the Protestants throughout the Province."

The chief benefits conferred by this Act were: (1) Dispensing with the yearly notification from supporters; (2) Exempting trustees from swearing to the correctness of their report; (3) Permitting the union of adjacent rural sections, and allowing any Catholic within three miles of the school to become a supporter; (4) Requiring of lay teachers the same qualifications as for Common schools; (5) Giving a share in all public appropriations for elementary education. The schools were at the same time made subject to inspection and to such regulations as the Chief Superintendent might impose. The opinion of this official was that, while correcting the anomalies and inequalities of the law of 1855, this Act did not extend the principle of Separate schools, and would be really beneficial to the Common school system by diverting opposition.

When, some two years later, Dr. Ryerson publicly asserted that Bishop Lynch had accepted this Act as "a finality," the latter wrote:—"When earnestly pressed to accept the bill as a finality I studiously avoided the term, and was taken to task by a city journal for so doing. The term savored too much of the perfection of human progress, and seemed to place a bar to the claims and exigencies of the future. I said I was content with the bill, as were also my brethren in the episcopate, so far as I knew their sentiments. . . . But I consider that we should be wanting greatly in zeal for the good of posterity were we to content ourselves with anything less than the Protestant minority of Lower Canada have. I therefore rejoice that I did not use the word 'finality,' which, even had I used, could not certainly be interpreted to mean final under any and all circumstances, but final only so long as the position of the two provinces remained unchanged."

When the plan of Confederation was about to be adopted, Bishop Lynch and the other prelates of Canada, fearing that, when educational legislation was entrusted to each separate Province, the Catholic minority in Ontario need expect no very liberal treatment, made strenuous efforts to have the question of Catholic schools put on a satisfactory footing. But, though they required merely a guarantee that Separate schools in the west should have the same rights and privileges as had been solemnly assured to the Protestant minority in the east, they were not successful. Confederation was a compromise on many very important questions, accepted by men of all parties and creeds, but an essential part of it, without which the measure would not have been agreed to, was the provision guaranteeing by Imperial enactment Separate schools to the respective minorities in Ontario and Quebec. This constitution reserves to the Dominion Parliament a most important power—giving not only the right to veto injurious legislation, but also the authority to pass remedial measures if found necessary; while the power to abolish such Separate schools is vested only in the Imperial Parliament, on whose honor Catholics rely for a continuance of their recognized rights and privileges.

Later Legislation.

The law of 1863 remained unchanged for fourteen years; then the amendments of 1877 relieved Separate school trustees from supplying a yearly list of their supporters, imposing this duty on the assessor. The Court of Revision was empowered to determine all complaints in regard to persons alleged to be wrongfully placed upon, or omitted from, the roll. But under the operation of this act frequent mistakes still occurred in rating the supporters of Separate schools. Accordingly the law was further amended in 1879, and the efficiency of these schools was improved by the following:

(1) Election of trustees in cities, towns and villages to be held as in the case of Public school Boards; and in townships, as in rural school sections; (2) Trustees authorized to borrow on the security of the school premises or rates; (3) A non-resident owner of unoccupied land may require the school rates thereon to be paid to the Separate school; (4) Any Separate school rates charged upon real estate and uncollected at the end of any one year, as in the like case of Public school rates, to be advanced by the township; (5) So much of the general county rate for salaries of Public school teachers levied from Separate school supporters to be paid over to the Separate school trustees; (6) Where the trustees of Separate schools exercise their option of having the rates collected by municipal machinery, the assessor is authorized to accept the knowledge of a person being a Roman Catholic as *prima facie* evidence of his being a Separate school supporter; (7) A Separate school may become a Model school for the preliminary training of

Catholic teachers; and the Minister of Education may appoint a Catholic member of the County Board of Examiners.

As originally introduced, the bills both of 1855 and 1863 provided that all Catholics within the legal boundaries should be considered as Separate school supporters, following in this matter the law of Lower Canada. But strong objection having been taken to these clauses they were finally omitted. Again in 1879 it was moved that every Roman Catholic should be deemed *ipso facto* a Separate school supporter, and that only on his giving written notice of joining a Public school could he be rated for its support. This was voted down, the Government contending that the fundamental principle of Separate schools was permissive support.

Under regulations framed by Dr. Ryerson and continued after the Department passed in 1876 under a responsible Minister, the inspection of Separate schools in cities and towns was confided to the High school Inspectors, while in rural sections the duty was entrusted to the Public school Inspectors. But, as the work of the High school Inspectors had greatly increased, and as the two duties were not very compatible, the Government, upon due representation of the facts, and at the request of the Archbishop, in 1882 created the office of Separate school Inspector—the writer being the first appointed. But the large number of schools made it impossible for one to discharge properly all the duties of the position, and two years later a second was named—Mr. C. Donovan, M.A., who had for many years ably filled the position of Headmaster in Hamilton Separate school.

In 1886 the law was again amended in the following particulars: (1) A company may require the proportion of stock or personal property of its Catholic members to be assessed for Separate schools; (2) Where a majority of a municipal council are not Separate school supporters they may agree to pay to the Separate school trustees such a proportion of the school taxes of the whole municipality as may fairly represent the relative assessment of the Catholic property; (3) In places where High schools are established, the Separate school Board may appoint a trustee, but not one of themselves.

In the general Provincial elections of 1886 and 1890, attempts were made by the Opposition to gain political capital by accusing the Government of unduly fostering Separate schools to the injury of the Public school system. But in both contests these unworthy appeals to passion and religious bigotry utterly failed, and the Government was sustained by such majorities as showed that the great body of Protestant electors could not at this date be influenced by such unscrupulous tactics.

Again, in 1890 the great feature of the debates in the House was "the battle of the schools." A large majority of the Conservative party maintained that Separate schools had been accorded too many privileges to the detriment of Public schools, and some even advocated their entire abolition. The Equal Rights party was established chiefly on this latter principle; and they alleged that, by amendments to the law of 1863, the support of Separate schools was no longer voluntary, but really compulsory on all Catholics. The clause referred to reads: "The assessor shall accept the statement of, or made on behalf of, any ratepayer, that he is a Roman Catholic, as sufficient *prima facie* evidence for placing such person in the proper column of the assessment roll for Separate school supporters." . . . The question having been referred to the Judges of the High Court, they decided that written notice is still necessary to make a Catholic a valid supporter of a Separate school; yet, if the assessor knows a man to be a Catholic, this is sufficient *prima facie* evidence for placing him on the list of Separate school supporters, though appeal can be made against such rating. Thereupon the Government passed a bill requiring the clerk of each municipality to keep an index book with the names of persons who have given such written notice of supporting Separate schools, and directing the assessor in compiling his roll to be guided simply by this entry of notices.

In the same session a member of the Opposition moved that all teachers of Separate schools should pass the same examination as those for Public schools. This amendment was designed to deprive the religious teaching orders of the privileges granted them by the Act of 1863, confirmed by the British North America Act, and thus placed beyond the authority of the Assembly to affect prejudicially. In opposing this motion, the Minister of Education stated that a considerable number of these religious had previously obtained certificates as teachers, and that during their novitiate they have not only a literary, but also a professional, training under competent instructors. He showed from the reports of the High school Inspectors, when examining Separate schools, that the standing of these classes was not inferior; while the results of public examinations for entrance to High schools and for teachers' certificates gave very satisfactory evidence of the success of Separate schools and the competency of religious teachers. The motion was accordingly voted down.

GROWTH OF ROMAN CATHOLIC SEPARATE SCHOOLS.

YEAR	Schools open	Teachers.	Pupils.	RECEIPTS.		Expenditure.
				Government Grant.	Taxes, etc.	
1841	1	1				
1850	21	26				
1860	115	162	14,708	$7,419	$23,941	$31,360
1870	165	236	20,652	8,906	49,594	58,498
1880	196	344	25,311	14,102	122,771	128,463
1890	259	569	34,571	18,652	294,674	289,703

This steady and rapid growth of the system must be highly gratifying to all friends of Catholic education. It is due to the hearty co-operation and noble sacrifices of clergy and laity, animated by a sense of their solemn duty in this sacred cause; and, while the present standing of these schools is most satisfactory, especially when viewed in the light of their great struggles for a proper measure of freedom, their future prospects appear equally encouraging.

SCHOOLS OF THE ARCHDIOCESE.

Of the early Catholic teachers and schools in Toronto it is difficult at the present day to get full and reliable information. The first Catholic teacher was John Harvey, who taught in an old frame building on Jarvis street, standing at the head of what was then called Nelson street, and situated near the farm belonging to the late S. P. Jarvis, Esq. He taught about 1830. Then came Joseph Seyers, who taught on York street, between King and Richmond. Mr. Butler, a ripe scholar, taught on the corner of Jordan and Melinda streets. He resigned and became a priest, Peterborough being the field of his ministry. Afterwards Mr. Denis Heffernan opened a

private school. In 1843 this came under the operation of the Separate school
law; the attendance was about forty, mostly boys; the girls were taught in
another room by the teacher's wife. The old fashioned method then prevailed of punishing by hoisting the culprit on another boy's back and liberally
applying the birch; and this master had the reputation of being rather severe.
He was, however, one of the ablest of his day in mathematics, and was
succeeded by Mr. Timothy McCarthy, also a clever Irish mathematician,
who held the position until 1847. Next followed Mr. Taaffe, and after him
Mr. O'Halloran, who held the place until the coming of the Christian
Brothers. One of the first Catholic classical academies was opened by Mr.
Patrick Lee, in a brick house on Jarvis street at the corner of Richmond,
the building to the south being a Commercial school taught by Mr. Higgins.
Both these schools were started with the aid and encouragement of Hon.
John Elmsley, to whose zeal and liberal assistance early Catholic education
in this city owes so much. Next followed Mr. Dussaulx, who taught in the
coach house of St. Michael's Palace, which was suitably fitted up. Besides
giving instruction in classics he trained the first Catholic temperance band.
In 1850 came Rev. Father Molony, who kept the school on Queen street
until the arrival of the Basilian Fathers.

Separate schools are established in seven rural sections and in many of
the towns and villages of the Archdiocese. In Toronto there are thirteen
schools attended by about four thousand five hundred pupils, with a total
staff of seventy-nine teachers, of whom forty-five are Sisters of St. Joseph,
eleven of the order of Loretto, twenty-one Christian Brothers and two
secular teachers. Of late years great improvement has been made both in
the buildings and in the equipment; in these respects Catholics have no
reason to feel ashamed of their schools. Among the most important of
these buildings is the De La Salle Institute, serving as a primary school for
the Cathedral parish and for the boys' high classes as well as for the
Christian Brothers' novitiate. In St. Paul's the large brick school, situate
near the splendid new Church, provides ample accommodation for over six
hundred pupils in charge of thirteen teachers. In St. Mary's there are
three schools, two of the buildings ranking among the best of the kind in the
city. Other parishes are also well supplied, for primary schools are scattered
over the city wherever the population requires. Nor have the orphans been
neglected; the home at Sunnyside has school rooms that are unsurpassed
by any in the Province. In addition to these primary schools there are

central high classes for boys and for girls, who are admitted on passing a written examination corresponding to that for entrance to the ordinary High schools. The girls' divisions of these high classes are taught by the Sisters of St. Joseph. The course of study comprises both the ordinary commercial branches, including typewriting, &c., and the programme for teachers' non-professional certificates. In both these departments, as shown by the results of the public examinations, the Sisters have been particularly successful. In the corresponding class of boys, the course has been chiefly commercial work, but with special attention to freehand and industrial drawing. The success of the training here given is evidenced by the many responsible positions ably filled by the graduates.

If it may be permitted to single out any one to whom special credit is due for the interest taken in the work of the Catholic schools of this city, it is the venerable Father Rooney, Vicar-General of the Archdiocese. For many years Chairman of the Board of Separate schools in Toronto, he has witnessed their growth from small and humble beginnings to their present prominent rank in numbers and efficiency, and has, by his influential position in the Church and on the Board, been largely instrumental in bringing about this happy state of affairs.

St. Catharines has three schools, and with the completion of St. Bridget's, it can boast of having accommodations among the best of any place in the Province. Much of the credit for this most favorable showing must be given to the Very Rev. Dean Harris, under whose administration all these buildings have been erected, and who is indefatigable in his efforts to bring his schools to the highest degree of excellence. The Sisters of St. Joseph have charge of two of these schools, and the Christian Brothers take the management of the boys' classes; the attendance in all reaches nearly five hundred.

In Barrie, where the school has done very successful work, there is a staff of three teachers, two of whom are Sisters of St. Joseph, having charge of the girls' departments. For many years this school was under the careful and constant supervision of the Right Rev. Bishop O'Connor of Peterborough, then Dean of Barrie, and it is largely owing to his fostering care and protection that the school has had so prosperous a career. Orillia has an excellent brick school house, with fine play grounds; there are three secular teachers in charge and the standing of the school is highly creditable.

Rev. Father Campbell has labored most zealously and constantly to advance the interests of Catholic education in his parish, with the most gratifying results. The school in Thorold is taught by four of the Community of St. Joseph and a male teacher. A large addition has recently been made to the brick building, so that now the accommodations and equipment are very good. Rev. Father Sullivan has ever been most solicitous about the education of his flock, and the standing of his school is highly satisfactory. At Merritton there is an excellent building, provided at a considerable sacrifice by the comparatively few ratepayers. The Sisters of St. Joseph are the teachers, and it is needless to say that under their management the school has steadily improved. The Loretto Sisters who are in charge of the Separate school at Niagara Falls are zealous and capable teachers, under whom the school has reached a highly creditable standing. The same community has a school at Falls View, kept in the Convent, which has been of great benefit to the Catholics of that neighborhood. Newmarket, Whitby, Port Colborne and Weston have had Separate schools, established many years ago, all taught by secular teachers. There is a fine brick building with attractive grounds at Newmarket; the others are frame. At Lafontaine in Tiny township there is a settlement of French Canadians, who have a largely attended Separate school directed by the nuns of the Holy Cross order—the only house of this community in the Archdiocese. A recently erected brick school house gives suitable accommodations; and the earnest work of these religious has been of great benefit in this somewhat remote district. In Mara (Brechin) and Adjala (Colgan) there are good brick school buildings, well equipped and largely attended. Toronto Gore (Gribbin) and Vespra have schools established many years ago and still doing useful work. North Toronto has excellent accommodations for its school, which is under the care of the Sisters of St. Joseph.

SUMMARY FOR THE ARCHDIOCESE.

	1880.	1890.	Ten Years' Increase.	Increase per cent
No. of Schools	31	36	5	16
No. of Teachers	76	112	36	47
No. of Pupils	5559	6,731	1,172	21
Total Receipts	$32,120	$68,442	$36,322	113
Total Expenditure	$30,916	$65,130	$34,214	111

It may be fitting to conclude this chapter by some extracts from a most eloquent and comprehensive pastoral on Education issued by his Grace Archbishop Walsh in January, 1872, when presiding over the See of London:

"The question of Catholic education is the great absorbing question of the present day for Catholics throughout the world, and on the manner in which it shall be solved must depend the ruin or salvation of thousands. . . . . Hence the Church wishes that religion shall be the tutelary spirit in the school house, that it shall knead and mould the plastic character of our children; that it shall spread its blessed radiance, its transfiguring power, on their young minds, and consecrate them by the baptism of holy faith, so that during their school days their innocence and purity, tender and delicate as the flowers of Spring, may be sheltered from all stain and blight; that their uncertain and timid footsteps may be directed to the path of rectitude and virtue, and of religious principles, which leads to Christian manhood and honorable old age, and conducts to a blessed immortality. She demands that the secular sciences should hold their subordinate places, and that religion should, like the sun, be the orb around which they should, as satellites, revolve, and from which they should borrow an additional light and beauty. . . . The duty of inculcating religion must be exercised in the school-room, and not relegated to parents, wearied with their day's hard work, and perhaps unable or unwilling to fulfil it. This duty must not be confined to Sunday, for the impressions made during that day are too easily effaced during the subsequent week. . . . The morality inculcated in Common schools must necessarily be based on the assumption that all Christian denominations are equally good, an assumption which of course is utterly untrue, and must necessarily result in religious indifferentism. There is another consideration to be added here, it is the baneful impressions that may be made on the young mind by non-Catholic teachers. The child is naturally disposed to respect the teacher, to look up to him as the embodiment of wisdom, and to consider his words as oracular utterances not to be questioned for a moment. It is easy then to see what fatal and perhaps lasting impressions may be made on pupils by a casual expression, a suggestive hint, a sneer at 'Popish practices,' a general tone of contempt for Catholic usages, indulged in by a teacher who is not a Catholic. . . . The Church prizes education, and is the mother of Christian civilization, but she brands with anathemas godless education, which destroys the souls of so many children. 'The Church,' says John Henry Newman, ' regards this world and all that is in it as a mere shade, as dust and ashes, compared with the value of one single soul. She holds that it were better for the sun and moon to drop from heaven, for the earth to fail, and for all its many millions who are on it to die of starvation in extremest agony, as far as temporal affliction goes, *than that one soul should be lost.'* Directed and animated by this principle, our Holy Father, Pope Pius IX., has declared in the famous Syllabus that Catholics cannot 'approve of a system of educating youth unconnected with Catholic faith and the power of the Church, and which regards the knowledge of merely natural things; and only, or at least primarily, the ends of social life.' . . . In the face of one of these solemn utterances of the infallible head of the Church, and of our own Canadian hierarchy, no Catholic can conscientiously patronize the Common or mixed schools, so long as he has Catholic schools in which to educate his children. . . . You have hitherto done wonders, you and our faithful clergy, to establish Separate schools and to encourage and support them. Let us exhort you to persevere in this great and good work; by doing so you will bring blessings innumerable upon yourselves and the children committed to your care. . . . Thus honor, conscience, faith, the example of our forefathers, the voice of our Holy Church, and the commands of God, all considerations of our honor as men, and of our duty as Catholics, call upon us to be faithful to our trust as Catholic parents, to support and encourage our Separate schools, and our Catholic colleges and convents. By so doing we shall plant the faith deep in this soil, we shall leave behind us a legacy of great price, more precious far than all the riches of the earth. . . . It is true that the shibboleth of the age is the maxim ' knowledge is power.' But the greatest and most beneficial power of all is the religion of the Crucified, which has triumphed over the powers of earth and hell. This is the power which triumphs over our base passions, which enables us to resist evil inclinations, which breathes hope into the despairing, which consoles in deep sorrow, which wipes the tear from the eye of grief, which staunches the wounds of the afflicted heart, walks with us like an angel of light through the darksome journey of time, sustains us amid the perils and bitter trials of life, assists at our death-bed like the angel of consolation at the agony of our Saviour, fans with its heavenly wings the heat of our dying hour, and wafts the liberated soul to its eternal home. This is the power which should take precedence of all others—in the school-room first, and then on the stage of mature life. This, says St. John, is the victory which overcometh the world, our faith."

CRITICAL NOTE.—In one of the debates regarding Confederation, Hon. Mr Rose, speaking on behalf of his Protestant co-religionists of Lower Canada, said:—"I believe we have always had our fair share of the public grants in so far as the French element could control them, and not only the liberty but every facility for the establishment of Separate dissentient schools wherever they were deemed desirable. A single person has the right under the law of establishing a dissentient school, and obtaining a fair share of the educational grant, if he can gather together fifteen children who desire instruction in it. . . . So far as being handed over to the French in the Local Parliament and our rights being interfered with, I feel every assurance that the spirit of the answer will be carried out." This answer was a guarantee given by the Government that all the rights and privileges then enjoyed by Protestants in regard to their schools would be maintained inviolate. And on May 29th, 1892, Mr. Scriver, a Protestant member from Quebec, bore this testimony as to how these promises had been fulfilled:—"The Protestant minority of Quebec have been treated since Confederation with perfect fairness and with the utmost liberality by the majority of that Province. Protestants could not live there were it not for the privileges they enjoyed."

THE DEANERY OF TORONTO.

EDITED BY

REV. J. R. TEEFY, B.A., C.S.B.

VERY REVEREND EDWARD CASSIDY,
DEAN OF TORONTO.

CHAPTER IX.

THE DEANERY OF TORONTO.

Introductory—St. Michael's Cathedral—Other City Parishes—The Parishes of the Counties of York, Peel and South Ontario—Adjala, Brock, Orangeville.

INTRODUCTION.

AS the formation of the Diocese is fully given in Chapter IV.,* we refer our readers to the account therein contained. The limits, as officially defined, were: West of Newcastle, from Lake Ontario to Lake Muskoka; thence by a line direct North-west through Lakes Moon and Muskoka to western branch of Two Rivers, emptying into the Ottawa; all west of that, including Lake Superior districts. This embraced the counties west of Durham, and all the Districts of Muskoka, Parry Sound, Algoma, and the rest of the territory now forming the northern portion of the Diocese of Peterborough. When, in 1856, Hamilton and London were erected into Dioceses, all west of the County of Peel and north of the County of Simcoe, except the Counties of Lincoln and Welland on the Niagara peninsula, was taken from Toronto. Thenceforth the limits of Toronto Diocese comprised the Counties of Ontario, York, Peel, Lincoln, Welland, Simcoe and Cardwell. In this area there are at present forty-two parishes, of which nine are in the city. These various districts are divided into three deaneries—Toronto, St. Catharines and Barrie—each of which occupies a chapter in this volume, with a brief sketch of a history of the different parishes.

* Vid. p. 112.

Toronto was erected into an Archdiocese on March 18, 1870, with the following Sees for Suffragans: Kingston, Peterborough, Hamilton and London. In 1889, Kingston being raised to a Metropolitan See, Peterborough ceased to be a suffragan of Toronto; so that the ecclesiastical Province of Toronto consists of the Sees of Toronto, Hamilton and London.

The officers of the Diocese are: The Most Rev. John Walsh, D.D., Archbishop; Auxiliary Bishop, Right Rev. T. O'Mahony, D.D., Bishop of Eudocia; Vicars-General, Very Rev. F. P. Rooney and Very Rev. J. J. McCann; Archdeacon, Ven. K. A. Campbell; Secretary, Rev. Jas. Walsh; Deans, Very Rev. W. R. Harris, E. J. Cassidy and W. Bergin; Bishop's Council, The Very Reverends, the Vicars-General and the Deans.

The Deanery of Toronto comprises the parishes of the City of Toronto; also Adjala, Brock, Caledon, Dixie, Duffin's Creek, Gore of Toronto, Newmarket, Orangeville, Oshawa, Schomberg, Thornhill, Uxbridge and Whitby.

The Deanery of St. Catharines comprises the parishes of Fort Erie, Merritton, Niagara Falls, Port Colborne, Smithville, St. Catharines, St. Mary's (in St. Catharines), and Thorold.

The Deanery of Barrie comprises the parishes of Alliston, Barrie, Brentwood, etc., Brechin, Collingwood, Flos, Mara, Midland, Orillia, Penetanguishene, Stayner, and Ste. Croix.

The following figures give the general statistics of the Diocese:—Priests—Regular, 23; Secular, 54. Total, 77. Churches and Chapels, 95. Catholic population, 60,000.

St. Michael's Cathedral.

An account of the purchase of the property upon which the Cathedral is built, and the laying* of the corner stone on May 8th, 1845, by Bishop Power, will be found in an earlier portion of this work. Some of our older readers will remember the ceremony, and how they roasted an ox whole upon the auspicious occasion; and how, as the building grew, it did not lack sad recollections as well as most pleasing ones; how one of the builders, Mr. Hughes, was killed by falling from its roof; and how the saintly prelate who had founded it died before its completion. The corner stone contains amongst other things fragments of a stone pier from the nave of the Cathedral of York, and of the English oak roof of the same, which was built in 1340, and also a fragment of one of the earliest Roman temples in England built before the conversion of the Britons. The style of architecture is gothic of the early part of the 14th century. It is a very different looking building to-day from what it was when on St. Michael's Day, September 29th, 1848, it was solemnly dedicated by Bishop Bourget of Montreal. Each of the Bishops in turn has done much for the beautifying and improving of the Cathedral. As already noted, Bishop de Charbonnel turned it into a building of the florid gothic style, and imported from France the magnificent stained glass window back of the main altar, representing the Crucifixion, and which was made by a celebrated artist, Thevenot. And the last official act which his Lordship performed in Toronto was to consecrate the grand altar on February 10, 1860.

Archbishop Lynch followed out the plan by completing the tower and graceful spire which, crowned by a beautiful gilt cross, rises to a height of over 260 feet. During his time also an iron fence was built around the Cathedral, and a fine organ placed in the gallery.

One of the first objects which engaged the attention of Archbishop Walsh, on taking possession of the See of Toronto, was the renovation of the Cathedral. A neat morning chapel, 71 feet by 28 feet, was built to the north, a cloister connecting it with the Bishop's house. The whole interior of the Cathedral was renewed and frescoed in far more cheerful colors than before; so that now its graceful pillars and finely proportioned arches show

---

* The silver trowel used upon the occasion is still carefully preserved and frequently used. The last occasion upon which it was employed was the laying of the corner stone of the Basilian Novitiate, May 8th, 1892.

to advantage, and the appearance of the church is in keeping with its metropolitan dignity. It was formally opened on June 7th, 1891, with imposing ceremonies in presence of a large number of prelates and priests. The Right Rev. Dr. McQuaid, Bishop of Rochester, preached upon the occasion. The total expense upon the improvement of the Cathedral and the erection of the chapel was about $40,000.

A beautiful stained glass window has been placed in the north side to the memory of the late Archbishop Lynch. The central portion consists of a representation of the Last Supper. Below this is a good portrait in glass of his Grace, surrounded on either side by his patron saints, John and Joseph. The inscription beneath tells its purpose. It is the gift of the Right Rev. Bishop O'Connor of Peterborough.

The exterior of the Cathedral is 190 feet long and 115 feet wide; interiorly it is 182 feet by 80, exclusive of the transepts. It is capable of seating sixteen hundred. There are eight large decorated arches in the building, giving an elevation of 66 feet to the nave and 45 feet to the side aisles.

There are four chapels, that of the Blessed Virgin and of St. Joseph being to the gospel and epistle side of the main altar respectively; a mortuary chapel in the north transept, and one dedicated to the Sacred Heart in the south. A few tablets on the pillars and walls perpetuate the memory of some of the early leading Catholics—one to the Very Rev. John James Hay, first Archdeacon of Toronto. One is erected to the remembrance of

> "GREGORY GRANT FOOTE MACDONALD,
> ROYAL NAVY, LATE ONE OF HER
> MAJESTY'S HONORABLE CORPS OF
> GENTLEMEN-AT-ARMS,"

who died in 1858. To the right of the Blessed Virgin's Altar is a marble tablet, inlaid upon black stone, sacred to the memory of Sir Charles Chichester, Lieutenant-Colonel and Brigadier General in Spain, who died in 1847, and who was buried with military honors.

Two prelates have been consecrated within its sanctuary—Archbishops Lynch and Walsh; and two lie buried here—Bishop Power, who rests in the crypt below, and Archbishop Lynch, beneath the shadow of the north wall. The other chief religious ceremonies celebrated were the Dogma of

the Immaculate Conception in February, 1855, and a funeral Mass for the late holy Father, Pius IX., in 1878.

Various synods, and the Provincial Council of 1875, held their public sittings within this church.

Turning to the priests who have been stationed at the Cathedral, it would be impossible to notice all. Amongst the most prominent names is that of the Very Rev. Father Jamot, Vicar-General, and afterwards Bishop of Peterborough.

John Francis Jamot was born at Creux in France on June 23rd, 1828. Most of his studies were made in his native land, but he completed his theology in All Hallows College near Dublin, Ireland. He was sent to this institution by Bishop de Charbonnel, who met him on a tour which his Lordship made through France after his consecration. Soon after coming to Canada he was ordained priest in 1853. In the year 1855 he took charge of Barrie mission, which at that time included the northern part of the County of Simcoe. This was the school of zeal and self-devotion in which the apostolic Father Jamot learned the great heroic virtues which characterized him in the wider field and higher sphere to which he was afterwards called. Early mission life has been already pictured for our readers; it is unnecessary to dwell upon it; but none passed through its labors and difficulties with more energy and success than the saintly subject of this paragraph. A hardy constitution enabled him to undergo the privations which his duties necessarily entailed, and his solid, priestly piety prevented him yielding to the fatigue which ultimately undermined his health and brought him to the grave while yet in the prime of life. In 1860 he was appointed Vicar-General of the Diocese, and came four years after to take charge of the Cathedral. The people of this parish remember his untiring devotion to duty during his residence of fourteen years here, while the spire and the iron fence are lasting monuments of his administration. On the 25th of January, 1874, the Holy Father, Pius IX., erected the Vicariate of Western Canada, and Father Jamot was named Bishop of Sarepta *in partibus infidelium* and Vicar Apostolic of the new Vicariate. His Lordship was consecrated on the 24th of February following by Archbishop Lynch, assisted by Bishop de Charbonnel. "We had," writes Dr. Jamot in his first pastoral, "the honor of receiving the episcopal consecration in one of the sanctuaries devoted to the Queen of Heaven, in the

Church of Our Lady of the Sacred Heart at Issondun. We by no means expected this favor; we had even taken steps towards having the ceremony in another place, the Little Seminary de Felletin, which is very dear to us, since it was in this house we found those pious and devout masters who have lavished their pains upon us during our classical studies." His Lordship first had his See at Sault Ste. Marie, and afterwards at Bracebridge. But in 1882 a portion of Kingston Diocese was assigned to Bishop Jamot, and the whole territory erected into a diocese, with Peterborough for a Cathedral city. His Lordship continued the exercise not only of his episcopal but also of his priestly functions with the same zeal, humility and piety as when a young curate or simple missionary. The hardships of his early and later apostleship cut him off at the age of forty-eight. His death took place on May 4th, 1886.

Another name still fresh in the memory of the Cathedral is that of the late Father Laurent. The place of his birth is not certain. The year given for it is 1822. In 1856 he came to Canada from France, where he had belonged to a religious community of Brothers who instruct deaf mutes. Father Laurent was ordained priest in 1860. He was stationed in the Cathedral for some time; but the parish with which his name and work are most closely connected is St. Patrick's church, Toronto, to the account of which we refer our readers. In 1881 he was removed back to the Cathedral, and made Vicar-General of the Diocese, where he remained until his sudden death on December 19th, 1890. Indefatigable in his labors, Father Laurent really died in harness. After hearing confessions at the Convent of the Good Shepherd, Parkdale, he was proceeding home when he was taken ill upon the street. Upon being carried into a gentleman's residence he died of heart disease within a few minutes. Pending the appointment of a successor to the late Archbishop Lynch Vicar-General Laurent was co-administrator of the Archdiocese. For many years he was an efficient member of the Separate School Board, and also of the Board of the House of Industry, where his charity and affability commanded the respect and admiration of all.

The present rector of the Cathedral is the Very Rev. J. J. McCann, Vicar-General, who celebrated last July the twenty-fifth anniversary of his ordination. His classical studies were pursued with success in St. Michael's College, entering in 1859 and spending there five years. He early showed a

Very Rev. J.J. McCann, V.G.

talent which has been of great service to him as a preacher and which gives his sermons a poetic and figurative character. Rich in imagination, and choice in language and diction, Father McCann holds a deservedly high rank amongst the Canadian Catholic pulpit orators. From Toronto he proceeded to Montreal Grand Seminary for the pursuance of his theological studies. He was ordained priest in St. Mary's Church, Toronto, by the late Archbishop Lynch on July the 21st, 1867. His missionary work was begun at St. Catharines, where he was assistant to the late Dean Mulligan; thence he was removed to St. Mary's, Toronto. He left this to take his first pastoral charge of the Gore parish. In 1869 he was Rector of the Cathedral, and again in 1877; afterwards pastor of St. Helen's, Brockton, when he was made Dean of Toronto. After the death of Father Laurent Father McCann once more took charge of the Cathedral and was appointed Vicar-General.

On the 21st of July, 1892, the very reverend gentleman celebrated the silver jubilee of his priesthood. Most generous presents, most pleasing addresses, most cordial congratulations bespoke the esteem in which Father McCann is held by his Superior, by his equals amongst the clergy, and by the people for whom he labors.

Attached to the staff of the Cathedral is the Rev. Francis F. Rohleder. He was born in Prussia in 1846 and came to Toronto in 1866. After finishing his classical studies in St. Michael's College he went to Montreal to prosecute his theological course. He was ordained priest on the 29th of June, 1873. His first curacy was at St. Paul's, Toronto; from which place, after nine months, he was transferred to the Cathedral. Here he remained for seven years. In 1881 he was appointed pastor of Brock, where he labored zealously for ten years, until his return to the Cathedral in January, 1891.

The third member is Father Francis Ryan, whose burning eloquence and thorough theological training are a great aid towards the spiritual welfare of the parish. He was a prominent member of the Society of Jesus, and came to St. Michael's Cathedral in the early part of the present year.

St. Paul's Parish, Toronto.

St. Paul's, Toronto, is the premier parish, and one of the largest and most important in the Archdiocese. For many years its history may be said to be almost the history of the Archdiocese, as it was for some time the Cathedral parish and the scene of many important events, as related in the third and fourth chapters of this work. Its history dates from the early years of the present century; and, indeed, if we date from the first time a priest officiated at Toronto, we have to go far back into the eighteenth century. When the first Mass was said on the site of the modern city it is not easy to say. The famous Father Piquet, of the Congregation of St. Sulpice, in making a tour of the missions on Lake Ontario in a boat supplied to him for the purpose by order of the King of France, arrived at the French trading post of Fort Rouille, or Toronto (erected 1749) on June 26th 1752.* It seems quite certain that Father Piquet said Mass on this occasion, as we find him conferring with the Mississaga Indians, whom he found here, with reference to the erection of a regular mission at the post. These Indians complained that they were not as well treated as the Iroquois, in that the latter had been provided with missionaries, while they (the Mississagas) had not even a church erected for them, but had to be content with a canteen. This would lead us to suppose that other missionaries had passed through here, and that consequently Mass had been said at an even earlier period. But, to come down to a later date: it is related that when Rev. Edmund Burke, afterwards Vicar Apostolic of Nova Scotia, was stationed at Niagara in 1797, he occasionally visited York, and undoubtedly said Mass for the few Catholics who had taken up their residence here.

The next priest to visit York, of whom we have any record, was Father Alexander Macdonell, afterwards first Bishop of Kingston, who, as related elsewhere, shortly after his arrival in Canada, proceeded to York to arrange with the authorities for the land granted to the Catholic Highlanders by the Home Government. This brings us into the present century. Other missionaries visited York at intervals on their tours of the Province, then a vast wilderness, but no regular mission was established until Father James Crowley came as the first resident priest, and, gathering the few Catholics around him, formed them into the infant Parish of St. Paul.

---
* The site of Fort **Rouille** is included in the present Exhibition Grounds, and is marked by a handsome granite monument. See Dr. Scadding's "Old French Fort and its Monument." Toronto: 1887.

St. Paul's Church

This was in the second decade of the century. Some years before (December 11th, 1806) Vicar-General Macdonell had secured from the Government a block of land, being lot 5, Dundas street, York, on which to erect a church and school. Dundas street is the modern Queen street, which at that time existed only on the map of the surveyor. On this block of land now stand St. Paul's church, school and presbytery, and the House of Providence. It was also the site of the first Catholic cemetery in Toronto.

The first church built in York is said to have been a wooden building, which, however, soon gave place to the substantial brick structure which did duty for so many years, and ceased to be the parish church only on the completion of the magnificent new edifice which, thanks to the energy and the faith of his Lordship Bishop O'Mahony, now adorns the corner of Queen and Power streets. The old church, built between 1820 and 1826, and some years ago considerably enlarged, is now transformed into a parish hall.

The more important incidents in the history of the parish under Father Crowley and his successors, Fathers O'Grady, McDonagh and Kirwan, have already been related in the earlier part of this work, and need not here be repeated. It continued to be the only parish in the city until Bishop Power's time, when that much lamented prelate began the erection of St. Michael's cathedral. St. Paul's church was Bishop Power's cathedral, and in it took place his funeral service. At the time of the Bishop's death, Father J. J. Kirwan was its pastor; and after him came Father Harkin for a year or two, and then Father Thomas Fitzhenry, who remained for some years. On the latter's withdrawal in Bishop de Charbonnel's time, Father (now Archbishop) Walsh took charge for a brief period, and then the parish passed under the care of Father F. P. Rooney, now the venerable and much respected senior Vicar-General of the Diocese. Father Rooney continued as Pastor of St. Paul's for nearly twelve years, and during that time put the parish on a firm and enduring footing. After his removal to St. Mary's church, St. Paul's had many changes in its pastors until the advent of his Lordship Bishop O'Mahony. Fathers McCann, Kelly and Conway each spent a year or more in the parish, the latter being the immediate predecessor of the Bishop of Eudocia.

The advent of Bishop O'Mahony marks an epoch in the history of St. Paul's. Apart from the distinction of the parish having a Bishop for its pastor, the many great works set on foot during his regime must ever mark it as a memorable period in its annals.

Bishop O'Mahony is a native of Cork, and spent many years of his priestly life in that city. Possessed of talents of a high order, and being ever conspicuous for his energy and piety, he was selected by Pope Pius IX., of holy memory, as the first Bishop of the Diocese of Armidale, Australia. There he labored with great fruit for some years; but the hot climate, and the exposure consequent upon his visitations of so vast a diocese, told upon his constitution and obliged him to resign his charge and return to Europe. To use his own words, he returned to the Eternal City to die. But a few years' rest in Rome somewhat restored his health, and at the request of the late Archbishop Lynch he came to Canada in 1879 to co-operate in the work of the Archdiocese of Toronto. On his arrival here, he at once took charge of St. Paul's parish, where he has ever since remained. The result of his twelve years' pastorate is seen in the commodious schools on Queen street, in the splendid new church, in the general condition of the surroundings, but, above all, in the thorough organization and administration of the parish, and the spirit of faith and devotion which animates its people.

On taking charge of St. Paul's Bishop O'Mahony found the old church entirely inadequate to the requirements of the parish. One of his first thoughts, therefore, was the erection of a new building which would be more worthy of Almighty God, and at the same time afford proper accommodation to his people. To this end his Lordship instituted a weekly collection, which was continued for several years, enabling him in 1887 to break ground for the foundation of the new church. The corner stone was laid on October 9th of the same year by his Eminence Cardinal Taschereau, assisted by his Grace Archbishop Lynch, their Lordships Bishops Walsh and O'Mahony, and Mgr. O'Bryen, Papal Ablegate; and such was the energy with which the work was prosecuted that on December 22nd, 1889, the new temple was solemnly dedicated to the service of Almighty God by his Grace the Archbishop of Kingston. The church is not yet completed according to the original design; but even as it stands, it is much the finest ecclesiastical building in the city. It is on the symbolic cruciform plan, and consists of vast nave and spreading aisles and transepts, apsidal chancel and side chapels, lofty campanile and roomy sacristies. The basement contains a spacious cryptical church, sub-sacristy and elaborate steam

Very Rev. J.J McCann V.G.

heating apparatus. The external dimensions are as follows: Total length, 174 feet; width across nave and aisle, 70 feet; width across transept, 100 feet; height of campanile (still unfinished), 129 feet. It has a seating capacity of 1,250, while the basement will seat 1,000. The cost to date has been considerably in excess of one hundred thousand dollars. The architect is Mr. Joseph Connolly, R.C.A.

Although Bishop O'Mahony has been enabled to see his new church practically completed, it has been at the cost of his own health. When he entered upon the work he was comparatively a vigorous man, but now, unhappily, he is broken in health and a confirmed invalid, and the work of the parish devolves at present entirely upon his assistants, Fathers Lynch and Minehan. But whether his Lordship's time be long or short, his memory will ever be gratefully and affectionately cherished by his people, to whom he has been a faithful and devoted pastor; and he will be remembered as a prelate of great learning and ability, and as a friend singularly constant and urbane.

The Catholic population of Toronto mission (which included all the territory lying about the city) in 1834 was 3,240; in 1844, according to the assessor's returns, the Catholics of the city alone numbered 3,678; in 1845 they had increased to 4,046 out of a total population of 19,706. (See Brown's Directory, 1845.) The latest census of St. Paul's parish within its present boundaries gives about a thousand families, exclusive of those of French origin, who, though residing within the parish limits, worship at the church of the Sacred Heart, under the direction of Rev. Father Lamarche. The number of individuals is not stated. These figures give an idea at once of the general expansion of the city, and in particular of the growth and prosperity of St. Paul's under a succession of zealous and devoted pastors.

St. Mary's Parish.

This parish, the third in order of time, dates from the year 1852. Thus far the growth of the Catholic population of Toronto was confined to the east and the centre. All that portion of the city west of Spadina avenue was an extensive common, used chiefly for military parades, and unbroken, save by a few isolated houses, and outlined streets which then had dim prospects of becoming great public thoroughfares. But, "Westward the course of empire takes it way;" and the church that spread from St. Paul's, on the extreme east, to St. Michael's in the centre, now extended still further west to St. Mary's on Bathurst street. The venerable Bishop Macdonell, during his episcopacy, manifested great foresight and zeal by securing portions of land in several localities for church purposes whenever the future would point to their convenience or necessity. One such grant was situated at the head of Adelaide street, on the west side of Bathurst street, and is now known as Macdonell Square.* Here Bishop de Charbonnel resolved to build a church, a white brick edifice of modest design and dimensions, which, when completed, was to be dedicated to the Immaculate Conception. The hope which his Lordship entertained, that when a Church was there a congregation would soon be found, was most happily realized. Thus was established the nucleus of the now flourishing parish of St. Mary's. The corner stone of this Church was laid in May, 1852. The preacher upon the occasion was Rev. Father Lynch, uncle of his Lordship Bishop Dowling of Hamilton.

The new parish, by no means populous, made up for its want of subjects by its extent of territory; being bounded on the east by Simcoe street, on the west by the River Humber, on the north by the Davenport road, and on the south by Lake Ontario.

The Church which was then erected manifested before many years such evident signs of unsafe construction that it was necessary to pull it down and erect a new one in its place. Whether these indications resulted from the insecurity of the foundation or from the unskilled character of the workmanship, it is impossible now to determine. The old building was torn down in 1858, and a second church built upon its site. The walls were commenced on the old foundations, which had never been very secure; and as these walls were longer and higher than the former, the second building, soon after its completion, gave signs of weakness, which would have terminated with similar results if due precaution had not been taken. The heavy brick walls and the weighty roof proved too great a burden for the weak foundation. Iron girders were inserted, binding the walls together and saving the structure until, in answer to their prayers, they should be in possession of a Church, solid and permanent, and worthy of themselves and

---

* It is described in the City Directory as running west from 130 Bathurst street to Defoe street. Vid. p. 101 of this volume.

St Mary's Church and School

those in charge. This church was completed and dedicated, and in 1860 was solemnly consecrated by the late Archbishop Lynch. The Most Rev. Dr. Timon, Bishop of Buffalo, N.Y., preached upon the occasion a very eloquent sermon on the holy sacrifice of the Mass. After some years the weakness of the foundation, the fault of construction and the giving way of the roof, made it incumbent upon those concerned to take steps to build a third Church. At last the initiative was begun by erecting a temporary shed on Bathurst street, which was to be used as a chapel until the new Church would be finished, which now stands a model of architectural style, one of the principal ornaments of the western part of the city. It was designed by Joseph Connolly, Esq., who has done so much for church architecture in Canada.

This, the third Church of St. Mary's, is of the French gothic style, and is composed of nave and aisles with a clere-story, transepts, chancel and side chapels, tower and baptistery. Connected with the Church is a charming winter chapel, with a beautiful altar, and with confessionals projecting outwards from the side and end walls of the nave, each entered by a triplet of gothic arches. A sacristy and a cloistered passage connecting the church and presbytery are in the plan. The main Church is about 160 feet by 74 feet at the transepts, and 55 feet in the other parts of the nave. The building is white brick, with Ohio sandstone and granite for dressing—the walls standing on the most firm foundations. Finely varnished pine gives the roof a light, handsome appearance; while the oiled oak of the pews and of the heavily carved communion railing sets the whole building off with a charm of solid beauty. The aisles and transepts are separated by two rows of stately arches springing from polished granite pillars, with moulded and carved capitals and bases. The polished red granite pillars supporting the arch of the chancel rest on large yet graceful corbels, each wrought with a figure of an angel bearing sacred symbols. The corbels supporting the main timbers of the roof are richly carved. The ground floor of the tower forms the chief vestibule of the church, surrounded on either side by an entrance for stormy weather. The view on entering the Church through the main door is very pleasing—embracing the graceful arches, the lofty nave, the stately transepts, and in the distance the rich and beautiful chancel with its polygonal apse lighted by traceried windows of graceful design, and with a richly vaulted and groined roof forming a suitable canopy for the whole. The chancel has recently been beautifully frescoed in chaste colors embodying prominent subjects from sacred history. The cost of the building when complete will be about $70,000. It will remain for generations a monument to the zealous pastor and generous people of St. Mary's.

The corner stone was laid on the 15th of August, 1885; and the opening services took place with great ceremony on February 17th, 1889. The Right Rev. Dr. Dowling, Bishop of Hamilton, performed the ceremony of dedication; the Most Rev. Dr. Cleary, Archbishop of Kingston, celebrated pontifical high Mass. The sermon of the day was preached by his Grace Archbishop Walsh, who at that time still held the see of London. It was one of his best and happiest efforts. The Right Rev. Dr. Richard A. O'Connor, Bishop of Peterborough, presided at Vespers, when the Very Rev. Father Henning, C.SS.R., preached upon the Blessed Virgin. This closed a memorable day in the annals of St. Mary's, when, with the people assembled for the first time in their magnificent temple, the holy sacrifice was offered and evening song chanted in gratitude to God, who had crowned the work with His blessing and with success.

Turning our attention to the various priests who have had charge of this parish, we learn that it was first the intention of Bishop de Charbonnel to establish the Basilian Fathers here and give them charge of the Little Seminary which formed part of his plan. With this end in view a large frame building was constructed in the Church grounds of St. Mary's. This plan was not carried out; the Basilians opened their College in St. Michael's Palace. The house was then given in charge to the Sisters of Loretto. From that time up to the present, on account of Loretto Abbey being situated in the parish, the pastors of St. Mary's have had more or less charge of these devout religious. After the removal of the Loretto nuns to Bond street this house was for a time vacant. However, it was soon occupied by the Sisters of Charity who converted it into an industrial school for girls. Then those Sisters of St. Joseph who were engaged in St. Mary's Schools took possession. At length, after being connected with nearly all the Communities in the city, the old building was sold and removed to make room for the handsome presbytery which was erected by Father Rooney on its site.

After the dedication of the first church St. Mary's was attended for a time from the Cathedral, and chiefly by Father McLaughlin. The first pastor was the late Father John O'Neil. During his incumbency he built a frame parish house on the north-west corner of Bathurst street and Macdonell square. Father O'Neil was a zealous priest and was highly esteemed for his good qualities and brilliant attainments. But his health soon became impaired by the multiplicity of his arduous labors, and he was obliged to retire from active duty.

He was succeeded by Father Louis della Vagna, a Capuchin friar. This saintly priest was born at Genoa in Italy in the year 1801. He entered the Franciscan Order, and being in due time ordained priest, was nominated to the mission of the northwestern coasts of Europe. While in Paris he met Bishop de Charbonnel, who urged upon him to come to Canada. The missionary, after working hard in England for a few years, fulfilled his promise, and came to Canada in the spring of 1856. On Ascension Day of that year he was introduced by his Lordship in St. Paul's Church, and the following Sunday was inducted into the pastoral charge of St. Mary's. "To recount his prayers," tells his biographer,* "his exhortations, his multiform duties, while pastor of St. Mary's, is impossible. Suffice it to say that while all the day long he worked and preached, it may be said that all the night long he prayed and wept for the faults of his people, and with the deepest humility, while living the life of a saint, he accounted himself the lowliest Christian amongst them." But the great difference between the Canadian and the Italian climate, not to speak of the rigorous mortifications which he practised, was too much for his health. On March the 13th, 1857, he was taken down with inflammation of the lungs and died four days after on the feast of St. Patrick. While his body lay in state at St. Michael's Cathedral crowds pressed eagerly around, if only to touch the hem of his garment, or snatch a thread as a relic from his coarse habit. The body was temporarily placed in the crypt of the Cathedral, and solemnly removed to St. Mary's Church on April 16th. Here the late Monsignore Bruyere sang Mass, and his Grace Archbishop Walsh preached upon the occasion. He was then buried under St. Mary's Church ; and when in 1887 the workmen were making excavations for the new church, they came upon the iron coffin in which the corpse had been interred thirty years before. The slide was opened and the face seen to be in precisely the state in which it had been buried.

---

* Vid. Life of Father della Vagna, p. 13.

When the sanctuary of the new church was built, the coffin was placed in a vault beneath, which had been prepared for it. The following is the tablet over his grave :

✝

Beneath are Deposited the Remains of
THE VERY REVEREND FATHER LOUIS DELLA VAGNA,
of the Order of Capuchins.
A native of Genoa —He loved Poverty, Obedience, Chastity. He led a mortified life, and was a strict observer of the rule of St. Francis

He died on the 17th of March, 1857. Jesus and Mary receive his soul.

After the death of Father Louis, Father Ouellette administered the parish for a short time until the appointment of Father Walsh, now happily reigning as Archbishop. At that time a young priest of great promise, prudence and piety, an eloquent preacher, he was welcomed to St. Mary's with great joy. Soon after Bishop Lynch's consecration Father Walsh was removed to the Cathedral, of which he was appointed rector. His absence from St. Mary's was felt all the more keenly, as his presence and energy were considered necessary to assist them in paying off the debt upon their second church, which had but lately been built. The people besought his return, and his Lordship Bishop Lynch granted their request. Father Walsh continued in the charge of St. Mary's until, in 1867, he was raised to the episcopacy. Upon resuming his charge he labored assiduously in the discharge of his many duties, in the establishment of new schools and the general supervision of parochial matters, while, on account of his amiability and suavity, he was beloved by all. In the interval of Father Walsh's first and second charge of the parish Father Hobin was temporarily appointed, who built a fine school house of four rooms quite adequate for the time and well furnished with all necessary equipments. He was made parish priest of Niagara.

During his first incumbency Father Walsh had as assistants Father Ouellette, who withdrew afterwards to the College of St. Hyacinthe, Quebec, where he taught as professor and where he is now superior, and Canon of the Diocese of St. Hyacinthe. The next curate was Father Sauvadet, who was transferred to St. Patrick's ; and after him came Father Michel, who left here to be parish priest of the Gore of Toronto. When Father Walsh returned to St. Mary's he brought with him Father Proulx,

Monsignore Rooney, V G.

who succeeded to the pastorate. Father Proulx administered the parish with considerable success. His long career as missionary amongst the Indians and in other places made him a man of great experience and ripe judgment. He was transferred to the Cathedral about the year 1873, and not long after made Dean of Toronto, and then promoted to the higher dignity of Roman Prelate. His health failing, he returned to his friends in the Province of Quebec, and died in 1881 at the ripe age of seventy-three.

During his incumbency of St. Mary's Father Proulx had consecutively for assistants Fathers White, O'Donohoe, Kelly and Sullivan. The first of these left the diocese and joined the Benedictine Order, with whom he served most faithfully, and amongst whom he died last year a holy death. Father Kelly is now chaplain of the Christian Brothers; and Father Sullivan's name and labors will be found in the account of the Thorold parish. Father James O'Donohoe, still remembered by those who knew him as an able and eloquent man, died some years ago in Barrie.

To Father Proulx succeeded the present revered pastor, Vicar-General Rooney, concerning whose life and work something more is required than a mere passing word.

Francis Patrick Rooney was born in the County of Armagh, Ireland, where, also, he received his classical education in the diocesan Seminary. About the time that he was finishing, it was commonly reported that Father Dowd, who was well known in that part of the country, was to be co-adjutor Bishop of Toronto. This determined Father Rooney to come to Canada; and on writing Bishop de Charbonnel, he received a letter in reply which was a most cordial invitation. He reached Toronto in July, 1853. When St. Michael's College opened the following September, Father Rooney, then entering upon his theology, became prefect of studies. He continued in the College as Professor until after his ordination as priest, which took place on the Feast of St. Rose of Lima, August 30th, 1857. He remained still in the College; and for one year in addition to teaching he had charge of St. Basil's parish. The following summer he was called upon by Bishop de Charbonnel to be pastor of St. Paul's. This parish at the time was in a state of excitement and anger. It required prudence and firmness to settle matters, and bring them to that habit of discipline and respect which are such necessary dispositions for the fruitfulness of God's word. Father Rooney, notwithstanding his inexperience in the holy priesthood, acted with such caution and determination, that in a short time he had the satisfaction of reigning over a peaceful and united people. For twelve years he labored here earnestly, zealously and successfully. When he arrived there was no presbytery; he built a large one, which is ever since the parish house. He provided for the spiritual wants of the people in repairing and decorating the Church, in establishing new schools where necessary and enlarging old ones, and equipping all at his personal expense. At this time the Separate schools were in their infancy; the means at their disposal for their sustentation were very limited. And in order to supplement their revenues the pastors of the several parishes in the city found it necessary out of their limited revenues to contribute to their support. Be this ever recorded to the credit of such men as Father Rooney, that it may not be forgotten by younger generations, how these zealous priests purchased property for school sites, and erected school houses, and by their fostering care brought them out of the swaddling clothes of poverty, weakness and inefficiency, and helped most materially to place them in the satisfactory position they occupy to-day.

Soon after Bishop Walsh's consecration in 1867 Archbishop Lynch showed his confidence in Father Rooney by making him Vicar-General of the Diocese. Nor was this confidence at all misplaced. From the time of the appointment to the death of the venerable prelate who conferred it, Father Rooney served him with the most constant and devoted loyalty. When Archbishop Walsh took possession of the See he continued Father Rooney in his dignity of Vicar-General. In the interval between the decease of Archbishop Lynch and the accession of Dr. Walsh he was co-administrator of the diocese with Father Laurent; but the whole work practically fell upon him as senior priest, and as having already administered the diocese several times when his Grace had been absent.

Resuming the history of his parochial work, we find Vicar-General Rooney, in 1870, called from St. Paul's to St. Mary's. Here he saw many important works necessary for the benefit of the parish. One of the first was to erect St. Helen's in the village of Brockton for the service of the northwestern portion of St. Mary's people. We refer our readers to the account of this now active and flourishing parish, which formed for several years a part of St. Mary's. The next work which engaged the pastor's attention was a presbytery. It was completed in a short time, and is not the least of the west end improvements. But now that the people northwest of the Church were accommodated, the necessity was soon found of a school directly north of St. Mary's, as the distance was too great and many of the children too young to attend regularly; and what was a more serious consideration, many were at the neighboring public schools. Father Rooney purchased land on the corner of Bathurst and Bloor streets extensive enough not only for a school but also for a church and presbytery, thus forming the nucleus of a parish. A building was erected upon it which serves as a school during the week, and in which Mass can be offered when necessary. When completed it was dedicated to St. Peter and blessed by Archbishop Lynch on the 4th of January, 1872; since which time two Masses are regularly celebrated in it on Sundays and holidays. Here is an energetic Conference of Vincent de Paul Society, with Mr. Joseph Rodgers as President.

The next matter requiring attention was further school accommodation. Property was purchased on Manning avenue and St. Francis' school built, containing four rooms, and well equipped with all modern improvements. The schools in the grounds around St. Mary's Church occupy twelve rooms, and are filled to overflowing. The Christian Brothers have a house near by; while the Sisters of St. Joseph have within the past few years erected a very comfortable and substantial Convent on Bathurst street for those Sisters who teach in the parish of St. Mary's, and also for the purposes of a select school.

The spiritual state of the parish is in keeping with the material. A flourishing Conference of the St. Vincent de Paul Society, having an active membership of 70, with Mr. Martin J. Burns as President, attends to the wants of the poor. There is also a League of the Sacred Heart, with over a thousand members. An Altar Society of four hundred, and a Sodality of one hundred and fifty, complete the most prominent and energetic societies in the parish.

All this is to a large extent due to the zeal and prudence of the Vicar-General, who has watched and fostered it for the past twenty-two years. Venerable in age and connected with well nigh forty years of the history of Toronto,[*] Father Rooney commands the esteem and affection of all who know him. In the parishes where he has served his name is a household

---

[*] His services on the School Board are noted in Chapter viii., p. 270.

word; while amongst the priests, like Nestor of old, he has seen two generations pass away, and he now reigns amongst a third.

The present curates at St. Mary's are the Rev. Fathers D. Sheahan, J. Cruise and P. Coyle. The first is a native of Ireland, where he completed his education before coming to this country. Father Cruise is from Nova Scotia, and is a convert to the faith. After studying in Toronto and St. Hyacinthe, he went to Genoa, Italy, for his theology; returning to Toronto, he was ordained priest in 1887 by the late Archbishop Lynch. Father Coyle is "to the manner born." He made his classical and philosophical courses in St. Michael's College, and was then sent to complete his theology in the same institution with Father Cruise, and was raised to the holy priesthood in Italy in 1891.

St. Basil's Parish.

This is the northern apex of the original ecclesiastical triangle into which the city was divided, and of which St. Paul's and St. Mary's form the other angular points. The parish is under the direction of the Basilian Fathers who have charge of St. Michael's College. To a priest of the Community is given the special duty of attending to the spiritual wants of the parishioners; and the different professors taking a share in the Sunday services, the imposing ceremonies of the Church are carried out with suitable pomp and impressiveness.

We refer our readers to the pages devoted to the Basilian community for an account of this parish, whose history and efficiency are so closely connected with St. Michael's College. We propose here briefly to supplement it.

As the Church and College now stand, they present a very different appearance from that of the original plan designed by Mr. William Hay, Architect. The buildings were arranged in the form of a quadrangle, after the manner of the ancient English colleges. The Church, occupying one side of this square, consists of nave and aisles, with an extended chancel. The style of the sacred edifice is severe first pointed, or that which prevailed in England about the middle of the thirteenth century. The principal entrance, a very handsome one, is through the tower at the south-east corner, reached by a circular walk and drive from St. Joseph street. This entrance is through a cut stone doorway, whose arch is supported by granite pillars. The tower above is of pressed brick, surmounted by a slated spire, 150 feet high to the top of the cross. From this entrance, which is 12 feet square, we pass by a flight of stone steps to the vestibule or narthex, which is 25 feet long by 16 feet wide, with three doors opening to the church proper, and stairways leading to the gallery above, and the Society rooms in the basement beneath respectively. The roof is of open timber construction of bold design, supported by eighteen pillars, with several dormer windows, which throw a chastened light over the otherwise sombre scene.

The sanctuary has a dimension of 32 feet by 25. The main altar is of wood, handsomely carved and richly gilt, with pannelings on the gospel and epistle sides, and above the tabernacle a deep niche containing a statue of the Sacred Heart. The reredos, terminating in various pinnacles and crosses, mounting higher toward the centre, gives the whole, especially when illuminated, a most devotional effect. Behind and above this altar is a richly colored window of three niches representing St. Michael, St. Basil and St. Charles, the gift of the Very Rev. Father Laurent of Toronto, the Very Rev. Father Rooney of Toronto, and the Very Rev. Father Heenan of Hamilton. All the windows of the church are gifts of old students of the College who became priests, and whose names are at the foot of each; while the slab in the entrance retains the names of other benefactors who, out of regard for their Alma Mater, contributed most generously to the completion of the College church.

The altars of the Blessed Virgin and St. Joseph neatly adorn the ends of the sanctuary. They are white, with gilt ornamentations. The various statues and the life size crucifix tend very much to the solemn aspect of the interior.

Just outside the sanctuary near the Blessed Virgin's Altar is a marble tablet with the following inscription in raised gilt letters*:

HON. JOANNI ELMSLEY.
CUJUS COR HIC
DEPOSITUM EST, SOCIETAS S. BASILII GRATA.
Visi sunt oculis insipientium mori; illi autem sunt in pace.—Sap. iii. 2, 3.
R. I. P.

* The following is the translation: "The Society of St. Basil in gratitude to John Elmsley, whose heart is here deposited."
In the sight of the unwise they seem to die; but they are in peace. —Wisdom iii. 2, 3.

Mr. Elmsley had made provision by will that his heart should be taken from his body and placed in St. Basil's Church, which, during his life, he so dearly loved. After his death his heart was hermetically sealed in alcohol, and deposited in a niche behind the tablet where it now rests. The body is buried in the crypt of the Cathedral.

The history of this parish is briefly told: it being a continued advance for many years as the city grew and business forced the population farther outward. If we regard the interior causes for the efficient state of the Church, it is largely due to the energy of Father Lawrence Brennan, C.S.B., who is now parish priest of St. Basil's. The front extension in 1886, with all the material improvements which were made at that time, was the work of his zeal. The parish is well organized, with largely attended Sodalities and an excellent Conference of the St. Vincent de Paul Society, which has an active membership of twenty-five under the Presidency of Mr. J. J. Murphy. This Society has charge of the Parish Library, containing over one thousand volumes. There is also a Ladies' Sewing Society that meets every week during the winter for serving the poor with clothes.

This year the Basilians erected a novitiate for their Community upon their property on St. Clair avenue. It is a handsome four story building, with a neat chapel sufficiently large, not only for the private use of those residing in the house, but also for the Catholic public in the neighborhood. It will thus form the beginning of a parish in the northwestern section of St. Basil's.

The corner stone was laid on May 8th, 1892, by the Right Rev. Denis O'Connor, C.S.B., Bishop of London. A large procession formed at St. Michael's College, consisting of a number of the Benevolent Societies of the City, and, headed by the College Band, marched to the grounds. After the ceremony his Grace Archbishop Walsh preached an eloquent sermon upon the great work of Catholic education. This discourse was followed by addresses from Father Flannery, sole survivor of the pioneers of the Basilian Community in this country, and by Dr. Cassidy and J. J. Foy, Q.C., on the part of the old students of the College. Thus closed a memorable day in the annals of this parish and the Community in whose charge it is placed.

ST. PATRICK'S PARISH.

The western half of the central portion of the city was formed into a parish in the latter part of Bishop de Charbonnel's reign, and placed under the invocation of Ireland's patron Saint. It was originally composed of portions both of the Cathedral and St. Mary's parishes; and is bounded on the north by College street, on the east by Elizabeth and York streets, on the south by the Bay, and on the west by Peter street and Spadina avenue.

The people of this parish were served for a short time by the late Father Proulx. After him came Father Sauvadet, from 1861 to 1865. This priest afterwards went to Cleveland, Ohio, to which diocese we still find in the clerical directory his name attached as chaplain of a hospital in Toledo. Father Sauvadet was succeeded by Father Rey, who remained till 1867; when he was replaced by Father Laurent, who was parish priest of St. Patrick's for fourteen years, from 1867 to 1881, when he was made rector of the Cathedral and Vicar-General. During this time Father Laurent so devoted himself to the spiritual and material progress of the parish, so won the affections of his people, that when he, in obedience to duty, left them for a higher position, his flock were extremely loth to part with him. Upon the removal of Father Laurent the congregation was placed under the charge of the Redemptorist Fathers, who entered upon their work on February 1st, 1881, with the late Very Rev. Eugene Grimm as Superior, and Fathers F. X. Miller, S. J. Krein, A. J. McInerney and J. Hayden as assistants. Amongst these, Fathers McInerney and Krein are at St. Patrick's for a second term, the former being the present Superior. Father Grimm was succeeded by Father Sigl, and he by Father Henning; after whom comes Father A. J. McInerney, who was ordained May 20th, 1875. His assistants are Fathers Krein, McCarthy, Cook and Grogan. There are also three lay brothers in the house. The Redemptorist Fathers of the province of Baltimore, Maryland, were called by his Grace Archbishop Lynch to take charge of the parish and to give missions in the diocese. The regret which the parishioners felt at losing Father Laurent yielded to respect and affection, when they became acquainted with the fervent community in whose charge they had been placed.

The church of this parish, situated on William street, between Caer Howell and Anderson streets, is a neat brick building of gothic design.

The first church erected here, a frame one, was destroyed by fire on June 22nd, 1865. In 1869 Father Laurent started to build a new church, which was completed the following year, and dedicated November 20th, 1870, by Archbishop Lynch. Bishop Farrell of Hamilton sang the Mass, while the sermon was preached by his Grace Archbishop Walsh, then Bishop of London. Bishop McQuaid of Rochester preached in the evening.

Since that time the Church has been frescoed in chaste design, and two neat oratories have been erected on either side of the main altar. These give the sanctuary a more roomy appearance; and when, at solemn evening services, the altars are lighted, the effect is most pleasing.

When the Redemptorists came, the presbytery proved altogether too small and inconvenient for a community. In 1886 Father Sigl, who was then Superior, erected the present handsome convent upon McCaul street. The basement contains a fine hall, where the various societies can hold public as well as ordinary meetings. The rest of the house is devoted to Community purposes, having on the second story a small but tasteful private chapel.

There is one Separate school on William street, north of the Church, built in 1867. Until the opening of the new church it served for religious purposes on Sundays and Feast days. There is an attendance of 400 children at the various classes, which are taught by the Christian Brothers and the Sisters of St. Joseph.

The following religious and literary societies are connected with the parish : St. Patrick's Conference of the St. Vincent de Paul Society, under the presidency of Mr. William Burns, with an active membership of forty-seven ; Children of Mary ; three branches of the Arch-Confraternity of the Holy Family ; the St. Alphonsus Young Men's Catholic Association, and the St. Catharine's Young Ladies' Literary Association—the last two meeting at stated times in the parish hall for religious, mental and physical improvement. All these societies are under the direction of the Fathers. The Catholic population of the parish is given at 2,300 souls.

St. Helen's Parish.

About twenty years ago Mr. Alexander Macdonell gave some land for church purposes in what was then the village of Brockton, situated on the corner of Lansdowne avenue and Dundas street. To this property Father Rooney, who was at the time parish priest of S. Mary's, added by purchase an acre and a half. In 1872 he built a church here, which was dedicated to St. Francis and St. Helen, the former being the patron saint of the pastor, and the latter being added in accordance with the donor's wishes. The title of St. Francis has practically dropped out, and the parish church is better known as St. Helen's. Archbishop Lynch performed the dedicatory services, and Archbishop Walsh, who had preached at the laying of the corner stone, was the preacher upon the occasion.

SANCTUARY OF ST. HELEN'S CHURCH, BROCKTON.

This church, a neat red brick structure, prominent by its position on rising ground, served very well until the growth of the population called for more accommodation. Accordingly, in 1888, the Very Rev. Father McCann commenced the building of a new one, the rear portion of which, consisting of a fine sanctuary and transepts, as given in the preceding view, is all that is yet finished. This, joined to the old church, forms but one edifice, and is quite sufficient for the present wants of the congregation.

In constructing the first building the basement was so arranged that it made a very good school, which lasted for several years. But the history of Brockton Separate school dates much farther back. It had been established in 1857 by his Grace Archbishop Walsh, when pastor of St. Mary's, in a frame building on St. Clarence avenue. Father McCann, in 1883, secured the erection of a substantial school of four rooms, to the north of the church. A second building of similar dimensions is in course of erection, and will be finished before the close of the present year.

The Christian Brothers have charge of the boys; and the Sisters of Loretto, of the girls.

For a few years after the erection of St. Helen's it was attended from St. Mary's Church. But in November, 1875, it was erected into a separate parish, under the care of Father J. J. Shea. This name, familiar to many of our readers, recalls a most amiable and generous character, whose career was cut off a few years ago by sudden death while still little beyond the prime of life.

In 1880 Father Shea was succeeded by the Very Rev. Father Conway, who was appointed Dean of Toronto in 1882. The Very Rev. Father McCann followed shortly after. He enlarged the presbytery, which had been erected by his predecessor. His other improvements have been already noticed. All this time the parish had been rapidly increasing, so that a second priest was necessary, Father Harold being appointed in 1881.

When Father McCann was, in January, 1891, appointed Rector of the Cathedral, Father Cassidy took charge of St. Helen's, and was made Dean of Toronto.

Edward Cassidy is an old Toronto boy, being born in this city October 4th, 1845. He received his classical education at St. Michael's College, and studied theology in the Grand Seminary at Montreal. His ordination as priest took place on the 4th of October, 1868. Thornhill, Pickering, Dixie, Adjala, Barrie, were all in order, previous to Brockton, scenes of Father Cassidy's priestly labors. In all of these parishes he commanded the respect of his different flocks, and in many he left substantial marks of his zeal. It is difficult to sketch the character of a living man; but history will know Dean Cassidy as a prudent, careful priest, whose career is fittingly honored with the dignity bestowed upon him.

The present assistant at St. Helen's is Father Joseph F. McBride, who is a native of Scotland. His early education was received in Streetsville High school. He attended the College of the Holy Angels at Niagara Falls, and completed his theology in the Grand Seminary at Montreal. In 1877 he was raised to the holy priesthood, after which he was made Secretary to the late Archbishop. This position he held, with the exception of a few years' residence in Penetanguishene, until the death of Dr. Lynch. Since that time Father McBride, on leaving Our Lady of Lourdes, where he was parish priest, took charge of Dixie, and afterwards, at his own request, was appointed curate at Brockton. Besides his clerical duties he is at present editor of "The Catholic Weekly Review" of Toronto.

In addition to St. Helen's church the priests of Brockton have charge of Weston, where a church was erected by the Very Rev. Father Soulerin, Superior of St. Michael's College, in 1853, and dedicated to St. John the Evangelist. Up to the appointment of a resident pastor of Brockton, this Church was served by the Basilian Fathers. A Separate school also was organized at Weston in 1856, and has ever since been maintained. So far the sacristy has been used for a school room; but steps are being taken for the erection of a school house proper.

A large Separate school was built in 1888 in the extreme north-west part of the city, immediately adjoining Toronto Junction. This building is temporarily used as a church for the accommodation of the Catholics between Brockton and Weston.

Thus we find springing from the parent stock of St. Mary's not the mere mission chapel of St. Helen's, but a flourishing parish with promising future, and other churches branching from it in turn. A Conference of the St. Vincent de Paul Society, with an active membership of twenty-five, under the presidency of Mr. V. P. Fayle, a flourishing League of the Sacred Heart, and other Sodalities bespeak the satisfactory state of religion, the bright prospects for the future, and the zeal of the priests and people in this rising young parish of the west.

St. Joseph's Parish, Leslieville.

Leaving the western parish, the next in order of time is St. Joseph's, Leslieville, in the eastern extremity of the city. It began practically when the Separate school was opened on Curzon street about the year 1863; for soon afterwards Mass was celebrated in it every Sunday for the accommodation of those parishioners of St. Paul's who lived beyond the Don. A new school house containing two rooms was built in 1871, which was also used for divine services. It continued to be attended by the priests of St. Paul's until November 10th, 1878, when it was erected into a separate parish, under the invocation of St. Joseph. But the church was not built until the year 1884, when the corner stone was laid. It was dedicated in July, 1886, by his Lordship Bishop O'Mahony.

The parish has since so far increased that a second church was needed still farther east, near the village of York. As early as 1853 or 1854 the late Mr. Terence O'Neil, who then lived in the neighborhood, gave some land for a church, beautifully situated on high ground which overlooks the lake. But it had little prospect of ever being devoted to the sacred purposes for which it was intended; sparseness of Catholics, scarcity of priests, and the slow growth of the city in that direction prevented any action being taken. However, the donor himself, when speaking upon the subject, hoped against hope, and with faith used always remark that some day or other Mass would be offered over that spot for the repose of his soul. Nearly forty years went by; Mr. O'Neil himself passed away; but at length his conviction proved a prophecy. A neat chapel was erected, and dedicated to St. John the Evangelist by his Grace Archbishop Walsh on Sunday, May 22nd, 1892. On the following Wednesday the holy sacrifice was offered for the repose of the soul of the generous giver of the land.

The population of the whole parish is about two hundred and twenty families, although it fluctuates, on account of the neigborhood being a favorite summer resort.

The present pastor, Father M. McC. O'Reilly, has been parish priest since its separation from St. Paul's. This good priest was born at Granard in the County of Longford, Ireland. After completing his classical education in St. Mel's Seminary, Longford, he came to this

Church of Our Lady of Lourdes Toronto.

D.

country, and entered St. Michael's College, Toronto, for his philosophy. He studied theology in the Seminary of the Holy Angels, Niagara Falls, and also at Montreal. Archbishop Lynch ordained him priest September 21st, 1865. Since that time he has been stationed at Thorold, for a short while, Stayner for seven years, and St. Joseph's, Leslieville, for the last fourteen. He has been always an active church builder—Merritton, Stayner, Brentwood and the two churches of his present parish being the enduring evidence of his devoted work in the priesthood.

Parish of Our Lady of Lourdes.

This parish dates from the year 1886. When his Grace the late Archbishop Lynch celebrated the Silver Jubilee of his episcopate in 1884, the erection of a memorial church was decided upon as the most fitting way in which to commemorate the event. The site chosen was the Sherbourne street front of the ecclesiastical property known as St. John's Grove, the private residence of the Archbishop. Hitherto the north-eastern part of the city had had no regular place of worship, though Catholic residents were generally admitted to the private Mass of his Grace or of his resident Chaplain in the basement of the archiepiscopal house. But the room was small and inconvenient, and as the neighborhood grew and developed, the necessity of a larger and better adapted chapel became apparent. Having, therefore, decided upon the erection of a church as stated above, the Archbishop entrusted to Commander Law, R.N., the preparation of plans and specifications. The handsome Church of Our Lady of Lourdes is the result of that gentleman's work, and stands to-day a monument to his architectural skill. The corner stone was laid on June 21st, 1885, by his Grace Archbishop Lynch, assisted by his Lordship Bishop O'Mahony, the latter of whom preached the sermon. On October 29th, 1886, the solemn dedication services took place, Archbishop Lynch again officiating, assisted by their Lordships Bishop Walsh of London and Carbery of Hamilton. The sermon on this occasion was preached by the Bishop of London.

The church is in the classic Italian style of architecture, and is modelled after that of Santa Maria del Popolo in Rome. It consists of transept and nave, and is surmounted by a spacious dome 97 feet in height and 26 and one half in diameter. The interior length of the structure is

100 feet and the width 35 feet, the whole, with its unique scheme of coloring and artistic woodwork, forming a most charming interior. The external appearance is likewise pleasing, the symmetrical dome and stately facade, surmounted by the words: "Gloria in Excelsis Deo," presenting a prominent feature in that part of Sherbourne street. The cost of the structure was about $40,000.

Contemporaneously with the opening of the church was proclaimed the erection of a new parish under the invocation of Our Lady of Lourdes and St. John the Evangelist. Its boundaries were defined as follows: On the east, the River Don; on the south, Carleton street to Church street; thence up Church street (including both sides) to Bloor street; thence along Bloor street to Gwynne street; thence to the old northerly boundary of St. Paul's parish.

The first rector was Rev. J. F. McBride, so long and favorably known as Secretay to the late Archbishop Lynch, and, on the latter's death, to the Very Rev. Administrators of the Archdiocese. Father McBride is referred to at length elsewhere, and we have here to do only with his incumbency of the church under survey. Under his fostering care the parish grew rapidly, and many good works were inaugurated, which have not failed to bear fruit during subsequent years.

Upon the appointment of the Most Rev. John Walsh as Archbishop of Toronto in 1889, Father McBride was replaced by Father James Walsh, nephew and Secretary of the Archbishop, and who became second Rector of the parish. These offices he still holds, and has firmly established himself in the affections of his people.

Father Walsh was born in 1857 at Mooncoin in Ireland, in the same house in which had been born, twenty-seven years before, his illustrious uncle. He studied for four years at St. Patrick's College, Carlow, and thence proceeded to Rome, where, at the College of the Propaganda, he remained four years, completing his theological studies and preparing himself for the priesthood. He was ordained on March 13th, 1881, by his Eminence Cardinal LaValetta, in the Basilica of St. John Lateran, the Cathedral Church of the Popes as Bishops of Rome. He came to Canada in September of the same year and proceeded to London, of which Diocese his uncle was at that time Bishop. He remained there as assistant priest of St.

Peter's Cathedral and Chaplain, first of St. Joseph's Orphan Asylum, Mount Hope, and latterly of the Sacred Heart Convent; and, on the removal of Bishop Walsh to Toronto, accompanied him hither, and was installed into his present charge. He is known and esteemed both in London and in Toronto as a zealous, pious and devoted priest, an efficient Diocesan Secretary, and an eloquent pulpit orator.

Under Father Walsh the parish has made steady progress, and now numbers 150 families. In addition to the Archbishop's residence, it contains an Academy on Wellesley street, conducted by the Nuns of Loretto, and a Separate school; and in connection with the Church there are a Conference of the Society of St. Vincent de Paul, the Sacred Heart Altar Society, a Sodality of the Blessed Virgin Mary, and a Branch of the C. M. B. A.

THE SACRED HEART PARISH.

This, the last of the city parishes, differs in this respect: that the basis of its separation from the others is not in regard to place, but to language. The Sacred Heart parish has been erected for the benefit of the French speaking Catholics of Toronto, whose interests are more carefully attended to when they have a priest of their own language and nationality. And this city having more or less French, it was a continued source of anxiety on the part of the bishops, as it was the wish of the people themselves, to have their own church, wherein they would hear their mother tongue. For several years the Basilian Fathers used to gather several French families in their College chapel, and, after a few prayers, preach to them. But this met with no degree of success: the few and the good came; the many and those who needed special attention remained away. At length, in 1887, a French Canadian priest was brought from Montreal and given special charge over all the French Catholics of the city. On the 26th of June he held his first services in the St. Vincent de Paul Chapel in St. Michael's Palace, where they remained for fifteen months. Then an old Presbyterian church on King street, between Power street and the Don, was purchased; and, having been refitted, was blessed on October 7th, 1888, by the late Vicar-General Laurent.

The population attached to the parish numbers one hundred and thirty families, and is continually increasing. When we consider the difficulties and religious dangers for a foreign speaking people in a mixed community, we readily discern the good which this parish has done and is doing amongst a class who, at home, have always been remarkable for their spirit of simple faith. Their priest, since first the parish was organized, is Father Philippe LaMarche, a native of Montreal. He prosecuted his studies, both classical and theological, in Joliette College, where also he was raised to the holy priesthood by Archbishop Fabre May 19th, 1883. Between this date and his coming to Toronto, four years after, he remained in Montreal as curate, and was attached to various churches in that city.

There is a Separate school in this parish taught by two Sisters of St. Joseph, where the scholars are instructed in both English and French. It was opened in the year 1891, and already numbers one hundred pupils. The parish has two societies, which are devoted to the various wants of the poor: a benevolent society under the patronage of St. Joseph, for the benefit of the French Canadians, with a membership of sixty ; and a Conference of the St. Vincent de Paul Society, having 30 active members, under the presidency of Mr. P. Jobin.

The League of the Sacred Heart and the usual parochial Sodalities are well established, and give evidence of their earnestness and activity.

A notable event worthy of chronicling in connection with this parish is the visit of his Eminence Cardinal Taschereau, October 9th, 1887, when he came to Toronto for the purpose of laying the corner stone of St. Paul's new church. This first Canadian Prince of the Church kindly paid his fellow countrymen a special visit, and gave them a special blessing for their union, encouragement and success, which, as time advances, is producing its fruit under the care of their zealous pastor.

The Parish of Adjala.

In the sketches of the country parishes, instead of taking them according to the time of their establishment, as was done with those of the city, we follow the alphabetical order. This plan very appropriately opens with the prosperous and historical parish of Adjala, situated in the south-western part of the County of Simcoe.

The Catholic settlement in the township after which the parish is named dates from the early part of this century. Bishop Macdonell wishing that, in advancing to the back portions of the country, his people should not be scattered, advised particular sections. Amongst these was the fertile township of Adjala. In order still further to secure his object, a verbal agreement was entered into with the English church authorities that all Protestant settlers should be advised to go to the neighboring townships of Mulmur and Mono, and all Catholics to Adjala. We may relate a typical case, that of the late Mr. Hugh Ferguson, father of the Rev. M. J. Ferguson, C.S.B. Mr. Ferguson, with some neighbors, had been lumbering in Maine, but turned towards Upper Canada in the hope of getting better land. They applied at Kingston for information, and were recommended to go to Adjala, where Bishop Macdonell had, on his visitation not long before, found the land very good. A number of families also came from the Welland Canal. In this way Adjala grew up to be a Catholic township, peopled with the nobles of the soil, a race hardy and brave, with not much book learning, but well trained in the simplicity, honor and faith of their Irish forefathers.

For these good settlers, many of whom he had been instrumental in sending there, Bishop Macdonell obtained, in 1834, about 185 acres of land, described as "broken lots 10, 11 and 13 in the 8th Adjala, in trust for a church and school house." The following year is the date given for the first church. A second was built upon its site about 1850, as a subscription list of the year previous is to be found in the parochial archives. The present sacred edifice, a handsome brick building, was erected by Father Cassidy in 1888. It was blessed by the Very Rev. Father Rooney, then co-administrator of the Archdiocese, in the early part of 1889, and dedicated to St. James.

Bishop Macdonell visited this parish during its earliest days. The next episcopal visit was that of his co-adjutor, Bishop Gaulin, who administered Confirmation here on the 27th of August, 1837. Bishop Power of Toronto made his first pastoral visitation to Adjala in 1844.

The first priest's name is that of Father Lawlor, Missionary Apostolic, who attended this mission from June, 1833, to February, 1837. After him we have the following series of priests: Father Fitzpatrick from March, 1837, to March, 1840; Father O'Dwyer from the last date till October, 1841; Father James Bennett, the first resident pastor, from March, 1842, to June, 1843; Father Flynn till 1846; Father Mills from 1847 to 1849; Father Rattigan to 1855; F. X. Pourret to 1859; M. M. O'Shea till 1860.

This last was succeeded by Father John F. Synott, whose pastoral charge of six years terminated sadly by him being thrown from his buggy and killed. Father J. Michel was next appointed, but remained only a year and a half, when he was followed by Father Richard A. O'Connor, now Bishop of Peterborough. In 1870 he was replaced by Father Harris, now Dean of St. Catharines, who remained till 1875; after him came Father McSpiritt till 1887. In November of that year Father Edward Cassidy, now Dean of Toronto, was appointed pastor, and was succeeded in January, 1890, by the present incumbent, Father James Kilcullen.

Father Kilcullen made his classical course in the Seminary of the Diocese of Achonry, Mayo County, Ireland. He then came to this country, and studied philosophy and theology in the Grand Seminary of St. Sulpice, Montreal. His ordination to the holy priesthood took place May 30th, 1869, after which he was appointed curate in the Brock mission. His first and only parish, previous to Adjala, was Port Colborne, of which he had charge for eighteen years.

Besides the parish church of St. James, situated in the centre of a fine farming district, there are two others. That of St. Francis at Tottenham, a village on the Hamilton and North-western railroad, and about three miles from the presbytery, is a neat brick structure, erected in 1884. On the western border of the parish, at Achil, is the second, a frame chapel, St. Mary's, of unpretentious appearance, built some twenty years ago.

The Catholic population is about 1050, distributed as follows: 450 belong to St. James' or the parochial church; 350 to St. Mary's at Achil; and 250 to St. Francis', Tottenham.

The majority of the school sections being entirely Catholic, the schools are classed as Public, and are taught by Catholics. Of these there are five, and there is in the parish but one Separate school, strictly called.

At present the mission consists of the southern section of Adjala township and part of Tecumseh, about four miles in length by three in width. But in the beginning it comprised the townships of Tecumseh, Adjala North and South, Mono, Mulmur, Essa, King and Tossorontio.

It may not be unworthy of mention that Adjala parish (including North as well as South) is the birthplace of six priests—by far the greatest

number from any one mission in the Archdiocese. Three of them are members of the Basilian Community, still doing active duty—Fathers Ferguson, Hayden and Kelly--a fourth was also a Basilian, Father Morrow, who died some years ago. The fifth was the late Father Skelly, a priest of the Archdiocese, who passed away not long after his ordination. The last is Father John O'Leary, at present parish priest of Freelton in the Diocese of Hamilton.

The Parish of Brock.

This parish derives its name from the township of Brock in the County of Ontario, where the parochial church and residence are situated.

It dates as far back as 1855, when Father Walsh, now Archbishop of Toronto, was appointed its first resident pastor. Before his time it used to be visited occasionally from Oshawa by a priest, who said Mass in a small frame church, which had been erected some years before. When Father Walsh entered upon his parochial charge there was no priest's house, and he was obliged to board with one of the Catholic families in the neighborhood. At this time the district extended over the townships of Brock, Reach, Uxbridge, Scott, Georgina, North Gwillimbury, Thorah and Mara. To accommodate a large number of Catholics he built a frame church in Georgina township, not far from Lake Simcoe, on two acres of land given by a Mr. Anthony Charpentier.

Father Walsh, being called to take charge of St. Mary's in Toronto, was succeeded in Brock by Father John Lee in 1857. Through the generosity of one of his parishioners, Sterling Pangman, who gave him two acres of land at Vroomanton, Father Lee built a parsonage. He erected also a frame church in Thorah. In 1860 Father Louis Braire was appointed to the mission, and labored hard in it for twenty-one years. During his long incumbency churches sprang up under his zeal and energy; and two missions, that of Mara on the north, and Uxbridge on the south, were cut off from Brock. Thus the mission now includes the Townships of North Gwillimbury, Georgina, Thorah and Brock, with three churches—one in Georgina, a second in Thorah, and the other, with the presbytery, at Vroomanton in Brock.

Father Braire was succeeded by Father Rohleder, and he, in 1891, by the present incumbent, Father Patrick Kiernan.

Brock, like Adjala, has been the birthplace of several priests. Vicar-General McCann spent here his early boyhood; Archdeacon Campbell of Orillia; Fathers Donald McRae of Parkhill, in the Diocese of London; Kenneth McRae of Smithville; and P. Coyle of St. Mary's, Toronto, were all born in Brock.

THE PARISH OF CALEDON.

This parish, situated in the Township of Caledon and County of Peel, belonged to the Gore of Toronto until its establishment in 1867.

The Catholic settlement in this part of the country is very old, and has a similar origin to the larger Catholic colony of Adjala. As in all other districts, the holy sacrifice was first offered in private houses. But as early as 1834 a log church was built and served by Father Lawlor. This made way for a frame one which Father Eugene O'Reilly erected in 1843, and which did duty for over forty years. In the year 1885 it was torn down, and a substantial brick church, dedicated to St. Cornelius, raised upon its site.

Belonging to the parish there is a second church, that of St. Alphonsus, in the township of Albion, built also in 1834. It was the first sacred edifice in Albion, and is still in good preservation.

The first pastor of Caledon was Father McSpiritt, who had charge for five years. Fathers Laboureau and Rey came next in order, but remained only one year each. Father Egan succeeded, and held the mission for six years, when he was replaced by Father Eugene Gallagher. It was during his incumbency that the present fine church of Caledon was erected. After laboring zealously for seven years he was, in 1887, followed by the present parish priest, Father Patrick Whitney.

Father Whitney studied theology in Genoa, where he was also ordained priest, September 23rd, 1882. After filling several curacies he was made pastor of the Gore in 1886, which he changed the following year for Caledon and Albion.

THE PARISH OF DIXIE.

One of the oldest churches in the Diocese was that on the Fifth line of Toronto township, in the County of Peel, and which derived its name from its situation. It was built about the year 1830, and was the original parish church of this district. Since that time the parochial residence has changed from the Fifth line to Streetsville, and from Streetsville to Dixie, where, for the last twenty years, it is firmly established.

The first priest's name on the registers is one well known to many parts of the country, Father John McNulty, who attended the parish from 1856 to July, 1858. Though he was not resident pastor, he built a frame presbytery at the Fifth line, and the present brick church of Streetsville. The names of many of the priests who preceded him have passed into oblivion; but Father Gordon, afterwards Vicar-General of Hamilton, and Father Eugene O'Reilly of Toronto Gore are still held in cherished recollection by many of the old inhabitants. The latter, having direct charge of this church, as part of his parish, visited it regularly; the former only from time to time, according as his duties called him in this direction.

Father McNulty afterwards went to Hamilton diocese, and was parish priest of Caledonia for many years. Having purchased a property in Dundas, he bestowed it upon the Sisters of St. Joseph for a House of Providence. Here he spent the last two years of his long life, the greater portion of which had been zealously devoted to the arduous duties of a homeless missionary.

After him came Father Michel, who attended this parish from the Gore. Then we find Father Conway parish priest of Streetsville in 1859, and Father J. J. Shea pastor of the Fifth line from March, 1860, till May, 1861, when he was succeeded by Father Flannery, whose name is already familiar to our readers. He purchased the church property at Dixie, where he built the present presbytery. It is situated on Dundas street, about twelve miles from the city of Toronto. Father Flannery remained until 1867, and was replaced by Father Finan, and he by Father T. J. Morris. The last named priest erected a portion of the present church at Dixie, which was completed, except the sanctuary and tower, by Father McEntee, his successor. It was opened in October, 1872. Father Cassidy came to this parish in 1877, and remained ten years. During his charge he built the present church at Port Credit, a neat brick church at the Fifth line, and a frame church at Lambton, where he formed a new congregation. He also improved the presbytery, and erected new altars in the churches of Dixie, Streetsville and Port Credit. Father Cassidy was followed by Father Harold, who erected the sanctuary and sacristy of the Dixie church.

Between the last named and the present incumbent, Father Trayling, who was appointed February 1st, 1891, the pastorates were brief and unmarked by any event of historical importance.

The Parish of Newmarket.

On the first of November, 1838, a meeting of the Catholics of Newmarket was held at the residence of Mr. John Walsh, store-keeper, to take into consideration the advisability of building a church there. All the Catholics in the vicinity, numbering but six, were present, whose names tradition still preserves—John Walsh, Patrick Gibbons, Michael Gibbons, Michael Cannon, William Wallis and Francis Rafferty. The sum of sixty dollars was subscribed, but was considered too small to commence with. A second meeting was held the following year at the house of Mr. William Wallis. In addition to the six named above three more were present—and it was resolved to proceed. A grant of half an acre of land was obtained from Mr. George Lount, and preparations were made to build. Accordingly, in 1840, the little band of Catholics of Newmarket had the happiness of possessing a neat rough-cast church of the modest dimensions of 30 feet by 20, where the holy Mass was offered occasionally. After the erection of the church more Catholics settled around Newmarket, and a small congregation was formed. A large number of immigrants came in 1847 and the following year; but the fever, which was raging at the time, crowded the cemetery rather than filled the church.

The first priest stationed here was Father Quinlan, who entered upon his charge at the time the church was built—about the year 1840. He was succeeded in 1845 by Father Nightingale, who remained only a short time. Father Proulx came in 1847, and had his headquarters here for four years. After him there was a vacancy until the appointment of Father O'Loughlin in 1853. Then, in 1855, Father McNulty, diocesan missionary, attended Newmarket, two or three years. After a short interval we have a series of pastors beginning with Father Wardy (from 1858 to 1862) and ending with the present incumbent, Father D. Morris. Father Keane, who had charge of the parish for nine years (1867—1876), replaced the old church by a handsome gothic brick structure, dedicated to St. John Chrysostom. His immediate successor, Father Harris, was here for the same length of time, and built an excellent Separate school house, the classes of which had been till then taught in the old church.

Father D. Morris was educated at All Hallows College, Dublin, Ireland, and was raised to the holy priesthood June 24th, 1884. After ordination he was assistant at St. Paul's, Toronto, until 1890, when he was made pastor of Orangeville, from which place he was removed to Newmarket the following year.

There is a Conference of the St. Vincent de Paul Society, having twelve active members, under the presidency of Mr. P. J. O'Malley.

Besides the parish church there is another dedicated to the Forty Martyrs at Bradford in the County of Simcoe, built about the year 1860, which is attended by thirty-five families. The Catholic population of the parish is given at one hundred and sixty-five families, of whom one hundred and thirty belong to Newmarket, and the remainder to Bradford.

THE PARISH OF ORANGEVILLE.

This parish was erected in June, 1885, by his Grace the late Archbishop Lynch. It includes also the missions of Mono West, Brampton and Cataract. The first pastor was Rev. Michael Jeffcott, who, about a year ago, was succeeded by Rev. Henry J. McPhillips, still the incumbent.

Orangeville was formerly attended from Caledon. For many years Mass was said in the house of one of the Catholic residents, until twelve years ago Rev. J. J. Egan, at that time in charge of the parish, erected the brick church which still continues in use. On his advent, in 1885, Father Jeffcott purchased the house which is now used as a presbytery.

Mono West contained at one time nearly thirty Catholic families. It was originally attached to the parish of Adjala, and subsequently to that of North Adjala, until united with Orangeville under the care of Father Jeffcott. The old log church was built about thirty years ago upon a plot of land of four acres, donated for the purpose by Mr. Patrick McCabe of this township.

Brampton has been attended from various points. In the beginning the priest from the Fifth line visited it occasionally; then it was attended from the Gore, from Toronto, and from Caledon, in the order named. Although a town of some dimensions, Brampton has few Catholic families, not sufficient to form a distinct parish, and is therefore united with Orangeville. The first church, a brick one, was erected twenty-seven years ago; but, in the year 1875, it was burned by an incendiary. Subsequently an edifice formerly used by the Presbyterians was purchased and transformed into a Catholic church, which continues in use to the present time.

The small mission of Cataract, which contains a brick church, built in the year 1882, was formerly attended from Caledon, but within the last three years it has been attached to Orangeville.

Father Henry J. McPhillips, the present pastor of these missions, is a native of Alabama, United States, and was ordained priest on July 10th, 1887. After studying at the Seminary of the Holy Angels, Niagara Falls, he completed his theology at Montreal. He was for a few years assistant priest at St. Helen's, Toronto, and while there was elected to a seat on the Separate school board. He is an active, energetic young priest, entirely devoted to his work.

The Parish of Oshawa.

The parish records not going beyond 1843, it is difficult to trace the history of Catholicity in Oshawa; for it is certain that as early as 1825 the few settlers here were visited by a Catholic priest. In 1830 Mass was first celebrated in this mission, in the house of the late Mr. Daniel Leonard, by Father O'Grady. He visited the town subsequently at intervals to administer sacraments to the dying, and to afford the scattered families opportunity of complying with the precept of Easter Communion. Father Butler of Peterborough also attended this settlement occasionally in the course of his missionary tours. Tradition, piously treasured by the few remaining pioneers, makes mention of Fathers McDonagh, Gibney and Quinlan of Toronto. From 1836 to 1842 Oshawa seems to have been under the pastors of Cobourg. In 1841 Father Kirwan commenced the erection of the present church. Previous to its opening, which took place the following year, the holy sacrifice used to be offered up once a month for a period of five or six years in McGregor's school house. The old building still stands, a venerable witness of the early struggles of the Catholic immigrants who settled in this locality.

The first resident priest was Father Henry Fitzpatrick, who was appointed in 1843. He was succeeded the following year by Father Nightingale, whose first entry on the baptismal records appears November 1st,

1844. These two priests alternated in the charge of the mission until April, 1847. Between this date and the appointment of Father Proulx, August 20th, 1848, local tradition assigns the pastorate to Father Smith; but of his administration no record remains. When Father Proulx took possession Oshawa included the whole County of Ontario, where there are now eight parish priests attending fifteen churches. In 1852 he enlarged the church; and in 1859 he built the first Catholic school of the town. To preside over the education of the young he established the Sisters of St. Joseph. This venerable priest remained in Oshawa until 1860, when he was succeeded by Father Eugene O'Keefe—a man of literary taste and oratorical power, still remembered for his scholarly lectures. He was the first priest to have Mass every Sunday in Whitby, where he established also a Separate school, in existence to the present. He resigned his charge in 1862; and was replaced by Father J. J. Shea. This last remained for ten years, and in 1868 he erected a Catholic church in Whitby. After Father Shea came Father McCann, who was appointed November 1st, 1872. During his pastorate he built a good parochial house, improved and enlarged the school, and procured ground for a Catholic cemetery. To him succeeded Father McEntee, in 1877, who remained till January, 1890, and was then replaced by the present incumbent, Father John L. Hand, who had been, up to his charge of this parish, assistant at the Cathedral, from his ordination in 1883.

In 1882 Whitby was separated from Oshawa and erected into a distinct parish, with Father J. J. McCall as its first pastor. Father Patrick Kiernan succeeded him, but was transferred to Brock April, 1891, when Whitby was again attended from Oshawa.

The Parish of Pickering.

This mission comprises the townships of Pickering and Scarborough. It was formerly known as Duffin's Creek, and in the old days formed part of the Oshawa mission.

The first church in Pickering (St. Winefrid's) was a frame building erected in the year 1849 by the venerable Father Proulx, at that time stationed at Oshawa. This beloved missionary continued to minister to the spiritual wants of the people in this section until his removal to

Toronto in 1858. Soon after (1860) Pickering was erected into a separate parish, with Rev. P. D. Laurent (now parish priest of Lindsay and Vicar-General of the Diocese of Peterborough) as first pastor. Father Laurent had formerly been assistant to Father Proulx at Oshawa. On taking charge of Pickering he built a presbytery and put the parish into a thorough state of organization. He was succeeded by the saintly Father Philip Cummins, who, however, died about a year afterwards. The next pastor was Rev. A. P. Finan, who remained about five years, being followed by Rev. William Flannery, now of St. Thomas. Father Flannery soon gave place to Rev. Father Conway, and he, in 1868, to Rev. Father Hayden, who remained until 1875, when Rev. E. Cassidy took charge for one year, being followed by Rev. William Bergin, who, in November, 1877, was succeeded by the late Rev. James Beausang. During Father Beausang's pastorate a good addition to the presbytery was built. The next pastor was Rev. D. J. Sheahan, who was appointed in 1885. He remained until January, 1890, when the present pastor, Rev. Michael Jeffcott, was installed.

A tradition in connection with Pickering is worth recording. Although the first priest to officiate in the section of whom there is any record was the first incumbent of the parish of Oshawa, it is said that in olden times, when Canada was under French dominion, Rev. Pere Fenelon, brother of the famous Archbishop of Cambray, landed at Frenchman's Bay, and said Mass there.

The present church, under the patronage of St. Francis de Sales, is a handsome brick building, erected in 1871, during the pastorate of Father Hayden.

Pickering has given many of her sons and daughters to the church. In this respect it is perhaps unsurpassed by any parish in the province of the same extent. The present Bishop of London, Right Rev. Dr. O'Connor, is a native of Pickering; so also is Rev. Robert McBrady, C.S.B., of St. Michael's College, Toronto. It was also the birthplace of the late Rev. John O'Connor, parish priest of Maidstone, as well as of Rev. M. J. Redden, of the Archdiocese of Toronto, and Father Walsh, C.S.B., who was born at Highland Creek. It would be impossible here to enumerate all the ladies who from this parish have entered the religious orders.

The present church (St. Joseph's) at Highland Creek in the Township of Scarborough, was built by Father Proulx about 1854. It is a frame building still in a fair state of preservation.

The present parish priest, Father Michael Jeffcott, was born in Tralee, Ireland, in 1857. After finishing his classical course in St. Brendan's College, Killarney, he studied philosophy and theology in the Grand Seminary, Namur, Belgium, for six years, and was ordained priest on July 9th, 1882, by Right Rev. Dr. Higgins, Bishop of Killarney. After coming to the Archdiocese of Toronto he was assistant priest to Rev. Father Laboureau, Penetanguishene; then chaplain to the House of Providence, Toronto; and, for a short time, Secretary to the late Archbishop Lynch. His pastorate of Orangeville is referred to elsewhere. In January, 1890, he became pastor of Pickering. His career is marked by a faithful and energetic discharge of the duties of the sacred ministry.

The Catholic population of Pickering is about 350, and that of Scarborough about 100.

THE PARISH OF SCHOMBERG.

This mission comprises a portion of the Township of King in York County, and also a part of the Township of Tecumseh in the County of Simcoe.

It originally belonged to Adjala parish, from which it was cut off about fifteen years ago. The Church of St. Margaret in Tecumseh dates as far back as 1836; while St. Mary's in King is some twenty years later. Old settlers tell of Father Gordon of Hamilton as the first priest visiting this part of the country. When Father Lawlor became parish priest of Adjala* this section was attended regularly.

The first pastor of Schomberg, as a separate mission, was Father Sheahan, followed by Fathers Mullen, McGinley, P. Kiernan and Eugene F. Gallagher. The last named is at present in charge. He studied classics and philosophy in St. Macartan's Seminary, County of Monaghan, Ireland, and theology at the Grand Seminary in Montreal, Canada. After his ordination to the holy priesthood, September 21st, 1877, he was assistant at St. Catharines, then pastor of Niagara, Caledon and finally Schomberg.

* Vid. sketch of Adjala, p. 309.

The Parish of Thornhill.

The early history of this mission is connected with Newmarket, by the priests of which place it was visited periodically. In 1849 we find Father Byrne residing for a short time in Thornhill; but the priest who may be regarded as the first pastor of this parish was Father Louis Griffa, a native of Turin, Italy. He came to this country in 1858, and was placed in charge of this district, but remained only two years.* The church was commenced nearly forty-five years ago by Father Quinlan, and was completed by Father Proulx, who succeeded him. The list of priests whose names are still on the records corresponds very closely with the Newmarket series. We select Father McNulty from amongst them, as being longer connected with Thornhill, coming in 1853 and leaving in 1858. He built an addition to the church, and attached a wing which served as the pastoral residence for many years. It was only in 1879 that it was vacated for the neat brick presbytery built by Father McGinley while parish priest from 1876 to 1881. He had been preceded by a long list of clergymen who were each in charge for a short term, and was followed by the Rev. J. J. Egan, the present incumbent.

Father Egan is a native of Ireland, and studied in the Diocesan College of Ennis in the County of Clare. In 1869 he came to Canada, and after completing philosophy at St. Michael's College, he attended the Grand Seminary at Montreal for theology. Archbishop Lynch ordained him priest at St. Michael's Cathedral, June 29th, 1873, and sent him as assistant at Thorold. His first pastoral charge was Caledon, during which, as has been already noted, he erected the church of Orangeville. The other names which are most associated with Thornhill are those of Father James O'Donohoe, who had charge for about four years (1860—1864), and Dean Cassidy from 1871 to 1875.

There is a second church attached to the mission, that of St. Mary's at Richmond Hill, a village four miles north of Thornhill. Two acres of land were purchased ostensibly for other purposes, and a church erected, which was blessed in 1857 by the Very Rev. Father Rooney.

---

* **Father Griffa, or** as he is better known to his old parishioners, Father Louis, was next at St. Michael's Cathedral for a short time. He afterwards went to London Diocese and then to the United States. He lived to celebrate his golden jubilee as priest, and died only two **years** since (1890) at Chatham, New York, in the Diocese of Albany, where he was pastor.

Nearly at the same time as the building of the church of Richmond Hill, Father McNulty purchased a lot at Markham village, with the intention of erecting a church upon it. During Father O'Donohoe's incumbency this plan was carried out, and for years Markham belonged to the Thornhill mission, but in 1881 was attached to Uxbridge.

THE PARISH OF UXBRIDGE.

The southern portion of Brock parish was separated from it, and, with Markham village, erected into a distinct mission, having one church at Markham, another at Port Perry, and a third at Uxbridge, where the pastor resides.

The earliest history of our religion in this district is connected with Father Proulx, who, while in Oshawa, used to visit it occasionally. In those and later days Mass used to be celebrated in the house of Mr. Michael O'Neil until the church was built in 1864. The present Markham church dates from 1870, while that of Port Perry was erected ten years ago.

The following is a list of the priests who have been in charge of this mission: Fathers P. Kiernan, Finan, O'Reilly, McEntee, Egan, McCall, Allain and Keane, the present pastor.

Father Keane, after studying in San Francisco, California, came to Toronto and completed his philosophical and sacerdotal education at St. Michael's College and the Seminary of the Holy Angels at Niagara Falls. After his ordination as priest on the 6th of April, 1862, he was first stationed as curate of St. Paul's, Toronto. Subsequently his name and works are found connected with the parishes of Port Colborne, Newmarket, the Gore, and now Uxbridge.

THE PARISH OF TORONTO GORE.

We regret that owing to the manuscript having been mislaid our sketch of this parish does not appear in its proper order.

This mission like many others of the country districts dates from the earlier part of the present century, when many immigrants formed Catholic settlements, here and there, throughout the Province. Amongst such colonies few were more prosperous than the Gore, which derives its name from the Township of Toronto Gore in the County of Peel. In its early days the parish included all the diocese west of the city of Toronto and south of Adjala. But its boundaries have been since very much decreased by the erection of new parishes in the neighborhood, and its numbers have diminished by the emigration of the people. Here, near Wildfield post office, stands one of the oldest land marks in the archdiocese—St. Patrick's church, which was built in 1837, and attended by Father Lawlor. But the first resident pastor of the Gore of Toronto was Father Eugene O'Reilly, who completed the church, and who, after serving the mission for many years, died about the year 1860. A number of parish priests followed in order until, in 1887, Father McSpiritt, the present incumbent, was appointed.

The Rev. Francis McSpiritt received his classical education in the Diocesan Seminary of Cavan; and on coming to this country studied philosophy at St. Michael's College, Toronto, and theology in the Grand Seminary of Montreal. He was ordained in January, 1865. Besides the Gore of Toronto, which he now attends, Caledon, Niagara Falls and South Adjala have been the parishes over which he has ruled during his priestly career.

There is in this mission a small Separate school, established thirty-three years ago, and ever since maintained with a success varying in proportion to the population of the district.

THE DEANERY OF ST. CATHARINES.

EDITED BY

REV. J. R. TEEFY, B.A., C.S.B.

VERY REVEREND WILLIAM R. HARRIS,
DEAN OF ST. CATHARINES.

CHAPTER X.

THE DEANERY OF ST. CATHARINES.

St. Catharines — Merritton — Niagara-on-the-Lake — Niagara Falls — Port Colborne — Smithville — Thorold.

THE PARISH OF ST. CATHARINES.

IN 1822 St. Catharines had a population of from two to three hundred, among whom were a mere handful of Catholics, who were visited at rare intervals by Father Polin, then stationed at Niagara. In 1827 Father Campion, who was for some time pastor of Niagara, took up his residence, and lived in a small frame house built on the ground now known as the "Monte Bello Gardens." In 1828 Father Burke said Mass here about once every three months.

We find that, from this date, the mission was attended for some years by Rev. John Cullen, who had Niagara, Guelph and Dundas in his spiritual care. He was succeeded by Father Crowley, who remained some time, and left in 1834 for Ireland. In 1835 the first church, a frame edifice, was built by Father Gordon, then stationed at Niagara. From 1840 to 1841 Fathers Cullen and Cassidy were resident here, the former for six months and the latter for nine. In August, 1842, the frame church built by Father Gordon was burned down, supposed to have been the act of an incendiary, as party spirit ran very high in those days. Rev. Dr. Lee was then, and had been for some time previously, the pastor of this mission, which included within its limit nearly all the Niagara peninsula. He died at Marshville in the fall of 1842, and his remains were brought to St. Catharines and buried in the graveyard adjoining the church, whence they were transferred to their present resting place beneath the high altar.

During the latter part of 1842 and a portion of the following year the mission was attended by Father Gordon and others, who came from Niagara once a month, and offered up the holy sacrifice, sometimes in private houses, at others in Schickluna's sail loft, and lastly in a barn on the premises of G. S. Adams on Ontario street, now owned by Ridley College. In the fall of 1843 Father McDonough was appointed pastor, and continued until 1850, when he was succeeded by Father Mousard, and he in turn by Father Wardy, who, remaining but a short time, was replaced in 1852 by Father Grattan. This last named clergyman was the first Dean of the Niagara peninsula, and is still remembered with feelings of respect by the older members of the parish. His charge included not only St. Catharines, but also Thorold, Port Colborne and Smithville. In the duties which this vast extent of country entailed he had as curate his nephew, Father Conway, whose name is already familiar to our readers. Father Grattan was succeeded by Dean Mulligan, who labored faithfully and zealously in this parish for nineteen years. Owing to ill health he retired in 1884, and the present pastor, Father Harris, was chosen to fill his place.

The Very Rev. William R. Harris was born at Cork, Ireland, on the 3rd of March, 1847, but came to this country with his parents at an early age. His classical studies were pursued at St. Michael's College, Toronto; his theological at St. Anne's Seminary, Quebec, and also at the College of the Propaganda, Rome, where he took the degree of Bachelor of Divinity. After his ordination, which occurred in 1870, he continued as Secretary to Archbishop Lynch. Previous to the Deanship which he now holds, he was pastor of Adjala, rector of St. Michael's Cathedral for a short time, and parish priest of Newmarket, where he remained eight years. Dean Harris was elected by acclamation President of the Association of Mechanics' Institutes of Ontario for the years 1885 and 1886. His work and success in his present position may be best appreciated by a paragraph upon the church and schools of St. Catharines.

The main portion of this tasteful though irregularly constructed church was built in 1844 by Father McDonough. Deans Grattan and Mulligan each added a wing; and Father Harris, during his charge, has spent twenty-two thousand dollars on its further enlargement and decoration. As it stands, with its beautiful marble altars, its richly adorned sanctuary, and its chastely frescoed walls, much is due, not only to the generosity of the people, but also to the zeal and financial talent of its urbane Dean and pastor.

As an instance of the liberality of the parishioners we may mention that the magnificent main altar was the gift of Mr. William Ahern, who is still living at the age of eighty-six, and whose name we find among the list of contributors to the support of religion here for the year 1844. The altar of the Blessed Virgin was built by Captain King, and the third by Mrs. Scott to the memory of her husband.

The Separate schools of St. Catharines date from the pastorate of Dean Grattan, under whom one was opened in a brick building which he erected. A new era, however, was marked in their history when Dean Harris constructed the present fine building at a cost of twenty thousand dollars, with eight splendid rooms, which has lately been opened. There are five hundred children attending the schools of this parish, taught by the Christian Brothers and the Sisters of St. Joseph. The large recreation ground of the Separate school was donated by Mr. Edward McArdle at a cost of twelve hundred dollars.

St. Catharines has been the school in which many who are now pastors were first trained as curates. As the majority of these names are met in the various parishes, we mention only two, who were cut off so early in their priestly career that they could not fulfil the promise which their talent and virtues had already given. These are Fathers O'Hagarty and Shanahan. The latter was a Toronto boy, who, after completing his classical education at St. Michael's College, where he distinguished himself, proceeded to Genoa, Italy, for the study of theology. He was ordained in St. Paul's church, Toronto, by Bishop O'Mahony on the 8th of December, 1883. At the time of his death, which took place August 1st, 1890, he was pastor of Merritton, but had been in charge only six months.

Father O'Hagarty was born at Montreal, but spent his youth in Ireland, where also he was educated. Meeting Archbishop Lynch at All Hallows College, Dublin, he decided to come to Toronto, and was ordained by his Grace at Lough Derg, Ireland, in 1882. Upon returning to this country he held various positions in the archdiocese before being made pastor of St. Mary's church in the city of St. Catharines, which he held until his death on the 5th of February, 1890.

The city of St. Catharines contains a second parish, St. Mary's, whose history is too brief to call for a section of its own. It first formed a distinct mission in 1885; but the church dates back to the year 1867, when it was built by Dean Mulligan. There is attached to this parish a second church at Port Dalhousie, which was erected in 1875, and dedicated to Mary the Star of the Sea.

The first pastor was the late Father McGinley, who was followed by Father O'Hagarty, and he by the present incumbent, Father Allain. This good priest is an Acadian by birth, in whose public schools he received his early education. He afterwards attended St. Lawrence College, Montreal, and that of the Jesuits in the same city. He was raised to the holy priesthood September 21st, 1878, by Bishop Rogers, in his native city of Chatham, New Brunswick. Soon after his ordination he came to Toronto, and has worked successfully and zealously in the parishes of Uxbridge and Merritton and the present scene of his labors.

There is one Separate school in St. Mary's, under the charge of two Sisters of St. Joseph, who reside in the Convent at St. Catharines.

Dean Mulligan also built a third church, St. Patrick's, situated in the direction of Niagara, which is served by the Dean of the city and his assistant.

The Parish of Merritton.

This parish is situated, between St. Catharines and Thorold, in the manufacturing village from which it derives its name. Long before it was separated from Thorold, in 1883, Mass used to be celebrated in the frame church which served during the week as a school house. This building was moved from Port Colborne about twenty years ago to the site which it now occupies. Since the erection of the parish it was renovated by Father Allain, and a sacristy added to it by the late Father Shanahan.

The first pastor was the Rev. A. P. Finan, who labored devotedly for the firm establishment and proper organization of the parish, and built a neat brick presbytery while in charge of Merritton. To him succeeded Father Allain. He was chiefly instrumental in erecting a handsome Catholic school, so that the former building was left free for the sacred purposes of religion. This school is conducted by two Sisters of St. Joseph, who come every day from St. Catharines. Father Allain was replaced by the Rev. T. J. Shanahan, whose death rendered a second change necessary, and Father McColl, the present incumbent, was appointed to fill the vacancy in September, 1890.

The Rev. P. J. McColl pursued his studies in Fort Edward Institute and at St. Marie de Monier College, near Montreal, and thereupon entered St. Joseph's Seminary, Troy, New York, for his theology. He was ordained priest May 12th, 1878, in St. Mary's church, Toronto, and soon afterwards appointed pastor of Uxbridge. Owing to ill health he resigned, and was appointed chaplain of the Central Prison and the Mercer Institute, and in 1883 placed in charge of the newly erected parish of Whitby, which he held until being transferred to Merritton.

Parish of Niagara-on-the-Lake.

This parish embraces the north-eastern portion of the township of Niagara in the county of Lincoln, and the church and presbytery are situated in the old capital of Upper Canada, the town of Niagara, or as some call it "Niagara-on-the-Lake," in order to distinguish it from Niagara Falls, a town twelve miles distant.

During the first quarter of the present century the few Catholics settled in the district were provided with Sacraments and other ministrations of our holy religion by priests who held stations at rare intervals, after a long and tedious journey from Dundas. Some of the records of those early days are still preserved, and speak more eloquently than words, of the faith of the flock and the ardent zeal of the pastors. Here is the first entry in the time worn register: "The first day of June, 1827, by me, Roman Catholic Missionary at Niagara, Dundas, etc., etc., has been baptized Mary Anne Hughes, born the 2nd day of January, 1827, of the lawful marriage of Jas. Hughes of Niagara and Mary May. JAMES W. CAMPION, M. Pt."

Another child was baptized the same day, and not till the 12th of August does the signature indicate the next visit of the Missionary. It appears the Right Rev. Bishop Macdonell was at Niagara about this date, for several baptisms performed by him are entered and certified by Father Campion, whose name appears for the last time on the 18th of August, 1830. It is well to note that this zealous priest signs as P. P. of Niagara, etc., on and after the 27th December, 1828.

The next priest whose name appears on the records is Rev. Father Edward Gordon, afterwards Vicar-General of Hamilton. He subscribes a baptism performed by him May 30th, 1830. This must have been a casual visit, as Father Campion was here as late as August 18th of that year.

November 16th, 1832, we have the name of " M. Lalor, Miss. Ap.," who appears to have resided in the town from that date till May 6th, 1833. A certain " P. Polin, P.P.," then assumed charge, and seems to have been the only priest from July till November 5th.

On April 23rd, 1834, the Rev. Edward Gordon took charge of the mission of Niagara and its vicinity, according to his own statement written at the head of page 97 in the old register. He resided in the presbytery built shortly after the erection of the church, and kept a detailed and exact account of all transactions affecting religion in this parish till the 27th October, 1846.

On the 8th of November of the same year Rev. Father Carroll assumed charge, and remained until March, 1852. The next priests in charge of the mission were Rev. L. Mousard* and Rev. C. Wardy, whose administrations reached the year 1857. Father Mulligan, afterwards Dean of St. Catharines, was in charge from September, 1857, till December, 1860, assisted occasionally by Father Juhel.

Rev. Louis Griffa's name appears in the new baptismal register, provided by Father Mulligan, from 22nd December, 1860, till August 15th, 1861. Rev. Father Hobin succeeded Father Griffa; and the names of Fathers T. J. Sullivan, J. Kelly, Thos. Laboureau, Wm. Bergin, A. J. O'Reilly, M. Ap., P. Kiernan, E. Gallagher, A. Murphy, O.C.C., and T. Shanahan bring down the succession of pastors to the present incumbent, Rev. P. J. Harold.

The old frame church still stands by dint of constant repairing, and at its altar about 200 souls receive the Sacraments.

The present pastor, Rev. P. J. Harold, made his preparatory and commercial course in Detroit (Christian Brothers' Academy), classics at the Collegiate Institute, St. Catharines, rhetoric and ecclesiastical studies at St. Michael's College, Toronto, and the Grand Seminary, Montreal.

---

* This name appears in the "Canadian Almanac" spelled in various ways. We have adopted it according to the records of the parish of St. Catharines. —ED.

He was assistant at St. Michael's Cathedral in 1876, Thorold in 1877, Brockton in 1881, and was pastor of Dixie in 1888.

THE PARISH OF NIAGARA FALLS.

This mission requires less the pen of an historian than brush of an artist, who would graphically picture the wonders of the waters, whose thundering torrents the little parish church overlooks. Tradition tells us that the first white man to discover the Falls was a priest. Whether he ever offered the holy sacrifice, or what were his feelings, his dreams of the future, it matters not; for we do not record the event as the starting link of our historic chain. We also leave aside all mention of the later missionaries who, in the days of Father Hennipen and the venerable Bishop Neumann, hallowed this picturesque spot with the sacred rites of our holy religion, and we open our brief sketch with events still fresh in the memory of living men. The oldest settlers of this district, as is well remembered, travelled to Kingston that they might fulfil their duty of Easter communion. But the name which heads the list of those who have, down to the present, regularly officiated at Niagara Falls is Father Campion, about the year 1829. He used to say Mass in a yellow cottage where now stands the residence of Mr. Sutherland Macklem. Then Father Gordon, while pastor of Niagara-on-the-Lake, used to come and officiate every second Sunday. He it was who built the church on the River bank, just above the Horse Shoe Falls. The corner stone was laid the 13th of June, 1837, and the building, when completed, was dedicated to the priest's patron, St. Edward. This title was changed at the time of the American civil war by the late Archbishop Lynch to "Our Lady of Peace." A frame addition was afterwards made to the church by Father Juhel in 1860. The church, of cruciform shape, is quaint in appearance; and, beautifully situated within the sound and sight of Niagara's mighty flood, it lends devotion to the prayerful worshipper and adds the awe of grace to the surrounding majesty of nature. Its dimensions are seventy-five feet by twenty-two; and the arms of the cross sixty by fifteen.

After Vicar-General Gordon the congregation continued to be served from old Niagara until 1858, when the Falls was erected into a distinct parish and Father Juhel appointed pastor. This good priest died here in the odor of sanctity, January, 1862, and is buried beneath the church.

Between him and the Carmelites, who took charge in October, 1875, we have the following list: Father Mulligan till December, 1865; Father R. A. O'Connor (now Bishop of Peterborough) till September, 1868; Father Michel till July, 1872; and Father McSpiritt.

One of the cherished ideas of Archbishop Lynch was to erect a Hospice at Falls View, similar in spirit and rule to the ancient Hospice of Mount Carmel in the Holy Land, which still exists and dispenses the traditional hospitality of the monks of old. For the purpose of carrying out this intention, Dr. Lynch introduced a small branch of the Carmelites, one of the oldest orders in the church, whose devotion and history are closely interwoven with the Brown Scapular. His Grace gave the community a farm of two hundred acres of land on the banks of the Niagara. The first to take charge was the Very Rev. Ignatius Beerhorst, O.C.C. Several followed, amongst whom may be mentioned Father Mayer, O.C.C., at present Provincial of the Order in America, and Father A. J. Smits, so favorably known to many of the parishes of the Archdiocese by the missions which he preached. The present prior is the Very Rev. Anastasius J. Kreidt, O.C.C. He finished his studies at Rome, was ordained in Holland, and was shortly afterwards sent to Montpellier, France, where he remained until his community was expelled. In 1879 he came to America, and has since been stationed in many of the houses of his order in this country. Some years ago he was honored by Rome with the title of *Sanctæ Theologiæ Magister* (Doctor of Holy Theology). There are also two other priests, who reside in the monastery, Fathers Philip A. Best, O.C.C., and D. F. Best, O.C.C.: they are natives of Hamilton and are brothers.

The little church of Our Lady of Peace was endowed by Pius IX., of holy memory, with all the privileges of a pilgrimage, where may be gained the indulgences attached to the oldest shrines of Europe.

There is a small but successful Separate school here, taught by the Sisters of Loretto, who have given a large room in their convent for this purpose.

Besides Our Lady of Peace there is a second church, St. Patrick's, situated at Clifton, which district was erected into a distinct parish in 1863; but since the coming of the Carmelites it has been attended from its parent mission of Falls View.

A third church, St. Joseph's, stands at the intersection of the roads leading from Stevensville, Chippewa, Black Creek and Netherby, whose congregation is made up of Germans. Till 1880 they were in charge of the Jesuits at Buffalo, but were then placed under the zealous care of the Carmelites.

Directly opposite the city of Buffalo are the remains of a fort, from which the village of Fort Erie derives its name. Here was, until last year, a small parish, which included all the territory from Lake Erie on the south to the International Bridge on the north, and from Niagara River on the east to Ridgeway. A frame church was built here in 1858, but afterwards burned. The present church, a brick building, was erected ten years later. Its first pastor was the Rev. G. A. Voisard, who, serving it faithfully, retired a few years ago on account of bad health. Many others priests had charge of Fort Erie at different times, until, February 1st, 1891, Father Trayling, the last secular pastor, was replaced by the Carmelites, to whose parish of Falls View it is now attached.

It was within the limits of the mission of Niagara Falls that the Fenian raid took place. Father (now Bishop) O'Connor relates how, "In June, 1866, part of the volunteers and regulars encamped in a field adjoining the German Catholic Church." He goes on to tell that in the afternoon he heard in the tents the confessions of many of the Catholic soldiers who belonged to the 16th and 47th regulars. The following morning, in company with Vicar-General Jamot, he said Mass in presence of a few dozen lay persons and a handful of Catholic soldiers, as all but seventy-five had proceeded on Saturday night towards Fort Erie.

In Niagara River, a few miles above the Falls, lies Navy Island, important as being associated with the early history of this country. It is also worthy of note that the few Catholics living there have received religious ministration from time to time.

THE PARISH OF PORT COLBORNE AND WELLAND.

Like many other missions in the Niagara peninsula, the early history of Port Colborne and Welland is connected with St. Catharines. As far back as 1844 we are told of Father McDonough celebrating Mass in the Colored Barracks of Welland, and also in Quinn's Hotel, and a school house on the Creek Road leading to Port Robinson. Dean Grattan and Father Conway continued in the same line until 1861, when the present church lot, with a school house upon it, was purchased. The school served for religious as well as educational purposes until the new church was built by Father Wardy of Thorold, which, when finished, was dedicated to the Japanese Martyrs in 1864.

Port Colborne, or as it was then called, Gravelly Bay, dates from the same time and priest as Welland. In the days of Father McDonough and his successor Mass used to be offered in various places, an old mill upon the pier, a school house, and at the residences of different families, whose homes were sanctified in those primeval days by the tread of the Son of Man—spots more hallowed than broken column or ancient battle field. But this order of things gave way for a better when, in 1856, Father Conway erected a frame church at Port Colborne, which served until 1879, when, on July 20th, Archbishop Lynch laid the corner stone of the neat brick structure where the faithful of the western extremity of the diocese now worship. It was dedicated under the patronage of St. Patrick by Bishop O'Mahony, March the 14th, 1880.

Port Colborne and Fort Erie were erected into a parish in 1859, with Father Voisard as pastor. His residence was in the former of these places, his house being a small addition to the church. He was succeeded (1865) by Father Keane, who remained two years, after which a vacancy occurred, and it was attended from Thorold. Father Voisard returned (1868) and remained till 1871. Fort Erie was then made a distinct mission, being separated from Port Colborne, which received Welland as an adjunct, and the parish assumed its present form. Father Kilcullen was appointed pastor, and his eighteen years of administration were marked by great advancement and works of zeal. The church at Port Colborne is due to him; the enlargement of the presbytery and the decoration of the church at Welland are also some of the fruits of his pastorate. This good priest, upon his removal to Adjala, January, 1890, was succeeded at Port Colborne by Father McEntee.

The Rev. John J. McEntee received his primary education in the Separate schools of Toronto, whence he entered St. Michael's College for his classical and philosophical studies. Upon completing these he proceeded, in 1871, to the Grand Seminary of Montreal for theology. Here he remained two years, when he returned to his former college for the completion of his studies. He was ordained priest October 18th, 1870, in St. Michael's Cathedral by Archbishop Lynch. He was assistant at St. Paul's and Thorold, and in 1872 appointed pastor of Dixie, where he remained five years; and after a brief charge of Uxbridge, he was made parish priest of Oshawa and Whitby. His reign in this mission lasted twelve years, when he was transferred to his present field of labor.

There is a Separate school at Port Colborne, started in 1864, whose classes are conducted in the old frame church, forming, by its lofty ceiling, an airy room: it has an attendance at present of seventy.

THE PARISH OF SMITHVILLE.

This mission, situated in the County of Lincoln, comprises the townships of North and South Grimsby, Clinton, Gainsborough and Caistor. Its population does not rate in proportion to its territory, this vast area containing at present only two hundred and sixty Catholics.

It was established as a separate parish in September, 1866, and has two churches, St. Martin's at Smithville, where the priest resides, and a small stone chapel, under the patronage of St. Joseph, at Grimsby. Land has been purchased for a third church, to be built at Beamsville.

The spiritual needs of the few Catholics scattered through this section, before being erected into a distinct mission, were attended from St. Catharines, then for a short time from Cayuga in the Diocese of Hamilton, and finally from Thorold. But the first priest to visit these parts was Father Gordon, while he was chaplain to the troops stationed at Niagara. The priests of Cayuga who attended Smithville were Fathers McIntosh and McLoughlin. In 1857 Father Grattan of St. Catharines took charge, and built the two churches already mentioned. Before the erection of that at Smithville Mass used to be celebrated in the residence of the late Mr. Martin Tolly, then in his cooper-shop, and for a time in the old Methodist church. At Grimsby the religious services varied between different private houses and the Town Hall. At Beamsville, even to this day, on account of the small number of the faithful, a similar state of affairs exists.

The first parish priest of Smithville was Father Laboureau, who remained between four and five years. He was transferred to Thorold, from which place this mission was thenceforward attended. But in 1875 it was reopened as a distinct parish, and Father Beausang appointed. During his brief pastorate of two years a presbytery was built, which was afterwards destroyed by fire during the administration of Father McMahon. Father McMahon was preceded by Fathers Skelly and Davis; and followed by the present parish priest, the Rev. Kenneth McRae. This young clergyman is a native of the diocese, being, as already stated, born in Brock mission. He received his classical education partially at Assumption College, Sandwich, and partially at St. Michael's College, Toronto. After spending a few months at All Hallows College, Dublin, he was sent to Genoa, Italy, where he made a course of five years in philosophy and theology, and where he was ordained priest, December 18th, 1886. Returning to Canada, he was appointed curate in Adjala for a very short time, and then placed in charge of the small but no less important mission whose history we have briefly outlined.

The Parish of Thorold.

Prior to the beginning of this century a few pioneers had entered the forests of the vicinity where to-day stands the town of Thorold. Of these settlers and their immediate followers, most, if not all, were non-Catholics; so that, for the first quarter of the century, accounts are so few and uncertain, that we have little better than conjecture that the primitive missionaries passing between the earlier colonies of Niagara and Dundas may have left their regular route in search of souls in newer settlements.

In time, some Catholics began to move into this place, for some years known as Stumptown; and as their number increased, they were given as frequent and regular attendance as the few priests in these districts could afford. Stations were held by the nearest clergyman, that is, from Niagara; and to that place the people had to go for baptisms, until, in 1835, the first church was built at St. Catharines, only four miles distant. Thenceforward until Thorold had a priest resident, this mission came under the jurisdiction of St. Catharines; and Thorold people attended church there till about 1843, when their first place for worship, a frame structure, was built. Thus the birth and early progress of Catholicity in Thorold are associated with the opening chapters of our religious history in St. Catharines, to which sketch we refer our readers. The names of the same pastors, as Fathers Campion, Burke and Cullen, appear on the records, and live in local tradition; while the labors of the venerable Father Gordon, who is of later date, are still fresh in the memory of most of our older people. Then the Rev. Dr. Lee commenced his arduous duties, which soon terminated in his untimely death, an account of which has already appeared in these pages. It is mentioned here again, because his body lay in state for one night in Thorold church, when the funeral was on its way to St. Catharines.

St. Catharines being again without a resident priest, this place also had to look to Father Gordon of Niagara, for attendance until, in the fall of 1843, at the appointment of Father McDonough to St. Catharines, Thorold was again attended from there. Father McDonough retained the charge until 1852, it being under his administration that the first church was completed here, for the building of which much good will seems to have existed on the part of Protestants.

The Catholics who took an active part in the erection of the first church were Messrs. Thomas O'Brien, William Heenan, James Boyle and Amandus Schwaller, the last of whom alone survives.

In 1853 Thorold, for the first time, had a resident priest in the person of Reverend Michael McLaughlin, who, during his stay here, resided with a private family. During this same year the Very Rev. B. Grattan was appointed to St. Catharines, and made first Dean of this district. Owing to the increasing labor in caring for the large numbers employed along the Welland canal and in its thriving villages—for Thorold had, in 1851, become a village—Father Grattan was given as assistant, his nephew, Rev. Patrick Conway, whose name appears frequently in the parish registers between the years 1855 and 1860. It was during Dean Grattan's care of this place in 1853 that the first Catholic school was built on the same premises as those upon which the church stood. In January, 1860, Father Eugene O'Keefe arrived, but gave place, in April of the same year, to Father Christie, who at once engaged himself in building a priest's residence of brick, and one which was considered in those days to be palatial. Father Christie was relieved between 1862 and 1865 by Father Wardy; and returning, remained for three years, when ill health obliged him to retire to his native diocese in France, where he died not long after. His place here was filled in August, 1867, by Father Gribbin, who, in the spring of 1869, was followed by Father Michael O'Reilly, now of St. Joseph's Church, Toronto. In two years again a change occurs, and Father O'Reilly is succeeded by Father Laboureau, who remained until the fall. This brings us to the period of the present pastor, one from which dates the substantial progress in every department of the parish.

In November, 1871, Father T. J. Sullivan was transferred from Adjala to Thorold, and has since been its permanent pastor. His first efforts in the interests of his new mission were directed towards the welfare of the young. By 1874 a convent, of brick, was completed, and in the year following some Sisters of St. Joseph procured, who, since that time, have, with the aid of a master for larger boys, conducted the schools. The building occupied for this purpose was a frame one, and was made to serve until 1882, when the first part of the present brick structure was put up on a new site, directly opposite the convent. This school was enlarged in 1890 so as to accommodate 250 children.

On Rosary Sunday, 1878, his Grace the late Archbishop Lynch laid the corner stone of the new church. Father Sullivan's aim being to keep it free from debt so that it could be consecrated when finished, its erection was necessarily slow. The building was roofed in 1881, and for ten years Mass was said in the basement, work being done on the upper part whenever circumstances permitted.

Through the assistance of kind friends in Canada and the United States, Father Sullivan was so far able to complete his church that it was ready this year for consecration. It is a handsome red stone building, of gothic architecture, beautifully situated on a hill which overlooks a charming stretch of country and the city of St. Catharines in the distance. The interior of the nave and chancel is very chaste and devotional—the delicate wooden pillars allowing a free view of the altar from every portion of the church, and the clere-story windows casting a gentle light upon column and wall. The altar is marble, consisting of blue Italian, Mexican onyx and white American, whose varied colors add the charm of beauty to stability of material, while the effect of the scene is further heightened by the tasteful surroundings of the sanctuary. A silver plate upon the handsomely carved altar railing records the fact that it was the gift of the late Mr. John Battle of Thorold.

Port Colborne and Thorold

On June the 19th of the present year the crown of solemn consecration was placed upon this great work, which had engaged the energies of a zealous priest and the generosity of a faithful people for fourteen years. The sacred ceremony was performed by the Right Reverend R. A. O'Connor, Bishop of Peterborough, who also sang Pontifical Mass, with the Reverend Father Carroll of Providence, Rhode Island, as deacon, and Father McColl of Fort Erie, as sub-deacon. The Archbishop of Toronto, the Most Reverend Dr. Walsh, occupied the throne; and a number of clergymen were present in the sanctuary.

The sermon at the Mass was delivered by the Very Rev. Father McInerney, C.SS.R., of Toronto, who took for his subject the Church as the house of God. He complimented the pastor, the parish and the town of Thorold upon the religious completion of the church in which they assembled that day as a congregation for the first time.

His Grace also took the opportunity to address a few words of congratulation upon the church which they had just consecrated. He paid a glowing tribute to Father Sullivan, "who had worked so earnestly on the labor of love. The people had upheld him in his efforts, and the entire Catholic church appreciated what he had done." "Here," concluded the venerable prelate, "when all that is mortal of us shall be laid at rest, will the grand monument of your devotion stand, and aloft on the hilltop raise the spire, bringing to men christian hopes and aspirations, and thoughts of those whose hands and hearts did their share in the erection of this glorious temple of Almighty God."

In the evening Vespers were sung by the Very Reverend Vicar-General Rooney, and a discourse delivered by Father Ryan upon Our Lady of the Rosary, to whom the church was solemnly dedicated. And then, with Benediction of the Most Blessed Sacrament, given by the Archbishop, closed a memorable day for the parish and people of Thorold.

The Reverend Timothy J. Sullivan was born in the County of Cork, Ireland; but received his education in this country at the College of Our Lady of the Angels, Niagara Falls, New York. He was ordained priest at St. Catharines on the Feast of the Assumption (August 15th), 1868. The greater part of his sacerdotal career is told in the above sketch of Thorold parish, where he has now been pastor twenty-one years. Not only are the material structures proofs of his zeal, but his spiritual care of his people, his earnest and continued efforts in the cause of education, are likewise a higher evidence of his pious character and priestly energy.

Father Sullivan's appointment in 1871 included charge over Merritton, which place he held until 1883. He secured an acre of ground and erected a temporary church, all of which were paid for by him before resigning the mission. Also Grimsby and Smithville fell to his care, until 1875, when he was relieved of that mission by the appointment of a pastor, and Port Robinson was given to him, where he expended a large sum for a church, and the property upon which it is erected.

ADDENDUM.

The sketches of the parishes, as they appear, are taken from reports made out last year (1891). Since that time the following changes have taken place in this Deanery:—Father McColl has been transferred from Merritton to Fort Erie,* which again forms a distinct parish, and is succeeded in the former mission by Father Lynett.

* Vid. p. 433, where Fort Erie is mentioned as attached to Niagara Falls.—ED.

THE DEANERY OF BARRIE.

EDITED BY

REV. J. R. TEEFY, B.A., C.S.B.

VERY REVEREND WILLIAM BERGIN.
DEAN OF BARRIE.

CHAPTER XI.

THE DEANERY OF BARRIE.

Barrie—Alliston—Brechin—Brentwood—Collingwood—Flos—Mara—Midland—Orillia—Penetanguishene—Ste. Croix—Stayner.

THE PARISH OF BARRIE.

THE spiritual wants of the few scattered settlers who formed the pioneer band of this now flourishing parish were attended to by the priests of Penetanguishene. In such times the holy sacrifice used to be offered at the residence of the late Mr. James Bergin, who lived on the Penetanguishene road. At his house a Father Dempsey, who had gone to Penetanguishene in 1832, died two years later. The following account is given of his death by Mrs. Bergin, who has had her home at St. Joseph's Convent, Toronto, for many years, and who, though now (1892) over ninety years of age, still remembers the early demise of this young priest. Upon one occasion Father Dempsey had been down in Toronto on business, and while at Holland Landing, waiting for the boat to take him up Lake Simcoe, he heard of this family, who had settled in the neighborhood of Barrie; so he determined to visit them. His ordinary route home in those days was from Orillia by the Coldwater Road. Instead, therefore, of continuing up Lake Simcoe to Lake Couchiching, the missionary turned his boat into Kempenfeldt Bay and landed at Barrie, which then contained one store and a few houses.* He found his way to Mr. Bergin's, who welcomed him most warmly, as he had not seen a priest during the seven years he had been living in that district. Father Dempsey

---

* In 1837 its population was, according to "Smith's Gazetteer," twenty-eight families.

was taken ill the very night he arrived; and, although he said one Mass, he never left the house, but grew worse, and died in less than three weeks. His body was taken to Penetanguishene, where it lies buried beneath the sanctuary of the Catholic church.

Father Proulx, who at this time was settled amongst the Indians, was the next to serve the mission. The Rev. Amable Charest, during the first four years of his long residence at Penetanguishene (1837—1854), used to visit Barrie regularly. Then Father Quinlan, who resided at Newmarket, attended and celebrated Mass in the houses of the principal Catholics. After a while a Protestant, Mr. Charles Thompson, gave the Catholics the use of his large stable, where Mass was offered up and services held for some time. Bishop Power of Toronto visited Barrie in 1845, and administered Confirmation to several candidates in a private house belonging to Mr. John O'Neil.

Father McNulty was the next missionary who served Barrie. As the Catholics were beginning to increase in numbers he urged upon them the necessity of a church. Two half acre lots were granted by the Government for this purpose, described as lots Nos. 127 and 128, on the north side of Macdonell street, upon which the present church and school house are situated. The church was begun in 1849, and was completed the following year. It was constructed of a heavy timber frame, which the farmers themselves had hewn, sheeted on the outside, and was fifty feet long by thirty-six feet wide. Henceforth the good settlers had the privilege of a priest about once a month, and sometimes even more frequently. Shortly after the Catholics became so numerous that Bishop de Charbonnel resolved to place a resident priest to attend Barrie and the surrounding country. Accordingly, in 1855, Father Jamot was sent as pastor, but was obliged to board amongst the Catholic families until a residence was provided. The mission then included the village of Barrie and the townships of Vespra, Innisfil, Oro, Essa, West Gwillimbury, Sunnidale, Flos, Medonte, Nottawasaga and the villages of Collingwood and Belle Ewart.

In July, 1855, Father Hobin, then just ordained, was sent as curate to Father Jamot. The latter's first step was to procure a dwelling, and accordingly he purchased a site on the west side of Mulcaster street, where the Convent of St. Joseph's now stands. The house, a small frame building,

Rt. Rev. R. A. O'Connor, D.D.
Bishop of Peterborough

bishop. The priests of the Barrie Deanery made his Lordship a special offering of a very handsome episcopal ring. By his old parishioners Bishop O'Connor's gain was particularly felt to be their loss, and although they rejoiced at the well deserved honor he was to receive, they sincerely mourned that their Dean, who had been so loved by his own flock and respected by all, should be removed from those whom he had ruled with such gentleness, and whom he had led in the ways of God for so long a time. To manifest their esteem for his many services the Catholics of Barrie presented his Lordship with a farewell address and a purse of five hundred dollars. Many other kind words were spoken and kind acts done by various societies to join in the hearty wish of all for the success of the new Bishop of Peterborough. With his work, now that he has left Toronto, this volume is not closely concerned; but all, priests and people, who knew him, feel a continued joy in his continued success.

Resuming our sketch, we learn that, before being transferred to Toronto, Dean Northgraves had already made certain preparations for a new church, which the growth of the Catholic population of Barrie rendered necessary. His successor, the Very Rev. R. A. O'Connor, continued these preparations with such promptness that the corner stone was laid the spring following his entry to the parish, June 3rd, 1871. The ceremony was performed by Archbishop Lynch, while Father Northgraves preached the sermon of the day. The church was completed the following year, and was dedicated to the Sacred Hearts of Jesus and Mary on December 15th, 1872. The building is of gothic design—red brick with white trimmings. Since the opening the following improvements have been made in and around it: the spire finished, and a neat iron fence upon a stone foundation enclosing the grounds, in 1876; and in 1888 the frescoing of the interior with handsome paintings of different Saints on large panels.

After Bishop O'Connor left, the church was served from Toronto until Archbishop Walsh, in January, 1890, installed Father Edward Cassidy Dean of Barrie. During his brief pastorate of less than a year Father Cassidy made several improvements in both the church and presbytery. He, being transferred to his present charge of St. Helen's, Brockton, was succeeded in the Deanship of Barrie by the Very Rev. William Bergin on January 17th, 1891.

Father Bergin is a native of Cashel in the County of Tipperary, Ireland, where he was born November 16th, 1847. His classical course was begun at the Abbey, Tipperary, and finished at the Diocesan College. Upon finishing his course he came to America, and joining the Archdiocese of Toronto he went to Montreal in 1868 for the completion of his theological studies. In 1870 he was ordained priest at London by the present Archbishop of Toronto. He was immediately appointed to a position in St. Michael's Cathedral. After fulfilling well his duties there he was assigned various charges in the diocese until, in 1891, his Grace Archbishop Walsh, showing his confidence in Father Bergin, honored him with the Deanship of Barrie. For several years during his residence in the city of Toronto he was financial secretary and treasurer of the Separate school board, for which he proved himself admirably fitted by his administrative ability.

As early as 1857 the Sisters of St. Joseph established a branch of their Community at Barrie; and Father Jamot had the old school house on the west side of Mulcaster street enlarged and fitted up for their residence. This building lasted until, in 1885, Dean O'Connor took steps to erect the present fine brick convent directly opposite the church, a pleasant home for the half dozen Sisters who form the Community, of which two were the pioneer band. Besides the Nuns teaching in the Separate school, a head master has been employed for the past twelve years for the older pupils.

There is also a second Separate school in the parish, established by Father Jamot in 1860, and which has ever since been maintained, and which is for the benefit of the Catholics on the tenth concession of Vespra and the district. A new frame school house was built here in 1879 to replace the log one, which had till that time been the humble hall of learning. In this building the holy sacrifice is offered up occasionally for the people of the neighborhood, who can thus attend to their Easter obligation.

Some twenty miles north of Barrie is the village of Brentwood, where, in 1864, Father Northgraves purchased land for the building of a church, which was afterwards erected in 1871 by Dean O'Connor. It is a small frame structure dedicated to Our Lady of the Assumption; but is large enough for the congregation, which consists principally of French Canadians. About the same distance south of Barrie is another village, Belle Ewart, on Lake Simcoe, with a small Catholic chapel and a small congregation.

To serve these two places Archbishop Lynch sent, in 1872, a priest, whose home was to be in Barrie, and who would officiate at Brentwood and Belle Ewart on alternate Sundays. Father Louis Gibra, a native of France, has ever since filled the position with self-denying zeal, devotion and piety. Barrie is thus saved the necessity of an ordinary curate, who was removed when Stayner was erected into a separate parish; and the two outlying districts on the north and south are thus more frequently and regularly attended.

THE PARISH OF ALLISTON.

This parish, up to the year 1883, was known as the parish of North Adjala, where the priest resided; but this being a purely country place, it was thought desirable to build a presbytery in the then growing town of Alliston, which was accordingly done, and from that date it has been known as that of Alliston. At present writing there are two churches in the jurisdiction of the pastor — St. Paul's of Alliston and the Immaculate Conception in North Adjala, four miles distant.

St. Mary's of the Immaculate Conception was built in 1855, under the auspices of the Pastor of South Adjala of that date, the Rev. Father Rattigan.

A preliminary meeting was held on the eve of St. Patrick's Day, 1854, at the residence of Mr. Hugh Ferguson, and a committee organized for the erection of the church. The work was under way when Father Rattigan was removed in August, 1855. He was succeeded by Father Pourret, under whose pastorate the church was completed, and the first Mass said in it by him on the 25th of November, 1855. It is situated on two acres of land donated by Mr. Ferguson, in whose house a station used to be held and Mass celebrated every three months previous to its erection. After the opening of the church it was attended every third Sunday from South Adjala until 1865, when North Adjala was formed into a distinct parish, with the Rev. Patrick Conway as pastor. During his incumbency of a year and a half a brick presbytery was built. Father Rey succeeded to the charge of the parish in July, 1866, and remained until the summer of 1873, when the present pastor, the Rev. H. J. Gibney, was appointed. While here Father Rey built an addition to the church, and erected a belfry, in which he placed a very fine bell, whose tones could be heard for miles as it rang out the angelus or summoned the people to prayer.

In 1875 Father Gibney, looking to the future, took steps, not only to build a second church, but to transfer the parochial headquarters from the rural district where they had been so far located to Alliston. On the 28th of May, 1876, the corner stone of the new church was laid with imposing ceremony by Archbishop Lynch, and an eloquent sermon preached by the present Archbishop, then Bishop of London. It was dedicated to St. Paul on New Year's Day, the Feast of the Circumcision, 1877, by the late Dr. Crinnon, Bishop of Hamilton.

The church is a gothic structure, ninety feet by forty, and has a fine spire one hundred and thirty feet high. The erection of this church has been the means of increasing the Catholic population of Alliston, who numbered but five families at the date of commencing, but which, in 1891, amounted to sixty.

Up to the year 1882 the pastoral residence was beside the church in North Adjala, when it was transferred to Alliston, where a handsome presbytery was erected.

The old frame church of North Adjala, being destroyed by fire in February, 1885, was replaced the following summer by a neat brick one; and was blessed by Bishop O'Mahony on the 13th of December of the same year.

The Rev. H. J. Gibney was born at Toronto on the 10th of August, 1846. He was educated at St. Michael's College, Toronto, from which place, after completing his studies in 1869, he proceeded for his theology to the Grand Seminary, Montreal. He was ordained priest by Archbishop Lynch on August 25th, 1872. Adjala was his first parish, where still, in the early prime of life, he commands the respect of all who know him, and the affection of his people, whom he has faithfully served for the past eighteen years.

The Parish of Brechin.

About forty years ago the Rev. Father Proulx, who resided in Oshawa, attended to the spiritual wants of the Catholics of Brechin. This good priest, as we are told, encountered severe trials in the performance of his sacerdotal duties, but so burning was his zeal for the salvation of souls that nothing could deter him from doing the work of his ministry. There being no church in the place at this time the devoted missionary was obliged to offer the sacrifice of the Mass in private residences wherever it was most convenient for the people. This was the order of things until the new mission of Brock[*] was formed. Father Walsh, its first pastor, like his predecessor, laboured hard, late and early, for the people over whom he had charge, offering the Holy Sacrifice for them in their humble homes, preaching to them the word of God, and bringing consolation and happiness in their hour of distress.

From Brock was formed the parish of Mara, to which Brechin was attached. In 1884 Brechin was separated from its parent stock and erected into a distinct mission, with Father Davis as pastor. It was Father Campbell who, while in charge of Mara, built the parish church of Brechin. Father Rey came next, and it was during his time that the mission of Brechin was separated from Uptergrove, when, in 1884, the late Archbishop Lynch appointed Rev. Father Davis as the pastor of Brechin. Father Davis laboured here for nearly four years, during which time the presbytery and Separate school were built. In November, 1887, he was replaced by Father McMahon who is still the parish priest, and under whose charge considerable improvements have been made since he took the management of the mission.

The Rev. P. McMahon was ordained priest in All Hallows College, Dublin, in June, 1878, and has manifested in his labors the spirit of his Alma Mater. His first appointment was assistant to Dean Mulligan of St. Catharines, and his next appointment to the parish of Smithville, whence he came to Brechin.

As in every other Catholic mission so in Brechin, there are members who leave behind them monuments of their generosity. The name of James Patrick Foley, who died on the 6th of August, 1889, is a household word throughout this mission. Being an ardent enthusiast for Catholic education he built the Separate school known as the "Foley Institute," at the cost of four thousand dollars, and gave it over to the parish; and still more, wishing that it would never fail, and in order that it might be a

---

[*] Vid. p. 311.

self-supporting institution, he endowed it with the large sum of ten thousand dollars, the interest of which is only to be drawn, and the principal to remain intact for all time to come.

The Parish of Collingwood.

The Catholic history of this town, one of the ports on Georgian Bay, dates back only to the year 1886, when, on its separation from Stayner, it was formed into a distinct parish, with the Rev. Edward J. Kiernan as its pastor. Prior to this time it was connected with Barrie and afterwards with Stayner. When Collingwood was erected into a parish, Mr. Thomas J. Long immediately gave land for a church and parochial residence, upon which his brother, Mr. John J. Long, built a handsome presbytery at his own expense. They then deeded all to the episcopal corporation.

As early as 1859 a small frame church was built in the western suburb, which was quite ample for the few Catholics of the place. This, with an addition which was made by Father Jamot, served the congregation until 1888, when the present pastor undertook the heavy task of erecting a handsome brick church on the land given by Mr. Long. The corner stone was laid on the 24th of May, 1888, by Bishop Dowling of Hamilton, and an eloquent sermon was delivered by the Very Rev. Father McCann. On December the 16th, in the same year, it was solemnly blessed, under the title of St. Mary's, by the then Dean of Barrie, now Bishop O'Connor of Peterborough. The writer of this sketch preached in the morning, and Father Moyna, parish priest of Stayner, in the evening delivered an eloquent discourse upon the growth of the church, so aptly illustrated in the very town of Collingwood, where, from the private residence of Mr. Patton, one of the early settlers, they moved into the little chapel which had tender memories for so many, and thence to their present place of worship, which reflected such credit upon priest and people.

Father Kiernan, before having charge of this mission, had been from 1882 pastor of Stayner. He is a native of Ireland, where he received his classical education. Upon coming to this country he went to the Seminary of St. Sulpice in Montreal, and was ordained priest on March 19th, 1878, by his Grace Archbishop Lynch.

THE PARISH OF FLOS.

As we journey north of Barrie and enter upon several of the missions in this district, most notably Penetanguishene, Ste. Croix and Flos, we feel that: "Where'er we tread 'tis haunted, holy ground." Here were enacted the tragic scenes recorded in the first chapter of this work; here was the cradle of that civilization whose glory perished in its infancy, but whose hallowed memories it has been our endeavour to transmit as a legacy to the faithful children of this diocese. Here, within the limits of this very parish of Flos, once stood the Huron village of St. Mary's, where flowed the blood and burned the bones of the saintly martyrs, Brebeuf and Lalemant. It is not our task now to repeat the harrowing tale, but to write of a new and better order of things—an order less exciting in events, but much more hopeful and, we trust, more lasting in its results.

This part of the County of Simcoe, embracing the townships of Flos and Medonte, and portions of Oro and Vespra, contains at present about one thousand Catholics. Like many other of our country missions, its origin dates to the early part of this century, when numbers of Irish immigrants took up land here on account of the timber with which the district was so rich. The first priest who attended these pioneers was a Father O'Keegan. Then followed in order the priests of Penetanguishene, until the appointment of Father Jamot to Barrie, to which place Flos was assigned. In 1863 Father Gribbin had special charge of this mission, with his home in Barrie; and two years after he took up his residence here, when it was erected into a separate parish. The Rev. A. P. Mullen succeeded him in a short time, and remained until 1875, when he retired to the House of Providence, Toronto, and died some years after. A number followed, amongst whom was the late Father John Skelly, who died May 9th, 1885, while in charge of this mission, having been ordained only a few years. From the 28th of April, 1884, he had as assistant Father M. J. Gearin, who succeeded him as parish priest.

The early life of this zealous priest was spent in Thorold, where, under Father Harold, he studied classics. In due time he proceeded to the Grand Seminary of Montreal for theology, and was ordained March 25th, 1884.

Before the first church was built (1857) by Father McNulty Mass used to be said in a log house belonging to Mr. McAvoy in the township of

Medonte. There are three churches attached to the mission: the parish church, St. Patrick's, in the township of Flos; Our Lady of Purity in Vigo, which was built by Father Mullen in 1871; and St. Louis' in Medonte. This last is the third which has been erected upon this site, following the usual order—the first being a log building, which made way for a frame one, and this, being destroyed by fire, was replaced by the present brick structure. The corner stone of a new church was laid by his Grace Archbishop Walsh, in 1891, to replace St. Patrick's, which had served its faithful worshippers for so many years.

THE PARISH OF MARA.

On the east side of Lake Simcoe lies a fine stretch of rolling land where, in early days, a number of Scotch and Irish Catholics settled and formed the northern part of the Brock mission. It was first constituted a parish in 1856, with the Rev. J. Synnot as pastor, who is named in the "Canadian Almanac" as having charge of Orillia, Medonte and North Mara. Little interest can be taken by the general reader in the sketch of a parish like Mara. Generation of faithful worshippers succeeds generation—their numbers vary and their pastors change—but the humble frame chapel, whose tin spire glistens from the distant hills on the opposite shore of the little lake, stands just as it stood when, in 1857, it rose from amidst the swarthy pines of the forest; and the priest offers there the same sacrifice, and the people break the same heavenly bread in hope and faith and love. Rather let us sketch the unvarnished tale of its simple history than touch the chord of religious sentiment.

To Father Synnot succeeded the Rev. Joseph Michel, who built the presbytery at Uptergrove. Several priests followed, until Father Rey took charge in 1875, and remained for eleven years. The Rev. Philibert Rey was a native of the province of Burgundy in France, and received his education, partially at Privas, France, and partially at St. Michael's College, Toronto. He was the first candidate whom Bishop Lynch ordained priest. The ceremony took place in Barrie on the 8th of January, 1860, where for some time he remained as curate. Besides Mara the other principal mission of which he had charge during his career of twenty-one years was North Adjala. In 1886 ill health obliged him to resign Mara, when he was then given the easier duties of the chaplaincy at the Penetanguishene Reformatory. Here he died October 26th, 1887.

His successor was the Rev. William Joseph McGinley, who was born in the County of Donegal, Ireland, but who came to this country in his early youth. His classics were completed at Bardstown, Kentucky, and his theology in Lower Canada. Archbishop Lynch ordained him priest on September the 8th, 1875. He held various missions in the Archdiocese, before being appointed to Mara in 1886, which he retained until his death, January 7th, 1891.

The present pastor is a venerable priest, Father James Hogan, whose education in Montreal and Paris ranks him amongst the most learned of our clergy. He was ordained May 17th, 1856, and the earlier years of his priesthood were connected with St. Ann's church in the city of Montreal, and his latter years with the church of the Immaculate Conception in New York.

There is a second church, St. Joseph's, in the township of Rama, north of Mara, which is attended by the pastor once a month.

The Parish of Midland.

The second chapter of the history of this parish dates from very recent times; the first belongs to the Jesuit missions amongst the Hurons in the seventeenth century, for near Midland stood the Fort of St. Ignace, which was erected in 1644. In order to preserve some of the relics of this heroic period the late Father Proulx bought the land surrounding the old Fort and gave it to the Jesuits. There are also traces in a graveyard at Waubashene of many Catholics buried there.

But we treat of modern days, when adventurous white men sought these districts for the more worldly motives which the forests of timber offered, and settling, formed a congregation at Waubashene, whose members are principally French Canadians. Here the late Father Kennedy, while in charge of Penetanguishene, erected a small church in 1865. In the following decade the Midland Railway opened up the country, having its terminus on the Georgian Bay, at a point where there is one of the finest harbors upon our lakes. The more than thousand islands which stretch in seemingly unbroken chain as far as the eye can reach, give to the water a natural variety of barren rock and wooded green. Here grew up the town, and within the town, the mission of Midland. The three churches belonging to it—St. Margaret's at Midland, St. Mary's at Victoria Harbor, and St. John's at Waubashene—are the work of Father Laboureau, and were erected by him in 1882. The following year Midland was separated from its mother church of Penetanguishene, and formed into a distinct parish, with Father Lynett as pastor. His zeal and energy, during the eight years in which he had charge, were marked by the most satisfactory improvement of the mission in the material as well as the spiritual order.

The Rev. John Francis Lynett is the youngest son of one of the pioneers of Catholicity in the County of York, Mr. Nicholas Lynett, and was born near Richmond Hill the 10th of February, 1857. His early education was received in the high school of his native village. He then entered the Sulpitian College of Montreal, and finished his preparatory course at St. Michael's College, Toronto, after which he studied theology in the Grand Seminary in the former city. Here he received all the orders, being raised to the priesthood by Archbishop Fabre, December the 17th, 1881. After his ordination he was appointed curate at St. Paul's for two years, at St. Michael's for a short time, and then placed over the trying mission of Midland. Last year (1891) he was transferred to Merritton in the Deanery of St. Catharines, when the Rev. Father J. Colin from Montreal was named his successor.

The Parish of Orillia.

One of the fairest scenes in our fair Canada is the view from the parish church of Orillia, where, away on the right, slopes the hill to Lake Simcoe in the distance, and sinks more quickly in front to Lake Couchiching, which is skirted by the fields and forests of Rama and Mara on the opposite shore. How changed from the times when hunter or missionary passed this way on his route to the waters of the Upper Lakes; or when, for the first time within the range of modern tradition, Father Dempsey visited the place in the autumn of 1833. What it was then it is hard to describe—forest of moaning pines, foot path of weary scout, and murmuring waters of lonely lake—all can be better imagined than portrayed. To-day, overlooking a flourishing town, a neat brick church, with a handsome presbytery on its left, and farther up the street a large four room Separate school, all the work and devotion of one man, Father Campbell, and his faithful people of Orillia.

After Father Dempsey Monsignore Proulx paid a visit to the few settlers here in the winter of 1835, and continued them at various intervals for a period of about two years. His successor, Father Charest, called for the first time in 1837, and returned occasionally until 1852. For the next three years Father McNulty attended the mission as frequently as his scattered posts of duty would allow; and Father John Synnot was named first pastor of Orillia, with charge of Mara as well. The Reverend M. Coyac, came next but remained for a short time, and was replaced (1865) by Father Michel. In 1866 he was succeeded by the present pastor, who retained both Mara and Orillia until, in 1874, they were separated, and Father Campbell was assigned to the latter mission.

The holy sacrifice of the Mass used to be offered in the house of Mr. John Kenny on the Coldwater Road, where the Catholic cemetery is now located. In time a log building was erected near by, which served as a mission chapel until the church of the Angels Guardian was erected by Father Campbell. It was dedicated by Archbishop Lynch July 28th, 1872. It has since been frescoed and presents a very neat and devotional interior.

There is a succursal chapel at a small village called Warminster, which was built in 1882, and dedicated to the Sacred Heart of Jesus.

The Very Reverend Kenneth A. Campbell, to whom the progress and present efficiency of this parish are so largely due, is of Scotch descent, and was born in the County of Ontario, Canada, November 30th, 1837. He received his classical education at St. Michael's College, Toronto, and studied theology under the Sulpitians at Montreal. On the 22nd of September, 1864, he was raised to the holy priesthood at St. Joseph's Church, Beaverton, within a short distance of his boyhood's early home. With the exception of the first two years, when he was curate at Barrie, his sacerdotal career has been passed in the parish of Orillia. Here, with constancy, he cultivated the vineyard entrusted to him, until church and home and school* have grown up under his zealous care, and generations of his people have learned the

---

* Vid. pp. 270 and 271 for the state of the Orillia Separate Schools.

great lessons of piety and spiritual life from the devoted example of their pastor. In the early part of 1890 Father Campbell was appointed Archdeacon of the Diocese.

The Parish of Penetanguishene.

In 1818 Penetanguishene (the place of the rolling sand) was selected by the British authorities as their naval and military station on the Georgian Bay. But its settlement really took place ten years after, when several families of half-breeds, who spoke French, and some French Canadians, who had married squaws, were brought here from Drummond Island at the time of its cession to the United States. These poor settlers, who were nearly all Catholics, found only two or three traders; but even in their small numbers they formed a permanent colony upon the land which was given them by the English Crown. A new band entered towards the year 1840; and from that time until between 1860 and 1870 an almost uninterrupted stream of immigration continued to flow, so that now there are several missions where at first scarcely one was needed.

The first priest to visit Penetanguishene was Bishop Macdonell, who, accompanied by Father Crevier, passed through this district about the year 1830. Nearly two hundred years had passed away since the feet of them that preached the Gospel had trodden that forest soil; and these two hundred years of spring leaf and summer flower had overgrown the land and covered up the traces which religion had made in the march of its simple yet true civilization. The venerable Monseigneur Macdonell, in the short stay which he made here, administered confirmation, and so encouraged the few settlers that we find them, shortly after, erecting a small log church on a village lot given by Peter Giroux. In this they were directed by a Mr. D. Revol, who, having a little education, used to instruct the people in Catechism, and so keep more brightly burning the lamp of faith in this remote but historic mission. The following year (1831) a priest, Father Cullen, passed that way and attended to the spiritual wants of the people. Shortly after him Father Dempsey came to reside amongst the settlers of Penetanguishene; but he had all the County of Simcoe north of Adjala, and a part of the County of Grey, for his field of duty. Bishop Gaulin of Kingston, accompanied by a priest, visited the mission in September, 1835, and, as may be seen by the parish register, baptized several children. He promised the people a priest; and accordingly Father Proulx, two months after, became resident pastor. At this time, in and around Penetanguishene, as well as upon the neighboring islands in the Georgian Bay, lived large numbers of Indians, who were gathered afterwards upon Manitoulin Island. To the care of these poor souls the zealous Father Proulx devoted his time and energies, and followed them to their new home. From the Island he used to come to attend to the Indians who remained in the village and its vicinity—which is done to the present day by the Jesuit Fathers, who have charge of the Indian missions in this northern country; and the names of Fathers Duranquet, Point, Hannipaux, Nadeau are household words for generations amongst these tawny children of the forest. After Father Proulx the Rev. Amable Charest was appointed parish priest in 1837, and remained till February, 1854. He was succeeded by Father Claude Ternet in June, 1854—the interval being supplied by the Rev. N. Fremiot, S. J., who is placed amongst the list of Jesuits on the Manitoulin Island for that year. In the mean time the mission was divided, and Father Ternet's ministrations were confined to the townships of Tiny and Tay, and portions of Flos and Medonte, with the churches of Penetanguishene and Ste. Croix. The eastern part of the mission was attended by Father Synnot. In October, 1857, Father Lebaudy was appointed pastor, and was succeeded in 1860 by Father J. P. Kennedy, who, in addition to being parish priest, was chaplain to the Provincial Reformatory for boys, then established at Penetanguishene by the Government of Canada. In the following year the mission was again divided, and Ste. Croix erected into a parish, with the Rev. Louis Gibra as pastor. In this year (1861) also a new church was built beside the old one, and was blessed by the present Archbishop of Toronto, then Father Walsh. Father Kennedy labored faithfully in his arduous mission until June 25th, 1873, when he lost his life in an heroic act of generosity. He and a boy were out on the Georgian Bay attending some of the parishioners, and the lad falling over, Father Kennedy, in his attempt to rescue him, was drowned. After a brief interval, during which Father Proulx had charge, the present pastor, Father Laboureau, was appointed. Since his entry to Penetanguishene the Reformatory was detached from the parish, and has a resident chaplain, the Rev. James Gibbons, a native of Hamilton. He was educated at St. Michael's College, Toronto, and at Chicoutimi in the Province of Quebec, and after his ordination as priest in 1883 was adopted by Archbishop Lynch. The second change in the parish was the separation of Midland district, and the erection of the latter place into a distinct mission, thus leaving Port Severn and Wyevale as the only chapels attached to Penetanguishene.

Father Laboureau's greatest work—which is not yet completed—was undertaken in 1884. As Penetanguishene was the point around which centred the traditions of the Huron missions, and as this was the first parish re-established in the old Huron country, thus forming the connecting link between the dead past and the living present, it was proposed to erect a Memorial Church as a fitting monument to the martyrs who perished in this part of Canada. The corner stone of the new church was laid by Archbishop Lynch in presence of the Lieutenant-Governor of Ontario, the Honorable John Beverley Robinson, and a large concourse of people, on September the 6th, 1886. The work, still unfinished, progresses with that steady pace which warrants hopes of a successful termination. Standing in a prominent position it will readily attract the attention of travellers, and tell the story of devoted heroism, which ought to be the pride and boast of every Canadian. The style of the building is modern romanesque.

The Reverend Theophilus Francis Laboureau, who, with prudent energy, is carrying on this work, more provincial than parochial in its interest, is a native of the Diocese of Dijon in the old province of Burgundy, France, where he was born, 1837. His studies were prosecuted in the Little Seminary of Plombieres, which he quitted to enter the Grand Seminary of Dijon. Upon coming to this country in 1858 he went to Montreal, where he completed his sacerdotal education, and was ordained priest January the 14th, 1866. The greater part of his life has since been passed in the once arduous but now easier parish of Penetanguishene, where he has ever worked with piety, zeal and success, and where he is doing so much to perpetuate the names of his saintly countrymen who perished in this neighborhood two hundred years before.

THE PARISH OF STAYNER.

On the 15th of June, 1871, the Reverend M. McC. O'Reilly was installed pastor of Stayner, which was detached from Barrie and erected into a separate parish. At that time it included the towns of Stayner and Collingwood and the townships of Nottawasaga and Sunnidale.

The first occasion of a priest coming to this neighborhood was when Father Proulx, accompanied by an Indian chief, crossed the Nottawasaga River on a raft and opened an Indian mission here, where no white man had yet settled. But Father Charest of Penetanguishene had formal charge of this district, and paid his first visit in 1839. After this he came once a year for four years, and then twice, to attend to the spiritual wants of the few faithful scattered through this wild forest of pine. Under his supervision a log chapel was built on the fourth line of Nottawasaga in 1848 on a farm belonging to Matthew Dowling, in whose barn the holy sacrifice used sometimes to be offered. In the few years following, besides Father Charest, missionaries visited Stayner from Toronto, amongst whom are mentioned Fathers O'Dwyer, McNulty, Flannery, Synnot, and Archbishop Walsh in the earliest days of his priesthood. Occasionally the priests of Adjala attended the mission; it was a pastor of Adjala, Father Fitzpatrick, who was the first to say Mass in Sunnidale at the residence of Herbert Cain, and in Nottawasaga at John Bertles' lumber shanty, near Duntroon, January, 1839.

When, in 1855, a mission was established at Barrie, Stayner became a portion of it, and was regularly attended every third Sunday. Things then advanced steadily until the number of Catholic settlers was such that a resident priest at Stayner became a necessity. As soon as Father O'Reilly took up his home in this mission he started a church. The corner stone was laid by Archbishop Lynch in June, 1872; and it was opened for divine service New Year's Day, 1873, by Archbishop Walsh (then Bishop of London). It is a neat brick structure one hundred feet by fifty.

The separation of the new parish of Collingwood from Stayner has already been mentioned in our sketch. When Father Edward Kiernan took Collingwood the Rev. Michael Moyna was appointed to Stayner, and is the pastor at the present time. Father Moyna was born September 24th, 1853, in the County of Monaghan, Ireland, where also he made his primary studies. Upon coming to this country he taught school for some time; but resigned for the purpose of advancing to the holy priesthood. He then entered St. Michael's College, Toronto, for the study of philosophy, upon the completion of which Archbishop Lynch sent him for theology to Genoa in Italy. Here he spent some years in the Collegio Brignole, where he was ordained priest

July 27th, 1884, by the Archbishop of Genoa. Prior to being stationed at Stayner he was assistant to Bishop O'Mahony in St. Paul's, Toronto.

THE PARISH OF STE. CROIX.

We have led you, patient reader, by many a weary path where earnest, devoted priests spent and are spending their energies in uninteresting routine upon religion's material and immaterial temples; we have moved in a vast circle of persons, places and events; we now arrive at the same point from which we started. Here in this, the last parish which it is our duty to sketch, were the missionary labors of the brave Brebeuf. Little remains for us to write, as the history of Ste. Croix is a simple tale of early settlers clinging to the faith amidst the hardships of forest life, and of a later generation forming a parish with two churches, and a convent of Sisters who have charge of the Separate school.

This mission, until 1850, formed part of Penetanguishene; but it was eleven years after this date that a pastor was permanently appointed. In the interval Father Ternet resided for a short time at Lafontaine, where he built a log church. When, in 1861, Father Gibra took charge he labored most zealously for the spiritual and material welfare of his flock: he extended the little church, built a vestry, which he occupied as his house, and erected a second chapel at St. Patrick's, about seven miles from Lafontaine. Frequently in those early days this good priest was obliged to walk this distance to say a second Mass for this portion of his congregation. Father Gibra being transferred (1871) to his present position at Barrie, Rev. Joseph Michel was made pastor of Ste. Croix. He built a presbytery, and replaced the old church by a handsome brick one, which was completed in 1877. A new frame chapel at St. Patrick's, a convent at Lafontaine, and the establishment of an efficient Separate school are the other works of the zealous Father Michel's administration. After laboring for thirteen years his health failed; but an assistant, Father Gibbons, was sent, who remained two years, when Father Michel resumed his full charge. It was too late; nature gave way; but, like the faithful servant that he was, he worked till near the last. On the 13th of May, 1889, he passed away, beloved and mourned by the people he had served so long and well. He was a native of France, where he received his early training. Coming to this country at the request of Bishop de Charbonnel, he was sent to the Sulpitian Seminary at Baltimore for the study of theology, upon the completion of which he was ordained priest at London, Ontario, by Bishop Pinsonneault in 1857. His sacerdotal life was spent in various missions of the archdiocese of Toronto, where his works remain, a monument to his apostolic zeal and devotion. Not long after his death the Rev. Joseph E. Beaudoin of Montreal succeeded him, and is the present pastor of Ste. Croix.

In Memoriam.

I.

In our sketch of St. Paul's Parish mention is made of Bishop O'Mahony's serious illness, which, since that portion of our work was written, terminated in the death of the venerable prelate on the morning of September the 8th, 1892. Although the sad event did not come as a surprise, nevertheless it gave a shock to all who knew his Lordship, for it removed from the higher ranks of the clergy a man of great ability and distinguished attainments; it stopped the beating of a noble and generous heart; and brought rest to one who in health knew no rest in the exercise of his priestly functions.

Timothy O'Mahony was born in the parish of Kilmurray, County of Cork, on November 1st, 1825; and was therefore at the time of his death in the sixty-seventh year of his age. After pursuing his early studies at Cork, he proceeded at the age of sixteen to Rome, where, upon the completion of his ecclesiastical education, he was ordained priest in 1849. Returning to Ireland he first served in some of the rural parishes of his native diocese, and was then attached to St. Finbar's Church in the city of Cork, where his piety and zeal produced the most edifying results. Since his elevation to the purple in 1871 his career may be briefly summed up as the life of a devoted missionary in Australia and self-sacrificing pastor in Canada.

The funeral took place on September the 10th, when, besides Archbishops Walsh and Cleary, and Bishops Dowling, Richard A. O'Connor and Denis O'Connor, a large number of priests assisted at the solemn burial service. The Mass was sung by Archbishop Cleary, the life-long friend of the deceased; and his Grace the Archbishop of Toronto preached the sermon. He paid a fitting tribute to the virtues and good works of the dead prelate; to his personal qualities of mind and heart; and to his taste and culture, which expressed themselves in the very temple which had risen under his influence, until it stood the pride and glory of the people and the greatest architectural monument of the city of Toronto.

Mass being finished and the touching absolutions being administered by the prelates present, the body was carried in procession and deposited in a vault at the south-west corner of St. Paul's. Here he rests on the sunny side of the church he loved so well, and which cost him his life; while it rises above him to perpetuate his name, to plead the cause of his pious zeal, and to ask the prayers of his faithful people.

II.

Our task, we thought, was done; but just as we were finishing our memorial paragraph of Bishop O'Mahony there came a message of sorrow from Penetanguishene that a leading member of the Committee to whom the preparation of this book was entrusted, Dr. O'Sullivan, had died of typhoid fever on September the 13th, 1892. It would therefore ill become us to close our work without a slight tribute to him who had taken a deep interest in it from the very beginning. His experience first gave it practical form, his pen afforded us one of our most interesting chapters, his advice guided us in our general plan, and the results of his study and research are to be found in almost every page. In noticing his death one of the city papers justly remarked: "He was one of the first stars in the literary firmament of the country. A man of ripe scholarship, temperate judgment and studious accuracy in discussion, his views always carried weight wherever delivered. His loss will be all the more keenly felt by reason of the fact that he had only reached that stage of manhood which discloses the future as a certainty rather than a promise."

At the time of his death Denis Ambrose O'Sullivan was in his forty-fifth year, being born in the County of Northumberland, Ontario, on the 21st of February, 1848. After receiving his early education at St. Michael's College, he entered Toronto University, where he graduated in 1872 with the degree of Bachelor of Arts. During his study of law, or following shortly upon his admission to the Bar, he took the course for the LL.B. in the University of Toronto, in which he distinguished himself with high honors. The degree of Doctor of Laws was conferred upon him by the Universities of Laval (Quebec) and Ottawa. He devoted his leisure hours to literature, which he preferred to the more arduous duties of his profession, in which he held a high position as Queen's Counsel. His principal works are " Government in Canada," "Manual on Conveyancing," and " How to Draw a Simple Will." His articles on the " Church in Canada," written first for " The American Catholic Quarterly," have been collected into one volume, wherein he treats many interesting historical questions from a legal point of view. He was prominent in public life as a member of the Senate of the University of Toronto, of the General Hospital Board, of the House of Industry and of the Board of the Public Library, of which last body he was chairman at the time of his death.

In him, as Archbishop Walsh remarked at his funeral, the Church lost a dutiful and devoted son, the Bar an able and brilliant member, the city a useful and upright citizen, and the family—their loss is irreparable.

> " Naught can avail them now but prayer.
> *Miserere, Domine.*"

www.ingramcontent.com/pod-product-compliance
Lightning Source LLC
Chambersburg PA
CBHW032131010526
44111CB00034B/580